Enforcing Freedom

Dear Liam!
Thank you for
your support &
friendship through
many years...

Kevin

Studies in Transgression

Studies in Transgression

EDITOR: DAVID BROTHERTON
FOUNDING EDITOR: JOCK YOUNG

The Studies in Transgression series will present a range of exciting new crime-related titles that offer an alternative to the mainstream, mostly positivistic approaches to social problems in the United States and beyond. The series will raise awareness of key crime-related issues and explore challenging research topics in an interdisciplinary way. Where possible, books in the series will allow the global voiceless to have their views heard, offering analyses of human subjects who have too often been marginalized and pathologized. Further, series authors will suggest ways to influence public policy. The editors welcome new as well as experienced authors who can write innovatively and accessibly. We anticipate that these books will appeal to those working within criminology, criminal justice, sociology, or related disciplines, as well as the educated public.

Terry Williams and Trevor B. Milton, *The Con Men: Hustling in New York City*

Christopher P. Dum, *Exiled in America: Life on the Margins in a Residential Motel*

Mark S. Hamm and Ramón Spaaij, *The Age of Lone Wolf Terrorism*

Peter J. Marina, *Down and Out in New Orleans*

David C. Brotherton and Philip Kretsedemas, editors, *Immigration Policy in the Age of Punishment*

Robert J. Durán, *The Gang Paradox: Inequalities and Miracles on the U.S.-Mexico Border*

Enforcing Freedom

Drug Courts, Therapeutic Communities, and the Intimacies of the State

KERWIN KAYE

Columbia
University
Press
New York

Columbia University Press
Publishers Since 1893
New York Chichester, West Sussex
cup.columbia.edu

Library of Congress Cataloging-in-Publication Data
Names: Kaye, Kerwin, author.
Title: Enforcing freedom : drug courts, therapeutic communities, and the intimacies of the state / Kerwin Kaye.
Description: New York : Columbia University Press, [2019] | Series: Studies in transgression | Includes bibliographical references and index.
Identifiers: LCCN 2019005950 | ISBN 9780231172882 (cloth : alk. paper) | ISBN 9780231172899 (pbk. : alk. paper) | ISBN 9780231547093 (ebook)
Subjects: LCSH: Drug addicts—Rehabilitation—United States. | Drug courts—United States. | Discrimination in criminal justice administration—United States.
Classification: LCC HV5825 .K37 2019 | DDC 364.6—dc23
LC record available at https://lccn.loc.gov/2019005950

Columbia University Press books are printed on permanent and durable acid-free paper.
Printed in the United States of America

Cover design: Milenda Nan Ok Lee
Cover image: Dan Henson / © Alamy

Contents

Acknowledgments

A book of this sort is not accomplished by oneself, and I owe many debts to people who have helped me along the way. The mere process of gaining permission to sit in on court cases took an extended period, and it would not have been possible without the support of Justin Barry of the New York City Criminal Court, who generously approved this project and helped to move it through the state bureaucracy. Once I began the research process, an additional set of opportunities were offered that aided greatly in the project. At the drug court in which I conducted the majority of my research, the judge permitted me to not only attend pre-court sessions but to sit in the judge's bench (a position that allowed me to hear the many huddled conversations in which the judge would quietly confer with lawyers or with drug court participants). The director of the drug court's administrative side was also extremely welcoming in giving me "free range of the castle," not only helping me in finding any documents for which I might ask, but even offering a room in which I might conduct interviews with participants. Case managers at the court were generous not only in answering my many questions but in taking me under their wings and showing me how their end of the program worked. Though anonymity requires that I not use any specific names, I am especially grateful for the friendship offered me by DB, who allowed me to sit for many hours in her cubicle and share stories both related to the project and not. The welcoming atmosphere I experienced at the court greatly exceeded my expectations.

This generous attitude was also present at the treatment center at which I conducted the majority of my ethnography. Being given the ability to roam freely within a controlled facility—as well as occasional use of an office for interviews—is a rare experience, and I am indebted to the director of the program in particular for the opportunity. The people at the treatment center received me with a warmth that again surpassed any welcome I could have imagined. The staff members struck me as not only genuine, caring, funny, and deeply committed but as having tremendous personal integrity as well. I especially wish to thank B, L, F, and E for their great insights, assistance, and friendship.

The people undergoing treatment through both the drug court and the therapeutic community were of course the most central to the project, and I cannot adequately express the extent of my appreciation for the way in which many individuals opened their lives, sharing both jokes and challenging moments with me. Beyond our formal interviews, which sometimes involved a great deal of openness and candor, I felt privileged to be able to simply chat with them during quieter moments. I was especially grateful for the trust that was shown to me in revealing many of the "behind-the-screen" events and happenings within the facility. I am especially grateful for the friendship and comradery offered by AM, CM, I, and M, without whom this inquiry would have been both much less pleasant and less successful. Though this book is more of an institutional analysis than a study of individual lives, I hope that the work that follows successfully captures at least a part of what was most important to the residents who shared so meaningfully with me while passing through this program.

A debt of gratitude is also owed to the many others who also shared their perspectives and allowed me to interview them. Ranging from district attorneys and defense lawyers at the drug court to officials working at the New York State regulatory agency, OASAS, as well as to other professionals who have worked in other components of the criminal justice and treatment systems (whether as judges in drug courts, as program directors of treatment facilities or of other drug courts, as staff members, or as outside experts), I often relied upon the knowledge and wisdom of these experts and was grateful for their willingness to take time from their schedules to help educate this untutored student. A further debt of gratitude goes to several people who spoke with me about the Asklepieion program (a therapeutic community which ran from 1968 to 1972 in the maximum security prison at Marion, Illinois); though this material is found only in the dissertation and not this book, it formed a valuable point of reference for me in my thinking of the evolution of the TC, and I thank Edward Opton, Alan Eliado Gómez, CB, EG, LM, and PW for their thoughtful reflections. Additional thanks go to the program participants I interviewed at the court offices, who often gave me different perspectives than I heard through residents at the treatment facility. Anonymity again prevents me from naming anyone directly, but I want to thank each of them for helping me to better understand how the drug court/treatment system works at both formal and informal levels.

I also received a great deal of support in developing this project and writing it up, first as a dissertation and later as this book. Lisa Duggan provided powerful insights and consistently spot-on editorial suggestions as my dissertation chair, and the final product reflects her mentorship and support in many ways. The rest of my dissertation committee—Patricia Clough, Arlene Dávila, Emily Martin, and Andrew Ross—were also a source of outstanding assistance throughout the process. Patricia Clough provided intellectual and emotional support in abundance, continuing to offer advice and care as the dissertation became a book. Emily Martin offered a most careful reading of each chapter, additionally offering methodological suggestions based on her own ethnographic experience that were extremely useful throughout. Arlene Dávila offered both strong encouragement and intellectual insight, particularly in relation to my initial grapplings with the so-called culture of poverty, and further helped me navigate the convoluted bureaucratic hurdles that were placed in front of me. Andrew Ross's support and input, meanwhile, were critical in framing the entire project, particularly at earlier stages of the work. I am extremely fortunate to have had such intelligent and politically adept people to work with on this project, and am gratified to have learned from such able mentors.

In the course of writing the original dissertation, I obtained a predoctoral training fellowship in behavioral research through the National Institutes of Health and the National Institute on Drug Abuse, and I am thankful for both the financial support this provided as well as for the wisdom the institutions had in developing such training programs for junior scholars.

The fellowship itself was (and is still) administered by the National Development and Research Institutes (NDRI) in New York City. My time with NDRI was very helpful, most especially from the advice and suggestions I received from the other pre- and post-docs in the program as well as from the mentorship of our able and always helpful director, Greg Falkin. The general good spirits within the program were also a much appreciated benefit of our weekly meetings, and I wish to especially thank Stephanie Campos, Jennifer Cantrell, Melissa Ditmore, Alex Duncan, Luther Elliot, Juline Koken, Vivian Pacheco, Ben Singer, and Rafael Torruella for both their thoughts and friendship. George De Leon joined the program as a codirector halfway through my tenure and deserves special mention. George, one of the world's foremost authorities on (and an outspoken advocate for) therapeutic communities, spent extra time working with my project—reading early chapters, responding to my questions, offering insights and perspective—despite having concerns with my general analysis. He has always been willing to disagree in a most friendly way and to directly discuss any points of contention. I often wonder how I would react if someone were to challenge work I had devoted my life toward; should I find myself in such a position, I would hope to emulate his example.

Various iterations of writing groups have further helped me both directly and indirectly, first in creating concrete deadlines and in offering excellent feedback but also in providing much needed friendship, levity, and support. At various points, Robyn Autry, Rich Blint, André Carrington, Miabi Chatterji, Andy Cornell, Greg Goldberg, Rebecca de Guzman (also at NDRI), Miles Grier (MJ), Allison McKim, Dawn Peterson, Alton Phillips, and Craig Willse all read and made comments on various chapter drafts. A number of other friends and colleagues also read drafts and/or offered extensive thoughts and comments, including Ann Burlein, Jan Chargin, Tom Chargin, Christina Crosby, Teresa Gowan, Helena Hansen, Anthony Hatch, Janet Jakobsen, Leigh Claire LaBerge, Brad Lewis, Kelly Moore, Victoria Pitts-Taylor, Svati Shah, Ben Shepard, Rebecca Tiger, Rhys Williams, and the ever-transcendent Jackie Orr. The ideas and support each of these individuals has offered has been of enormous benefit throughout, and I am especially glad to have so many dear and wonderful friends through this time. I would also like to thank David Brotherton and Lowell Frye at Columbia University Press, as well as two readers for the press, for their support and useful suggestions. Many other individuals also helped me with various technical aspects of this book, including transcriptions, copyediting, compiling and formatting the bibliography, creating graphs, gathering research, helping me to obtain images, and so on, and in this regard I would like to thank Blaise Bayno-Krebs, Carter Deane, Amna Jehangir, Shoshana Lauter, Kathy Lo, Meryl Lodge, Nana Mensah, Dorothy Della Noce, Aaron Sandoval, Rachel Schiff, Muhammad Tayyab, Erin Ward, and the mysterious *Person X* (who prefers to remain undefined). I'd also like to thank Marc Eisner at Wesleyan for providing funds for indexing.

On a more personal note, I am thankful for the many close family members with whom I have shared my life, many of them sadly lost during the development of this text. I'd like to thank my mother, Kay Brook, and stepfather, Bill Lorber, both deceased. Bill had the kindness to read the entire dissertation and to offer very detailed comments, and I am glad for his very generous gift. My mother, meanwhile, has been my biggest influence throughout my life, and I am grateful for the innumerable ways she has shaped my life. I also thank my deceased father, Bryan Brook, and I am thankful for the gift of his many years of fun-loving care. I know my parents would be happy and proud to see this done. More happily, my closest friends, including Tracy Bartlett, Dovar Chen, Sealing Cheng, Clare Corcoran (who also offered editing and insight), Mark Padilla, Jim Sandler, Naneki Scialla (dearest sister!), and DW (who is also a source and therefore remains anonymous), also offered joy and profound support throughout the process. I am grateful to have such amazing people in my life. I likewise am grateful for the cuddly companionship offered by Sappho, the wisest of cats, as well as Hercules, Medium, and Ruffles (all now deceased) who collectively helped me to stay relatively sane while spending far too many hours sitting in front of a computer screen.

Lastly, my heartfelt thanks go to my dear partner, Elizabeth Bernstein. Elizabeth has been with me throughout the entire process of the original dissertation and now the book, helping me in the earliest moments when I was choosing a topic, spending long hours with me addressing particularly knotty practical or theoretical conundrums, offering emotional encouragement freely and often, and working to carefully comment upon and edit the entire book. My life is powerfully enriched through our relationship, and my heart delights in sharing so deeply and meaningfully with you every day.

Enforcing Freedom

1

Policing Addiction in a New Era of Therapeutic Jurisprudence

First Impressions

I wait in the courtroom for the judge to appear, somewhat anxiously trying to take in everything that I see and hear. Lawyers shift papers at the front, while approximately thirty or so people—mostly black and Latino men—talk quietly or sit bored waiting for the proceedings to begin. A sign behind the judge's bench reads "In God We Trust," and a U.S. flag is positioned to the side. Finally the judge enters from a door in back of the room. We stand as asked. A white woman of around fifty, the judge handles a few minor issues with the lawyers before the first program participant is called before her. "I am very impressed with the report I received," she says, looking directly at the individual, a thirty-year-old black man. The judge smiles broadly as she speaks and actually gives the man a thumbs up. "I see your mother is here, your family is here. Good." Then, speaking to his mother, she loudly proclaims, "You should be very proud of him. He has done fantastically well." Turning her attention back to the program participant, she tells him to approach the bench. As the man steps forward, she takes his hand, shaking it enthusiastically and then speaks to him in quiet tones. I overhear only a brief snippet, something to the effect of "I have kids too. It's tough." A few moments later, she allows the man to return to the defendant's table. "You're in the home stretch, and you look great," she says before leading a round of applause from those gathered in the courtroom.

Not only do both the prosecuting and defense attorneys join in, but to my surprise, even the bailiffs clap with what seems to be genuine feeling.

The second person called is a middle-aged Latino man dressed in a suit. The judge greets him energetically: "You look very dapper today, sir. You look nice. How is your job?" Calling this gentleman close in as well, she shakes his hand and speaks quietly. I cannot hear what they say, but the judge makes direct eye contact the entire time she is speaking, and she smiles throughout their conversation. Releasing him back to the defendant's desk, she returns to the topic being presently decided. "I have a note from your mother. You wish to move back in with her?" She turns to the prosecuting attorney, "The People have no objection to his moving back in with his mother?" (The district attorney signals no.) Then she addresses his treatment supervisor, "And I'm assuming the program has no objection to this?" (Her query is met with a shake of the head from the case manager.) With this assent, the judge permits the man to move back in with his mother. She sets another date for him to return, this one only two weeks away, and she moves onto the next case. The judge acts in much the same friendly manner with all of these initial cases. Spending perhaps three to four minutes on each case, she rapidly offers praise to each of the participants, often asking about their jobs or, in a few cases, about their educational pursuits. She leads the court in a round of applause for each and every person who is doing well, and some receive one-month, two-month, or three-month certificates of completion.

A thirty-five-year-old Latina woman soon follows. "The essay you wrote about lying was excellent," says the judge. "Not only was it well-written, but the statements you made were right on target. If you don't tell the truth, people will lose trust in you. It seemed to me that you learned your lesson. I am going to have you move into an outpatient program. This is not me saying that what you are doing is correct. It is a last chance for you. If you mess up, I'll have no choice but to send you back to jail. What happens to you is up to you, not me."

An even more strict tone is struck for the next individual, a thirty-year-old Latino man. "You will need to wait over here," the judge says, gesturing to a bench at the side of the court. "The threats you have made against your wife are unacceptable." It is unclear exactly what he has done, but from comments that the judge makes, it seems that his wife called to complain to one of the case managers about whatever happened. The judge has the power to decide what sort of penalty is merited in a case such as this, and—without hearing any explanations whatsoever from the man—she eventually informs him that he will be sent to jail for a one-week stay.

Another man, the only white participant I see during my ninety minutes of court viewing, is called up from the same side bench where the man accused of abuse was told to wait. He is one of a small number of people who have been brought in from the jail for possible participation in the treatment court. "Do you smoke marijuana?" the judge asks him. Seeming confused, he answers with a weak "No." "Treatment court is for addicts. If you don't use drugs, then we can't place you." The defense attorney has a quick hushed word with the man. The judge asks again, "Do you smoke marijuana?" "Yes," he offers this time, seeming only slightly more sure of himself. "Treatment court has three goals," offers the judge, "to get you off of drugs, to get you to become a regular member of society, and to get your case dismissed. It's a lot of time and effort. Now, do you want a quick sentence or do you want to go through our program?" After a bit of back and forth, the man at last opts to participate in the program. The judge arranges for an evaluation to be done in one week and returns the man to jail in the meantime.

Later, I walk into a side office of the Treatment Court, finding the staff too preoccupied to immediately greet me. One of the program participants is having difficulty with his urinalysis. After testing negative the day before, this eighteen-year-old black youth is now testing positive. He emphatically proclaims that he has not smoked marijuana since beginning the program and that he most definitely did not smoke it the night before. One of the staff members seems to believe him and is arguing with other staff members that the test result is actually somewhat indeterminate. The staff supervisor suggests that the youth pee into a second cup. A second man is also angry because his urinalysis has turned up positive, and he likewise insists he has not done any drugs. "I don't have time for this shit," he mutters aloud, "I have to get to work." On the wall hang two posters, one entitled "Health Dangers of Cocaine," the other "Health Dangers of Marijuana." Ironically—to me, in any event—a poster of a rather bedraggled cat is hung nearby, featuring a caption that reads "Before I get my morning coffee, I might as well be a dog." Eventually, the staff members address all of these testing challenges, and we have some time to speak about my project.

In what has come to be called a "quiet revolution" in the judiciary, the first drug treatment court began in Miami, Florida, in 1989 under the direction of then-State Attorney Janet Reno.[1] Indeed, this successful experiment was one of the key factors that eventually helped propel her to become U.S. attorney general (the first woman to serve as such) under President Clinton. As of 2014—twenty-five years after the establishment of the first such court—there are some 3,057 drug courts within the United States and its territories, covering 56 percent of all U.S. counties, and collectively handling just over 107,000 individuals on an annual basis.[2] In sending those arrested for drug-related crimes to a court-supervised treatment program rather than to jail or prison, drug courts are widely perceived to offer an alternative to the lawmaking trends of the 1980s, including the war on drugs, when harsh penalties were established for crimes that were previously considered to be relatively minor in nature. Perhaps best exemplified by New York State's Rockefeller Drug Laws and the more general war on drugs, this model of long-term incarceration rested upon a dual justification: it purportedly prevented crime by establishing punishments that deterred illegality, and it locked up those individuals who nevertheless committed crime, ideally keeping those deemed inherently dangerous off the streets for as long as possible.

While the decades-long campaign for law and order was generally initiated by conservatives, the 1990s saw Bill Clinton and other Democrats working hard to make sure that they would not be outflanked on the issue of crime, passing legislation such as 1994's infamous Violent Crime Control and Law Enforcement Act (VCCLEA) and taking the Democratic Party decidedly to the right in the process.[3] Yet while the war on drugs helped to initiate a more general trend toward punitive lawmaking, it never completely displaced an earlier logic favoring preventative and rehabilitative approaches to criminal justice. One rarely discussed aspect of the war on drugs in this regard has been the way that funding for treatment programs has generally expanded together with the overall budget for the drug war, even as other behavioral health programs have suffered severe cuts (see figure 1.1). Although most scholarship on the drug war has quite properly focused on the way that it has privileged law enforcement over treatment and prevention, the idea of softer rehabilitative approaches has remained politically relevant, even in moments when tough-on-crime policies were at their most dominant. Clinton attempted to enfold this support for rehabilitative efforts into his legislative agenda, even as he greatly expanded the coercive powers of the police apparatus. Thus, while the VCCLEA included funding for 100,000 new police officers and $9.7 billion for prisons, it also included $6.7 billion for crime prevention programs, including drug courts. Violent offenders were excluded in this initial mandate, ensuring that the courts would focus only on low-level offenders. Clinton offered increasing

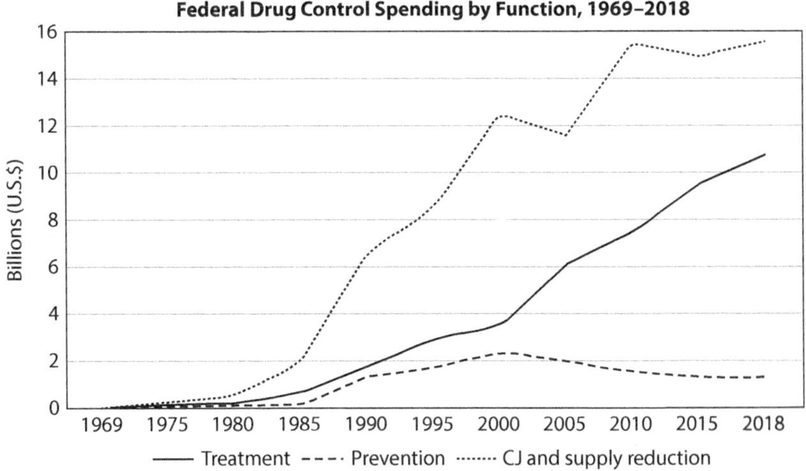

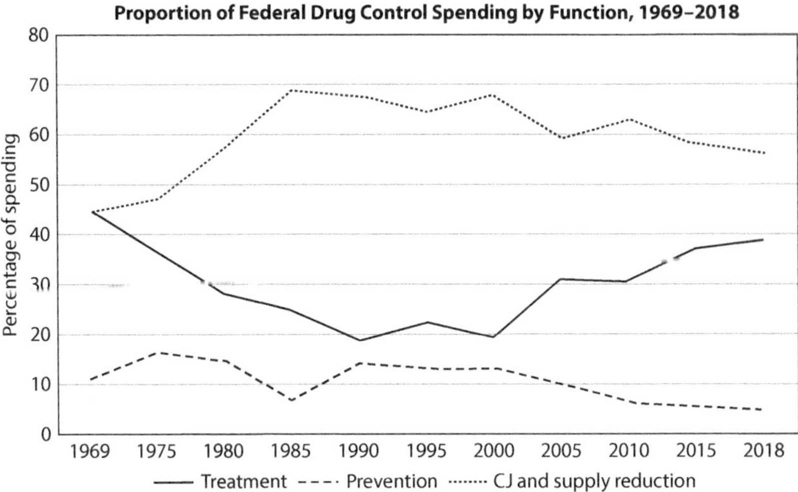

FIGURE 1.1 Federal spending on drug control and the proportion of spending by function. Significant accounting changes occurred in 1981 and 2003, with smaller changes occurring in other years, making comparisons between years imprecise. However, the figures nevertheless reveal broad funding trends in the War on Drugs. (Sources of data—1969–80: Gerstein and Harwood [1990: 217]; 1981–90: ONDCP [1994: 184]; 1991–2000: ONDCP [2000: 13]; 2001–2: ONDCP [2003: 6]; 2003: Kilmer, Midgette, and Saloga [2016: 12]; 2004–8: ONDCP [2015: 18]; 2009–18: ONDCP [2017: 19]. Walther [2012] offers a different set of data that is nevertheless in general agreement with the calculations provided here. Gerstein and Harwood also provide a graph showing overall trends including all sources of funding in both nominal and real dollars from 1969–1989 [1990: 214]).

support for drug courts during his tenure, and funding has continued to rise under both Republican and Democratic presidencies since.

By the time Obama arrived in office in 2009, support for the drug war, and mass incarceration more generally, had waned. Obama's director of national drug control policy, Gil Kerlikowske, pointedly argued against the use of the phrase "war on drugs," and declared drug courts part of a strategy that would move away from the " 'tough on crime,' enforcement-centric 'war on drugs' approach": "They need treatment, and they deserve a chance to recover and change their lives. That's why this Administration is working to expand innovative programs like drug court."[4] With New York's Rockefeller Laws significantly amended as of April 2009 (in a deal that established drug courts on a statewide basis), it appeared that treatment had at last won out over punishment. While many drug policy reformers were ultimately disappointed by the lack of substantive change they saw from the Obama administration, his presidency nevertheless seemed to mark a turning point toward a considerably less punitive drug policy.

The ascendance of Donald Trump has done much to alter this narrative. At the time of this writing, over a year into Trump's presidency, it is still too early to assess the exact direction drug policy will take within the new administration; but with campaign pledges promising aggressive police enforcement and "drug war dinosaur" Jeffrey Sessions as attorney general, a retreat from some of Obama's more progressive drug policies is a certainty.[5] Despite this, support for drug courts seems secure within the new administration. In a speech addressing the opioid epidemic, President Trump declared his support for "innovative approaches that have been proven to work, like drug courts."[6] In fact, Trump's 2018 budget request significantly raised financial support for the courts, offering $139 million in federal grants, slightly more than a 50 percent increase over the $92 million Obama appropriated in his final 2017 budget.[7] More recently, President Trump's White House Commission on Addiction and the Opioid Crisis (headed by former New Jersey governor Chris Christie prior to being disbanded in 2017) called for the expansion of drug courts into every federal district,[8] while Attorney General Sessions has similarly been a long-time supporter, helping to establish the first drug court in Alabama while acting as a U.S. federal attorney in the 1980s.[9]

Though drug courts have critics on both left and right, the diverse appeals that the courts offer to liberals and conservatives has generated a convincing political consensus. For liberals and progressives, the idea of moving from the "punishment for drug-involved offenders" to "helping offenders involved in drugs" has an immediate humanitarian appeal that has made drug courts generally well-liked.[10] Writing in the liberal weekly news magazine, *The Nation*, regular contributor Sasha Abramsky cites what he sees as a growing movement toward "restorative justice," arguing that "the era of 'Lock 'em up and throw away the key' " is slowly "drawing to a close," and that drug courts are an important part of this trend in "channeling more offenders into structured treatment."[11] The left-leaning Sentencing Project has likewise praised drug courts as a treatment-oriented alternative to incarceration, and the National Legal Aid & Defender Association (NLADA)—the primary professional organization for defense attorneys in the United States—has offered its endorsement for the courts.[12]

The movement toward treatment over incarceration has held appeal beyond those on the liberal left, however. California's 2000 vote on Proposition 36—which did not establish drug courts but created a similar option for supervised treatment instead of imprisonment—was passed by 61 percent of the electorate in conservative Orange County (as well as by 61 percent of the state overall).[13] Similarly, in 2001 Idaho legislators unanimously passed the Idaho Drug Court Act, further increasing funding for the courts on two occasions.[14] While law-and-order detractors have sometimes pejoratively referred to drug courts as "hug courts" or even "hug-a-thug" courts (and indeed, judges do sometimes offer hugs to drug court participants), drug courts have nevertheless gained support among many conservatives due in large part to the apparent efficacy of court-supervised treatment, both in terms of direct costs and lowered recidivism rates, when compared to incarceration.[15] David Muhlhausen, a senior policy analyst for the right-wing Heritage Foundation, has argued in support of drug courts, saying that "If you take the less serious offenders and put them into programs other than prison it would be a benefit to society."[16] James Nolan's 2001 contention, that "the model has received almost uniformly positive media coverage and overwhelming public support," remains largely true today.[17] In 2009, *Newsweek* thus referred to drug courts as "that vanishingly rare thing in Washington: an issue with near consensus."[18] Given the rancor of the current political moment, drug courts offer a remarkable example of ongoing bipartisan agreement.[19]

However, it is not entirely clear that drug courts represent a simple dichotomy that moves from punishment to treatment. Advocates for drug courts consistently argue that the program is not "soft on crime" but rather "an effort to stem the advance of drugs in a humane but hard-nosed way."[20] More generally, advocates for drug courts, working through the National Association of Drug Court Professionals (NADCP), have worked hard to argue that the shift toward judicially supervised, court-mandated treatment does not represent an end to the war on drugs. As noted by two early drug court promoters:

> Local drug court leaders have succeeded only where they've built constructive partnerships with other key players, including the community. For example, in Louisiana, [Judge William] Hunter[, who sought to introduce drug courts into the area,] made sure to win the support of the St. Mary Parish sheriff and local prosecutors—crucial allies in the fight to avoid a "soft on crime" label.[21]

As the primary national organization for those who work in drug courts, the NADCP also opposed California's Proposition 36 in 2000 (which established treatment rather than imprisonment for most nonviolent drug crimes but with fewer requirements for judicial supervision), California Proposition 47 in 2014 (which reduced penalties for most drug offenses), as well as all initiatives to decriminalize marijuana, including for medical purposes.[22] Drug court advocates are perhaps drug warriors of a different stripe, but they remain committed to the racially disparate forms of policing and carcerality that have characterized the post-1973 period of mass incarceration.[23]

In this vein, the court has come to define punishment as its most vital therapeutic tool, thereby rendering any division between the two terms somewhat suspect. In the words of one drug court judge (in comments disseminated by the NADCP)—drug courts offer "therapy with teeth."[24] A number of scholars have commented upon the convergence of these two otherwise distinct elements, introducing a model which presumes, as Rebecca Tiger notes, that "force is the best medicine."[25] Tiger critically dubs the result "enlightened coercion," while other commentators have termed it "therapeutic punishment."[26] As noted by Judge Jeffrey Tauber, former president of the NADCP, "Sanctions are not used to punish participants, or as an end in themselves, but as part of a therapeutic strategy to move participants toward a sober lifestyle through a motivational system of escalating sanctions."[27] Punishment becomes therapy, making "punishment" disappear.

At the same time that punishment is framed as therapeutic, however, it is simultaneously described as being punitive, playing a key role in showing that drug courts remain tough. As noted in a review of the courts conducted for the U.S. Department of Health and Human Services, "judges and prosecutors have seen that sanctions encourage participation in treatment and are necessary to gain public acceptance of treatment in lieu of punishment."[28] Although some conservative commentators suggest that the acceptance of a disease model of addiction signifies the ascendance of "guiltless justice," drug courts employ their own force-oriented rhetoric of accountability and are keen to apply sanctions for any and all infractions of the rules.[29] In adopting a newly-fashioned medical model of addiction as a relapsing disease, however, drug courts "attempt to moderate inflexible accountability rules" while continuing to emphasize that "defendants are held accountable for their actions."[30] *Accountability* here signals a therapeutic commitment to criminal justice sanctions (including, ultimately, to long-term incarceration for those who fail at treatment). The adoption of a disease model of addiction thereby seeks to justify the court's existence in retributive terms as well as rehabilitative, enabling it to speak to diverse audiences in different contexts. Drug courts thus achieve a truly magical trick, enabling punishment to appear and disappear at will.

Therapeutic Jurisprudence and the Stratification of Punishment

The scholarship of Boldt (1998), Moore (2007), Paik (2011), Tiger (2013), and Murphy (2015) has discussed the coherence—or lack thereof—of this "enlightened coercion," often highlighting its ambiguities and contradictions as well as the ways in which it masks ongoing forms of punishment. As Rebecca Tiger argues, the fusion of the therapeutic and the legal greatly expands the terrain of the court, orienting it not just toward *law*, but toward *norm* as well. The court here "oversees increasing aspects of defendants' lives . . . rely[ing] on the disease model to argue for enhanced judicial control of drug addicts."[31] The *productive incoherence* of therapeutic punishment thus introduces new logics in deploying a more extensive and intimate range of surveillance techniques, assessing their charges by a more comprehensive set of analytics than simple law-breaking.[32] At the same time, the ideological elasticity of punitive therapeutics has also made continuing reliance upon criminal justice solutions more palatable, making it possible for the courts to speak in rehabilitative terms as well as retributive, and rendering the ongoing production of racialized mass incarceration far less visible. Advocates for drug courts here play a dual game, combining disparate messages as necessary: notions of accountability and cost-savings typically draw in conservatives, while progressives and liberals tend to be drawn in by the idea that drug courts offer an alternative to mass incarceration that addresses the root causes of drug use and criminality in a more humane manner. Thus, while maintaining a hold on law-and-order conservatives, drug courts seeks to redeem the promise of criminal *justice* among liberals in particular, turning the threat of imprisonment into a therapeutic technique and repositioning the criminal courts in terms of individual and social improvement.

The links that drug courts have with the ongoing warehouse prison (in which few correctional services are offered and little effort is paid toward the social integration of inmates)[33] point toward the deceptiveness of these claims. Not only do drug courts rely upon the threat of imprisonment in the unreconstructed retributive prison, both in order to coerce initial participation and as a therapeutic punishment in and of itself (via short periods of "flash incarceration" used in sanctioning rule violations), but approximately half of all participants in the courts ultimately fail at treatment and are sentenced for their crimes,[34] generally without receiving any form of credit for the time they have been supervised by the court. As most drug courts require that their participants plead guilty as a condition of their involvement,[35] this half that fails—disproportionately black and poor (with white graduation rates approximately twice as high as nonwhite)[36]—faces terms in prison that are significantly longer than they would have received had they not undergone court-supervised treatment in the first place.[37] In some successful cases, the time a participant is incarcerated for infractions of drug court rules can exceed the amount of time they would have had to serve had they simply accepted a prison sentence.[38] To add insult to injury, some judges assume a punitive attitude toward those who fail at treatment, condemning them to even longer sentences than others who have not taken up court resources.[39] In other words, it is entirely possible for a participant to attempt treatment through drug court and spend a longer time in jail while under that court's supervision than they would have received in traditional sentencing, only to fail out of the program and receive an entirely new sentence based on a guilty plea to the most serious charges the DA could muster (without any chance to plea bargain), a fact that highlights the grave risks that drug courts can entail for participants.

In some (though not all) studies, the impact of race disappears when two of the other factors frequently shown to impact success in drug courts are statistically controlled: educational level and employment status.[40] Butzin, Saum, and Scarpitti summarize these findings by suggesting that those who do well in drug courts tend to possess what they call "stakeholder values": "That is, they are characterized by two of our society's most stabilizing attributes and values, education and work. . . . It may well be that because of their education and commitment to work, they use drugs less frequently. To a lesser extent, there was some evidence that married clients did better than did single clients."[41] In some sense, however, this seems to amount to saying that those who succeed in drug courts are, in fact, those who are least involved in and impacted by drugs.[42] Equally to the point, however, these disparities indicate the role of education and work, and to a lesser extent marriage, in helping people maintain the proper emotional and behavioral disposition (or *habitus*) that drug courts require for success. In both their admission criteria (which favor the admission of white participants)[43] and their procedural operations, drug courts provide a mechanism by which class- and race-privileged individuals who are caught up in the drug war might fairly consistently avoid the full penalty that was implicitly designed with the nonwhite poor in mind.[44]

In other words, drug courts act as a structure of *stratified penalization*, significantly intensifying the war on drugs for the nonwhite poor, even while lessening its burden for the moderately poor and working-class whites who are increasingly caught within a widening net of criminal justice.[45] From a different perspective, drug courts and many other forms of problem-solving justice can be said to mark an institutional turn away from what has been termed "revolving door justice," in which individuals cycle in and out of jail on a frequent basis.[46] Drug courts instead take low-level offenders and submit them to intensified levels of disciplinary training and surveillance before making a single, more consequential decision regarding long-term social exclusion. Far from serving as an alternative to incarceration, drug courts act as a sorting mechanism, carefully assessing which participants merit freedom and which should be locked up for an even longer time than before. Penal welfarism—David Garland's term for an orientation within criminal justice toward correction and rehabilitation—is seemingly reborn but only within a closely supervised context that threatens a more totalizing social exclusion for those who fail to receive aid in the desired way.[47]

Beyond this, there is also significant evidence that drug courts work to "widen the net," meaning that more attention is paid to low-level drug crimes as a result of their presence.[48] As one critical analysis of drug courts notes, once a court is in place, it operates by "providing the police and prosecutor with a costless alternative for those cases that would not go to court."[49] Another study of juvenile drug courts found that concerns about possible net-widening were expressed by drug court staff, defense attorneys, and treatment providers in all six of the courts that the researchers visited. As the researchers write:

> As word spreads in a community that the juvenile drug court employs a rigorous schedule of graduated sanctions, it becomes tempting for referring agencies to send a broader segment of the juvenile justice population to drug court. . . . This practice . . . exposes a much wider array of young offenders to the relatively intense methods and severe sanctions available in juvenile drug court.[50]

The fact that drug courts often widen the net is hardly a surprise given that the initial impetus for their development was to create a more efficient mechanism to handle the large numbers of new, low-level cases generated by the drug war.[51] Increasing judicial capacity was thus one of the key purposes of drug courts, removing something of an institutional bottleneck within the expanded war on drugs. With constant calls to be tough on crime, the rest of the criminal justice system can readily expand into the space they create. Drug treatment courts thus join a long line of intermediate sanctions that have worked to amplify criminal justice control.[52]

But even if drug courts do not mark a complete break with the earlier focus on punishment, it is nevertheless clear that a significant shift has occurred, one with much greater emphasis upon what the legal scholar David Wexler has favorably termed "therapeutic jurisprudence," an approach to law that seeks to maximize the reparative and healing benefits of the legal system.[53] Drug courts thereby significantly redefine the traditional judicial model, with judges no longer acting as seemingly impartial arbiters in a contested process of truth seeking and instead engaging intimately with program enrollees. No longer a site primarily devoted to the establishment of truth beyond a reasonable doubt nor a location for the purportedly neutral application of procedural rules, the court now seeks to learn and deploy pragmatic psychic truths in an effort to rehabilitate. Equally important, drug courts supervise participants while coercing them to attend drug treatment programs and to receive whatever vocational training and educational services the court deems necessary. In this regard, drug courts can perhaps best be said to act as a form of "judicial probation,"[54] a site where judges closely monitor those who have already plead guilty and ensure that they undergo what the court understands as suitable forms of discipline, training, and self-development. In pioneering this mode of therapeutic jurisprudence, drug courts have acted as forerunners for a whole panoply of problem solving courts—specialty courts focusing on a range of issues including mental illness, homelessness, domestic violence, prostitution, and even truancy—that no longer work to ascertain truth but which instead use the threat of imprisonment to force aid upon those it governs.

Administrative Research and Its Discontents

Interest in drug courts has spurred a large and growing body of scholarship and social scientific studies. Most commonly, attention focuses upon the program's efficacy, generally measured in terms of recidivism rates and subsequent cost-effectiveness. Many of these studies are funded by either the Department of Justice (DOJ) or the National Institute on Drug Abuse (NIDA), and are designed to provide information that is useful to the professionals and managers running the courts. These studies form what science studies scholar Thomas Kuhn might call "normal science," an approach in which basic propositions are left unexamined and investigations seek only to answer questions within a previously established frame.[55]

This administrative research generally leaves the terms and definitions of program success uninterrogated and fails to ask basic questions, such as the extent to which lowered recidivism corresponds with changes in peoples' lives that they themselves consider positive.[56] To the extent that more theoretical questions are addressed within this evaluative literature, they generally arise directly out of the challenges and dilemmas court and treatment professionals face, whether in the form of debates concerning the ethics of working with coerced clients or discussions regarding the new model of justice practiced within the courts. While the information gathered through this sort of research is important and valuable, it is notable how little attention such scholarship pays to the actual experiences of program participants, even within much of the clinical literature. The bureaucratic model that arises from this managerial shepherding ignores the issues participants confront on a day-to-day basis, reducing the input of those going through the programs to data points concerning re-arrest rates and other statistical measures designed to assess a program's worth.[57] Assessments of cost effectiveness similarly fail to include any costs (psychological or financial) incurred by participants, detailing only financial outlays incurred by the criminal justice institutions that they evaluate. Cost-benefit analyses thus help to identify efficiencies only in the narrow matter of social control, and the possibility of social citizenship is granted only to populations for whom "catch, train, and monitor" is more cost effective than "catch and exclude."[58] Such calculations financialize citizenship, enabling narrow forms of statistical expertise and an emphasis on results to replace questions of process and broader possibilities for democratic engagement.[59]

This narrowed scope of administrative research not only ignores the lives of participants, it similarly ignores the larger structural shifts that drug courts initiate within the neoliberal state as a whole. Far from simply marking a straightforward revival of the rehabilitative ideal within criminal justice, the rise of drug courts and other problem-solving courts represents a restructuring of what Loïc Wacquant refers to as the "carceral-assistential net," the series of criminal justice and welfare-oriented programs that together manage the (racialized) poor.[60] While Progressive Era efforts at rehabilitation took place within the context of a slowly burgeoning welfare state, drug courts have arisen at a time when racialized mass incarceration has been in place for several decades and services for the poor have been sharply diminished by a neoliberal assault on the post-WWII labor-capital compact. While drug courts share a number of features with Progressive Era courts (which innovated rehabilitative features still present to some extent in today's juvenile courts),[61] the transition from what Wacquant terms a "social state" to a "penal state" gives "problem solving justice" a very different function. The dramatic reduction in welfarist benefits offered to those who have *not* suffered from a criminal conviction, combined with significant growth in imprisonment (including its meager but very real penal-welfarism), result in a situation in which the criminal justice system plays a growing role of in the management of welfare services. Drug court not only enhances the significance of criminal justice within the overall architecture of the carceral-assistential net, it also creates a new role for criminal justice in the administration of welfare services, expanding the state's surveillance capacities in the process.[62] Wacquant rightly argues that this net presses people toward the formal labor market, working to "ensnare the marginal populations of the metropolis . . . either to render them 'useful' by steering them onto the track of deskilled employment through moral retraining and material suasion, or to warehouse them out of reach in the devastated core of the urban 'Black Belt' or in the penitentiaries that have become the latter's distant yet direct satellites."[63] In doing so, the cost-benefit analyses that the state relies upon make it clear that these services are only to be offered when the financial costs of social inclusion can be said to be less than the outlays required for long-term imprisonment and social exclusion.[64] Drug courts thus significantly reshape not only the nature of punishment and criminal justice but the grounds for social inclusion as well, initiating a fiscally-mediated citizenship that conforms with other trends relating to the dominance of finance within neoliberal state-making.[65]

If administrative research on drug courts tends to focus narrowly on questions of efficacy, they similarly focus attention narrowly upon the courts, generally ignoring the drug treatment programs to which participants are referred in the process. Within the evaluative literature on drug courts, in fact, the process of treatment is sometimes referred to as a little-known "black box" into which people enter and spend some time before leaving with magically reduced recidivism rates.[66] This emphasis upon the courts rather than the treatment programs derives from the court's role as an institutional nexus that oversees case management, coordinating both treatment and/or imprisonment. The court thus becomes the central focus in generating cost-benefit analyses, producing data that reveals the advantages of drug courts to the criminal justice system, but through an approach that only incidentally reflects the views and experiences of participants.

Developing a vein of inquiry outside of this managerial context requires an investigation that proceeds on entirely different terms. From the perspectives of those who are participants in drug court programs, for example, the court does not act alone; and indeed, the courtroom is not necessarily the most significant institution with which they interact. While the courts provide administrative direction and oversight, one of the primary activities that a drug court undertakes is simply to refer participants to drug rehabilitation programs, forcing clients to abide by the dictates of these comparatively unexamined institutions. Much of the action of the drug court, then, happens well beyond the confines of the court, in the residential and nonresidential facilities that the court relies upon to provide the day-to-day activities involved in treatment.

Although these treatment facilities are private institutions, it is common for many to receive 80 percent or more of their clients through the drug courts and other parts of the criminal justice system, making them more properly conceived of as adjuncts to criminal justice rather than completely distinct entities.[67] In the case of the drug court I most closely examine, approximately half of the participants are initially assigned to inpatient, residential treatment facilities, a figure that is on par with other urban drug courts. Furthermore, of the half initially sent to outpatient facilities, nearly 50 percent are eventually reassigned to residential facilities after suffering a relapse or otherwise breaking court rules, meaning that approximately three-quarters of all participants end up in long-term residential treatment (over thirty days). In most parts of the country, residential placement involves a form of treatment known as therapeutic communities (TCs), facilities which function as what the sociologist Erving Goffman might have described as "total institutions."[68] Given that drug court participants may spend months or even years living in TCs while visiting the drug court only once every several weeks, I have chosen to direct most of my attention toward these residential facilities. An examination of these institutions allows for a better perspective as to the reality that most people face within drug courts, particularly within urban areas where the use of TCs is most pronounced.

While focusing much of my attention in this book upon therapeutic communities, I continue to focus on the administrative role of the drug court in providing clients to the TCs as well as an overall rationale. The way in which participants are referred—or not referred—to therapeutic communities in fact reveals one of the critical functions of drug courts: stratifying punishment based upon both racial and what I term *para-racial* criteria (which envelop, extend, and partially reconfigure the domain of the racial). As Teresa Gowan and Sarah Whetstone comment, "While whiter and richer drug offenders are filtered out to non-custodial community care, the 'criminal addict' is held to strict accountability within the quasi-incarceration of the strong-arm rehab."[69] Such filtering occurs both within individual courts (where people of different backgrounds are routed to different sorts of treatment programs) and in larger, structural ways (where drug courts offer very different forms of treatment options in jurisdictions that are predominantly white or nonwhite, poor or working class). Data concerning this group level is somewhat limited, but a 2003 study conducted in New York State by Rempel et al. reveals the general trends (see table 1.1). This data shows not only disproportionate benefits for whites within each set of courts, but also that urban courts with large nonwhite populations are more restrictive than rural courts with large white populations. A very different set of bifurcated impacts on the lives of participants is thereby generated, with the nonwhite poor often channeled toward inpatient therapeutic communities while white working class populations are more commonly sent to outpatient facilities that intervene in their lives in far less totalizing ways.[70] Drug courts manage and direct this system of racially stratified punishment, while therapeutic communities (and prisons for those who fail) act as the day-to-day disciplinary force within this new therapeutic drug war. One needs to see how drug courts and TCs work as a coordinated unit, together with a pre-existing system of imprisonment, in order to understand this new institutional inflection within an ongoing system of racialized and classed mass incarceration.

The fact that many (disproportionately white) rural courts rely less upon residential treatment programs than (disproportionately nonwhite) urban ones does more than highlight how geography and racial oppression intersect; it suggests that drug courts play fundamentally distinct roles in different locales featuring different populations. A nonadministrative analysis of drug courts must necessarily forefront the very different roles

TABLE 1.1 Data concerning urban versus rural drug courts

	New York City	Rural New York
Racial proportion of jurisdiction, white	45.1%	80.9%
Racial proportion of drug court participants, white	7.1%	59.8%
Overall proportion graduating vs. failing at three years (other cases remain open)	47.1% vs. 45.4%	50.0% vs. 46.0%
White vs. nonwhite graduation rate at three years	69.8% vs. 44.6%	53.6% vs. 44.4%
White versus nonwhite failure rate at three years	24.8% vs. 47.6%	42.4% vs. 51.5%
Racial proportion of drug court graduates, white	14.4%	64.9%
Racial proportion of drug court failures, white	5.3%	55.8%
Proportion of participants sent to long-term residential treatment program with first referral	38.4%	4.6%
Proportion of participants sent to long-term residential treatment program at some point during drug court	61.5%	17.7%
Proportion of participants charged with drug sales	84.1%	Less than 1%
Proportion of participants listing marijuana as primary drug of choice	47.9%	29.9%
Proportion receiving jail as a sanction	60%	44%

Note: As noted in the table, examinations of racial differences within specific drug courts have yielded mixed results, sometimes showing direct racial discrimination and sometimes revealing that racial differences correlate to other factors such as employment (see also notes 41 and 70). Yet whether these effects are directly or indirectly related to race, it is clear that significant racial differences exist both within individual drug courts and in differences between drug courts that work with predominantly white or nonwhite populations. Rempel et al.'s (2003) data also shows that an urban county (Brooklyn) features the most punitive sanctioning practices and that a rural county (Ithaca) has the least. Though the data in the table are based on a limited sample, the fact that urban drug courts appear to have more racially disparate graduation rates than rural courts—a 25.2 percent differential versus a 9.2 percent differential—is striking. I would speculate that this intensified disparity derives primarily not from differences in the populations involved but from the fact that urban drug courts send nonwhites to long-term residential treatment in disproportionate numbers (see note 70), and that the heightened requirements of these programs produce more drug court failures. The fact that this apparent disparity has never been noticed or investigated is another mark of the narrow range of concern lying within the purview of administrative research on drug courts.

Sources: Figures calculated from Rempel et al. (2003: 30, 32, 33, 41–42, 54, 58, 68, 77, 86). Data concerning New York City excludes Staten Island (which is predominantly white), while data concerning rural counties represent an average of two of the three counties Rempel et al. examined (excluding Tonawanda because complete data for that locale was unavailable). Data concerning marijuana as the primary drug of choice excludes both Brooklyn (as that court automatically excludes those who use only marijuana) and Manhattan (as that court excludes those whose primary drug is alcohol, thereby distorting the overall figures; 35). Data concerning the use of jail as a sanction is derived from only two urban counties (Brooklyn and Queens) and only one rural county (Ithaca) because no other data is available.

that drug courts play in terms of an expanding drug war: just as the heavily racialized war on drugs begins to extend further into the lives of the white working class—with discussion of an (implicitly white) heroin and opioid crisis making headlines[71]—the criminal justice system finds a way to significantly distinguish between these two populations, instituting varied ways of handling participants in localities featuring distinct race and class profiles, on the one hand, and utilizing purportedly neutral and colorblind assessments of drug addiction as a lever with which to appraise and discriminate within individual courts, on the other. Even as my particular study most closely examines a predominantly nonwhite and urban setting, it is important to keep this broader context in mind.[72]

In addition to framing the court within a larger analysis that links it both to other institutions and to wider social processes (such as racial oppression), operating outside of a managerial frame enables one to seek answers to questions that are overwhelmingly ignored within the administrative literature. For example, how does the drug court alter the ways in which treatment is conducted, and how precisely do these treatment services operate? How are ideas about addiction and its treatment enacted in diverse ways across varied social terrains of race, class, gender, age, and sexuality? What kinds of discursive and material tools do drug courts and their associated treatment programs offer participants as they renegotiate their lives under circumstances of state supervision and threat, and how do participants make use of and/or resist the interventions that are imposed upon them? And at a more theoretical level, how does addiction and its treatment relate to classically liberal themes such as rationality, citizenship, familialism, and freedom? How might an examination of these key discourses within liberal political theory shed light on ways in which new forms of social domination have been generated through legal enactments of so-called justice within contemporary social life?

The Drugs Lifestyle, *Homo oeconomicus*, and Humanizing Violence

In asking these questions, I seek to critically examine the naturalized vocabularies of governance that structure practice within the drug court and treatment centers. I thus devote significant attention toward a consideration of the meaning of *addiction* utilized within these contexts. Far from taking the concept as a given, I follow others in developing an anthropology of addiction, detailing the concrete meanings given to the term by different actors within the drug court and treatment contexts.[73] My focus, however, is not on the complex and multilayered factors that lead to compulsive drug use, nor the ways that users come to understand themselves and their own patterns of consumption. Nor are such patterns and identities always at issue, with many drug dealers sentenced to intensive treatment by drug courts despite the fact that they have relatively insignificant histories of consumption.[74] Instead, I direct my attention toward the ways in which various state professionals—judges, district attorneys, case managers, and social workers—conceive of and operationalize the issues surrounding drug use and what is termed recovery. Drug courts and other criminal justice (CJ)–oriented treatment programs do not simply work to get individuals to stop using drugs; rather, they focus their attention on changing what case managers and social workers often frame as an entire "drugs lifestyle."[75] According to social workers and case managers who work with the court, this drugs lifestyle consists of a series of characteristics—impulsivity and an inability to delay gratification, an incapacity to establish a normative work ethic, a sense of irresponsibility—that were previously closely associated with the so-called culture of poverty.[76] Both the drugs lifestyle and the culture of poverty draw upon earlier racial stereotypes in creating new deracinated meanings that are both racial and para-racial in nature, offering a "biologization of poverty and race."[77]

The pejorative stereotypes identified as the drugs lifestyle seem to pertain more to ongoing engagement with the street economy and with state surveillance programs than with the intensive use of drugs per se (it is unclear, for example, how the concept would pertain to those who use drugs while maintaining a steady job). Numerous scholars have written about the ways in which street life shapes personal demeanors and individual habitus according to survival needs generated when confronted with limited resources and a significant fracturing of social solidarity. While emphasizing that people living in poor communities share numerous qualities with middle-class individuals, scholars over a long period of time have worked to resituate the supposed culture of poverty in relation to situational adaptations.[78] In this context, William Julius Wilson suggests that work "imposes disciplines and regularities" and "provides the anchor for the spatial and temporal aspects of daily life." Without work, he proclaims, a person lacks "a coherent organization of the present—that is, a system of concrete expectations and goals." This is so much the case, Wilson argues, that "Persistent unemployment and irregular employment hinder rational planning in daily life."[79]

But if persistent unemployment makes "rational planning" impossible, it makes other forms of living necessary. What Michel de Certeau calls "the art of making do" necessarily creates a world of intense bricolage.[80] Far from the regularities of E. P. Thompson's industrial time,[81] engagement in street life evokes a temporality that emphasizes a spontaneous capacity to capitalize on emerging opportunities and that searches for ways to manipulate situations to one's best advantage. In his essay detailing "the social art of the hustler," Loïc Wacquant speaks in this regard of the "mastery of a particular type of social capital, namely, the ability to manipulate others, to inveigh and deceive them, if need be by joining violence to chicanery and charm, in the pursuit of immediate pecuniary gain."[82] And with an ongoing lack of resources forcing people to scrutinize one another as possible sources of income, the need to maintain a reputation and to defend oneself from possible violence and other sorts of threats becomes primary.[83] Sharon Hays's work has valuably emphasized that there is no singular adaptation to ongoing poverty, and that various "cultures of poverty" can be said to exist.[84] Within this diversity, aspects of street life that commonly pertain to various forms of hustling seem to most directly correspond to the behaviors targeted by the drug court. As will be detailed further throughout this text, these aspects of street life—the way it fosters tactics of bypassing rules and "getting over," the way it makes being yelled at a sign of disrespect that must be immediately answered, the way it generates an intensity and excitement that can make low-wage work feel tedious[85]—form the core aspects of the so-called drugs lifestyle that drug court and court-ordered drug treatment aim to change.

Within this context, drug use forms a secondary concern, and those who work within the drug court go out of their way to emphasize that getting people off of drugs is insufficient, that the entire drugs lifestyle must be changed. In this sense, the idea of addiction acts as an obligatory passage point[86] that enables legal intervention. As Dawn Moore puts it in her analysis of Canadian drug courts, the identity of the *criminal addict* constitutes a "strategy of governing," one that "justifies all manner of interventions and exertions of power."[87] Thus, drug use is subordinated within drug court practice to the true object of attention: the culture(s) of street life. At a social level, this works due to a frequent substitution that takes a host of social and political problems—unemployment, housing instability, hunger, race and class discrimination, barriers to education, police harassment, among many others—and replaces them with the individualized problem of drugs, an exchange that moralizes drug use by erroneously equating it with (a degraded conception of) poverty. In overcoming the supposed drugs lifestyle, the court identifies work in the formal sector as one of its primary criteria for success, so much so that participants must obtain a job in order to graduate from the program. And as will be seen, drug treatment within therapeutic communities itself often centers upon readying residents for their future jobs within the lower tiers of the formal labor force.[88] Thus, the drug court acts to take the disproportionately nonwhite and poor who are swept up into the war on drugs, offers this group of low-level offenders treatment and services that orient participants toward work, carefully monitors and evaluates their responsiveness, and then releases those who succeed while imprisoning anyone who fails to measure up to the employment-oriented criteria that are established. In other words, drug treatment courts are not primarily about drugs but instead form a technique of social management over the racialized poor. This step in the medicalization of poverty[89] not only makes structural conditions invisible, it also pathologizes survival-based responses to social and economic marginalization and, in effect, offers professionalized management (judicial and otherwise) of low-level, subterranean political resistance. Beyond legitimizing the disciplinary measures developed by middle class experts, in reaffirming the value of work (even in its most degraded and abusive forms), the medicalization of poverty also conceals the many mortifications of self—including intensive drug use—that people rely upon in adjusting themselves to exploitative labor practices.[90] This second circuit of drug consumption, in which work causes drug use, is entirely unthinkable within the ideology of the drugs lifestyle. Just as critically, to whatever extent a certain form of rhetorical medicalization is achieved via drug courts, it is carefully conducted so as to maintain managerial control within the domain of criminal justice rather than the medical or "psy" establishments. Drug courts do not represent a public health approach to drug use (however fraught that possibility might also be) but instead use the rhetoric of medicalization in order to validate criminal justice measures.

As part of a system of racialized poverty management, drug courts draw on themes that are foundational to liberalism in characterizing those they oversee and in providing justification for their interventions. While property is central to early liberalism's way of thinking about both civil society and selfhood—creating what C. B. Macpherson famously referred to as "the possessive individual"[91]—much more is implied within this metaphor of ownership. As Shannon Winnubst notes in her careful exegesis of Locke, liberalism entails a wider chain of signifiers involving "individualism, private property, labor guided by clear intention and teleology, a futural temporality, and freedom as the ability to express one's power."[92] In this regard, Locke tellingly argues that " 'person' is a forensic [i.e., legal] term, having to do with actions and their merit; and so it applies only to active thinking beings that are capable of a law."[93] Personhood thus constitutes a "unit of accountability,"[94] while those without personhood of this sort live outside the law and therefore have no rights.[95] In generating a long series of "wild" personages who were understood to live not only outside the law but outside society as well, liberalism created a legal justification to murder, enslave, and steal the lands of those who failed in its eyes to achieve true personhood.

As Sylvia Wynter suggests, to live outside of legal personhood in this sense was to be consigned to the realms of the "not-quite-human" or even the "nonhuman."[96] Wynter further argues that personhood in the West is largely equated with an implicitly classed, gendered, and racialized figure of *homo oeconomicus*, a figure that has been dominant in some sense since the rise of capitalism.[97] In the context of court-ordered drug treatment, the "drugs lifestyle" thus conjures a visage of an old enemy, the *not-quite human* who stands somewhere between the animal and Man. This logic of exclusionary violence was applied most ruthlessly along racial lines, but according to liberal logics, other "savages" (the criminal, the insane, the drunkard, the addict, etc.) bore a general familial resemblance and were subject to parallel forms of treatment.[98] The personality traits of these purported *animals* were a mirror image of the propertied, liberal self: shiftless, dangerous, unpredictable, and prone to sin. More than mere stereotypes, these images act as a form of legal and moral argumentation, justifying the use of direct force within a society in which liberal ethical precepts are hegemonic. Put simply: racism, classism, colonialism, and a developing liberal political culture came together in creating an image of the lazy, unpropertied brute lacking in self-possession, and this visage has had a genealogical influence on a variety of contemporary figures, including that of the criminal addict and their supposed drugs lifestyle.[99] This genealogical link among an otherwise diverse set of figures becomes possible because these personages are similarly located within a hegemonic liberal legal and cultural regime. Whether as *criminal* or as *addict*, the drug court participant has no personhood in the liberal sense, and thus shares—in a loose, semantic sense—the verdict handed down in the infamous decision of *Dred Scott v. Sanford* (1857), which ruled that blacks held "no rights which the white man was bound to respect; and that the negro might justly and lawfully be reduced to slavery for his benefit."

Yet white supremacy envisions another mode of domination unlike that which was exercised over the slave. This alternate form of violence is envisioned as inclusive, as lifting the savage into a civilized state. There is a shift from the necropolitical to the biopolitical here, even as both forms of power enact coercive control over the colonial Other. The idea that a *humanizing violence* (or a *civilizing violence*) can lift the "inhuman savage" into proper "personhood" has a lengthy history within the colonial encounter. As Samera Esmeir argues in her analysis of "juridical humanity" in colonial Egypt, liberal legal regimes regularly deploy pain in the making of "the human":

> The project of juridical humanity did not aim at eliminating wounding but rather at preventing what it defined as unproductive and disproportional cruelty, that which exceeded or fell short of its objectives. As long as violence was administered and classified, and as long as it was potentially productive, it could be humane. Torture became a means of punishment, whipping a means of disciplining, chaining in irons a means of controlling.[100]

Following this logic, "pain was put to use and mobilized toward the end of making a human."[101] Indeed, Esmeir points out, "modern law's authorizing assumption was indeed that those who have been abandoned to the 'state of nature' must be rescued through inclusion in the empire protected by modern liberal law."[102] It thus is incumbent on good political subjects to aid "already-suffering" brutes in their quest to become "human." As yet another civilizing technology, drug courts and the treatment programs to which they refer participants partake in the *violent care* generated by these colonial logics.

Drug courts thus combine David Garland's "Criminologies of the Other" (the threatening outcaste) and "Criminologies of the Self" (who are "just like us")[103] in a way that might seem contradictory but which is common within assimilative colonial projects. In colonial versions, the colonized remains savage until properly disciplined and "civilized"; within the rhetoric of the drug court, drug users are Others, but only insofar as the illness of "addiction" has made them such.[104] Drug treatment has the symbolic potential to cure participants and to render them part of the general collectivity, but failure at treatment leaves them othered, even if no drugs are currently being used. In this sense, it might be said that drug use is not the key feature of addiction within the drug court; drug use merely offers an entrée point for a larger socializing project. Thus, *the addict* is one against whom sufficient violence has been rendered as to make living as "human" impossible. The court seeks to take those whose "personhood" is damaged by "drug use" and subject them to further corrective violence.

Brainwashing and the Pre-Conditions of Freedom

The historical development of the treatment programs utilized by drug courts reveal a different genealogical connection with liberalism. The first therapeutic community, Synanon—an organization that has had a foundational role in developing the model for contemporary treatment programs within the criminal justice system—seems to have adopted some of its techniques from reports of Chinese brainwashing techniques prevalent in media reports of the 1950s.[105] Accounts concerning these "communist" methods appear to have, in fact, been based upon CIA propaganda rather than actual fact, the reality being that the CIA itself began to develop these practices shortly after World War II, ultimately consolidating its experiments within the notorious MK-ULTRA program.[106] Not only did the United States utilize practices of "brainwashing" during the Korean and Vietnam Wars, it has continued to develop interrogation techniques based upon this research for use in Guantánamo and other CIA black sites around the world.[107] Techniques inspired by accounts of brainwashing—rebranded as "coercive persuasion" by Edgar Schein, who later became a central figure within the field of organizational psychology—were similarly recommended for use in U.S. prisons, to uncertain effect.[108] While brainwashing in *The Manchurian Candidate* sense of the term does not exist, the ongoing use of these highly abrasive and coercive techniques within CJ-oriented drug treatment programs establishes a state therapeutics that forcibly embeds itself into the daily lives of a population that the state itself considers "low risk."[109]

Coerced rehabilitation practices thus lie directly of the border between liberal and illiberal rule, marking the otherwise invisible set of preconditions that the state establishes before "freedom" can be exercised. As the legal scholar Mariana Valverde argues, liberalism here depends upon the application of force to those it excludes.

> The justification of "good despots" by reference to a defect of the will, a failure of desire, is the key to "workfare" programmes aimed at the remoralization of the long-term unemployed and others whose "habits" and whose very souls are perceived as requiring some combination of liberal-therapeutic, disciplinary and morally coercive techniques to bring them up to the level of liberal subjects.[110]

Valverde suggests that the subsequent combination of despotism and liberal forms of governance necessarily coexist, whether within the management of marginalized populations or in the childcare practices of elites. As she suggests, "liberal governance is in practice never merely liberal. . . . There are dialectical reversals that make liberal governance logically dependent upon despotism even within the heart of the liberal subject."[111] In this sense, Valverde's analysis points toward the way that drug courts address marginalized populations primarily through practices of threat and coercion, even when attempting to foster liberal forms of selfhood and self-governance.[112]

The techniques of brainwashing offer a common mechanism, first in the war against communism, then in the war against criminality, and then in the war against drugs. It is a complex genealogical circuit, one only loosely and haphazardly knitted together. But the homologies that Schein drew between communism and criminality, and that Dederich drew between communism and drug addiction, are latent possibilities constructed by the structure of liberal selfhood and its exclusions. The communist (a mental slave), the criminal (the uncontrolled savage), and the addict (whether monstrous dope fiend or enslaved victim) all suffer from what Valverde terms "diseases of the will," maladies that allegedly make self-governance unmanageable. Without self-control, freedom is rendered unobtainable, at least according to this liberal logic.[113] This notion of freedom acts as a coercive force, one used to justify intensive state interventions. As Saidiya Hartman argues, an "onus of accountability . . . rested upon the shoulders of the self-responsible individual—the task of proving oneself worthy of freedom."[114] "We are governed not against but *through* our freedom," suggests Valverde. "Individual freedom is not a utopian force threatening the status quo . . . but is rather the means through which the status quo perpetuates itself in our very souls."[115] In this vein, Rousseau intoned that in order to sustain the social contract, some must necessarily be "forced to be free."[116] In point of fact, however, liberalism provides two options: civilizing force which (in a highly gendered frame) makes *men* from *savages*, or exclusion from the body politic. Drug courts are remarkable in that they combine both assimilative and eliminatory options: an effort to rehabilitate the fallen addict as well as long-term incarceration and social segregation for those who fail at freedom. Foucault's disciplinary society is fortified by necropolitical possibilities.

In this context, brainwashing simply offered the most recent and powerful technology of freedom-making available, one capable of being adapted for use with a variety of liberty's Others. But while Cold War panic spread fears that the entire Soviet and Chinese populations had been brainwashed, the practical reality of the techniques required a high degree of control over a targeted person's social environment, rendering brainwashing feasible only with inmates. Even as brainwashing became a metaphor for various sorts of social manipulation (advertising, etc.), the therapeutic community—with its intense surveillance and severe punishments—ultimately found its primary home only within institutions capable of confinement.[117] Yet the intense levels of control exercised by these institutions sometimes left those who attempted to force (a particular version of) freedom onto others subject to criticism for themselves contradicting the basic principles of liberty. For example, Synanon was accused of becoming a cult, despite having been the model for hundreds of drug treatment programs around the globe.[118] The mirrored discursive logic on display—in which those who seek to instill "freedom" in others must resort to extreme coercion—again points toward the interpenetration of "despotism" and "freedom," the ways in which this vision of freedom necessarily rests upon a bedrock of unfreedom. Whereas Isaiah Berlin warned of the coercive dangers of positive liberty in his 1958 anticommunist essay "Two Concepts of Liberty," here it is revealed that even the notion of negative liberty—freedom from constraint—carries within it the potential for considerable regulatory principles and exclusions from "the social contract."[119]

Drug Courts and the Shifting Logics of Racialized Mass Incarceration

Of course the nature of unfreedom—whether for children within elite families, whose subordination is temporary, or for the mostly nonwhite poor ensnared by the institutions of criminal justice—varies enormously depending upon circumstance. Part of the task of this book is to document the consequences of liberal governance within the particular context of the drug court and its associated therapeutic practices within the TC, looking within these settings at the ways in which the practices of freedom take on particular forms in relation to the particular formations of capitalism, as well as in relation to issues pertaining to the interlinked formations of race, gender, class, and sexuality. The background social conditions in this case pertain to globalization (i.e., the dispersal of industry to the semicolonized periphery), and the ways in which this move rendered U.S black populations economically superfluous. Automation began causing similar dynamics in the 1960s, as presciently noted by the sociologists Sidney Willhelm and Edwin Powell in their 1964 article "Who Needs the Black Man?"[120] But if automation and the dynamics of racial capitalism began to give white supremacy a new configuration by the mid-1960s, one characterized by the economics of disposability rather than the economics of exploitation, globalization greatly exacerbated that nascent trend, creating a situation in which large-scale mass incarceration could be enacted (a measure that countered black protest and the potential for uprising while offering a not-so-coded form of racist populism to white populations).[121]

Several penologists have described the rise of racialized mass incarceration and the epochal shift in penal logics implicated in that change. While an earlier rehabilitative ethic (what David Garland refers to as "penal welfarism") arose in the late 1800s, by the 1970s it was being displaced by what Garland refers to as "the culture of control."[122] This neoliberal period of escalating incarceration was accompanied by theories of deterrence, risk management, and incapacitation that established a rationale for longer sentencing, intensified levels of enforcement, and warehousing practices within prisons. Theories of deterrence and risk management in particular guided efforts to alter the pattern of incentives and disincentives that a potential offender faced, either by passing harsher laws or by intensifying state surveillance. A series of measures—hiring greater numbers of police officers, installing more closed-circuit cameras and street lights, and using statistical methods to identify "high-risk" areas and patrolling them with greater intensity (including the use of stop-and-frisk)—all worked to change the overall behavioral environment, making it more likely that illegal acts would be discovered and punished with greater severity, at least against certain (invariably poor and nonwhite) populations. Significantly, the anticrime logics embedded in these approaches have no self-imposed limit: when it is believed that crime rates are going up, it signals a need for still stricter laws; yet when crime rates are shown to be going down, it indicates that "toughness" is working and needs to be pressed further.

Propelled in many ways by the war on drugs, this process began to reach its institutional, though not political, limits as early as the late 1980s—most notably in the form of a court system overfilled with drug offenders—and it was at this point that bureaucratic innovation was necessitated *within* the bounds of a neoliberal and highly incarcerative logic. A variety of drug diversion programs were initiated at precisely this time, eventually culminating with the apparent ascendancy of drug treatment courts.[123] With change necessitated by fiscal concerns—stemming from both the high costs of imprisonment and bottlenecks in legal processing (themselves caused by an unwillingness to spend more money in handling the increased caseloads)—I argue that the first wave of neoliberal penology—characterized by extreme punitiveness—has been followed by a second wave, this one introducing a carefully calculated and delimited focus on the individual. Whereas Feeley and Simon's "new penology" identified a statistical focus that targeted "high risk" populations with heightened security measures, this new variant directs it toward low-risk groups where costs might be cut through the provision of limited services. In this way, drug courts mark an important shift within neoliberal social policy. To the extent that cost-benefit analysis and other forms of marketized policy-making are established, in the current moment they represent an important limit upon a politics of law and order, the criminalization of poverty, and racialized mass incarceration. The use of cost-benefit analyses to justify certain rehabilitative programming—a trend Hadar Aviram identifies as *humonitarianism*[124]—is thus linked with broader trends toward austerity politics and the financialization of governance. Ironically, given the identification of mass incarceration with neoliberalism, humonitarianism might best be seen as a finance-led effort to impose austerity measures upon right-wing populism.

More generally, the move to provide progressive/liberal justification for the ever greater involvement of social management via the criminal justice system finds numerous examples, including the Violence against Women Act (VAWA), antitrafficking measures, and anti-hate crime policies, all of which offer a narrow vision of crime control to deal with complex social problems.[125] What links these diverse topics is the way in which the criminal justice system as currently constituted comes to be understood as a means of achieving justice more generally, a perspective that ignores the ways in which it offers a limited repertoire of possible interventions, all of which intimately bound with the pervasive oppression that is so fundamental to its routine operations. Elizabeth Bernstein has coined the term "carceral feminism" in pointing toward ways in which certain parts of the woman's movement have effectively been coopted in the construction of this new hegemonic form,[126] while James Kilgore has similarly noted trends toward supposedly humane, yet inevitably more controlling, forms within the criminal justice system, calling the result "carceral humanism."[127]

This rhetoric of humanitarian benefit enables criminal justice to identify itself more completely as a force for good in society. It works to quell unease around the role of policing, establishing it as a benefit to those who are most marginalized (and whose needs might otherwise go unaddressed if not for the benevolent role of the police). In their ground-breaking 1978 text *Policing the Crisis*, Stuart Hall et al. discussed the way in which law and order politics worked to displace the post-World War II welfarist consensus, pointing toward the cultural hegemony a notion of legitimate aggression against lawbreakers came to have within both the UK and the United States. Importantly, however, as the title suggests, Hall et al.'s analysis suggested that law and order thrived upon the notion of an emergency, a state of affairs beyond the usual foundations of the liberal order. "The 'ideology of the crisis' . . . leads to and supports and finally finds its fulfillment in a 'law and order' society."[128] The "sponsored moral panics" that generate support for this "exceptional" state exist only in moments of perceived (racialized, classed, gendered) threat, at "the time of mugging."[129] While Hall et al. argued that crisis led to the overturning of the post-war social order (roll-back), contemporary humanitarian logics enable action on marginalized populations *outside* of these moments of crisis or at moments when the primary "sponsored crisis" has been displaced onto other terrain, such as terrorism. In the face of an eased crisis, rhetorics of both humanitarianism and fiscal responsibility reappear on the public stage and work to stabilize neoliberal structures as not simply necessary but as advantageous for those impacted.

As Didier Fassin notes in his text *Humanitarian Reason*, "the politics of compassion is a politics of inequality."[130] Humanitarianism is not a language of obligatory rights but of voluntary benevolence; a language directed at assisting those who are placed outside of the political order without challenging that exclusion. It creates a "politics of pity" rather than a "politics of justice."[131] Humanitarianism both depends on and solidifies a sense in which the boundaries between giver and receiver are well defined, thus being subject to dispersal in moments of fear.[132] The inequalities implicit within humanitarian logics enable neoliberalism to deploy a carceral humanism that consolidates and even extends the position of the criminal justice system. Jonathan Simon's notion of "governing through crime" is maintained, but its operations no longer revolve solely around fear as he suggested, instead becoming at least partly infused with tender concern.[133] Having successfully rolled out mass incarceration during a time of panic, the neoliberal security state[134] now moves to further entrench itself, presenting drug courts and other allied programs as humanitarian and cost-effective solutions to problems it has itself engendered. Most deceptively (given its rehabilitative rhetoric), the courts then maintain a politics of fear in incarcerating those who fail to properly receive the state's benevolent aid.

These shifting logics of institutional change within the forms of governmental control have been cogently discussed by other commentators. For example, in their analysis of neoliberalization (a term they prefer to the static *neoliberalism*), geographers Jamie Peck and Adam Tickell distinguish between two phases of contemporary political-economic restructuring:

roll-back neoliberalization and roll-out neoliberalization. While the first roll-back phase is marked by governmental deregulation and privatization, the later roll-out processes involve active policy creation and occur once the governmental forms established during the relative truce between labor and capital that followed World War II are effectively dismantled. "In the course of this shift, the agenda has gradually moved from one preoccupied with the active *destruction and discreditation* of Keynesian-welfarist and social-collectivist institution (broadly defined) to one focused on the purposeful *construction and consolidation* of neoliberalized state forms, modes of governance, and regulatory relations."[135] Peck and Tickell suggest that this roll-out phase has promoted policies of mass incarceration in relation to other forms of labor discipline over marginalized populations:

> In social policy, the (re)criminalization of poverty, the normalization of contingent work, and its enforcement through welfare retrenchment, workfare programming, and active employment policies represent a comprehensive reconstitution of the boundary institutions of the labor market. . . . Market discipline, it seems, calls for new modes of state intervention in the form of large-scale incarceration, social surveillance, and a range of microregulatory interventions to ensure persistent "job readiness."[136]

While in some ways drug courts might be considered an elaboration of this roll-out phase, I argue that they represent a sufficiently distinct logic as to usefully be identified as a new phase, one that works to establish neoliberal hegemony. Drug courts remain consonant with the rollout of mass incarceration but feature considerably different logics and rhetorics. Peck and Tickell's schema might thus be modified to include three phases or, more simply, three dynamics: (1) delegitimation and deregulation, (2) construction and consolidation, and (3) hegemonification.[137]

Unlike historical efforts at penal welfarism, today's programs are overwhelmingly centered in reentry programs and problem-solving courts where they address either those leaving prison or those deemed low-risk.[138] The neoliberal emphasis on dangerousness and fear remains visible in the drug court's focus on so-called non, non, nons (those who have committed nonviolent, nonserious, and nonsexual crimes). While there has been some effort to expand drug courts to somewhat higher-risk participants,[139] federal grant guidelines for drug courts specify that only nonviolent offenders can become participants.[140] The transformation of criminal justice into therapeutic jurisprudence thus marks a two-fold movement: on the one hand, the state recognizes the inefficiencies involved in a strategy of widespread mass incarceration, moderating its impulses toward social exclusion in favor of a more selective approach; on the other hand, the state indicates its unwillingness to stray too far from a punitive and exclusionary model, revealing the way in which neoliberalism has greatly diminished its grammar of possible interaction in relation to those liminally included within the social order. In this context, drug courts can be seen as reformulating the relationship between practices of despotism and practices of liberty, promoting practices of self-governance to low-risk offenders (who arguably should not be addressed through criminal justice in the first place), yet simultaneously retaining the possibility of social exclusion for any who cannot meet the work-related requirements that the courts establish. Drug courts retain the securitization of the color line through a new, therapeutic drug war, one that also targets far more poor whites than previously, albeit with a lighter touch. The neoliberal state here establishes a three-tier system of governance: citizenship for those who successfully navigate the market and enact normative self-governance; "humanitarian" policing and aid on a probationary basis for low-risk yet criminalized individuals who are deemed potentially amenable to reform (offered on a cost-savings basis and within structures that clearly favor working-class whites over less affluent nonwhites); and a totalizing exclusion for a still large and disproportionately nonwhite population understood as criminal threats. Given the drug court's demand that participants obtain a job in order to graduate, the program can be seen as fine-tuning the capacity of the criminal justice system to control what Marx termed a surplus population, those unable to conform to the labor dictates of capital.

Investigating the Practices of Freedom: Methods and Chapter Outline

While discursive critiques of liberal exclusions mark one jumping off point, my aim in this book is to detail the specific forms that are entailed by this legal and social marginalization in relation to a concrete set of related sites: the drug court and the treatment programs to which it assigns participants. At a certain point during my fieldwork, I realized that the drug court offered case study after case study in which the contemporary political order was deciding who possessed the requisite social capacities for "freedom" and who did not. In this sense, this book in part constitutes an ethnography of freedom—not as an existential characteristic but as a political and legal category often enforced against those deemed incapable of exercising it. As seen above, and for an overabundance of reasons, work in the formal sector has become the primary criteria in appraising a drug court participant's fitness for freedom.[141] In the case of the court I examined, the local district attorney's office had insisted upon the requirement that participants find work prior to being released during the initial negotiations that created the program. As one of the DAs who participated in these negotiations explained, "I don't want to create more effective, less addicted drug dealers. I want to create viable citizens." This conception entirely circumvents some of the questions that might arise in relation to the category of addiction (e.g., why punish a disease?) in favor of a much older dichotomy between work and criminality, revealing that drug court participants remain *criminal* addicts. In a similar vein, speakers at a drug court graduation ceremony I attended made frequent reference to their pleasure in knowing that participants were now "taxpayers" and "productive members of society,"[142] again pointing toward an imaginary that work and drug use are incompatible (this despite the obvious fact that many people who work also use drugs, and despite the fact that some 20 percent of drug court participants are already legally employed at the time of their arrest, with nearly 10 percent more attending school).[143] During conferences and in writings, drug court practitioners sometimes refer to their aims in these regards as the creation of NORPs: normal, ordinary, responsible persons.

NORPness, viable citizenship, earning an income, and paying income taxes—together with the contrasting image of the poverty-inflected "drugs lifestyle"—collectively form a series of interrelated images that guide drug court practice. Very notably, for example, when I asked one of the district attorneys working with the court who would be appropriately placed within an outpatient facility as opposed to a residential facility, they responded without hesitation: "Someone with a job."[144] The impact of these recommendations becomes clear once one considers that approximately half of those participating in this particular drug court listed marijuana as their drug of choice (most of them being charged as dealers). Despite their limited use of drugs, these individuals were systematically routed toward residential facilities because they were not employed in formal sector labor.[145] In the case of the DAs, it seemed that their concern was more with the potential *dangerousness* of a given participant than with their clinical need, and they clearly relied upon the criteria of formal labor in making this assessment, supplanting any of the usual criteria in relation to "treatment need" in favor of an unspoken imposition of "public safety."[146] This decisive imposition of criminal justice concerns within considerations of treatment effectively turns many inpatient treatment facilities into de facto jails (despite the fact that drug courts are often promoted as an alternative to incarceration). The idea that residential drug treatment facilities serve as auxiliary prisons was explicitly acknowledged by several staff members working within the drug court I examined, as well as one of the assistant DAs who directly suggested that the facilities were "turning into mini-jails." Likewise, many of the treatment center staff members recounted ways in which the therapeutic order of the program had significantly disintegrated in the face of an increase in unmotivated residents channeled through criminal justice programs. Participants in the program similarly noted its custodial feel, frequently comparing life inside the residential facility to life within jail (generally favoring life at the treatment center, but not always). "This is a containment center," offered one of the more critical residents who I interviewed.[147]

In referring to these dynamics as practices of freedom, I am admittedly introducing an outside term into the drug courts and therapeutic communities: I do not believe I heard a single individual in either the drug courts nor the therapeutic communities utilize the word *freedom* (nor *liberty*) during any of my interviews or more casual conversations. Nevertheless, I hope to both illuminate the ways in which concepts rooted in classical liberalism shape everyday practices even when the terms are not directly used, as well as to offer a critique of contemporary liberalism, highlighting the ways in which its conceptual categories are used in producing outcomes that are oppressive and unjust. At another level, the following study straightforwardly constitutes an ethnography of state power—one that seeks to examine the role of rehabilitation following the punitive turn and the types of subjects it seeks to create.[148] Drug courts represent an aspect of neoliberal reform within the criminal justice system and provide a useful site for analysis of both the opportunities (which do exist) and limits present within allegedly humanitarian reforms, as well as their practical logics and dynamics. While at its most basic level neoliberalism is notable for its challenge to Keynesian advocacy for a welfare state and for its reemphasis upon a politics of austerity and the values of the market, drug courts instantiate a whole series of interrelated institutional and cultural shifts that help elaborate the precise forms taken by this new liberalism.

In order to assess the drug court's approach to the treatment of addiction, I conducted thirteen months of ethnographic field research in three interrelated sites: a drug treatment court in New York City, the court's ancillary case management office, and one of the nearly 100 treatment facilities to which the court referred its participants. After initially visiting my first drug court in the spring of 2003, I returned to the same court in August of 2007. Over a period of four months at the drug treatment court, I sat in on court sessions, including precourt meetings during which the judge, defense and prosecuting attorneys, and the case managers assessed each case and made decisions regarding each individual's disposition. I interviewed all of the members of the court team and also visited three additional courts, interviewing judges and/or case managers at each site. At the drug court in which I conducted the majority of my research, the judge permitted me to sit with them on the bench during court proceedings (a position that allowed me to hear the many huddled conversations in which the judge would quietly confer with lawyers or with drug court participants). On rare occasions, I saw individuals in court who I knew through my other ethnographic work at the treatment center. In these instances, to my relief, the persons seemed pleased to see me sitting with the judge (in later conversation, it seemed that being seen with the judge made my study seem even more "official" and important). Later, I also visited a community court (which applied the drug court model to additional sorts of misdemeanor offenses) and interviewed several staff members there. Over time, I attended four drug court related conferences, two sponsored by the NADCP and two jointly sponsored by the Addiction Treatment Providers Association and the New York Association of Drug Treatment Court Professionals. I also attended two panel sessions sponsored by the New York State Office of Alcoholism and Substance Abuse Services (OASAS).

In a second component of my ethnographic research, I spent approximately four months observing and talking with the court-affiliated case managers and social workers. The director of the drug court's administrative side was also extremely welcoming in giving me "free range of the castle," not only helping me in finding any documents but even offering a room where I could conduct interviews with participants (which involved approaching individuals while they were waiting to conduct their urine tests and asking if they would be willing to speak with me about their experiences with the court).[149] Though it was not possible for me to directly sit in on interactions between the court's case managers and clients, I also had months of informal conversations with case managers about their work and conducted formal interviews with seven staff members, including five case managers and both the director and the assistant director of the organization.

In the third and most involving phase of the ethnographic research, I spent some eight months regularly visiting a therapeutic community to which the drug court referred individuals. Only a handful of the program's residents had been referred through the drug court where I conducted my other research, but some 80 percent had been referred through some component of the criminal justice system (usually as part of an agreement regarding probation or parole). I worked to form viable ties with both staff members and clients, sometimes sitting in the office with staff members at this residential treatment center, participating with residents in program activities or meals, and sometimes chatting informally with residents during unstructured moments.[150] During these months of ethnographic observation at the treatment center, I also conducted formal interviews with forty-four residents.[151] I further attended most staff meetings and interviewed nearly all of the staff at the facility. I supplemented this research with visits to two other residential treatment programs, interviewing staff members at each, and additionally interviewing staff members at a third prison-based treatment program (where I was unable to receive permission to visit). Lastly, I interviewed state officials at OASAS whose responsibility involved regulation and oversight over these private facilities. As part of this ethnography, I conducted ninety-three formal interviews, including forty-one interviews with professionals of various sorts and fifty-two participants in drug treatment programs.

Two key caveats must be added regarding the ethnographic components of this study. The drug court and the therapeutic community that I examined both focused heavily upon nonwhite populations. Whereas nationally, white participation in drug courts hovers at around 70 percent,[152] in both the drug court and the therapeutic community I examined the figure was closer to 5 percent. As referenced earlier, the places I examined are fairly typical in these regards for courts located in urban areas; however, it should again be emphasized that a significant number of courts operate in suburban and rural areas with predominantly white participants (perhaps operating in significantly different ways as a result). Additionally, I did not examine the outpatient drug treatment facilities to which the court referred people, though, admittedly, approximately 25 percent of people participating in the drug court—those more class-privileged to begin with—had experience with only outpatient institutions (and as noted, drug courts in rural areas rely upon outpatient facilities even more regularly). This emphasis resulted from my own interest in examining the way the drug courts impacted the least class-privileged sectors coming through the courts. It does, however, represent a limitation of the study in terms of its applicability. Readers might wish to think of this as a study of urban drug courts rather than of drug courts as such, keeping in mind that white populations in suburban and rural areas are treated with a distinctly lighter touch by these same courts.

A second issue arose as I began to conduct these ethnographic explorations. While ethnography enabled me to better see how the two programs were operating in the current moment, to observe the mechanisms they used to achieve their effects and the ways in which participants related to the programs, I found it increasingly necessary to situate my observations in a deeper historical field. I felt it important to undertake this historical exploration in relation to the therapeutic community in particular, as its practices might otherwise seem somewhat idiosyncratic and incomprehensible. (How is it that drug treatment at some facilities came to involve wearing dunce caps, for example?) Not wishing simply to document a history of humiliating and otherwise abusive practices within the facilities, I sought also to explicate the logic of such abuses and to show how the criminal justice system made use of and modified such practices. I therefore offer a chapter detailing part of this history, examining the practices of drug treatment developed at Synanon, most of which continue to organize CJ-oriented drug treatment in the present period, despite significant changes in the field (professionalization, managed care, etc.). I also briefly detail the historical relationship between therapeutic communities and the criminal justice system, showing how a set of practices developed at the cultural fringe came to be so central within contemporary programming.

This historical chapter not only illuminates the nature of contemporary regimes of punitive rehabilitation, but it aims to contextualize it and highlight the historical alternatives over which it gained institutional dominance. Additionally, I found it rather striking that an institution (Synanon) that partially modeled itself on brainwashing and that was routinely referred to as a cult in mainstream media nevertheless became the model relied upon for contemporary CJ-oriented drug rehabilitation programs. In this chapter, I seek to bring this surprising history forward, and to better contextualize the overall position of the TC within criminal justice.

In compiling this history, I rely upon the work of earlier historians who have written about Synanon in particular, as well as the abundant literature that was created by advocates for these programs at the time they were being developed. I supplement this research by examining many first-person accounts that have been written by both staff members and those undergoing treatment concerning these early programs, as well as by surveying some of the early accounts by investigators who took a more critical attitude toward these programs. Given the critical tone of my presentation concerning these early programs, it should be noted that the vast majority of the material that I use comes from sources that were strongly favorable toward the early TCs; the critiques that I make derive largely from differences of interpretation rather than differences of fact (terms such as *indoctrination* and *brainwashing*, for example, were openly used by advocates of such programs).

Thus, a total of five chapters follow this introductory chapter. In chapter 2, I rely on an ethnographic approach to examine the ways in which drug courts operate, providing a general overview before specifically examining the ways in which the courts seek to manage their own capacity to threaten participants and to direct this punitive capacity therapeutically. In this chapter, I discuss the ways in which drug courts extend state control by bypassing ordinary controls against judicial power and through the careful management of threat. I further discuss the therapeutic aims of drug courts, highlighting the way they work to target the drugs lifestyle and enforce citizenship in terms of para-racial criteria in the process. Chapter 3 constitutes the historical section of the book, providing a crucial contextualization for my ethnographic accounts. In chapter 3 I discuss the history of the first therapeutic community designed to address drug abuse, Synanon. Although changes have been made to the TC program, many of the practices developed at Synanon are still utilized in numerous drug treatment facilities today, particularly in TCs that work closely with the criminal justice system. I thus use this chapter to examine the basic logic of the TC approach before detailing the changes that have been made more recently. I also detail the historically tight links between TCs and the criminal justice system, emphasizing both the structural conditions and the extremely contingent and even happenstance events that ultimately made TCs successful. In chapters 4 and 5 I return to my ethnographic research, examining a contemporary therapeutic community and the ways in which residents coped with its challenging demands. Chapter 4 is focused on links between the issue of discipline and drug treatment within the contemporary TC, further detailing the complex ways in which residents sometimes resist and sometimes adapt to the TC's stringent goals, and highlighting the institution's efforts to produce specific forms of agency (as well as its rejection of *fugitive agencies*). Chapter 5 directs attention to issues pertaining to the nexus of work, gender, and sexuality, highlighting ways in which the TC mobilizes gender-based shame and offers highly gendered promises in order to achieve its effects. Among other issues, I use this chapter to critique the concept of hegemonic masculinity, highlighting the ways in which it fails to capture the contradictory dynamics confronted by men at the facility. I also detail the structure of intimacies of the state in relation to issues of privatization and the hollowing out of state functions. Lastly, in chapter 6, I offer an evaluation of drug courts and of their associated TCs. Although drug courts indeed feature a number of positive elements—most notably in relation to the comparatively non-punitive nature of the rhetoric they utilize—in this book I argue that drug courts in their current formulation represent a devil's bargain; and as with most deals with the devil, it is one in which the fine print reveals a situation much more disadvantageous than might at first be evident. While enabling certain conditional forms of social inclusion, drug courts' ultimate reliance on and commitment to the necropolitical—particularly in relation to black bodies—must be highlighted and condemned. In a more analytic mode, drug courts might be seen as a revelatory site insofar as they deploy multiple liberal logics in creating a novel institutional form, one that variously disciplines and excludes according to a financialized, biopolitical calculation. The courts bring these diverse modalities together in the name of security and an ongoing fight against *the criminal*, albeit a criminal who is discursively humanized by their purported victimization to demon drugs. As a reform *within* a framework of securitization, drug courts necessarily position themselves as the safeguards of an upright citizenry against beastly outsiders, even as they simultaneously offer the possibility of redemption for those who successfully "civilize" themselves. Thus, despite their apparent shift away from conservative tough-on-crime narratives, drug courts in fact adhere to these very same standards of "toughness." Disrupting the court's commitment to what is ultimately an exercise of state violence against predominantly black and brown bodies will require a far greater disruption to liberal logics than is conceivable within the penal reforms currently on offer.

2

Drug Court Paternalism and the Management of Threat

Graduation Ceremony

On a rainy day in the summer of 2009, about a hundred people make their way to one of the city's large courtrooms, all wanting to witness and participate in this final ceremony despite the inclement weather. Nearly half of the drug court's sixty-one graduates have chosen to attend the graduation ceremony even though there is no legal requirement that they be there, with most bringing supportive family and friends to celebrate their achievement. Nearly everyone has dressed up for the occasion, and I overhear one of the court case managers offer a friendly reproach—"I told you everyone would be dressed up"—to one of the few graduates who arrives in a t-shirt and jeans. For some time, the drug court graduates stand waiting in the hallway while their supporters, including family, friends, court personnel, and staff from the various rehabilitation programs, sit expectantly in the courtroom. The room is filled with a palpable excitement that echoes against the somber architecture of the room: an imposing judge's bench, a U.S. flag, and the words "In God We Trust" presiding above all.

At some point, the judge enters the room from her chambers in the rear (given the ongoing buzz, however, few seem to even notice). Wearing a semiformal skirted suit but no black gown, the judge chats for a bit with a number of the court personnel who stand with her behind the partition that divides the court from public onlookers. Eventually she approaches a lectern that has been specially brought out for the occasion and quiets the crowd: "This is a special day. An exciting and very rewarding day. And I'm happy to see so many friends and family members here, and I welcome you. Please rise and welcome our graduates." The graduates—twenty-two men and four women—walk into the room to a rousing round of applause, including from the judge herself. This ceremony commemorates the achievement of the graduates, not the power of the magistrate. "We didn't make things easy for you," begins the judge, "in fact we put up a lot of hurdles. You had to look into yourselves—which is very hard work—you had to get educational training and vocational training. You had to save money and get a job. And now you are working, paying rent, and to my great joy," she jokes, "you are paying taxes. You have accomplished something here, and you should be proud. Your family should be proud of you, and I am very proud of you. And when you're tempted to do something bad, you should remember how you felt here today, and all the good work you've done."

A second guest speaker, another judge, addresses the assembled audience with a similar message: "Your family and friends are ecstatic that you are here, full and whole. You can now be a help to your children, and to your spouses. I applaud what you have done for yourselves, for your families, for your children, and for your future children. Your success makes our communities better. . . . I encourage you to be happy. To work hard and be happy doing so. I encourage you to be good to yourself and to those around you. And I encourage you to not put any limits on yourself and what you can accomplish."

A third judge, the person who oversees the other judges in the several drug courts in the area, also speaks. "Drug courts are life altering, both for the individuals going through it and for me, as a judge. They are the only way to intervene in and stop the endless cycle of addiction, crime, arrest, and re-arrest. It's a noble cause, and the only opportunity we judges really have to change or save a person's life. . . . We can appropriately punish—harshly when necessary—but we can also rehabilitate. We can have public safety, restored lives, and sound communities as we seek to heal the heartache brought on by the scourge of drug addiction."

Three graduates are the next to speak. The first is a young Latino man who seems to be about twenty-five years old. "I want to thank the court for giving me this life changing opportunity. I was a high-ranking gang member, a drug user without responsibilities. In short, I was a child. Now I'm employed full-time, and I am a father with responsibilities. I'm a grown man, clean and sober." A black woman who looks to be in her mid-thirties speaks next: "I was addicted to both selling drugs and to using drugs. I surrounded myself with people who took advantage of me, and I entered this program heartbroken. This court was a beacon of light and a blessing for my soul. I learned to love myself, and that I deserve the best. I'm now in control of my life, spiritually, emotionally, and personally. . . . I especially want to thank my case manager, now a dear friend and my guardian angel. You believed in me when I didn't believe in myself. You were a soldier for me, going to battle for me. You gave me your words of wisdom, and I am forever grateful for you and your fatherly love." A white man, one of only two whites among the graduates and the only one who seems to be of a professional-class background (I later learn he had been a stock-broker) speaks after her: "I'm grateful for the second chance that we've been given here. I now feel more relaxed and much more positive than ever before. I found a deeper will to overcome the stresses of life than I ever knew I had. I want to thank the court staff, the judge, my family, and most of all, my girlfriend, who stood beside me through all this." Some people in the audience are tearing up or openly crying as the graduates recount their stories, including myself. It's a powerful narrative of healing, of suffering that seemed never-ending transformed into possibility and joy, and I and many others are moved.

Finally the graduates are called up one by one, their names read aloud as they are invited to approach the judge. Each graduate is roundly applauded by those assembled—some have their own cheering sections who stand and shout their approval—as the judge shakes each of their hands, and then presents each one with a diploma marking their completion of the program. Most of the graduates smile broadly as they hold their certificates and take a picture with the judge who has overseen their progress (the same person who, in most cases, punished them at some point and offered stern words for transgressive behavior). A tremendous round of applause follows after the final graduate returns to his seat, and all are congratulated by the judge. With the ceremony complete, a happy din begins again as all are invited to a reception in a different courtroom downstairs. Many people there partake of the cake and soft drinks that the court has provided for the occasion, and participants chat happily with both their families and the court staff. "Call me if you ever want to talk," says one of the case managers to a graduating client, "I mean it. Whatever it is, I'm always here." "Thank you." "You promise?" she presses. "Yes, I will." And after much celebrating, the crowd eventually drifts off to face the rainy return home.

When drug courts work, they often work *very* well, offering consequential assistance to participants in a manner that is simply unavailable in other parts of the criminal justice system. Judges and social workers take clear pride in their participants' success stories, and as the above narrative indicates, their efforts are often deeply appreciated by participants. In conducting interviews with people going through the program, the intensity of gratitude some felt was palpable, challenging my admittedly skeptical orientation toward the court. "Thank God that I was arrested!" said more than one. "If they hadn't arrested me, I'd be dead," said a couple of others. Comments such as these speak to the intense level of involvement and commitment that at least some participants develop with the court and its affiliated treatment programs, as well as the deeply meaningful ways in which the drug court impacts their lives. Even if aspects of this problem-solving court must be substantially reconfigured, the court's ability to substantially assist participants speaks to the program's significance in moving beyond punitive notions of justice. In short, for many participants, the support that the court offers does help many, even if these assistance-oriented strategies do not alter fundamental imbalances of societal power.

Drug courts, however, are not the only way through which meaningful services could be offered. Advocates of public health approaches to drug abuse recommend many of the same measures—not only treatment but also access to educational and vocational services or even housing programs—but all offered on a voluntary basis.[1] Advocates of drug courts assert that coercion is a necessary component, claiming that harsh drug laws are necessary in order to force help upon recalcitrant drug users. When California voters considered a significant reduction to drug penalties in 2008, the National Association of Drug Court Professionals (NADCP) called the measure "a drug-decriminalization measure disguised in sheep's clothing." Indeed, one of the primary spokespersons against the measure was the actor and NADCP ambassador, Martin Sheen.[2] Governor Jerry Brown criticized the law in similar terms, saying:

> Proposition 5 provides very weak incentives for drug addicts to discontinue using drugs while in treatment. We know that the hammer of incarceration is often what is needed to assist an addict to get off his dependency. . . . [The measure] was drafted without any public process and without seriously taking into account the well-considered opinions of drug court judges who deal with drug abusers on a daily basis.[3]

Following this same logic, the NADCP similarly opposed earlier efforts in California to create a diversion program for drug offenses that was slightly more lenient than drug courts,[4] as well as efforts to decriminalize marijuana.[5] These drug court proponents have consistently worked to maintain all of the weapons used in the war on drugs, albeit in the name of therapeutic need.

It was no surprise then, that when New York State significantly altered the infamous Rockefeller Drug Laws in 2009—eliminating mandatory minimums for some offenses, reducing sentences for others, and making drug courts available on a statewide basis—that one of the district attorneys working with the court I was examining foresaw doom: "The reform has effectively killed the program. . . . I'll be pleasantly surprised if it doesn't." In fact, referrals to drug courts in New York City saw 53 percent more participants under the new rules.[6] Nevertheless, the need for coercion is taken as a matter of course by most drug court practitioners. The chief clerk of the court I examined noted that those with small misdemeanors typically do not wish to participate in the program: "We're requiring that an individual participate in months of treatment. And if they fail to complete months of treatment, they're going to wind up going to jail. Why go to treatment if you can get rid of the case with a ten-day jail sentence or community service or something like that?" One of the case managers similarly observed that "Nine times out of ten, nobody wants to be made to go to a program. . . . When you come here, the voluntary aspect of treatment has gone out the window. You're here because you have to be here." Drug courts thus build upon, rather than challenge, the problematic reliance of the criminal justice system on plea bargaining, where penalties are so extreme as to coerce accused individuals into pleading guilty even when they are innocent.[7] While practitioners sometimes overstate the effect of specific policy changes on participation in the courts, they are well-aware that without this pressure—really a threat of violence—the courts would collapse.

While the court's ability to reinvigorate a failing drug war is distressing, particularly in light of its potential toward net widening (bringing larger numbers of people into the criminal justice system) and its demonstrated consequence of net deepening (applying harsher punishments against at least some participants), the court also incorporates a number of features that are not entirely punitive but which nevertheless result in complicated and mixed effects. In this chapter, I detail the ways these courts fit into new patterns of policing and incarceration, or what has sometimes been termed *the new penology* or even *postmodern justice*.[8] As a form of rehabilitative practice that depends critically upon the threat of incarceration in the warehouse prison in order to coerce participation, drug courts are broadly neoliberal in orientation, offering both new risks and new opportunities for those subjected to their disciplinary modalities.

In this chapter I combine a critical reading of texts written by drug court advocates and court professionals with my own ethnographic snapshots in order to examine the nature of the disciplinary regime that drug courts rely upon—both the way in which punishment is made "therapeutic" as well as the specific vision of addiction embedded within the court's treatment goals. As will be seen, drug courts attempt to achieve their effects through the structured management of threat, on the one hand, and by an effort to encourage participants to develop an emotionally charged relationship with the person who imposes that threat, the judge, on the other. This dual orientation is augmented by an intensified effort to monitor the lives of its participants in order to better enforce its mandates, generating a form of therapeutic surveillance to accompany the court's efforts at therapeutic punishment. Ultimately, the court hopes to engage with drug offenders in ways that shape their investments with dominant social institutions such as the family, work, and the law. This hoped-for investment in the dominant institutions of society represents, as I will show, an incorporation of self into the nation-state, with the offer of respect and release from immediate state control as inducements for compliance with the program.

Medicalizing Punishment through the Therapeutic Management of Threat

According to drug court advocates, the therapeutic emphasis deployed within this system turns an offender's involvement in the criminal justice system into an "opportunity for intervention."[9] The U.S. Justice Department has made arguments along these lines: "It must not escape our attention that the criminal justice system may represent the best opportunity these individuals will ever have to confront and overcome their drug use."[10] Drug court advocates make two claims in this regard: that drug court participants benefit because they are made to stay in treatment programs longer than they would otherwise (and in their view, this is salutary), and that the system of punishment utilized within drug courts is itself beneficial, creating a new system of "accountability" that works to counter addiction. Rather than contemplating alternative modes of intervention or service delivery, such reasoning yields ideological support for the ongoing war on drugs and, indeed, for the further expansion of that "war" (i.e., if coercion benefits drug users, then arresting even more people aids even more people). Given that supportive services can be offered without coercion, the claim that close monitoring and sanctioning aids in overcoming addiction (or is even necessary for it) begs careful scrutiny.

Perhaps the most unique feature of the drug court model is the way in which it re-envisions its own sentencing practices as therapeutic interventions, essential elements in a journey toward a recovery of self. Dorf and Sabel, two legal scholars who support drug courts, point toward the specific route through which punishment came to be seen as advantageous:

> Sanctions were necessary to demonstrate palpably that relapse was costly, but forbearance was necessary to help the addict learn through experience to anticipate the conditions that triggered relapse and the mechanisms for effectively avoiding it. Thus, whereas the criminal justice system (and many treatment providers) previously saw infractions of the rules of sobriety as a failure of will . . . relapse came to be seen as providing a window into the mechanisms by which the addict could learn to control addiction. The result was a rapprochement between the criminal justice system—which began to abandon the view that deterrence and punishment were the only effective "therapies"—and treatment providers—who not only softened their conviction that an uncoerced will to self-correction was indispensable to recovery, but came to think that *coercion and its associated crisis could, like relapse itself, provoke beneficial self-reflection.*[11]

As Dorf and Sabel's comments make clear, this rapprochement (which largely occurred in the 1990s) involved a willingness on the part of the court system to tolerate some level of drug use (adopting the frame of "relapse" in justifying a reduced penalty) and a willingness on the part of treatment professionals to accept the use of criminal justice penalties in order to deliberately provoke crises.

The intentional infliction of trauma thus comes to serve a therapeutic purpose, as the NADCP itself suggests:

> Arrest can be a traumatic event in a person's life. It creates an immediate crisis and can force substance abusing behavior into the open, making denial difficult. The period immediately after an arrest, or after

> apprehension for a probation violation, provides a crucial window of opportunity for intervening and introducing the value of AOD [alcohol and other drugs] treatment. Judicial action, taken promptly after arrest, capitalizes on the crisis nature of the arrest and booking process.[12]

The way in which the court seeks to take advantage of the psychic distress caused by an existing part of the criminal justice system (rather than to eliminate that source of trauma) bears some relationship to what in other contexts has been called *disaster capitalism*.[13] With drug courts, a type of governance through crisis is deliberately induced, one which uses trauma to disrupt a person's life before then seeking to reestablish it on terms that are more state-and-capital friendly. This conversion of police practices into therapeutic opportunities is striking and parallels court practice itself, where intentional efforts to generate shock—as with the brief periods of "shock incarceration" that the court imposes for rule infractions[14]—can be seen as a sort of shock doctrine of the psyche that roughly correspond to dynamics that Naomi Klein describes in the realm of capital. In this sense, it is not so much the drug court participants who are medicalized as much as the punishments that are doled out by the state; judges still retain ultimate control over participants, however jail sentences and other penalties are now understood as forms of therapy. This shift works to rhetorically justify the court and obscures the ongoing fact of punishment, but it also signals a shift in the court's aims: distress that is deliberately imposed by the state is no longer oriented toward simple deterrence but toward a more comprehensive restructuring of self, one that works to eliminate the so-called drugs lifestyle and to prepare people for low-wage labor.

At a basic procedural level, the court operates in a fairly straightforward manner:

1. Potential participants are first screened based on the type of offense for which they have been detained. Defendants who are deemed eligible are given the voluntary option to enroll in the drug court program, with the incentives that (a) they will not have to go to prison and may even receive outpatient treatment, and (b) their offense will be expunged from their record upon successfully completing the program.
2. Generally, the individual pleads guilty (though some courts offer a pre-adjudicative option in which no assessment of guilt or innocence is made),

after which an evaluation is ordered. The judge then sentences the person to a treatment program, with decisions about inpatient versus outpatient treatment often following the recommendation of court social workers, though the participation of the prosecutor's office (and sometimes a defense attorney) is also relevant in many cases.

3. The drug court staff monitors participants by gathering reports from the treatment facilities and through ongoing drug testing (testing may be done at the treatment center as well).
4. Participants are required to report to the judge on a periodic basis (perhaps once a week for newer participants and perhaps once every six weeks for participants who seem to be performing well).
5. Sanctions of various sorts are imposed on participants who are deemed to be performing inadequately, while rewards are offered to those who are judged favorably. Decisions about particular sanctions are ultimately decided on by the judge; however, they are usually arrived at in a relatively consensual process at a precourt meeting that includes the judge, the court's case managers, the prosecutor's office, and a defense attorney. Sanctions escalate when participants continue to break program rules and can ultimately include expulsion from the program and subsequent imprisonment.[15]

Although drug court advocates often emphasize the program's ability to individualize treatment,[16] its philosophy of punishment follows a very impersonal, bureaucratic structure derived from behaviorist principles of contingency management. Bureaucratic rules governing the use of sanctions are further meant to show participants that their treatment is fair, an element which, it is argued, "promote[s] buy-in to the drug court process"[17] and makes participants "more likely to comply with court orders."[18] Tension thus exists between needs for judicial discretion and for bureaucratic standardization in the sanctioning process, and individual drug courts thus vary significantly in the extent to which they consider individual circumstance when considering a punishment.[19] Advocates of either approach make arguments that mirror one another, with both sides suggesting that either discretion or standardization is necessary in order for participants to find the procedure fair and therefore be more willing to comply. A consensus position calling for an unspecified degree of balance between the two poles has thus emerged.[20]

Yet if drug courts attempt to mobilize behaviorist principles, they do so in a way that differs from more conventional criminal justice practices. One of the central features of the court, of course, involves the presence of a judge. This judicial presence enables the quick imposition of small, graduated punishments and it is this shift from severe, all-or-nothing punishments to a stepped sanctioning process that has been promoted by advocates as constituting "a new theory of deterrence."[21] These graduated sanctions must then be applied in a way that is "predictable, swift, and certain" in order to achieve their effects.[22] In making the shift from final execution to what might be termed *judicial probation*, punishment is thus converted into an allegedly therapeutic form: as noted by one drug court judge, "Smart punishment [i.e., punishment which follows these guidelines] is not really punishment at all, but a therapeutic response to the realistic behavior of drug offenders in the grip of addiction."[23]

Importantly, however, the key to this therapeutic turn involves an *extension* of criminal justice capacity. As the legal scholar and drug court supporter Richard Boldt suggests, the use of graduated sanctions becomes "rehabilitative" in that it initiates an ongoing (though not unlimited) process of offender management, rather than one which decides upon a singular punishment at one moment in time:

> [T]reatment court planners have developed procedures designed to delay the final disposition of cases and have arranged for judges to maintain frequent ongoing contact with defendants. This feature enables treatment court judges to retain jurisdictional leverage over participants as they navigate their way through relapse and recovery.[24]

In this way, drug courts shift toward a model in which threat is extended and utilized to a fuller capacity, deploying small sanctions in ways that are both punishing in and of themselves and deliberately suggestive of future possibilities (as occurs with *shock incarceration* in which participants are locked up in jail for periods as short as a day or up to perhaps a week). The careful management of threat is necessary in maintaining ongoing control over participants while not depleting the court's capacity for future threat. Crucially, however, the court must balance its temporal extension of threat with the need to inflict real pain: "Too slow to escalate, and the defendant could become habituated to punishment; too quick, and the judge runs the risk of exhausting his or her options."[25] Graduated sanctions and a tolerance for drug use (now construed as "relapse") allow the drug courts to keep participants in the program while continuing to provide "motivation" through ongoing surveillance and escalating punishment. Or put differently, the procedure "utilizes the coercive power of the court to encourage the addicted offender to succeed in completing the treatment program."[26] Drug courts thus deploy state resources in an effort to maximize their capacity to threaten participants, ultimately abandoning them to spaces of neglect—long-term imprisonment in what Jonathan Simon has termed the "waste management prison"—should they fail to respond.[27]

To step back and take an historical view of this development for a moment, the dominant approaches to crime since the 1980s have largely eschewed any conjecture upon psychological or sociological motivation for criminality, instead focusing solely upon the presumed costs and benefits associated with breaking the law. The move toward law and order involved an emphasis on deterrence that helped to displace most of the rehabilitative ethos which had been at least somewhat dominant within the field of corrections from the end of the 1800s until the 1970s.[28] While efforts at rehabilitation had taken a variety of approaches, psychiatric and then social-psychological models had predominated since the 1950s, with practitioners often exploring early childhood issues and attempting to change an offender's "deep self." The antirehabilitative models of crime control that emerged in the 1970s and 1980s did not directly engage in the criminal psyche but instead worked to raise the costs associated with crime. In doing so, neoliberal crime control tended to ignore questions of subjectivity, instead simply presuming a rational actor who would make calculations about the possible repercussions that might follow from criminalized activity.[29] As detailed in one of the central NADCP documents defining the ten key components of a drug court, "Eventually, participants learn to manage cravings, avoid or deal more effectively with high-risk situations, and maintain sobriety for increasing lengths of time."[30] This is a far cry from the ethic of self-actualization that some have seen in the drug court,[31] and works toward the creation of a self to be managed—a *managerial self* that understands and takes account of its own risks—rather than an emotivist or expressivist one.[32]

In important respects, the second wave of neoliberal criminology, characterized by drug courts and the increasing use of graduated sanctions in probation and parole, continues to eschew any emphasis on early psychic development or symbolic meaning, instead operating on criminological habits and patterns of thought. "In principle, graduated sanctions operate in a fashion similar to operant conditioning," suggests Faye Taxman, one of the leading academic researchers supporting drug courts. "The sanctions are a response to non-compliance and therefore are a stimulus to increase offenders' commitment to compliance with court-ordered conditions of release."[33] That is, graduated sanctions achieve their effects by altering the balance of rewards and punishments that surround an individual, just as with first wave neoliberal efforts to enhance criminal penalties and to alter the physical environment. Refusing the domain of the deep psyche enables the court to standardize punishment, thereby creating a structure that allows for quicker, more routinized processing of participants.

Perhaps surprisingly then, the principles involved with graduated sanctions are essentially devoid of a significant link to any theory of addiction, instead relying on behaviorist theories that have been developed in other contexts. A review essay on the use of graduated sanctions within drug courts, for example, published by the National Drug Court Institute, acknowledges that much of the research in this area has been conducted "in the animal laboratory or in institutionalized settings for mentally ill or developmentally delayed persons," but that nevertheless, "the basic behavioral principles that have emerged from this research appear to apply across a variety of settings and species."[34] Likewise, at the 2006 annual meeting of the NADCP, one presenter offered a power-point presentation in which they jokingly compared the process of treating addicted offenders with training a dog.[35] The ability of this behaviorist framework to move in such an unchanged manner through such inordinately diverse contexts, even across species, indicates that the model of the addicted self varies little from the model of nonaddicted selves: both will respond "rationally" to a clearly defined set of incentives if applied consistently and properly. While "drug addiction" plays a justifying role for this neotherapeutic court, the concept of addiction in no way animates the treatment methodology. Indeed, it is a telling fact that the same model of graduated sanctions is being developed within other parts of the criminal justice system that do not revolve around drug use in any way.[36]

Indeed, one of the only times that the concept of addiction, and particularly its status as a genuine brain disease, seems to take on any operational meaning occurs in relation to challenges from the law-and-order right, which sometimes accuses drug courts of effectively decriminalizing illicit substances (in that, particularly during early parts of the program, relatively small sanctions may be doled out if a participant is discovered to have used an illegal drug).[37] In response, drug court proponents often argue that addiction is a chronic and relapsing condition. "There was unlikely to be a straight path from addiction to recovery; rather, addicts undertaking recovery could be expected to relapse into addiction, often many times."[38] Notably, there is nothing new in addiction science—nothing new that has been revealed by brain scans or other technology—that led to this sentencing philosophy, and it had long been known that addicts frequently relapse. Instead, bureaucratic need and fiscal crisis led the courts to adopt a new strategy that was then attached to (and indeed, helped foster) a new definition of addiction, one designed to offer a new orientation toward supervisory control that relied primarily upon intermediate punishments rather than immediately returning those who broke the rules to prison. Beyond justifying the use of graduated sanctions over and against more either-or enforcement patterns, the invocation of the addiction concept performs additional ideological work for the court—not only providing a narrative for the court's existence but further converting the court's sanctioning process into a rehabilitative project. Indeed, in contrast to drug courts, which have become popular based partly on their ability to frame their procedures and raison d'être in terms of addiction, reentry courts have had difficulty in finding a similar justificatory narrative, a fact that has been identified as a key difficulty in preventing their rapid expansion.[39]

The court's thoroughgoing reliance on behaviorism suggests the very shallow notion of self that is meant to be engaged by the drug courts: for some, at least, it involves no more deep meaning than is involved in training a dog. Drug offenders are positioned as being *potentially* capable of responding "rationally" to reward and punishment, but they are not addressed as intelligent beings engaged in a lifelong process of meaning-making. A uniform narrative is instead surreptitiously supplied by the court: drugs have made the person irrational, but with treatment they will become rational once again. And of course, imprisonment remains the plan for those whose psyches are somehow so intent upon "antisocial" behavior as to fail this test. In large part, the rehabilitative frame that animates the behaviorist drug court thus sits comfortably with the theoretical orientations developed in the first wave of neoliberal penology: in its focus on risk management and deterrence, its engagement with a shallow self, and with a newly created dichotomization between ultimately "rational offenders" who can be reformed and "irrational criminals" who require long-term warehousing. The frame articulates smoothly with earlier neoliberal strategies while developing a carefully delimited space for rehabilitative modalities. The institutional structure of this return to rehabilitation, however—in which only low-level offenders are addressed and in which those who fail to properly respond to the state's efforts suffer even longer periods of incarceration—suggests that drug courts work more toward the targeted intensification of the criminal justice system than toward its reformation.

Drug Courts and the Extension of State Control

Pretrial conferencing takes place in a small room located directly behind the court and with a door that leads to the judge's chambers. Surrounding a central table in the otherwise unadorned room are the judge who presides over the drug court, one of the district attorneys working with the program, a public defender, and a supervisor from the court's case management office (a small number of people have private attorneys who briefly join the meeting to discuss their clients). The judge presiding over the court has told me that this group meets to "pretty much" decide what will happen in each case ahead of time. Having not yet met the attorneys, I briefly introduce myself before the meeting begins and sit to the side while furiously scribbling notes since a recording device is not allowed. Typically, the case manager's office presents each case first while the district attorney and defense lawyer chime in after. (What follows is a distillation of some of the cases presented during my eight visits to these precourt sessions).

In the first case, a middle-aged man had been placed in jail overnight due to a failed drug test. The case management office wishes to place him in a residential facility, but he has been rejected by three agencies because he is very agitated and speaks in a way that they could not understand. He was accepted by a fourth agency, but the case supervisor believes that program to be too confrontational for this particular individual: "He doesn't play well in the sandbox with others." The supervisor wishes to try to get him admitted into yet another program. "He seems somewhat nonchalant about his addiction," the supervisor argues, "but I think he's just going to go back to the same if he doesn't internalize the lessons they're teaching him." "OK, I'll speak with him about all this," offers the judge. "He just completed his GED too. You could make a big deal over this one. I didn't think he would do it." "I'll talk with him about that too," says the judge.

Next, a young man who has been in the court attending an outpatient program for two months, someone who is also on probation, is in violation of that probation due to a misdemeanor trespassing charge. "We think he should be sentenced," offers the DA. The judge is noncommittal: "Well, we shall see. . . ." "If you want to send him to residential, that would also be OK with us." "OK, we'll see. . . ."

They quickly move on to the following case, a forty-year-old woman who is new to a residential program. It is not clear if the program will agree to continue seeing her, however, due to her severe anxiety attacks. "Many of the programs don't want to touch her because of her recent suicide attempt," says the case manager. "They're looking to make sure that she's more stable." "How is she going to get stable if she's not getting any help?" queries the judge. "They're very touchy on the suicide issue." It seems as if nothing else can happen at the moment with that case, except for all to hope that the program where she currently resides will continue to accept her.

Another young man in the program has also been arrested for trespassing. "We no longer feel that he is a good candidate," argues the DA. "He denied using alcohol after testing positive." The defense attorney chimes in: "He was very polite and remained calm while others were saying bad things about him." "What about denying the alcohol?" asks the judge. "He claimed he was using Vicks 44." "What would need to happen if he got in?" The case manager answers the judge: "He needs to keep up with his GED classes. That was the only thing holding him up." The defense attorney again: "He has lost his apartment due to the incarceration." "Where would he live if released?" asks the case manager. "He could live with his father while getting a new place." "If he continues," asks the judge, "how long until he finishes?" "About six months. He was doing well until his rearrest." "I'd like him to admit to the alcohol use. The Vicks story doesn't wash." "I don't think that will be a problem," suggests the defense attorney.[40]

The cases continue quickly, each one taking just a couple of minutes. Next is a woman who is receiving money for job training from a man. "The reason I focus on this," says the DA, "is because of a prior case that was similar at DTAP [Drug Treatment Alternative to Prison].[41] *A woman had two men giving her money, sort of like her johns." The judge quickly looked over her case file: "She is doing job training and applying for disability. Is she doing job training for herself or just to get through our program?" "She wants to be independent," offered the case manager. "Well, I'll talk with her," concluded the judge.*

Another young man had been beaten up by police. Pictures were taken, and he is filing a civil suit. He was arrested at 12:50 a.m., long after the 10 p.m. curfew imposed by the court. "It sounds to me like he should be sentenced," says the DA, "He threw a punch at the officer after being arrested. The arrest is valid, and he was missing his curfew." The case manager took a more sympathetic tack: "He got his GED, and he did both residential and aftercare. He only needs a job. He quit his first job because he couldn't get time off to go to a wedding." "That's unacceptable," says the judge. Then to the DA: "What is he charged with?" "Obstruction of justice, assault in the third degree, and resisting arrest." "You're requesting sentencing?" "Yes." "I'll talk with him about it," concludes the judge.[42]

The cases keep coming, with an impressive paper trail helping everyone keep track of all of the individual circumstances faced by people going through the court. Recommendations range from following up on excuses offered as to why people failed to show up for a GED class (e.g., issuing a subpoena to see if a person had really visited his sick grandmother in the hospital on the day he suggested), asking the judge to verbally admonish someone in court, sending others to jail for short periods of incarceration (as occurred in one case of apparent domestic violence, as well as to others who failed their drug tests on multiple occasions), allowing some to graduate, and having others kicked out of the program and incarcerated. Some of the cases pertain to difficulties with the treatment programs, while others attempt to manage the contingencies that arise in the lives of poor and disenfranchised people. Many cases involve surveilling and policing the lives of court participants, and some cases involve more than one aspect of the above. In one case, a woman who has liver and kidney problems has been prescribed oxycodone after a doctor insisted that the pain was too severe to be treated through ibuprofen, a fact that will cause her drug tests to be positive for some time (the fact that the medical notes show she asked for ibuprofen weighs in her favor as they discuss this). In another case, the court's case managers have discovered that a woman in the program was not living where she said she was. They had her bring in energy bills to see her name on the account, but she said she was living with a friend and brought in bills with that other woman's name on it. Upon more investigation, the case managers decided that she was not living with the friend at all. "She seems to be living at a shelter, so she must go to residential." "She'll have to get off of her antianxiety med before she can go to residential," notes the DA. "Residential won't take her?" asks the judge. "No." "Then she'll need to speak with a doctor about finding a substitute," the judge concludes.

After about an hour of quick-paced discussion, we finally reach the last case before the court session actually begins. A woman hasn't registered for GED classes, claiming that it would interfere with her part-time job as a telemarketer. "She feels that we're not sensitive to her needs," says the case manager. "She wants to live by herself, so she doesn't want to quit. There's certain things she doesn't want to do, and we're trying to convince her to do them and then later it can get better. The last time she came in she had a very negative attitude and ended up crying. She has very low self-esteem because she's overweight." "It sounds like she reacts by getting into conflicts." "She's normally very shy and quiet," interjects the defense attorney. "Telemarketing is a terrible job," says the judge, "She needs to understand that that isn't a long-term job." "It's her first job," says the case manager, "She's hanging on. She can't be around her family." The case manager asks that she be placed on the bench during the court session in order to convince her to take the GED classes, and the judge says they will accede to this request. And indeed, the judge later makes the woman sit on a bench to the side of the courtroom for the duration of the session, a couple of hours.

David Garland's work has pointed toward the ways in which the current, resurrected vision of rehabilitative practice shifts the emphasis away from welfarist benefit toward "the efficient enhancement of social control."[43] And indeed, considered as a form of judicial probation, drug courts represent a tremendous expansion of state control over the low-level offenders it chooses to supervise in this manner. While the shift away from the traditional courtroom—in which judges act as allegedly neutral arbiters within an antagonistic legal process—toward a new therapeutic posture has generated intense interest (particularly within the judiciary), it is really the shift from ordinary probation toward a court-supervised process that is key. As O'Hear comments, drug treatment courts "are less a diversion from prison than a diversion from other alternatives to prison."[44] Considered as a form of probation, drug courts and other forms of therapeutic jurisprudence appear in a very different light than when compared to automatic sentencing. Not only does the comparison to conventional forms of community supervision fundamentally alter cost-benefit analyses—currently existing probation programs cost much less than drug courts (at least when considering up-front costs)[45]—but it also becomes immediately clear that drug courts involve a significant escalation of state power. In the words of one drug court advocate: "Drug courts were 'invented' to reinvent a justice role similar to the one formerly played by probation services, but this time entrusted with the power, authority, symbolism, and centrality of the criminal court and intervening at an earlier stage."[46]

The involvement of judges as probation officials enables a different type of surveillance and punishment than would otherwise be legally possible. In most jurisdictions, for example, probation officers are formally constituted as members of law enforcement, with limited legal capacities, thus limiting their ability to surveil those they supervise and preventing them from directly imposing a penalty for any given transgression. Punishment within probation thus tends to be somewhat slow and an all-or-nothing affair: probation officers must call for a hearing in which a judge decides if a penalty is warranted, and they typically do so only after an individual has broken rules on several occasions or when a major change in the person's status (such as revocation of probation) is deemed necessary.[47] In contrast, having supervision handled by someone with the legal authority of a judge not only allows the drug court's case managers to rapidly impose penalties for any infractions they encounter, it also allows them to request subpoenas for otherwise restricted information (e.g., hospital records showing whether a person visited on a given day or not).[48]

The use of the judiciary for the supervision of probation thereby accentuates a number of other effects that are already present within current probationary models to a lesser degree. As seen above, the presence of a judge gives the state greater capacity to enforce dictates in areas ranging from employment and education (rejecting telemarketing, for example; or, in another case, insisting that a participant obtain a GED even though he already ran his own construction company and earned more than $150k annually), to the people one lives with (such as deciding whether a participant could live with his mother, as seen in the vignette that opens this book), to the types of intimate relationships one has and the nature of those exchanges (e.g., questioning the financial support a woman was receiving from a man for no apparent reason other than a general suspicion of prostitution among female participants). Dawn Moore argues that the conjunction of the therapeutic and the legal "has decidedly punitive effects, amplifying control and erasing protections in the name of curing the offender."[49] Rebecca Tiger similarly notes that the therapeutic forms of "enlightened coercion" practiced by the court regularly intrude into domains usually considered "private."[50] In a manner that parallels the way in which African Americans have been denied many privacy rights due to the ways that white supremacy has denied them access to a domestic sphere,[51] here a "para-racial" logic draws from racist imagery in defining "the addict" as acting in such a way as to require forceful correction into this supposedly private sphere.[52]

As Tiger argues, the drug court's expanded jurisdiction gives it purview to enforce both norm and law. The drug court is similarly better able to ensure that other state rules and regulations are being followed by participants—checking up on the woman who was applying for disability while undertaking job training, for example. These types of intrusions occur regularly within ordinary probation as well, but the monitoring and enforcement mechanisms are far greater in drug court, where case managers (or probation officers)[53] supervise each client and where judges are quick to enact punishments for even minor infractions.[54] The greater authority of the court also gives the state more power to infringe upon medical decisions involving painkillers or other psychiatric medications, dictating or otherwise shaping the health choices of those participating in the court, as seen with the woman who asked for ibuprofen instead of oxycodone (a request that was overruled by her doctor).[55] This issue has also arisen in that many judges have resisted pharmaceutical forms of drug treatment such as methadone or buprenorphine, making it a requirement that individuals refrain from any such medications as a requirement in order to participate or to graduate.[56] Resistance to such Medication Assisted Treatment (MAT) has been shifting rapidly, however, with a small number of drug courts requiring at least some participants to take antiaddiction medications such as Vivitrol in order to participate.[57] The power of the court to make such wide-ranging decisions regarding the nature of the therapeutic, and its ability to enforce these decisions, has also resulted in some instances where judges impose conditions that are arguably abusive or exploitive.[58]

A key factor in all of these procedures, though not thoroughly commented upon in most discussions of drug courts, are the court's case managers. Handling far fewer caseloads than conventional probation—the case managers at the court I examined handled supervised 30–35 cases at a time, whereas probation officers in New York City typically averaged 150[59]—the case management office is far better equipped than most probation departments to follow up with participants and ensure they do what the court orders them to do. And indeed, the case managers I witnessed spent more of their time verifying excuses from participants than any other activity. Calling doctor's offices to confirm scribbled notes, calling parents or other family members (and then making judgments as to whether or not those individuals could be trusted), calling employers, even infrequently visiting places of purported employment to see if a job actually exists, case managers mobilize their lower caseloads to more closely monitor their charges. The case managers' investigative work gives them a crucial role in adjudicating the court's punishments, especially since participants are under probationary control and any new punishments are administered without much possibility for due process.[60] In the court I examined, situations in which facts are ambiguous sometimes resulted in the person receiving the benefit of the doubt but seemed to more regularly result in punishment.

The efforts that drug courts make to strictly monitor their participants have a close parallel in earlier criminal justice programs. Beginning in the 1980s, as part of the general movement to reduce prison overcrowding while remaining "tough on crime" (just as with drug courts in the 1990s and 2000s), a new model of Intensive Supervisory Probation (ISP) was developed.[61] While there is significant variation between programs, ISP typically features caseloads that are lower than thirty (and sometimes as low as ten), allowing probation officers to monitor their charges closely. As with drug courts, questions remain concerning possible net-widening effects (in which more people are sentenced due to the presence of a low-cost alternative) and net-tightening (in which low-level offenders receive greater penalties than they would without the presence of an intermediate sanction).[62] But while the exact scale of these phenomena has been difficult to pin down, it is clear that intensive supervision reveals greater numbers of minor infractions, resulting in greater reincarceration for technical violations (rule-breaking that is not otherwise illegal, such as missing a curfew, being unemployed and not doing enough to look for a job, failing to attend drug treatment or to do one's community service, and so on). This crackdown on minor rule-breaking within probation and parole programs has had an enormous impact on mass incarceration overall, with technical violations constituting the single largest cause of imprisonment in many states.[63] But while ISPs have been successful at detecting low-level infractions and imprisoning people for them, they have generally not produced lower levels of actual criminality, instead simply making life for probationers and parolees more onerous and uncertain.[64] There have, however, been a small number of ISP programs that have produced better results in reducing recidivism—programs that emphasize the delivery of services (such as GED classes or vocational training) rather than simply the detection of rule-breaking.[65]

The implications in relation to drug courts are clear and bears repeating: *supportive services work*, whereas the imposition of control simply helps to uncover greater amounts of misdemeanor wrongdoing that is then punished. This of course leaves open the question as to whether support must be imposed by force in order to be effective, as is claimed by drug court advocates. Even if true, the negative consequences of the state's use of force are consistently avoided in narratives favorable to drug courts. For example, approximately two-thirds of participants in the court I examined had spent at least a day in jail. While most jail stays in that court averaged a total of eleven days or less, some drug courts imprison many of their participants for more time than they would have received as part of their original sentencing.[66] Furthermore, as noted in chapter 1, approximately half of all drug court participants are unsuccessful in meeting all of the demands of treatment and face the known harms of long-term incarceration, generally receiving no credit for any time served while being supervised by the court and in fact being penalized for having attempted treatment and failed.[67] With these penalties falling disproportionately upon nonwhites, it seems that any fair comparison with voluntary approaches would necessarily begin with a consideration of the harms caused by coercion, generating a strong presumption in favor of public health and against criminal justice.[68] On the other hand, the apparent success of voluntary public health approaches in both the United States and in countries such as Portugal seems to belie the claim that force is essential for assistance to be beneficial.[69] Even within the frame of criminal justice, the difference between deterrence-oriented and service-oriented ISPs makes one wonder if service provision might be helpful on its own accord and if increased levels of surveillance produce anything more than greater levels of imprisonment due to technical violations. Whatever the case, the comparison between service-oriented ISP and drug courts is instructive, revealing that similar reductions in recidivism can be achieved through the provision of services without the presence of a judge and with roughly similar expenditure.[70] Such comparisons also highlight the fact that drug courts are less unique and innovative than their advocates claim, instead closely paralleling other trends within criminal justice that accentuate that institution's power.[71] The failure to compare drug courts to these cognate programs and the emphasis upon their allegedly unique nature makes sense from the perspective of the judiciary (for whom the program is truly new) but not from the perspective of participants in these programs or from a consideration of their general role within a criminal justice system that continues to expand and intensify its reach.

Of Carrots and Grandeur: Drug Court Judges

In constructing their own vision of behaviorist practice, the drug courts have adopted a strategy in which the provision of incentives is just as important, if not more so, than the sanctions to which the court structure is more accustomed (at least in its own self-vision). B. F. Skinner—perhaps the most prominent behaviorist of the twentieth century—suggested that punishment was ineffective in promoting behavioral change, as people might find ways to work around the punishment or simply reengage a behavior once the threat of punishment was removed (as he notes, "A simple way to avoid punishment is to avoid punishers").[72] Skinner thus argues that punishment was "a questionable technique" whose "weakness . . . as a technique of social control" was further accompanied by many "unfortunate by-products."[73] Sanctions should thus be used only sparingly—if at all—and in association with a program of rewards. This focus on reinforcements generated an approach he felt to be much more effective in producing long-term change.[74]

The drug court, for its part, continues to rely on a robust and elaborate sanctioning process. However, it also makes a deliberate effort to offer numerous positive incentives, many delivered by the judge her- or himself. Whereas Skinner placed primary emphasis on incentives, the court appears to devote far less attention to rewards and instead continues to focus on its historical specialty: punishment. Even supporters of drug court programming have noted that some courts seem to pay little attention to rewarding positive behaviors among participants, instead focusing solely on sanctioning infractions.[75] And while it has been suggested that graduated incentives are "equally important" as graduated sanctions,[76] there is no existing essay or policy document that examines how to best establish incentive programs with the same level of detail as is devoted to sanctioning procedures. Instead, within studies focused on the therapeutic effects of legal coercion, one finds suggestions to the effect that future research "should also include measures of positive factors that can enhance retention, such as the incentives offered by many drug courts."[77] But such work appears to remain continually deferred into the future whereas the serious business of sanctions and coercion is studied in the here and now. The New York State Treatment Court guide likewise specifies that "Behavior does not change by punishment alone,"[78] a phraseology that, even as it attempts to insinuate the importance of incentives, stipulates that punishment remains the primary part of the program. Notably, the guide contains specific suggestions regarding sanctions, but none beyond "praise" and "prizes" concerning rewards (with no level of detail beyond those two words). Thus, despite frequent admonitions from advocates specifying that "drug courts must reward cooperation as well as respond to noncompliance,"[79] in practice this vague standing order to offer positive reinforcements "at every opportunity" stands in sharp contrast to its rather elaborated system of tiered sanctions utilized within the program. This is not to say, however, that rewards are infrequently utilized within drug courts; while some courts acknowledge that they are still "trying to incorporate more positive reinforcement into the process,"[80] others feature judges who offer extensive praise (as seen in the ethnographic vignettes above). The relative lack of attention upon rewards and incentives, however, has rendered their application far less formalized and thought through than the more formalized sanctioning procedures.

This emphasis on sanctions over rewards is determined by multiple factors. On the one hand, the long-standing raison d'être of the court system has been to punish. Particularly given the now decades-long emphasis upon punitive concerns with public safety, it is far from surprising that efforts at including positive reinforcement are haphazardly introduced through the action of individual judges (rather than through institutionalized activity). There is also a risk that any sort of positive reward will be seen as illegitimate in the face of demands to remain tough (recall the critiques of drug courts as operating via a "hug-a-thug" philosophy). In its guidebook for drug court judges, the National Drug Court Institute (a division of the NADCP) comments on these political objections:

> Perhaps the most enduring objection to rewards is one of equity. Citizens are not ordinarily given tangible incentives for abstaining from drugs and crime. Therefore, it may seem inequitable to reward some people for doing what is minimally expected of others—particularly when those being rewarded may be seen as the less desirable elements of society, such as drug addicts and criminal offenders.[81]

The document nevertheless suggests that "there is a serious concern that some drug courts may place an inordinate emphasis on squelching undesired behaviors to the detriment of reinforcing desired behaviors," and follows Skinner's early analysis in arguing that "to maintain treatment effects over time, it is essential that drug courts not merely punish crime and drug use, but also reward productive activities that are incompatible with crime and drug use."[82]

The combination of an institutional insistence on punishment with an exhortation for reinforcement places a great deal of pressure on individual judges in determining the nature of any incentive program, particularly insofar as many of the rewards consist simply of praise and interpersonal approval from the bench (as witnessed and augmented by a mostly captive "audience" that views the interaction). Rather than relying upon formal procedures, judges draw on other social roles and scripts that can significantly inform their interaction with participants. Former director of the NADCP, Judge Jeffrey Tauber, for example, writes: "It is not necessary that one be an expert in behavior modification to be an effective Drug Court judge (although some basic knowledge of behavioral theory would be helpful). Drug court judges rely on their common sense knowledge of what works in motivating people (e.g. as a parent, etc.)."[83]

Tauber is far from the only commentator to link the judge's role with parenthood. The reference is an overdetermined one, coming from the nature of the role but also, no doubt, from the legal doctrines of parens patriae (in which the state acts as parent to the nation). The language of parentalism (usually understood as a masculinized paternalism) is thus directly built into legal discourse. More than this, however, the image of the parent provides, in many ways, an informal repertoire of behaviors, expectations, and understandings that judges can readily draw upon and appropriate into the drug court context. "The judge is familiar with each defendant in an almost parental role," suggests one advocate.[84] Another likewise writes, "When discussing the case, drug treatment, family concerns, housing or other personal matters, the judge is, by turn, authoritative, paternal, and cajoling."[85] Beyond parentage, judges call upon many other social roles (most of them notably authoritative). As Tauber writes: "A Drug Court judge performs on the courtroom stage before an audience full of offenders. As appropriate, the judge assumes the role of confessor, task master, cheerleader, and mentor, in turn exhorting, threatening, encouraging and congratulating the participant for his or her progress, or lack thereof."[86]

Having eliminated much of the procedural formality in streamlining the court, drug court judges are encouraged to foster a relationship with participants that involves a significant degree of interpersonal intimacy.

The emotional relationship and dependencies that are fostered with the state are then to be utilized as touchstones that might promote compliance with judicial orders. Participants value "the direct, respectful interaction with an authority figure," suggests one advocate, leading (it is hoped) to the buy-in that "is a critical step in the long-term goal to reduce offending."[87] The New York State Treatment Court manual offers similar comments, suggesting that it is precisely the opportunity for respectful engagement with authority that is most critical within this relationship:

> The judge should maintain a balance between his or her role as caring authority figure and role as judge. The judge needs to gain participant's trust through effective communication and understanding the challenge of recovery. At the same time, the judge must resist being perceived as the participant's friend. . . . For many participants, motivation towards compliance stems from the fact that an individual with great authority cares about their well-being. If the relationship moves too close to perceived friendship, that motivation is diminished. Also, judges must remain mindful that they may one day have to sentence a participant to a lengthy period of incarceration.[88]

The intimacy developed through this engagement thus poses some risks to the state: judges may lose their authority or become caring in ways that mitigate (rather than enact) violence.

These risks are somewhat mitigated, however, by the nature of the relationship involved, which is deliberately hierarchical. Judges remain judges, and Tauber encourages them to "use the symbolism and the authority of the office to reach the entire audience, impressing upon them the importance of their cases, the judge's deep and abiding interest in them, and the very real consequences of success or failure."[89] Judicial symbolism—the architecture of the room, the bench from which the judge surveys the courtroom from a position in front of and above all others, the presence of the flag as a symbol of state authority, the black robes signaling the dignity of the office—is deliberately mobilized in establishing the parameters of this intimacy.[90] Furthermore, the engagement is consciously staged not only for the immediate participant but also for those watching and awaiting their turn. "Drug courts, it has been said many times, are theater. And the judge is the stage director and one of the primary actors."[91] Tauber recommends that "successes . . . and failures [be] prominently displayed" in order to "educate the audience."[92] The manual produced by New York State for drug court judges similarly likens the courts to theater, recommending that care be taken to ensure proper acoustics, and further suggests that judges avoid legal jargon in order to be better understood by the audience.[93]

While drug courts completely transform the judicial role from neutral arbiter to therapeutic practitioner, the court does not entirely abandon its magisterial position through this alchemy. Many observers point toward the authority of the judge as a crucial component of the drug court, one that imposes a certain formality and seriousness upon participants.[94] Berman and Feinblatt, two leading advocates for drug courts, claim that these venues "make aggressive use of a largely untapped resource: the power of judges to promote compliance with court orders."[95] "I've found that we as judges have enormous psychological power over the people in front of us," suggests one former judge. "It's not even coercive power. It's really the power of an authority figure and a role model. You have power not only over that person, but over their family in the audience, over all the people sitting in the courtroom."[96] As suggested previously, drug courts largely "reinvent a justice role similar to the one formerly played by probation services, but this time entrusted to the power, authority, symbolism and centrality of the criminal court judge."[97] Thus, drug courts do not eliminate legal control as much as reconfigure it toward a new purpose, utilizing the power and majesty of the courtroom—as well as its coercive capacity—toward "therapeutic" ends.

Beyond an extension of surveillance and a restructuring of the sanctioning process, what is particular to drug courts is the use of "caring authority" as an incentive. The suggestion is that compliance with the court's demands will bring public, socially-sanctioned respect, a promise most visibly fulfilled in instances when the judge leads the courtroom in applause for a participant's accomplishments but also present in periodic, emotionally-charged engagements in which participants stand before the judge and are evaluated in a "parental" manner:

> [D]ignity is a critical variable in improving compliance with the laws. That is, practices that allow offenders to retain their dignity, as opposed to those that attack their sense of worth and pride, promote compliance. Fair and respectful treatment, regardless of whether the outcome is an arrest or imprisonment, may reduce the natural anger often associated with any contact with legal authorities; in turn, that positive experience may increase the motivation for compliance.[98]

The state offers an emotionally charged engagement, one filled with threat, mercy, and respect—very unlike the unemotional, rationalist image of a bureaucracy—but this relationship is only sustained if the participant continues successfully within the program. Disobedience within the drug court ultimately calls forth the uncaring and abusive face of state power in the form of the warehouse prison that awaits those who fail to reform. While in the program, however, the state offers both an authoritative enactment of a respectful and caring relationship, as well as resources (in the forms of job training and assistance in negotiating receipt of other difficult-to-access state benefits such as housing or health services, all of which come bundled together as a part of treatment). The limits of this relationship must be emphasized; the performance of procedural justice (i.e., the apparent fairness of the courtroom process itself) is not linked in any way with substantive justice concerning the initial injustice that brings participants in front of the court, nor does procedural fairness in the courtroom address the oppressive nature of the threat that will be imposed upon unsatisfactory performance (a threat that hangs over and structures the entire interaction, giving shape and meaning to even the more positive interactions).

Nevertheless, while within the drug court program, participants witness a drama in which they and the other codefendants are offered a respectful, emotionally engaged, and deliberately coherent interaction with the state. The drama in which they partake marks their incorporation into the nation, though only on the condition that they work to cure their purported disease. Unsuitable subjects are rejected, both from the courtroom and—particularly in the case of first-time felons (who face disenfranchisement as part of their punishment)—from the nation.

Curing the Drugs Lifestyle: Para-Racial Citizenship in a Post-Racial World

All of this leaves aside the question as to what drug courts are attempting to achieve: To what end are the courts developing these relationships? As I conducted my ethnography, I confronted this question through a different lens: Given that most individuals have desisted in their drug use due to regular testing, how does the court decide if a given individual is improving? How is the concept of addiction operationalized by the court, particularly in the absence of actual drug use? Even at the level of measurement, what criteria does the court use to evaluate its own success, and how are these criteria established? As seen in the chapter 1, security concerns of district attorneys play a huge role in the operations of the court, often taking on a decisive role in terms of treatment placement (residential versus outpatient) and helping to establish employment as a court requirement for graduation (where it is understood to act as an informal anticrime measure). Although this security framing has shaped the court at a foundational level, the district attorney's introduction of security concerns into the domain of the therapeutic was not shared by others working within the court. Case managers and judges tended toward frames that focused on more conventionally understood notions of addiction and treatment, though the need to defer to the district attorney's office as a condition of their participation ensured that the DA's recommendations often (though not always) prevailed.

Nevertheless, these more medicalized understandings conceal an even more intensive focus on labor as an antidote to drug use. This concealed focus on labor occurs through an emphasis upon an alleged drugs lifestyle in treatment. "It's not just getting off of drugs," argued the program manager of the court I examined, "It's changing your whole lifestyle. Get a job, get a place to live, and get an education so you don't go back into the old lifestyle that wasn't really working for you." Hora and Schma, two judges working within drug courts, speak similarly of the need to focus on lifestyle: "Treatment regimes are not punishment, but the restructuring of the defendant's lifestyle. These lifestyle changes provide the defendant with the very best chance of avoiding any further contact with the criminal justice system."[99] Case managers in the court I examined frequently offered similar comments, emphasizing that ending drug use was insufficient, and that their primary aim was to disrupt what they termed a "drugs lifestyle." While literature written about drug courts does not typically mention a need to alter the daily patterns of participants' lives, this emphasis is deeply embedded within the court's practices. And when asked directly, all of the court officials were completely clear that overcoming the disease of addiction required significantly more than simply ending one's drug use.

In many ways, the presumed content of this so-called drugs lifestyle is simply a rebundling of themes that have been commonplace throughout the period of neoliberal retrenchment, targeting behaviors that have previously been encoded in relation to either "culture of poverty" or simply as black culture. While the imagery associated with the so-called culture of poverty included a greater focus upon purported matriarchal familial patterns, the emphasis on the cultural demands of employment remains strong in both biopolitical imaginaries. The anthropologist Oscar Lewis, who originated the term *culture of poverty*, highlighted an alleged lack of impulse control and an associated present-time orientation that left victims of this culture with "little ability to defer gratification and to plan for the future."[100] And while Daniel Patrick Moynihan's infamous musings on black culture (*The Negro Family*, aka the Moynihan Report) emphasized a dysfunctional "black matriarchy," he argued that this supposed matrifocal pattern among black families resulted in a failure to properly instill the "discipline and habits which are necessary for personality development"; the result, Moynihan infamously suggested, left black children in a "tangle of pathology" characterized by a "hunger for immediate gratification" that significantly inclined them toward "immature, criminal, and neurotic behavior," including "narcotic addiction."[101] At a time when civil rights and black power struggles against racism made overt bigotry less acceptable, such culture of poverty arguments took earlier racist themes and repositioned them as cultural.

The notion of a drugs lifestyle similarly takes earlier racist imagery concerning black shiftlessness, laziness, and immorality, and biologizes it in an apparently deracinated manner, now applying such representations in relation to drug use rather than race. In the context of the drug court, the specific contours of the drugs lifestyle refigures old racist stereotypes and redeploys them in relation to a courtroom setting where efforts to avoid surveillance are registered as pathology. Participants are thus said to fail to take responsibility, to constantly try to "get by" (i.e., break the rules), and to lie frequently. While the "culture of poverty" was an early example of a frame that mobilized racist themes while attempting to disarticulate them from race as such, the "drugs lifestyle" introduces yet another level of abstraction, creating an image that can exist comfortably within a post-civil rights context and that can even be applied when a majority of the case managers and counselors are black and Latino themselves (as was the case in the court that I most closely examined). The putatively race-neutral formation of the drugs lifestyle thus draws upon implicitly racist conceptions to establish the addict as in need of control by the court, while at the same time its medicalized and post-racial status facilitates its use in novel contexts.[102] The result might be termed a para-racial formation, one that invokes an earlier/continuing racialized formation that has been sheared of its most obvious racial markers.[103] Such para-racial figures mobilize much of the racial animus established through centuries of white supremacy in the form of a "colorblind" figure that might sometimes be applied to whites but that is nevertheless applied to nonwhites with particular speed and vehemence. The so-called drugs lifestyle thus draws from the destructive power of race in creating new, related forms of oppression, joining the culture of poverty in bringing otherwise racialized imagery to a more wide-ranging application that broadly targets many of the same peoples once deemed eugenically unfit. As Gowan and Whetstone persuasively argue, the new formation established by drug courts and rehabilitation "amplifies the taint of addiction into a new biologization of poverty and race."[104]

In a sense, the concept of the para-racial can be seen as an important addendum to the notion of colorblind racism, both incorporating and sitting adjacent to the ways in which contemporary racial liberalism enables ongoing white supremacy. Yet the idea of the para-racial points toward the ways that the patterns of oppression that have arisen in the post-racial era have done more than simply duplicate prior forms of discrimination in sotto voce (though they have done that as well). Para-racial formations—including both the culture of poverty and the drugs lifestyle—introduce arrangements, methods, and groupings that enable novel patterns of alliance and exclusion. Most generally, they generate a less strictly racialized understanding, replacing it with an approach that subjugates along an axis that includes both race and class as dimensions of oppression. Racial logics do not disappear into the para-racial but rather animate it and give it particular urgency. Para-racial formations can thus be said to incorporate the supposedly colorblind dynamics of white supremacy—which is ongoing—but additionally extend the exclusionary power of racialized imagery to impoverished whites, albeit with lesser force. Racial logics must be seen as not only remaining potent forces in their own right (in both explicit and colorblind form), they additionally work to charge the domain of the para-racial. Furthermore, race strongly shapes the contours and application of the para-racial, with damage intensified for nonwhites and mitigated for whites. Nevertheless, the idea of the para-racial is distinct from the idea of colorblind racism, emphasizing both the ways in which it extends racial logics to marginalized whites and the ways it offers a language that articulates many class conflicts within nonwhite communities. Perhaps the danger of a concept such as the para-racial is that it will be used to overemphasize the extent to which we have indeed entered a post-racial era. It is useful to keep in mind that the para-racial is a social derivative of the racial and that its power depends upon the ongoing presence of race, even as the para-racial partly transforms that domain. The concept of the para-racial is thus not meant to replace the notion of racism ("colorblind" or otherwise) but to supplement it, making it increasingly possible to identify some of the new ways in which race and class are operating in the contemporary period.[105]

Homo pharmacum as Anti-Citizen: Burdened Individualism and the Drugs Lifestyle

As noted earlier, the historical opposition between the racialized figure of the criminalized addict and the implicitly classed, gendered, and racialized figure of *homo oeconomicus* has been pointedly suggested by the cultural theorist Sylvia Wynter.[106] Unthinkable within this dichotomous frame is the possibility that work itself might lead one to use drugs.[107] Similarly, the cocaine-fueled partying commonly referenced in relation to Wall Street is decidedly *not* part of the imagined drugs lifestyle, nor are such privileged users targeted for policing (indeed, one judge who had presided over a drug court for three years noted to me that they had seen only one participant who had a college education). The drugs lifestyle thus must be seen in relation to long-standing efforts at controlling the racialized poor and not in relation to drug use as such. The reliance on formal labor as a primary criterion indicating success over the lifestyle issues allegedly created by drugs further highlights the ways in which the goals of the drug court are much better understood as a class project rather than as a psychiatric-medical one per se. The drug addict is here constituted as an anticitizen, one whose drug dependency is symbiotically related to nonproductive labor, the leaching of state resources, and criminality (i.e., unsanctioned violence and violations against property). Drug use is said to harm the humanity of addicts, but its most salient injury is to damage one's social status as human: nonwhite and poor users are positioned as semianimalistic creatures who require either control or cure.[108]

Keeping in mind that many users coerced into residential drug treatment have only minimal involvement with drugs, it might usefully be argued that court-ordered treatment focuses on issues of drug use only in a peripheral and secondary manner. Drugs present an obligatory passage point through which the criminal justice system necessarily travels,[109] but meanwhile, issues pertaining to the "drugs lifestyle" are the actual centerpiece of court concern. More concretely, this drugs lifestyle acts as a stand-in for labor dynamics identified by the anthropologist Philippe Bourgois in his aptly-titled book, *In Search of Respect*. In a key chapter, Bourgois traces the experiences of young Puerto Rican men who left employment in the lower tiers of the formal sector in favor of a career in drug dealing because they found formal employment to be personally degrading. While the question of gender is not explicitly invoked within Bourgois's discussion, his argument highlights questions pertaining to the status of nonwhite men and masculinities within a deindustrialized context, one that has replaced factory jobs with a smaller number of low-level office positions. As Bourgois sees it, a large-scale shift from a manufacturing to a service economy has worked to marginalize street masculinities: "Oppositionally defined cultural identities that were legitimate on the factory floor shop . . . are completely unacceptable in the FIRE [finance, insurance, and real estate] sector, where upper middle-class modes of interaction prevail with a vengeance."[110] More generally, the Puerto Rican men he examines suffer from a contradiction in the demands that are placed on their behavior: "Street culture is in direct opposition to the humble, obedient modes of subservient social interaction that are essential for upward mobility in high-rise office jobs."[111] Arguing in a parallel but slightly different vein, the sociologist William Julius Wilson highlights (among many other issues) the way in which black men in particular sometimes find contemporary work in the service economy to be degrading, in part because of prior norms that developed when black men had better access to blue collar jobs. "Thus, the attitudes that many inner-city black males express about their jobs and job prospects reflect their plummeting position in a changing labor market."[112]

Drug courts address these negative reactions to the shifting formal economy under the medicalized banner of "addiction," seeking to adjust participants to lower-tier employment by transforming their experience of that work, turning it from a form of poorly paid drudgery in which they must subordinate themselves to their supervisors into an achievement of sobriety and self-restraint. Most commonly, this involves disciplining participants in relation to work-related (or school-related) issues. Participants are informed, for example, that "It is your responsibility to keep all *scheduled* appointments and to *arrive on time*."[113] Beyond the practical necessity of imposing such a requirement, court staff indicated to me that this measure additionally serves a therapeutic purpose, forcing participants to develop the organizational skills necessary to maintain a regular schedule. "If you always show up late for work, no one's going to keep you on," suggested one case manager.[114]

Issues concerning dress form one of the low-level battlefields in the court's fight against the so-called drugs lifestyle. A program guide given to participants, for example, specifies that one must "dress appropriately for court and case management visits (no hats, do-rags, tank tops, shorts or pants that hang below your hips)."[115] The change in clothing also serves a therapeutic purpose, according to drug court staff, in that wearing respectable clothing helps participants to develop more of a professional identity and demeanor and to get them out of the "drugs lifestyle." For participants who are members of gangs, the court likewise prohibits all clothing that might identify one as being a gang affiliate (one may wear no red or blue whatsoever due to their association with gangs). Beyond these requirements, the court works to degrade gendered sartorial presentations associated with the "drugs lifestyle," linking street culture with disrespectability and waged labor (no matter how poorly paid) with respectability. As will be seen, this pattern of active shaming is far more prevalent within drug treatment itself, but its presence within the legal sphere of the court is also notable. This basic tactic of shaming particular genders can be seen in figure 2.1. The flyer—found posted on the wall of a drug court case manager's office—somewhat apocryphally attributes the origin of sagging pants to sexual victimization within prison. While somewhat idiosyncratic (only one of the drug courts I visited displayed the flyer), the idea is to link a fashion choice that is socially unacceptable within most working-class job environments—it operates as a sign of proud disrespectability and of cultural capital that explicitly rejects the norms of work—to a shunned masculine status that would be relevant to the presumed audience. The court's ability to impose these types of constraints, and its use of heterosexist and misogynistic motifs in doing so, left me concerned about the ability of its newfound therapeutic approach to extend its reach so far into everyday life.

Another point of intervention in participants' lifestyles concerns the others with whom they spend time. The court will not permit participants to spend much, if any, time with individuals it considers to be bad influences.[116] One eighteen- or nineteen-year-old was told he could no longer spend time with his friends as they were still using drugs, and that contact with them would surely lead him back to drug use eventually as well. Whatever the veracity of this assessment, I was somewhat taken aback by the power the drug court was exercising over this young man's life: If I were in his position, would I be able to obey such a command? I was not sure. Another participant asked for permission to move back in with his mother; this was granted, but only after the case managers had determined that she did not herself engage in illegal drug use nor encourage it in her son. Not only might the court have decided against allowing this young man to live with the person of his choosing, potentially even straining familial ties in the process, but his participation in the court led to the evaluation of his mother's suitability as well. Interventions of such intensity were somewhat rare, but they speak to the dramatically expanded

FIGURE 2.1 A flyer posted in a drug court case manager's office. The flyer seeks to mobilize homophobic anxieties and warns of heterosexual failure with ongoing commitment to the subculture and its norms, implicitly promising masculine and heterosexual success with the adoption of a new cultural ideal. The overall effect is to turn socially "disrespectable" behavior—sagging pants are banned in the court and its offices—into a form of masculine ruination. The narrative itself seems unlikely as it would be extremely difficult to explain how a supposed image of male sexual victimization and interpersonal subjugation would rise to become a symbol of male prestige. Much more likely is that the innovation arose within a subculture that had already achieved recognition as having high masculine status (*perhaps* within the prison, but not as a marker of being a socially dominated "punk"), and that a fanciful tale that mobilized heterosexist sentiment emerged amongst critics after the innovation was established. However unlikely at a factual level, the narrative attempts to use homophobic emotionalities to indelibly contaminate the meaning of the sag. See also Christian (2007), Goodwyn (2007). To be clear, the drug court did not generally press participants to become heterosexual, and I heard no complaints of prejudice or discrimination voiced from variously "queer" individuals who participated in the program. Despite promulgating this heterosexist flyer, case managers at the drug court seemed to handle queer individuals with a general respect. Some of the case managers were themselves openly lesbian, and voiced no complaints about heterosexism within the office. The heterosexism of the poster was simply not visible to those working with the court.

terrain within which problem-solving courts (including drug courts) operate: the entirety of an individual's daily life comes under the jurisdiction of the court, and any arena of experience is potentially subject to court order. Flyers posted in one drug court waiting area, for example, used shaming tactics in an effort to alter participants' speech patterns, advising against the use of "the N word" as "low class."[117]

Perhaps more pointedly, the focus on occupational concerns extends into the imposition of normative expectations regarding work. After quitting a job, for example, the judge told one eighteen-year-old Latino man, "You quit a job because you couldn't get a day off. That's not how we do things in the real world. You have one month to get another job or it's a year in jail." Another Latino man of approximately thirty years was required to turn in slips indicating the jobs for which he had applied; having turned in two scribbled notes, the judge said, "This is not professional. You need a book." Upon finding out that the man had in fact turned down a job he had been offered, the judge issued an ultimatum, telling him that, "You should take the job if it is offered," and that he had one month to find a job or be incarcerated. Much of the work that the court does thus involves the enforcement of work-oriented norms (whether it be involved in finding work, being able to provide documentation that certifies one's level of self-organization, continuing at a job, or in relation to obtaining a GED). This is indeed the most sustained focus that the court brings to its participants, taking up as much or more of the court's time than issues arising from ongoing drug use and positive drug tests.

While utilizing a rhetoric that emphasizes "addiction," the drug court model very much follows earlier models of criminal rehabilitation in insisting on formal labor as a criterion for release from criminal justice sanction. While advocates for drug courts often present such programs as compassionate responses to drug use, they also work to medicalize a long-standing criminal justice focus: work now becomes a therapeutic need in the treatment of addiction. At the same time, the structure of the drug court significantly repositions work within the overall disciplinary scheme, introducing intensive probationary surveillance and a system of rapid sanctions in a manner that brings much greater state control over the disproportionately nonwhite and poor populations that are targeted through the war on drugs. This restructuring has the apparent effect of decreasing overall cost, thereby enabling the state to expand the drug war and potentially widening the net of those caught within the penal apparatus. Far from an alternative to the war on drugs, drug courts thus often extend its reach. Participants often find their gendered expressions denigrated and are instead offered "rewards"—praise from a recognized authority who has power over their lives—in an effort to coerce and encourage them to live otherwise. As it stands, while drug courts can be said to offer participants a much needed hand at obtaining work, they imprison those who do not adapt themselves to the needs of work in what for the overwhelming majority is the low-wage sector. It occurred to me during my ethnographic observations that, given its definition, a jobs bill would do much to reduce "addiction" among the court's participants, not because it would necessarily reduce drug use but simply because more people would be employed. Of course, the court systematically ignores such factors, instead establishing a program that reduces costs by altering its approach to what Marx termed "surplus labor": first, a large swath of the racialized poor are brought into the supervisory apparatus of criminal justice through the war on drugs, and then those who can be made employable and actually obtain employment are allowed to go free while those who cannot are incarcerated. This approach offers benefits for some participants who are genuinely helped by the services the state provides in the process, but the costs for those who do not respond in the desired manner point toward the court's ongoing role in enforcing an onerous system of racialized class oppression.

Saidiya Hartman comments on the ways that the position of African Americans following the Civil War faced new forms of constraint that left them with a "burdened individuality" that constrained their ability to participate in a liberal social sphere.[118] She pointedly argues that the resultant crisis must be understood as resulting not only from restrictions on black liberty but on defects within the liberal conception of freedom itself, leaving newly freed slaves forced to navigate "between a travestied emancipation and an illusory freedom."[119] She writes:

> Prized designations like "independence," "autonomy," and "free will" are the lures of liberalism, yet the tantalizing suggestion of the individual as potentate and sovereign is drastically undermined by the forms of repression and terror that accompanied the advent of freedom, the techniques of discipline that bind the individual through conscience, self-knowledge, responsibility, and duty, and the management of racialized bodies and

> populations effected through the racism of the state and civil society. Liberalism, in general, and rights discourse, in particular, assure entitlements and privileges as they enable and efface elemental forms of domination primarily because of the atomistic portrayal of social relations, the inability to address collective interests and needs, and the sanctioning of subordination and the free reign of prejudice in the construction of the social or the private. Moreover, the universality or unencumbered individuality of liberalism relies on tacit exclusions and norms that preclude substantive equality; all do not equally partake of the resplendent, plenipotent, indivisible, and steely singularity that it proffers.[120]

The inability to alter the civil sphere impositions of white supremacist violence and coercion left newly freed black slaves unable to enact the sovereignty of "freedom," while the subtextual exclusions of liberal political theory worked to blame them for their inability to be free. As Hartman notes, "It was their duty to prove their worthiness for freedom rather than the nation's duty to guarantee, at minimum, the exercise of liberty and equality, if not opportunities for livelihood other than debt-peonage."[121] Liberalism thus relocates the burdens of freedom, placing them on "the enslaved as the originary locus of transgression, liability, and shame"[122] while deflecting attention away from the actual sources of injury. The requirements of "viable citizenship" not only exclude but redirect attention away from the originating source of the inequalities at issue.

Drug users in treatment courts face a contemporary version of this challenge. A rhetoric that equates addiction with enslavement justifies the imposition of violent forms of state control over drug users. The state then enforces its vision of freedom, which is closely linked to participation in formal labor. Unnoticed goes the role of both the state and civil society in creating conditions that lead to racialized structures of unemployment and underemployment (and that, at least in some cases, helped to generate the types of drug use that sometimes accompany intensive involvement with street life).[123] Instead, the burdens of freedom—most forcefully articulated in terms of a need to subordinate oneself within the lower tiers of the workforce—are placed upon the individual. In operational form, the drugs lifestyle stands as a form of racialized opposition to the "freedom" that the court seeks to impose, one that must be eliminated through disciplinary control. This drugs lifestyle is primarily identified as existing among nonwhites, but it is also applied, albeit with lesser intensity, to whites who partake of this alleged subculture, thereby extending the racial metaphors of liberal exclusion to new populations (while perhaps enabling at least some measure of inclusion for nonwhite middle class populations, who are less directly targeted by the war on drugs).[124] One of Oscar Lewis's proposals was that the alleged "culture of poverty" might be treated psychiatrically;[125] drug courts quietly enact this vision under cover of "addiction," framing any and all issues pertaining to illicit drug use in terms of NORP-ness (becoming a "Normal, Ordinary, Responsible Person") and work.

Beyond this, fears for "public safety" can be seen to surround the entire endeavor, with those who fail to be "free" automatically understood as *animals* at war with those around them (and hence needing to be sequestered from civil society). Those unable to enact this vision of freedom (*even after being given a chance!*) are deemed both unworthy and dangerous, subjects who stand outside of society and for whom penal control is a matter of "self-defense." As Locke argues, "the criminal who, having renounced reason, the common rule and measure God hath given to mankind," is in a "state of war," and "therefore may be destroyed as a lion or a tiger, one of those wild savage beasts with whom men can have no society nor security."[126] Locke refers to those criminals who have killed another, but the new "therapeutic" drug war that treatment courts embody continues to figure the unreformed drug user as an enemy of society, vastly misstating the actual dangers of drug use and cutting off alternative policy approaches (and alternative notions of citizenship and political inclusion) in the process.

3

Today Is the First Day of the Rest of Your Life

Rehabilitative Practice within Therapeutic Communities and the History of Synanon

Addiction and Treatment in the Therapeutic Community: Dishwashing as Social Technology

Julia was downstairs in the facility's large kitchen cleaning dishes. The fluorescent lights above her and the light green walls made the area not seem so depressingly dark, despite the fact that the basement itself had only a few small windows in the neighboring communal dining and rest areas. As I walked down the stairs and entered the basement, a couple shouts from residents of "Staff on the floor!" greeted me. I did not usually receive such shouts, and they were intended this time as a playful reminder of my borderline status: mingling with the counselors often and entering into staff spaces freely, I was clearly not one of the residents, yet I did not enforce any rules, and I had not broken any residents' trust in reporting violations of the rules. The calls today were delivered with a smile and a "Ways out, Kerwin," but they nevertheless enacted what remained some open questions: What is your status here? Can you be trusted? The warnings immediately reminded me of the calls of "Five-O" [slang for "Police!"[1]] that I had heard people exchange on the street during my prior fieldwork experience while living in the Tenderloin area of San Francisco. On the street, they signaled a police presence as well as communal opposition to it. Here, the calls seemed to me to mark a similar understanding as to the role of the staff, and generalized opposition to such policing—a warning to one another: "Shape up! You are being watched!"

I briefly acknowledged the teasing and walked in to find Julia. Julia was among the residents with whom I had developed the closest rapport during these first three months of fieldwork, and I came down to chat with her about her recent punishment, or rather her learning experience (as such occurrences were called). Julia was a nurse, and—unlike the majority of the people undergoing treatment here—she was a voluntary client; whereas anyone could walk out the front door of the facility unhindered, some 80 percent of the residents would face a police warrant for their arrest after having done so (another percentage, perhaps 5–10 percent, would face consequences in relation to custody rights over their children if they walked out, and many would face both consequences). With a college degree, Julia was also much more highly educated than the majority of the residents, many of whom did not even hold a GED (schooling for the GED was another thing the program offered to residents, as well as occupational training).

I had definitely found it easier to develop a ready connection with the small handful of middle-class residents in the program, and was aware that I needed to push myself a bit to branch out lest I make their experiences and perspectives overly central to my analysis. Nevertheless, the insights that this small group shared with me were somewhat seductive in that they came closest to confirming my own initial impressions of the program. The middle-class residents tended to be the most critical of the tight regimentation of daily life within the facility. They also tended to be the most critical of the way that staff would frequently yell at the residents and of the exercise of authority that sometimes seemed both so arbitrary and petty in its attention to minute detail. They were the only residents I heard who voiced direct criticism of the term learning experience *and who questioned the pernicious yet foolproof logic that turned any abuse by the staff into a therapeutic opportunity to learn control over one's anger. In my mind, the inescapability of this logic threatened to equate any resistance to the program with an addictive personality disorder. "This is the lowest I've ever been," offered one of these middle-class clients, "and it's good for me in a way because I want to do whatever I need to do so I don't have to be here ever again."*

Finding Julia hard at work with the dishes, I stood nearby as we chatted about the events that had earned her this learning experience. "Oh, I don't know, Kerwin," she started, "Nancy (one of the staff members) said something stupid to me so I told her it was stupid. I just couldn't take this place anymore, all their BS. So I told her that what she was saying was stupid." "That's it? What did she say?" "Well, I might have yelled it a little. But it was really stupid! She wanted me to mop the floor in the medical office again, but I had already mopped it and I had to get going in order to meet my kid. Plus the stuff on the floor that she thought was so dirty just doesn't come off, so it's not like I hadn't done a good job or anything. But so anyway, I told her it was stupid and walked away, and so here I am." Julia's learning experience for this infraction consisted of waking up forty-five minutes earlier than the already early usual wake-up time of 6 a.m., cleaning the kitchen, and then doing dishes and kitchen clean-up throughout the day. She was required to do this for an indefinite and unspecified period of time, at which point the staff would simply decide she had learned her lesson, so to speak, and tell her she could go back to the regular schedule. In this instance, Julia ended up "learning" in this manner for six days, during which time she additionally lost all privileges, including the visit with her daughter that she had initially been looking forward to. "And you know, I'm standing here doing all these dishes and I'm just wondering what the heck doing all this cleaning has to do with stopping me from doing drugs."

I thought about Julia's question a great deal over the coming months, and it became one cornerstone for the way that I came to understand how criminal justice–oriented drug treatment operates, as well as some of the tensions that the treatment model has faced as rehabilitation centers have increasingly come into the orbit of the criminal justice system. Having gotten to know Julia a little, it seemed clear that her question operated from a place in which her vision of treatment placed counseling at its foundation. In this model of addiction—frequently featured within the middle-class self-help literature—the cause of addiction rests in psychodynamic concerns related to an individual's emotionally-centered history, with drug use functioning as a symptom of disordered and unruly sentiments. Talk therapy and a detailed exploration of the past often take on a primary role in treatment within this frame as individuals attempt to gain insight into their personal histories and to resolve internal conflicts.

In sharp contrast, most treatment centers utilized by the criminal justice system draw upon the therapeutic community (TC) model first established in 1958 at a well-known organization with many spin-off groups called Synanon.[2] Like the psychodynamic model, the theory utilized within traditional therapeutic communities emphasizes a psychological approach over and against any biological disease model of addiction.[3] Unlike psychodynamic approaches, however, the traditional TC sees the drug addict as having a personality disorder, one that is itself characterized by a lack of self-insight and that is therefore not particularly susceptible to insight-oriented therapy.[4] While psychodynamic therapies emphasize an individual's personal history and emotional conflicts, the traditional TC concept is that the personality disorder known as addiction both stems from and causes an individual to be unable to successfully integrate into society. One of the more prolific authors on the theory and practice of therapeutic communities, Fernando Perfas, writes:

> Synanon [the first TC aimed at curing addiction] considered the addict's problem as not primarily the drug, although drug use contributed significantly to many of his [*sic*] personality, emotional, cognitive, and social problems. The drug addict is often apolitical with anarchistic tendencies and largely alienated from society. He is self-centered and encapsulated in his addictive past. . . . [A] person who is asocial with little communication and relationship with others, except for reasons of expediency in obtaining and sharing of drugs. . . . Drug abusers suffer from behavioral and attitudinal problems that inhibit productive social relationships with others and society in general.[5]

The basic orientation within the TC thus emphasizes (male) undersocialization or what Durkheim would have called "anomie." Hence, rather than placing the emphasis upon insight-oriented therapy, the TC model leads one to "focus on arming the client with the necessary behavioral and social skills, as well as the attitudes and values necessary for socialized living."[6]

Unlike psychoanalytic and other insight-oriented therapies, the traditional TC views the anomic personality of the drug addict in terms that emphasize a shallow rather than a deep analysis of emotions: emotions are not explored for their meaning, for a chain of associations that links them to a potentially infinite set of earlier experiences (or to a single set of traumatic experiences), but rather they are approached as essentially meaningless and potentially even deceptive responses that need to be managed rather than elaborated. The addict's failure to properly manage these surface-level emotions results in an inappropriate morality focused on self-centered, immediate gain.[7]

This Durkheimian perspective—in which social norms play a controlling role over otherwise ungovernable desires—forms a core theme in much of the TC literature on drug addiction. As George De Leon, one of the acknowledged leaders in the TC movement, puts it, addiction has not only made users poor, but turned them into "misfits" who are "unable or disinclined to live ordered lives or to identify with mainstream values" and for whom "conventional lifestyles are missing or unpursuable."[8] Whereas, he suggests, a lack of class stability for most disadvantaged individuals results from their lack of education and other marketable skills:

> Among substance abusers from the advantaged segments of the society, a middle class lifestyle has failed or been rejected. Drug involvement for these individuals more clearly reflects existential malaise or frank psychological disturbance arising from their break with family or class values and expectations. . . . Both clients, however, are disaffiliated, often manifested in social or antisocial ways and both need to learn how to participate in a community of others in order to acquire personal and social responsibility. . . . This requires a socialization process in the broad sense of that word—to assimilate the individual into a community with shared values, assumptions, and expectations in which the individual is an active, successful participant.[9]

De Leon acknowledges the political content of his approach, saying that the therapeutic community "concept of health and personal success implied mainstream conformity, stressing traditional values, which (until recently) were aspects of a fading American conservatism, e.g. the family, social responsibility, self-reliance."[10] The TC would instead promote "vertical mobility and aggressive pursuit of tangible social rewards of status, privilege and possession, reflect[ing] elements of American national character—entrepreneurial, pragmatic, acquisitive."[11] TCs, in other words, would make misfits fit, providing them with values that render them good Americans.

Unlike someone like Talcott Parsons, however, whose Durkheimian analysis was supplemented by an interest in a simplified model of Freudian psychodynamics, the traditional TC aligns itself closer to B. F. Skinner and his emphasis upon behaviorism and social learning.[12]

> Since addiction and its accompanying maladaptive behavioral, emotional, and cognitive patterns are learned, likewise, a more adaptive repertoire of behavioral and psychological patterns can be learned through positive social learning experiences to counteract the old patterns.[13]

Having identified addiction as a process by which socialization into anti-social patterns lead the addict to both drug use and more generalized anomie, the resultant treatment program seeks to inculcate a particular set of values through a behaviorist program of sticks and carrots. An explicit programmatic focus on the inculcation of normative moral values (called "right living" within the TC model) seeks to alter the entire personality structure of the addict. The aim thus "extends beyond abstinence from drug use," and instead the focus lies in using these behavioral techniques to facilitate "a change in lifestyle and identity . . . to assist the person to acquire the ways of proper living, acquire and practice pro-social values, and become a productive member of society."[14]

From the TC perspective, then, Julia's dishwashing had *everything* to do with her treatment. Julia's resistance to doing as she was told resulted from her self-oriented wish to put her own desires above the needs of the community (as decided upon by the staff). Her outburst at the staff member was linked to a generalized lack of self-discipline, an obvious character flaw that had made it impossible for her to delay gratification and pursue longer-term goals. Her apparent inability to control her own emotional reactions—even in the face of the near-certain loss of a visit with her daughter[15]—revealed the same emotional immaturity that led her to drugs in the first place. Two of the common refrains that floor staff used to admonish residents ran: "If you had followed the rules in the first place, you never would have been here" and "You have to follow the rules whether you find it convenient or not." Residents are frequently told they must learn "belly control" or to "hold their belly," meaning that they must not lash out in anger when something (or some rule) upsets them. While belly control may well be a useful social skill for anyone, from a certain perspective, the overall message essentially seems to equate rehabilitation with the ability to follow rules without complaint. As Perfas says in one of his texts designed to teach TC methods, "It is through the ability of the community to elicit compliance to and encourage the practice of its social norms and values in a social learning process that TC is able to maintain its therapeutic character."[16]

Within this frame—a frame very popular within the criminal justice system (which not only sends clients to stand-alone residential TCs but which also sends approximately 45,000 inmates to segregated therapeutic communities located within prison walls)[17]—"addiction" thus appears as a personality disorder defined by an individual's inability to obey norms. Drug treatment is therefore "more autocracy than democracy . . . not unlike military situations," according to De Leon, with a necessary emphasis on both "self control and acceptance of authoritative leadership."[18] Drug use is seen as a condition that simply exacerbates tendencies toward self-indulgence within this vision, accelerating antisocial personality traits that are already in place. The frame thus equates conformity to a normative value system with psychological health: "Drug abuse is a disorder of the whole person. . . . The TC espouses a holistic view of addiction. . . . The abuse of drugs is symptomatic of a psychological character disorder and/or social privation and alienation. . . . The disorder also extends to the person's warped sense of values and morals."[19]

One key aspect involved in the "treatment" of such a disorder involves close supervision of residents and punishments that are more swift and certain than under most circumstances (as seen with the drug court). Ideally, this corrective atmosphere works to establish an affective bond between the addict and the authority; as De Leon notes,

> Autonomy (which involves self-authority), is most effectively learned through a positive experience with credible 'other' authority figures seen as supportive, correcting and protecting. Becoming one's own authority is mediated through a successful experience with a rational authority. . . . Personal autonomy . . . requires guidance from those who are further along, that is, rational authorities."[20]

Julia's complaint—what the heck does all this cleaning have to do with stopping me from doing drugs?—stemmed in part from her sense that the TC's authority was *far* from rational and protective. Just as importantly, however, her criticism also stemmed from what is today a more middle class approach to addiction, one in which psychodynamics are seen to be primary within dysfunctional patterns such as addiction, and in which counseling (or informal self-exploration in peer support groups) is to play a primary role in treatment. TCs directly challenge this approach to addiction, emphasizing instead the use of autocratic means to instill "good values" and a particular version of self-control. Within this frame, it would be irresponsible for the TC to permit Julia to care for her child until she can successfully manage daily chores. As De Leon notes: "Self responsibility, evident in the health and consistency of daily habits of living, is a prereq uisite for having responsibility over others."[21] The cleanliness of Julia's room and work area directly relate to her overall fitness as a mother.[22]

Brainwashing, Coercive Care, and Questions of Abuse

The "holistic" view of addiction within the TC amounts to something of a totalizing view as to the role of treatment, for if "drug abuse is a disorder of the whole person," it follows that "a drug-addicted person in recovery must re-invent himself [*sic*]."[23] Earlier advocates for therapeutic communities similarly argued that TCs needed to take the "sociopathic personality" of the addict and "totally reconstitute it" or "turn it about at a 180 degree angle."[24] The ideology espoused at the first TC for drug addiction, Synanon, was even more blunt: "The addict who runs up and down back alleys, goes to jail, lies and cheats is an emotional infant," according to Jack Hurst, former president of the organization.[25] Straightforward indoctrination is required to turn such a person's life around. "Although tough, indoctrination is honest," argued UCLA sociologist Lewis Yablonsky (who later sat on the board of Synanon).[26] Yablonsky reports how Hurst would greet new prospects:

> Don't start thinking for yourself yet. You know, when you try to think, you attempt to use a muscle that hasn't been developed. You haven't any muscle there yet. You have a little quivering fiber that just buckles if you try to think. It gets so confused and tired. It just relaxes when you put dope in your arm. Don't try to think for a while. Let us do the thinking for you, for a while.[27]

Critics charged the group with brainwashing, to which the primary founder of the organization, Charles Dederich,[28] retorted that most people, especially drug addicts, *needed* to have their "brains washed out" every so often, just as the body needs to be bathed.[29] According to Yablonsky, the term *brainwashing* was in fact commonly used during the early days of Synanon, noting a conversation with Dederich in which he argued that " 'brainwashing' was precisely what they hoped to accomplish; they at Synanon wanted to wash out things in the brain that had caused his trouble up to now, and start fresh with new ideas, attitudes and values."[30] David Gerstel, who was an early resident at Synanon, likewise reports that members followed Dederich's lead in embracing the terminology of brainwashing: "Of course, Synanon practiced brainwashing. The brains of dope fiends who came into Synanon needed washing."[31] Whatever the reality of so-called brainwashing, it offered a model of coercive care that Dederich set to work elaborating.[32]

Initially formed in 1958 in Santa Monica, California, and growing greatly during the cultural upheaval and utopianism of the 1960s, Synanon managed to attract the support of many Hollywood stars, countercultural figures such as Timothy Leary, Black Panther leader Bobby Seale, United Farm Workers (UFW) leader César Chávez, and the psychologist Abraham Maslow.[33] The organization also received favorable coverage in mainstream magazines such as *Time, Life, The Nation*, and the *Saturday Evening Post*; was visited by Governor Pat Brown; and was favorably featured in several films and television documentaries (see figures 3.1 through 3.4). U.S. Senator Thomas Dodd (CT-D) went so far as to refer to the institution as "a miracle on the beach."[34] Dederich himself is credited with creating the well-known phrase: "Today is the first day of the rest of your life."[35]

By the mid-1970s, however, media coverage had turned against the organization, particularly after the group declared itself a religion—the Church of Synanon—in 1974. *Time* magazine, for example, ran a headline announcing their strongly altered opinion about the organization: "A once respected drug program turns into a kooky cult."[36] Earlier that year, Synanon had ordered all male residents who had lived at Synanon longer than five years to have a vasectomy and for all pregnant women to have abortions. Shortly thereafter, Dederich required that all established couples exchange partners, with Dederich himself deciding upon the new couplings.[37] An armed wing called the Imperial Marines was established within the organization, allegedly carrying out beatings against those who left.[38] In 1979, after a woman won a $300,000 settlement against the group for holding her against her will, two "marines" placed a four-and-a-half foot long rattlesnake with its rattle removed in the mailbox of her lawyer (who, though bitten, survived the incident); the two "marines" and Dederich himself eventually pled no contest to charges of assault and conspiracy to commit murder (Dederich avoided a jail sentence, receiving only a $10,000 fine and five years probation, after agreeing to step down as chairman of the organization).[39] Following these disruptions, Synanon continued as a marginal and legally troubled organization within the treatment

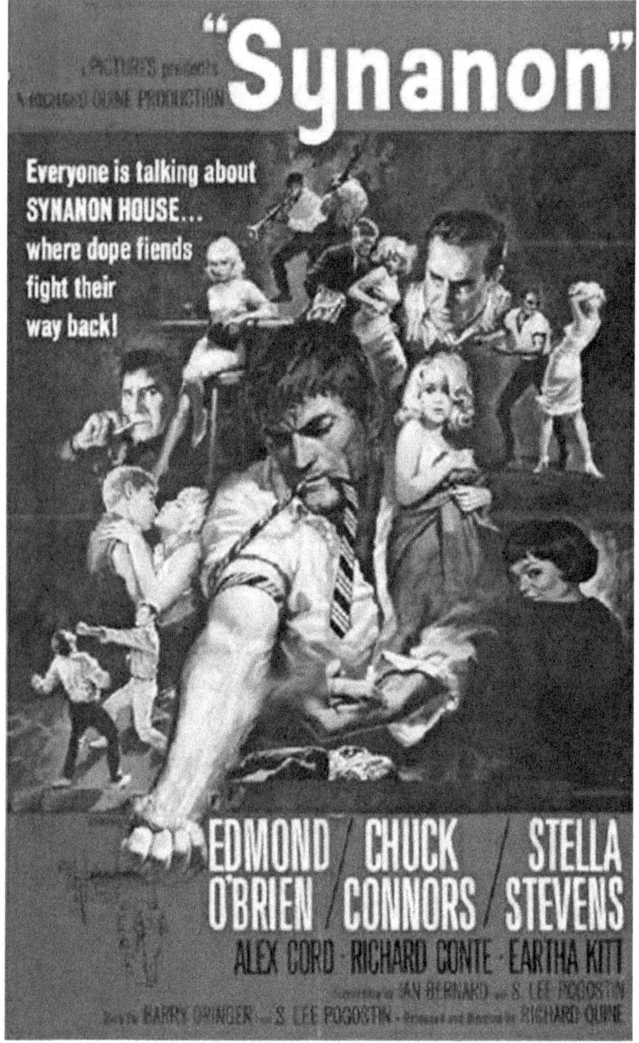

FIGURE 3.1 Promotional material for the made-for-television movie *Synanon* (1965), which was filmed at Synanon's Santa Monica facility. The trailer also refers to Synanon as "the coolest corporation in the world." Other film and television productions concerning Synanon includes the made-for-television film *Junky* (1964); *David* (1965), which followed an addict's first week at the facility; *Or Die!* (1966), "an hour-long documentary commercial for the Synanon approach" (Starks 1982: 196); and the documentaries *The Most Adult Game* (1967), a two-part television series); *House on the Beach* (1968); and *Children of Synanon* (1969), which showed children of residents confronting their parents during a "game" session. (See also *Here's Help* [NIMH, 1970] which featured several early TCs, including Synanon).

Source: Courtesy of Columbia Pictures,

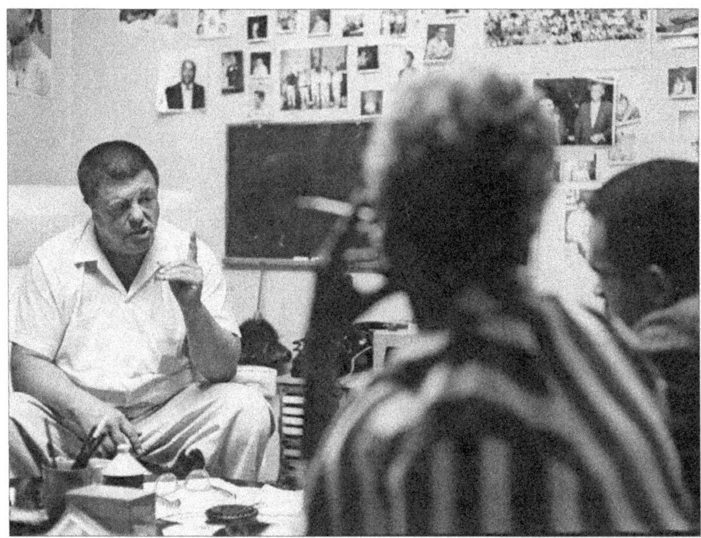

FIGURE 3.2 Chuck Dederich, founder of Synanon, speaking with an addict and his mother.

Source: Photo by Grey Villet/The LIFE Picture Collection/Getty Images

FIGURE 3.3 The Santa Monica building which housed Synanon between 1959 and 1979 (with top executives leaving for a Marin County compound in the mid-1970s). Though some lived at other facilities, Synanon had a total of some 500 residents in 1964, 800 in 1967, and 1400 in 1969.

Source: Courtesy of Santa Monica Public Library Image Archives. Photographed by Cynni Murphy. City of Santa Monica Landmarks Collection.

FIGURE 3.4 In the early years of Synanon, dances would often follow sessions of the game. Many non-drug users ("straights") came to participate in the game and an increasing number joined Synanon over the years. In its early years, Yablonsky helped bring Synanon techniques to "lost and alienated" students who did not use drugs on several UC campuses. Yablonsky posed Synanon as an alternative to "hurling themselves in front of trains or sit-ins," identifying such political actions as "destructive activities" (*Los Angeles Times* [1966]; see also *Nevada State Journal* [1966] and *New York Times* [1966]).

Source: Photo courtesy of *Los Angeles Times*, October 6, 1968.

field until its eventual dissolution in 1991, though a German branch of the organization continues to exist.[40] Dederich himself died of cardio-respiratory failure in 1997 at the age of eighty-three.[41]

Despite its eventual troubles, the early formation of Synanon attracted not only favorable attention but also many imitators. Organizations such as Daytop Village (created in 1963), Phoenix House (created in 1967), Odyssey House (created in 1967), and Covenant House (created in 1972)—all founded in New York City—as well as Delancey Street (created in San Francisco in 1971), Reality House (created in Columbia, Missouri in 1970), and the Gateway Foundation (created in Chicago in 1968), adopted much of the same treatment methodology and philosophy pioneered at Synanon. A survey for the National Institute of Mental Health in 1968–69 revealed no fewer than forty drug treatment programs that described themselves as therapeutic communities.[42] Known as second-generation TCs (with Synanon being the only first-generation TC), many of these subsequent programs had success in establishing further spin-off organizations (third- and more recently fourth-generation TCs). By the time of the Second National Drug Abuse Conference in 1975, over 300 organizations based on the Synanon model were in existence.[43] Synanon also established the first treatment-oriented boot camp for teens—called the Punk Squad—which served as a forerunner to countless other boot camp treatment programs.[44] More generally, Synanon worked to help develop the practice of attack therapy and disseminate it into a broader therapeutic context,[45] acting as a stimulus and forerunner to programs as diverse as Tough Love,[46] Scared Straight,[47] and possibly Erhard Seminars Training (EST).[48]

As the model developed by Synanon was copied and new TCs were established, they took the all-encompassing idea of the addict—linked as it was to a tough and all-encompassing idea of treatment—with them. The first of these organizations, Daytop Village, openly fashioned itself on Synanon's successful work as a "total institution."[49] Though the sociologist Erving Goffman coined the term and analyzed the methods of the total institution as a critique of such practices (taking a psychiatric hospital as a model),[50] here the techniques were deliberately copied and marshaled.[51] Barry Sugarman, for example, a sociologist and director of research at Marathon House (which itself grew out of Daytop Village), speaks openly of the "totalitarian" nature of the authority exercised over participants in the program, arguing that Daytop's method involves "using the whole therapeutic environment as a 'pressure cooker' to bring about perhaps ten normal years of character development within two years."[52]

Sugarman likewise speaks of the "mortification experiences" that new prospects were required to perform in order to enter the first- and second-generation TCs.[53] The intake interview here was not concerned with gathering information but rather involved a "dramatized dressing down" whose "function is to shock him [*sic*] into loosening his grip on his old defense mechanisms,"[54] or as Yablonsky states, "to pare newcomers down to their real emotional size."[55] Beyond this, "a tough approach is meant to inspire some motivation and commitment to joining the program"[56] and "is supposed to be a token of the strength of his sincerity in wanting to enter."[57] Within the early TCs, therefore, "token road blocks are thrown in the way of the person attempting to enter."[58] Persons showing up even a few minutes late for their appointments could be told to come back again the subsequent day.[59] When arriving on time, applicants were told to wait on a bench for an extended period, up to several hours.[60] Following this delay, what Yablonsky calls an "indoctrination" process would begin:[61]

> Inexorably the interviewers follow a basic strategy which leads eventually to admissions highly damaging to the prospect's former pride. Before he [*sic*] comes into the interview, his interrogators know his background and know what facts to focus on in order to cut him down to size. If he lived off his parents, sponging off them financially and letting his mother cook and clean for him, this will be presented as the situation of a dependent "baby." If he has been to jail for drug offenses and continued "sticking dirty needles in his arm," this is presented as the behavior of a "lunatic" who cannot learn from experience. Similarly if he acknowledges that friends or acquaintances of his have died of overdoses; this is the behavior of a *stupid* person; this is the behavior of a *baby*. These words hit him in the gut. They stick in his throat as he is made to say them in response to the leading questions of his interrogators. Until he does this, he cannot be accepted.
>
> "Why are you here?"
>
> "Because I'm all fucked up. Because my whole life is a mess."
>
> "What would you call the kind of person who acts the way you do and does the things you have told us about?"
>
> "A stupid person . . . a baby."
>
> . . . If he has long hair, he may be asked to agree to have it closely cropped. He may be asked to scream at the top of his lungs, "Help me" or "I need help."[62]

In this way, applicants to the original TCs were made to "fight" their way into the program.[63]

These highly masculinized degradation rituals were related to the gendered vision of the addict that the early TCs espoused. Not only was the prototypical addict male, but he was presumed to be a "tough guy," "cool guy," or "wise guy" who hides feelings of fear and loneliness behind a masculine act.[64] It is precisely the masculinity of the junkie that TCs sought to disrupt and break down in order to force a humbling of the masculine self:

> All the external "props" he has used to maintain his image formerly are taken away from him: his long hair is cut short, his beard and mustache are shaved, his clothing and ornaments are removed and he is issued standard work clothes. He is also deprived of his former social contacts, including fellow junkies, pushers, police, and parents, all of whom in their different ways may have helped to reinforce his unrealistic self-image.[65]

The male addict is instead aggressively placed into a low status via an assertion of superior masculinity on the part of the staff, both in terms of street standards and in terms of the new hierarchy within the TC:

> There are some questions that are fired off at the prospect. If he is the highly verbal, con-man type of junkie who has manipulated social workers quite easily in the past, he may start to spin a web of fabrications along the general line of "I've come to the end of the road . . . I can't stand myself anymore—the way I've been living . . . I'm determined to kick the filthy habit. . . ." The Daytoppers let him go on for a short while, then one of them will stop him short, shouting loudly and angrily,
>
> Knock off that shit, will you? Who do you think you're talking to? We ain't no bunch of bleeding heart social workers. The people you see here were dope fiends themselves, see? And at one time we all came in here sniveling just like you are doing now—"I want to rid myself of the horrors of drug addiction."
>
> All of the interviewers laugh. This transparent attempt at deception is a standing joke at Daytop.
>
> In this way the Daytop interviewers establish their claim to authority and credibility in the mind of the prospect. They commonly ask him about the nature and extent of his drug habit. This is generally ridiculed—especially if there is any hint of boasting or pride in the amount of drugs he [*sic*] claims to have used, which is quite common. "You seem to think you're some kind of big-time junkie, man. Why the people in here, we *spilled* more dope than you ever shot in your whole life."[66]

The yelling, the use of slang and profanity, the explicit disavowal of the implicitly feminized social workers (who are seen as easily duped in their emotionality) all work to establish the staff as both appropriately masculine and superior to the newcomer, who is identified as "an emotionally immature 'baby' who has to learn from the beginning how to live as an adult."[67] In a clearly gendered script, the male newcomer is told directly "Like you I was a baby but now I'm learning to be a man."[68]

Addicts Policing Addicts: Community as Agent

Within the original TCs themselves, residents were subject to ongoing surveillance and harsh punishment for any infractions of the rules, and staff at the institutions worked hard to ensure that the overall tone amongst the clients supported the program's regimen. This has been a particularly important feature of TCs, as the community itself is understood to act as the primary therapeutic agent. The program operated, in other words, by ensuring that norms against not only drug use but also against the entire way of life allegedly associated with that use were enforced by everyone within the organization. As the psychiatrists Henry Lennard and Steven Allen (who consulted for Phoenix House) wrote, "Treatment programs must compete successfully against the addictive social system of which its members are originally part. . . . The formation of subgroups which are loyal to the norms of the addict culture must be prevented."[69] Sugarman's discussion of the structure at Daytop shows how this is accomplished, particularly in relation to new recruits (who are discouraged from speaking to one another, and "put on a ban" and forbidden from socializing if they knew one another previously.[70] A strict system of surveillance enforced these rules:

> The monitoring of residents' behavior in Daytop is facilitated by a number of ecological factors in the living arrangements. The movements of residents are very strictly regulated: they are not allowed out of the house onto the grounds except on authorized business in the company of senior residents; and within the house nearly all their time is spent either in working or socializing in public view. On the premise that most deviant behavior takes place in secret, the living arrangements of Daytop are deliberately arranged to keep privacy to a minimum.[71]

> In addition to this general surveillance of each other's conduct, special responsibilities for monitoring the conduct of all residents is assigned to certain people. The expediting department has such a responsibility and so have all residents who hold any kind of status in the house—whether it is based on an official title such as department head or coordinator, or whether it is based on length of time in the house and the possession of certain privileges on the strength of this. Residents in the later categories are known as "strength" and, in return for the status accorded them and the privileges they enjoy over other residents . . . they are expected to set a good example.[72]

In the hierarchy of positions within the therapeutic community, senior residents were held responsible for monitoring newcomers and stood to lose their own status and privileges if they did not successfully keep those below them in line.[73]

The principle of residents informing on other residents was first established at Synanon during what became known as the "night of the great cop out." The evening involved a game (a group session of attack therapy) that successfully managed to get approximately twenty members who had been taking drugs to confess and implicate one another. As drug use within the facility threatened the existence of the entire program, it became an established duty to inform on anyone breaking a rule. "Not because you hate him . . . because you love him. That's how you save lives."[74] From that point, *all* residents, whatever their rank, were made responsible for reporting any infractions of the rules. As the sociologist Dan Waldorf of Phoenix House writes:

> [T]he resident is made to feel it is his [*sic*] responsibility to observe and criticize, or comment on, every other resident's behavior and attitudes. Only when a resident does this is he expressing "responsible concern" for other persons in the community, and a principle value in the community is to demonstrate concern for others.
>
> In application, the concept "responsibility and concern" is a conscious attempt by the community to overcome the code of the streets. . . . Despite heavy use by the police of informants, many addicts in the street maintain a . . . code of silence against police and official inquiry, and maintain an attitude of looking the other way regarding events that do not directly impinge upon them. Phoenix Houses reject this code and strive to make

> every resident reverse it. . . . Persons who do not disclose to the community behavior or rule breaking that is a threat to the community are punished as well as the rule breaker.[75]

Sugarman explains how this mode of peer surveillance—generally known as "responsible concern"—functions:

> [S]o long as there are within the house a minimum number of residents who act according to these norms, residents who fail to confront, pull-up [challenge] their peers, and report misconduct know that they take the risk of being reported themselves for misconduct. Even without assuming any degree of internalized commitment to the values of Daytop, someone who wants to make his [*sic*] stay in Daytop as tolerable as possible and who is aware of the vast range of positive and negative sanctions at the disposal of those who run Daytop, is likely to calculate just on the basis of expediency that he should conform a good part of the time. . . . Just a few people conforming even part of the time by exposing the misconduct of their peers allows considerable surveillance of the average Daytop resident.[76]

By thus working to ensure that any non-normative subcultures were kept to a minimum, and that no peer support or collaboration is established in relation to infractions of the rules, the TC worked to maintain a disciplinary order within the institution. "The tough guy or rebellious resident who enters the community is isolated," boasts Rosenthal. "He may look for, but will find no support for his former value system."[77]

The mechanism of surveillance within the TC thus moved beyond and greatly multiplied the power of the system envisioned within Jeremy Bentham's panopticon. Now immortalized in relation to Foucault's idea of a disciplinary society,[78] Bentham's approach relied upon reducing the mobility of prison inmates to a small cell in order to enable a single guard to monitor all inmates. By enlisting the coerced participation of all residents, the therapeutic community allowed for limited forms of (highly regulated) movement within and even outside of the institution while achieving a greater degree of surveillance. By instituting a requirement that linked a resident's advancement within the program to a requirement that they help enforce discipline on their peers—with staff members overseeing the effectiveness of the technique and intervening during moments of failure (as will be seen below)—the number of sites from which a disciplinary gaze extends was greatly increased and surveillance was largely accomplished by the residents themselves. As Waldorf notes: "Nearly everyone was constantly on guard to be on their good behavior . . . residents seldom relaxed because of the very pervasive controls in the community."[79] Coercive care of this sort requires active disciplinary surveillance of those around you and simultaneously places one on the defensive in relation to such surveillance from others.

To facilitate such surveillance and to extend its reach, residents were required to frequently tell other residents about their inner emotions. As seen from the following quote from Sugarman regarding Daytop, norms of "openness" and "honesty" were used to facilitate surveillance and discipline in a number of ways:

> Honesty and confrontation are connected to the norm of "relating." Residents are supposed to "relate" to each other at all times, except when they are hard at work; that is, to talk about themselves, how they are feeling, what has happened lately to make them feel good or bad, what they are learning about themselves and so forth. The norm of relating requires each resident to spend some time in relating to *all* the members of the house. The formation of exclusive cliques is expressly forbidden, though it is recognized that some individuals will form specially close relationships. . . . It is forbidden to "isolate" oneself or for small groups to get together away from the main areas where residents gather—unless they are accompanied by a senior resident. Isolated individuals are not relating and small groups which are away from the surveillance of senior members of the house may easily lapse into "negative" talk (talking about their old way of life in a nostalgic vein or criticizing Daytop rules).[80]

Like architectural designs emphasizing "openness," ongoing reports on one's emotional status worked to open the self to surveillance, with sharp confrontation at the ready for those who would not participate in ways deemed adequate or sufficiently sincere. The requirement that one must report upon one's feelings worked in tandem with requirements to report on any infractions of the rules, and was understood within the same context of surveillance and discipline. Surveillance-oriented versions of honesty and openness thus worked to reveal the self's intentions, to force residents to monitor and police one another, while norms regarding proper relating worked to prevent the development of an anti-institutional discourse or other forms of resistance to the TC value system. In these ways, coercive care worked assiduously to break down any barriers that established a zone of privacy, for such privacy could only shield a pathological self.

Of Signs, Dunce Caps, and Other Creative Humiliations

With an eye to the Durkheimian notion that sanctions should be directed toward those enforcing the rules and those witnessing the punishments as much as toward those who actually broke the rules, a move toward highly visible and deliberately humiliating punishments developed. In Synanon, where such mortifications were initially developed, the practices were referred to as "creative humiliation."[81] Sugarman offers some examples from Synanon and a rationale:

> A person may have to wear a large cardboard sign around the neck. This measures about three feet by eighteen inches and carries in large lettering a message pertinent to the individual's problem. It may say, for example, "I am a baby. I cannot control my feelings. Please help me." A sign is deliberately designed to be awkward and to get in a person's way constantly. It makes the performance of many ordinary tasks quite difficult. The purpose of this is to serve as a constant reminder to the person of what he [*sic*] must correct in his behavior and to give him an incentive to demonstrate that he is doing this so that he may be allowed the reward of being allowed to take off the sign.
>
> Similar thinking lies behind other kinds of learning experience which involve carrying around a symbol of the dereliction which got the person into trouble. For example, someone who persistently forgot to turn off lights was required to carry around a lightbulb at all times and to hold it at shoulder height. On another occasion, someone who persistently forgot to check in and out of the building was required to sit on a high stool by the check-in board and shout through a megaphone every time a person entered or left the house, "Don't forget to check in" or "Don't forget to check out." Learning experiences of this kind serve a dual function: as

> well as helping the individual to learn something, they also serve as constant reminders to the rest of the residents to avoid the same pitfalls. So the deviant individual is in a very real sense performing a useful service to his fellows.[82]

Another early sociological study at Phoenix House noted that "verbal haircuts" (as the rebukes came to be called) "are quite abusive and very explicit."[83]

> A resident who left the program and went home to his mother was forced to wear diapers for three days when he returned to the program and to carry big signs saying, "I'm a baby. Please help me." A resident who took something from another was forced to wear a sign saying, "I'm a thief! Don't trust me!" Contracts can be quite severe with residents being given such assignments as shining shoes of all the other residents."[84]

The precise nature of the punishment could often be ad hoc in nature. A person receiving training at Phoenix House, for example, relates a story in which a resident was made to wear a large silver bow of aluminum foil (two feet across) for a week after having used too much foil on their meal and having ignored two prior warnings.[85]

Sugarman assesses the therapeutic elements that were (at least theoretically) enacted at Daytop in association with such techniques:

> These learning experiences may seem unnecessarily harsh to outsiders but they are used only when more gentle methods have failed. They indicate not so much callousness to the feelings of the person receiving them but rather a determination to help him change in the way that he has said he wants to, however obtusely he may be acting. Embarrassment is the common feature of all these more forceful "learning experiences" and the slow-learning resident is made to feel foolish for what he has done. For anyone to laugh at him in this situation would be treated as a serious offence, though. The Daytop teaching is that such a person needs special attention from his fellows, who will ask him how he came to get himself in that position, and he will be expected to reply fully to each one of them, expressing his intention to change and acknowledging the blame.[86]

While creative humiliation formed a significant part of these punishments, it was linked to a further demand for a resident's verbal acquiescence to both the program and to the justness of the degradation.

Mobilizing Peer Anger Within the TC

While these punishments sought to mobilize shame by making one's humiliation visible to the community, another possibility was to mobilize the hostility of other residents against the offender through the use of collective punishments for an individual infraction. Sugarman provides an example:

> An example of how forceful a pull-up [a punishment for a minor infraction, considered less severe than a haircut] can be is provided by the following observation. One night, around one a.m., after most of the house has been in bed for about half an hour, we were awakened by a voice shouting, "Everyone into the bathroom." All of the male residents of the largest wing of the building, bleary-eyed, are crowded into the bathroom they use. The night expediter [a senior resident position in charge of ensuring that all rules are enforced] is holding an ashtray holding one cigarette butt and asking "Whose is this?" It was found in the bathroom after bedtime. In a broken voice, Louie says faintly, "It's mine."
>
> "Let's all thank Louie for getting us up," says the expediter and an obliging chorus of ironical voices chants, "Thank you, Louie."
>
> As if this is a familiar ritual, the expediter continues, "Good night, all." And a chorus responds "Good night, Louie."[87]

Fostering and channeling anger toward other residents was in fact directly encouraged within the early TCs. As Sugarman writes:

> The recipient knows, however, that he may deal with the hostile feelings which this experience invariably produces by taking the persons he feels most angry towards to the next encounter group [to be discussed further below] where he can scream back at them to his heart's content. Meanwhile, he must grit his teeth and take his medicine.[88]

Thus, anger that might otherwise be directed at the institution and the harsh enforcement of its rules was instead allowed a channel that further facilitated identification with the group norms of the TC; anger was allowed full force *if* its overt manifestation came in the form of enforcing the institutional norms. As Yablonsky notes:

> The misbehavior of a member sometimes . . . also gives the overall group a right to act as "righteous nonoffenders," attacking bad behavior. This somewhat holier-than-thou position seems to reinforce the group's own positive behavior. Witnessing the ridicule to which they themselves might be subjected if they misbehaved serves as a partial deterrent and control of their negative behaviors.[89]

Something of an in-group/out-group pattern was thereby established, with the residents marshalling their collective frustrations against those who undermine the authority of the institution (with "splitees" [those who flee the organization] being considered "dead").[90] Meanwhile, "residents are also expected not to 'jail' or 'bad rap' (talk negatively about) the program. They are supposed to be positive and constructive."[91] In turning all anger away from the institution and toward those who undercut the authority of the institution, the early TCs seem to echo Freud's insight regarding the social usefulness of scapegoats: "It is a convenient and relatively harmless satisfaction of the inclination to aggression, by means of which cohesion between the members of the community is made easier."[92] While Freud referred to the dynamics underlying racism and other similar cultural prejudices, here the facilitated aggression became mobile, tomorrow turning against the individual who today acted as a righteous nonoffender.

More common than either visibly humiliating measures or collective punishments, however, was the "haircut." In a practice that intensifies the humiliating practices of the initial intake interview, a person being punished was told sharply what they had done wrong:

> When a person walks into his haircut, he [*sic*] is faced by a semicircle of seated figures and told to stand up against the door [other organizations had people sit in a "hot seat"]. Then, in a prearranged sequence, each person in the semicircle delivers a tirade of verbal abuse at high volume, castigating the behavior which led to his appearance here. He will be called a "stupid asshole" and similar names. It will be pointed out to him that he is acting like a baby, which is what he came here to change. He will be

> warned that if he doesn't change this behavior forthwith sterner consequences will follow. He will be reminded that this kind of behavior is what got him into trouble in the first place and led to his being here. Through all of this the person receiving the haircut must remain silent and deferential. Generally the last person to speak is the coordinator-on-duty himself. When he has finished he dismisses the recipient of the haircut without his being permitted to say a word.[93]

The people administering the haircut included the coordinator on duty (a resident position), several other senior residents, the person who complained or who was wronged in the incident, and, very specifically, several other friends of the person being disciplined. The marshalling of numbers against a transgressor who was required to remain silent formed an essential component of the technique:

> [A]t each juncture where a Daytop resident has violated a norm and so challenged the authority structure of the house the consequences are meted out to him [*sic*] in a situation where he is outnumbered. This helps the person who is speaking for the Daytop authority structure to speak with assurance that he is in complete control of the situation, and it helps to psychically overwhelm the person receiving the sanction.[94]

The most serious infractions might have been dealt with in a general meeting (often referred to as a GM) in which all of the residents were assembled and pressure brought to bear upon those committing infractions. Waldorf describes one general meeting he observed:

> When two persons with writs of habeas corpus which challenged their state certifications to Hart Island [a Phoenix House program] left the program during one week it was perceived by the staff that the other holders of such writs were liable to undermine the morale and commitment of others in the program. A general meeting was called and four more writ holders were singled out from the group and exhorted in very vitriolic terms to give up their writs or leave the community. The attack was first mounted by the house directors and then by other residents. One female assistant director of a house compared the holders of writs to a malignant cancer that had to be cut or squeezed out of the house. It was a very

emotional meeting and one felt the very strong group pressures being exerted on the four to give up their writs.[95]

In the case of Hart Island, most of the residents were subject to arrest if they left the facility; however, the writs in question made it possible for these few to leave legally. Group pressure was therefore brought against the four to remove this legal option of escape. Waldorf notes: "The aftermath of the general meeting . . . was a general tightening of the house structure and a coalescence of residents in the houses of the Island against what was perceived as a possible threat to the community and the program."[96]

Disciplining the Disciplinarians

As seen in the above case, the administration of discipline is consciously designed to work on those enforcing the measures as well as those on the receiving end. As Sugarman writes:

> We should not forget, though, the effects of the haircut on those who help to administer it. It is a hard thing for them to do, especially if they are close friends of the deviant. It is important that they take part in the haircut for two reasons. First, this places them on one side of the fence, identifying them by their words and behavior with the normative order of Daytop. It makes it virtually impossible for them to commiserate with the deviant afterwards or to help him [*sic*] justify his behavior in any way. If anyone who is selected to participate in giving out the haircut fails to perform his role in a satisfactory way, he will himself receive a haircut from the coordinator on duty and other senior members of the group after the door has closed on the original offender.
>
> Within this structure it is very hard for residents to maintain the kind of "inmate solidarity" against the institutional regime which is typical of jails and most rehabilitative or educational institutions. On a psychological level, participation in a haircut helps the resident who is beginning to modify his behavior patterns to internalize the new values more thoroughly as he vocally rejects those aspects of his former self which he sees reflected in the deviant standing in front of the door.[97]

Requiring residents to participate in both surveillance and in enforcing the harsh punishments does not just extend the range of the disciplinary gaze; it also helps to further the internalization process. Whereas Foucault theorized internalization only in relation to the act of being observed, within the TC residents are forced to engage in actions that serve to socially identify them with the normative order and to make it difficult to maintain former allegiances. Beyond this, the emotionally-charged nature of these actions—e.g., being made to snitch on and betray one's companions—can generate a psychic allegiance to the new identities they portend. Lennard and Allen of Phoenix House write:

> [T]he issuing of sanctions has an impact as great, if not greater, on the person *issuing* the sanction as it does on the person being sanctioned; therefore, this function should not be the prerogative of "staff" or of higher-status members only. . . . To act *as* an agent of a system probably produces greater commitment to the system than being acted upon *by* an agent.[98]

Yablonsky notes the Durkheimian perspective at play in the enforcement of the rules: "Durkheim cogently pointed out how the societal process of punishment was an act that was often more significant for solidifying and validating society's norms than its effect on the offender."[99]

Tight Houses and Collective Punishments

Despite these efforts—Sugarman reports that six haircuts were dispensed almost every day[100]—occasional breakdowns still occurred. Many people simply left the organizations; at Daytop, for example, Sugarman notes that there were two to three splitees a week, over half of those admitted.[101] More threatening to the organization, however, is a general loss of discipline within the TC as a whole, that is, times when the TC:

> occasionally experiences a slackening of discipline and purposefulness among residents. This tends to happen every few months and it is one of the house director's most important functions to be alert to this development and to take steps to reverse the trend. The institutionalized means for doing this is by the "tight house." . . .

> When a "tight house" is to be inaugurated it may or may not be labeled as such. Commonly, though, the director will begin by saying that the house has become very "loose," that the people are "letting things slide." He will give examples of some recent incidents of neglect and carelessness. "People have forgotten what they're here for. They think this is a fucking country club." . . .
>
> The director will talk about the need to "get rid of the deadwood" in the house, the people who are not making any real investment in Daytop and who, consequently, are getting nothing for themselves and dragging everyone else down. "People will split during the tight house, the people who shouldn't be here anyway because their poor little bellies can't take it. They can't get a look at where they're at and start changing." This is the gist of what's usually said. Usually, too, there's talk of throwing some people out. Sometimes, in order to dramatize this possibility, expediters will be told to start up vehicles and the sound of motors starting up and running can be heard by everyone at the house meeting. This scares people severely and leads some to start "copping to things" they have been doing wrong or failing to do, when inevitably the "cop-out session" begins.[102]

During the tight house all privileges—phone calls, movie trips, television, visitors, etc.—are revoked, and most of the residents lose their previously earned positions while the staff run the organization with a reduced crew. According to Sugarman, "Residents are told that they are expected to be especially diligent at confronting and challenging each other." During these periods, "there is extra pressure on residents to 'cop to guilt' they are holding onto" and confess any wrong-doing, and the "scale of severity is now stepped up" for any punishments.[103] The intensity is rapidly made visible: "During the height of a tight house there may be ten people wearing signs, when only one or two would be seen in more normal times."[104]

Should this lengthy series of disciplinary measures fail, the early TCs had the option of throwing people out of the program. Sugarman notes:

> The fact that Daytop can be selective in whom it takes and whom it keeps is crucial to maintaining a high degree of at least outward compliance among the established members. This, in turn, is essential to its success as an ongoing community and to its success in bringing about attitude changes in its members.[105]

The option to terminate people from the program was used as a threat (as seen above, in Waldorf's description of a general meeting), but it was also open as an actual course of action for persons who simply did not respond to community discipline.

The Game: That Which Does Not Kill You . . .

Counseling techniques within the early TCs operated through this same logic of disciplinary action, and even if a resident did not commit any infractions and led an exemplary life by TC standards, she or he was still likely to be subjected to "treatment" akin to that received by those being punished. First known as the Synanon Game, or more simply as *the game*, these encounter groups operate through the same mechanism of attack therapy utilized within the verbal haircuts. Another sociological study situated at Phoenix House speaks about the nature of these groups:

> The encounter has been likened to a verbal street fight—screaming and yelling, and profanity are encouraged; the height of emotional intensity is incredible. . . . The use of profanity broadens the emotional spectrum and dramatically demonstrates that emotionally anything goes. . . . Laughter, tears, rages, compassion are all parts of the encounter. The very brutality of the verbal attack can soon be seen as an expression of love and concern. . . . The group will spare no verbal punches. . . . Encounters may sometimes be rigged, for example, by bringing all of the targets of a particular resident's hostility together. . . .
>
> It is amazing how quickly and easily facades of bravado, self-righteousness and rationalization crumble under the blistering scrutiny of the group. In the process, those who are attacking frequently gain greater insight and understanding than the attacked. Stripped of his stupid behavior the individual is now open to learn new techniques of controlling his feelings.[106]

Yablonsky adds that "elements of exaggeration and artful ridicule" are allowed within these sessions.[107] While most of these encounter groups last only a few hours, marathon sessions can last as long as two or three days, with only short breaks for sleep.[108] At Synanon itself, encounter groups were held three times a week,[109] while marathon sessions typically lasted seventy-two hours, with only one four-hour break for sleep allowed.[110] Yablonsky writes that "attack therapy in Synanon has the effect of 'toughening up' the person,"[111] adding that "crisis situations" such as that created by these confrontations "are manipulated and used in Synanon to help a person grow."[112] Thus, not only does the enforcement of discipline constitute the primary means of controlling the house and of offering daily opportunities for the internalization of a new set of values, but the entire counseling apparatus operates through this disciplinary regime that seeks to disrupt prior patterns, creating emotionally charged moments when identification with the institution might emerge. The process of "breaking down" an addict worked by forcefully unsettling any psychic structures protecting an individual's (clearly dysfunctional) sense of self.

Directed Action: Act As If You Meant It

In this sense, the entire therapeutic approach of both first- and second-generation TCs focused on and revolved around behavioral control and a strictly enforced regimen of coercive care. External discipline was enforced first, with the hope that internalization would follow. As Yablonsky wrote in relation to Synanon:

> Rather than working first on underlying emotional problems directly (as in psychoanalysis), Synanon concentrates *first* on the person's acting out of constructive behavior. The underlying assumption is that people mature psychologically after a sufficient period of constructive behavior. In short, positive behavior eventually effects internal psychological adjustment.[113]

A principle of acting "as-if" was enforced in which a resident was required "to act as if you were the kind of person you want to be, even though you know inside yourself that this is not the real you—yet."[114] Sugarman writes:

> Let us assume that a given resident is acting as if and, slowly building up a personal commitment to personal change for himself [*sic*]. He is developing his commitment to this new pattern. Meanwhile his fellow residents

> are mostly acting as if, while some of them are really committed. He does not know which is which unless he gets to know these individuals very well indeed. So he tends to take them at face value. The atmosphere at Daytop is thus one in which acceptance of the official norms and values is assumed and open rebellion nonexistent. In one sense, the resident has no choice but to take his fellows at face value, because a major part of their "act as if" consists of making pull-ups on him [minor disciplinary actions administered by peers of much less severity than a "haircut"] when his "act as if" is not good enough. And these pull-ups and other negative sanctions that may be invoked are real enough—even if the person instigating them is merely *acting* the role of a committed Daytop resident. Conversely, the resident who serves as the subject of our example demonstrates his "act as if" by pulling-up other residents. Residents do this because they are eventually rewarded for it with privileges and promotions to higher status jobs. More immediate rewards are general approbation, and not being pulled-up and confronted as much themselves. Also residents find that they get good feelings and begin to feel like part of the Daytop community as a result of consistent conformity and a developing identification with its values and its leaders.[115]

Control over participants was (at least envisioned as) so totalizing that any elements of resistance were to be rendered invisible, even to those sharing in the same conditions.

At all levels, then, mutual surveillance and punishment—together with techniques of gendered shaming—constitute the primary forms of treatment within the early TCs. Other modalities—such as work therapy—followed from, and were only possible in relation to, the establishment of this externally enforced discipline.[116] Forcing participants to scrutinize one another extended Foucault's panopticon into spheres where an authoritative eye could otherwise not penetrate, making it difficult for an oppositional discourse to exist. The requirement that participants police one another further worked to break down social bonds based on resistance and, it was hoped, psychologically enlisted participants into the dominant order established by the TC. Collective punishments likewise worked to break down any resistant forms of solidarity among participants, directing anger toward those whose rule-breaking allegedly caused the communal hardship. Lastly, the use of intense shaming, often through gendered tropes, worked to undercut prior forms of identification while positioning the TC's alternative as the only speakable alternative. The strategies involved in Synanon's program of "brainwashing" thus made use of Foucault's panopticon, but extended far beyond it, generating emotions (shame, anger, pleasure) in ways that were meant to undercut prior forms of identification and ironically mobilizing the very forms of peer pressure that are often blamed for drug use. Instead of locking people in isolated cells as was envisioned in the initial panopticon, community-as-method applied force in ways that were intended to make participants act as one another's jailers, enforcing social control upon one another even as they themselves are being controlled. The TC thus took possession over a participant's embodied actions, forcing an emotionally charged simulation of "right living" in hopes that the process of community-wide imitation would create a new set of identities that would then be internalized.

The therapeutic community highlights techniques that are missing from Foucault's vision of disciplinary society, emphasizing the significance not only of surveillance but of the manipulation of both social status and affect in generating control. The active efforts within the TC to make resistance invisible further emphasizes the importance of discourse in establishing the possibility of opposition. More than simple disciplinary society, the TC attempts to become what might be called a *totalizing institution*, one that attempts to work through a highly coercive form of communal simulation undergirded by deliberately structured mutual antagonism.[117]

Authoritarianism in the Hierarchical TC: A Few Defenses

The care involved in what I have termed *violent care* makes the presumption that peoples' lives will be better once they adhere to the established social norms, and it makes little effort to examine the harms that might be caused in the course of forcing people to conform. It envisions addicts as miscreants with no personal strengths and no innovative forms of social-psychological adaptation, and—in contrast—it proffers few criticisms of those who enforce such norms. Such a situation would seem to follow directly from the portrayal of addicts as anti-liberal villains; given a "savage" whose capacity for self-control is undeveloped, the effort at civilizing them must be as totalizing as possible (e.g., the Native American boarding school, the poorhouse, the asylum, etc.). From a different perspective, however, such a situation seems a form of oppression and abuse. On their own terms, then, the strongly authoritarian and disciplinary elements within the early hierarchical TCs might seem to necessitate some sort of safeguards against abuses of power. Perhaps not surprisingly, given the para-racial status of the criminal addict and the way in which the TC positioned itself as a guardian of normalcy, such safeguards were in fact poorly developed. Speaking in relation to Daytop, Sugarman acknowledges the limits and difficulties that someone experiencing mistreatment and abuse—even as defined by the TC itself—might have encountered in challenging their conditions:

> [T]he framework of discussion is restricted by the group ideology. Ideally a relatively junior resident may get a more senior resident to "cop to a mistake" in the way he treated him, either voluntarily or under pressure from a group leader more senior than both of them, but in no case will one get any senior resident to agree that some basic rule [or] requirement is unnecessary or wrong. The Concept itself is not open to challenge. . . .
>
> In theory there are grievance procedures which should ensure justice but in practice there are many loopholes through which unfair staff and senior residents can escape. They can represent the complaint as being a symptom of "baby attitudes" or a desire to "punch holes in the Concept." . . . The best grievance procedures in the world are not secure against unfair administrators. And it can be no surprise that some of the persons exercising authority in Daytop do so unfairly and defend themselves against legitimate grievances by unfair means. They are, after all, still in the course of their own treatment: they mostly have had little experience in exercising authority but plenty of experience as victims of unfair authority figures, and they are operating under a great deal of stress and anxiety.[118]

Sugarman goes on to straightforwardly note that "the Daytop power structure is monolithic and totalitarian."[119] In such a context, it is perhaps not surprising that Synanon and several of the organization's spin-off groups apparently devolved into practices of outright abuse (e.g., a TC developed in 1970 with federal funds on the grounds of the United States Narcotic Farm in Lexington, Kentucky ended in 1972 amid allegations that the group had held inmates against their will, sexually abused some residents, and engaged in "learning experiences" that amounted to torture (such as burning people with cigars).[120]

Even when they operated as intended, however, hierarchical TCs were sometimes subject to sharp criticism. In 1974, for example, a Congressional subcommittee examining behavioral modification programs concluded that the techniques used within TCs, and specifically the extended marathon encounter sessions, were in fact "similar to the highly refined 'brainwashing' techniques employed by the North Koreans in the early nineteen fifties."[121] Similarly, some psychological professionals responded very negatively to the idea of attack therapy (e.g., Yablonsky relates the opinion of one psychologist who saw the Synanon approach as the "most 'destructive approach to human behavior' he had ever witnessed in his twenty years of practice."[122] Sociologist Edgar Friedenberg likewise criticized Synanon for "counting the suppression of a symptom [drug use] as a therapeutic victory . . . no matter what the cure may have done to his more valuable attributes," thereby encouraging a psychological practice designed to force people to "throw their old self out with the bath water").[123]

Most advocates of TCs in the early years felt obliged to address these charges at some length. Speaking in relation to the early Daytop, for example, Sugarman offers a defense of such practices:

> It may well seem to the reader that the community we are describing is inhumane and its leaders sadistic. It must be remembered, however, that Daytop Village was created and exists in order to help drug addicts change their way of life and become able to live without drugs. Daytop residents are here because they say they want to achieve this. . . . A great majority of confirmed drug addicts become addicts because of the weakness of their character, and the lives they led as addicts served only to exaggerate and confirm these character weaknesses. Even when they find themselves in a place like Daytop, therefore, with all the group support and pressure toward certain kinds of behavior, it is still impossible for many residents to conform consistently to these norms. Drastic measures are used only because more gentle ones are ineffective. If it is hard to accept that some people have the right to impose such harsh sanctions on others, what should they then do? Throw them out? Or allow them to remain in Daytop, sabotaging the efforts of those who might benefit more from the community?[124]

In this discussion, the defense of such practices relies on the social stigma borne by "the great majority of drug addicts" and their reputation for an inability to conform. The image of the savage—in this case, savages who are themselves desperate to become civilized—thus inhabits the imaginary of the TC, justifying inhumane and sadistic treatment.[125]

Writing of Synanon, Yablonsky relates a more extended reflection from Dederich, adding his own analysis:

> A fist encounter with Synanon's hard-hitting approach to therapy is often shocking. A close appraisal of the method reveals some sound underlying logic.
>
> In a forthright statement on some aspects of this "hard line," Dederich commented: "Dope fiends shoot dope. As long as they are dope fiends, they are not much good; they are slobs and thieves, with the temperaments of nasty little children. When they stop using dope, they're something else again. They need self-respect and then general respect more than they do sympathy. . . . At Synanon, we may seem rough at times, but we have to be their guts, until they develop guts for themselves." . . .
>
> During my first synanon session . . . I too was shocked by the brutal treatment of individuals when they were placed on the "hot seat." . . . My reaction to the rugged synanon was to conclude that the attackers were after "blood" and that somehow this "fixed" their own emotional, sadistic needs. I also feared for the victim of the mob. I could see some of the therapeutic rationale for attacking "bad behavior"; but at the same time, I felt that the group was "rat-packing" a "victim" and was going too far.
>
> However, on the basis of my participation in about a hundred synanon sessions and "haircuts," I have revised my early personal opinions about what some professionals have labeled "verbal brutality." . . .
>
> After my first twenty-five sessions, I began to feel that, in many respects, the synanon "attack" was an act of love. Entwined in an attack was the assumption: "If we did not care about you or have concern with you, we would not bother to point out something that might reduce your psychic pain or clarify something for you that might save your life." In this context, the verbal "attack" seems to be an expression of great sympathy.[126]

While Dederich's response again invokes the savage, thereby denigrating everything about a drug user's life and capacity for any sort of mature emotionality, Yablonsky's own analysis simply fails to address the substance of the charge: while he claims that these attacks are motivated by love and concern, such a fact does not alter their potential status as abuse.[127]

Deitch and Solit offer a third defense of attack therapy at TCs, arguing:

> Regrettably, much of what has been written about therapeutic communities focuses only on its more sensational aspects—its intense behavior-management and behavior-shaping techniques, such as encounter and confrontation. . . . This is an extremely distorted image of the therapeutic community experience.
>
> The notion of having one's guts ripped out suggests that the individual is not volitionally involved in the process of disclosure. Furthermore, the image implies that the motivation of such disclosure is misdirected and/or negative. While the process *is* often challenging, it is not a challenge "to a person"; rather it is "for the person." The global goal is to help the individual wrestle with problems and experiences that cause them pain, conflict, and dysfunctional behavior. Demands *are* made on the individual, but these demands enhance their ability to communicate deep emotions and create prosocial activity.[128]

The idea that focusing on confrontation—at least within the early TCs—constitutes a distortion, however, is undercut by the absolute centrality of confrontation and behavioral control to the therapeutic approach.[129] The notion that individuals were choosing such treatment is also ironic given the more general evaluation of "the addict's" incapacity to make decisions for themselves (which is indeed what such treatment was intended to cure). In the end, the justification for brutal aspects of violent care rely upon the simple fact of its normative aims.

More than Discipline: The Love of Tough Love

It *is* very much the case, however, that focusing solely on the hostile and antagonistic aspects of the early TC—or even of the game—would significantly distort the experiences of those who lived within these communities. The opportunity to express anger and hatred with minimal consequence, for example, provided opportunities for some participants to explore their less visible emotional patterns or to simply emote in a way that might be experienced as constructive and positive. After years of feeling degraded as a prostitute and junkie, for example, Florrie Fisher (who later authored a memoir describing her experiences and warning youths away from what she saw as the inevitable consequences of drugs[130]) wrote that she found Synanon's attack therapy helpful precisely because it allowed her to go on the attack:

> [W]ithin about one week [of entering the program] all of my hostilities broke loose. New members are usually the most obscene, most vocal. I was so loud and so rank in my games that everytime I was in the game, they held it in the "crypt," the cellar, where it was most soundproof.
>
> I was really attacking people. After twenty-three years of hustling and dope and prison, I was full of hate. I hated everyone.
>
> For instance, I decided I hated men. Why not? After all the pimps and tricks I'd known, I had seen only the bad in men. When we'd get into a game, I'd crucify them.
>
> All they had to do was let me get started, and I was soon using the foulest, the filthiest language. I'd turn to a Negro. "You, nigger, shut up, shine my shoes, that's all you're good for."
>
> And they would laugh at me, just laugh at me.
>
> And I would repeat it and say it over and over until what I was saying didn't make any sense, even to me, and I'd have gotten rid of it, I'd have screamed it out of me. Synanon is completely integrated, with as many Negroes in top positions as whites, but nobody was mad about my built-in hate, they knew it would pass. . . .
>
> I was slowly getting rid of my hates, but it was a slow process, it took more than a year.[131]

In this regard, referencing attack therapy as *the game* emphasized its supposed social detachment from the rest of community life and suggested that experiences with what might be termed *serious play*[132] were not meant to completely define one's self outside of game time.[133] Rules in the early TCs specified that what happened within the attack therapy sessions was to remain within those sessions; at all other times, residents were to act as if they were the happy, productive, rule-abiding individuals that they were striving to become (indeed, Synanon gained a reputation for being filled with people who smiled at all times and were overly friendly, generating a disconcerting effect upon some observers).[134]

Beyond this, participants who appreciated the game and who became adept at playing it developed many more elements within the sessions than simply attack. Tourish and Wohlforth report, for example, that "once participants learned how to play, it could be fun," with developed tactics of attack and humor.[135] Speaking of his time at Synanon, Guy Endore similarly writes that:

> [T]he Synanon game is fun. A chance to match ourselves against everyone else and give as good as we receive. No wonder voices rise, tempers flare, and the language becomes salty. And many find that this is what they have been looking for all their lives, a chance to blow your cork in the company of people who are just as eager to blow theirs.[136]

Despite the fact that "behavior in the Game is loud, rude, and often hostile," Gates and Bourdette likewise note that "the Game is also played for fun, and laughter at the more ridiculous ironies of the human condition resounds from every Game room . . . a person learns to laugh at himself [*sic*]."[137]

Abraham Maslow, developer of the psychological theory of a hierarchy of needs and a leading light of the human potential movement, visited Daytop Village while it was still affiliated with Synanon. His impression of the Daytop encounter group was entirely positive:

> I have spent a whole lifetime learning to be pretty careful with people, to be sort of delicate and gentle, and to treat them as if they were like brittle china that would break easily. . . . The assumption in your group seems to be, on the contrary, that people are very tough, and not brittle. They can take an awful lot. The best thing to do is get right at them, and not to sneak up on them, or be delicate with them, or try to surround them from the rear. Get right smack into the middle of things right away. I've suggested that a name for this might be "no-crap therapy." It serves to clean out the defenses, the rationalizations, the veils, the evasions and politenesses of the world. . . . There was extremely direct talking, and it worked fine.[138]

Maslow went so far as to say that "In a way, this is a little Utopia, a place out of the world where you can get real straight-forwardness, real honesty and the respect that is implied by honesty, and the experience of a real group working together as a team."[139]

Thus, while *attack* formed a significant part of attack therapy, and often people saw the sessions primarily through that lens (not infrequently causing them to leave), other more affirming social dynamics were present as well. Meetings were "at once virulent, emotional and compassionate with admixtures of all three in any single session," suggests Waldorf.[140] Writing of Synanon, Yablonsky likewise argues that *attack* may be a misnomer, with seemingly aggressive interactions acting as "an effort to communicate some information useful to the person, information that he [*sic*] appears to have an emotional block to hearing."[141] Citing the "loving brute force" involved with the method,[142] he suggests that the "sympathetic counseling approach" often fails whereas "the combination of soft and hard—in proper proportion, at the right time—seems to do the job."[143] Gerstel similarly notes that "one had to learn to scale the force of his attack to the individual at whom it was aimed . . . A good Game player did not try to destroy others, but to improve them—to make them better Synanon people."[144]

Yablonsky offers an example of this mode of support:

> You stupid slob—you've run yourself into the ground by your behavior. Your tough-guy-dope-fiend style keeps getting you dropped off in a cage. You're not really bad; you're just stupid and ridiculous. Look at how ridiculous you are: like a rat, you ran up and down alleys stealing; you buy some white powder, and then you jam a needle with some fluid in your arm, conk out, and go back for more. Of course, you are killing yourself. You will either die by being locked up for life or die from an overdose in a back alley. Your *behavior* is ridiculous![145]

Yablonsky comments that this "This is cold, hard talk—on the surface, lacking in sympathy; yet in a definite way, it is realistic. More than that, it doesn't support the old pattern, which considerable unrealistic affection apparently does. . . . Love, affection, and involvement are also certainly practiced in the organization, but these approaches . . . are used in conjunction with the (seemingly) tough approach."[146] While comments that one will "either die by being locked up for life or die from an overdose" may be exaggerations based on worst-case scenarios—as well as a framing that both naturalizes incarceration and renders the life of an addict as essentially worthless and akin to that of a rat—it is certainly the case that such comments *might* be experienced as a deep expression of concern and even love.

In this same vein, it is also significant that people who were attacked within haircuts or encounter groups were generally approached afterward in what was called a *pick up*, either an attempt to express support or simply to offer "a compliment at a time when he least expects it . . . at a time of maximum effectiveness."[147] Yablonsky writes of Synanon's founder: "Chuck somehow has the exquisite sense of knowing just how hard to go, when to quit, and, of course, to pick up a man [*sic*] after he's run the man up against a wall. He doesn't leave him depressed after a haircut—he'll give him something to pick himself up with."[148] In an early UK facility (modeled on Phoenix House), a *patching up* time followed encounter groups, "where group participants were encouraged to share with the others in twos and threes what had happened to them and how they felt. A softer atmosphere was created, ending with food and soft drinks."[149] "Hearing the violence of the arguments at the synanons, and then seeing happy and relaxed people gather afterwards for refreshments, is a shock, until you understand that each has reached some sort of catharsis, or release," offered Winslow. Though the early TCs had "less emphasis on rewarding good behavior in formal ways and more emphasis on correcting bad behavior,"[150] these positive reinforcements formed an important part of the approach, significantly shaping how residents experienced the institution as a whole.

Not only was attack therapy not always experienced as negative by participants, but there were numerous elements of community joy and celebration as well (particularly at Synanon, as seen in figures figures 3.4 and 3.5). Yablonsky describes some of the positive incentives encouraging a new resident at Synanon to stay:

> At times I felt like splitting. . . . [but] Synanon was better than anything else I could do—at the time." Also, Synanon House was on the beach. The meals were good. In the evening many ex-addict top musicians would play cool jazz.[151] Also there were, according to Frankie, "broads to dance with and get to know."[152]

Though most later TCs (heavily shaped by their association with the criminal justice system, as will be discussed in the next chapter) eventually

Tribune photo by Robert Stinnett

Thousands of visitors to Synanon's Oakland fair crowded around Saturday to dig the sounds of Country Weather, one of many groups performing

Kids and Old Folks Jam Synanon Fiesta

FIGURE 3.5 More than 75,000 people in Oakland, CA attended a day-long concert sponsored by Synanon and headlined by Country Joe & the Fish in 1969. Earlier, in 1968, the organization sponsored another concert featuring Janis Joplin as part of "Synanon Week" (declared by San Francisco mayor Joseph Alioto), drawing approximately 60,000 people.

Source: Photo by *East Bay Times*.

prohibited sexual encounters between residents,[153] sexual relationships at Synanon, while highly regulated, were not entirely disallowed.[154]

While I have emphasized the punitive aspects of social control, and suggested that these formed the core of the techniques within the early therapeutic communities, the institutions cannot be understood solely through this lens. Rather, the discipline they exerted must be seen in a context in which love, affection, and involvement are also mobilized, both as therapeutic techniques and as ways to maintain the loyalty of residents to the organization. In their examination of the role of humiliation and verbal violence within the TC, Stine, Patrick, and Molina offer the useful admonition that practices such as the game must be situated and understood within the overall context of community life, rather than condemned without any exploration as to how people actually experience the techniques. While ultimately condemning "radical confrontation therapy," they nevertheless insist:

> Radical confrontation can have both positive and negative effects . . . an anthropological examination of just how it fits into the ritual life of the community—on the one hand, providing for a safe, ritualized expression of anger; on the other, raising ethical, legal, and clinical problems.[155]

While a large number of people—easily the majority of voluntary admissions—left the organization rapidly as a result of the harshness of TC tactics (many could not simply laugh off such verbal assaults), one cannot understand how those who remained understood the practices by making decontextualized assumptions based on the virulence of the techniques. No evaluation of TC practices would be complete without a more thorough examination as to how individuals experienced and related to the techniques in question.

Rise of the Therapeutic Communities

It is somewhat remarkable that the innovations developed at Synanon—an experimental community with clear links to the counterculture of the 1960s—rose to become standard fare within contemporary criminal justice programs oriented toward the treatment of drug abuse. The institutional rapprochement that TCs achieved with the criminal justice system reveals much about the elements that appealed to policy makers, even as other elements were necessarily shorn away. While I write about this history in greater detail in an earlier text,[156] it is worth mentioning a few points. Synanon and other TCs gained legitimacy by linking themselves to an earlier form of therapeutic community, one formed by psychiatrists in the late 1930s, 1940s, and 1950s and operating by significantly different principles. Sometimes called democratic therapeutic communities to distinguish them from the hierarchical TCs that followed Synanon,[157] these psychiatric facilities emphasized the *strengthening* of psychic defenses rather than their elimination and did not call for residents to police one another. In general, the roles established for staff were meant to be supportive, with psychiatrists literally removing their white coats.[158] Democratic TCs were introduced in a variety of contexts, including many state prison systems, particularly California's, where they were used in an effort to rehabilitate all inmates (not simply drug users).[159] But while California led the way in creating democratic TCs, they also led the way in closing the projects. The 1965 uprising in Watts, in particular, "gave conservative critics of California's efforts in rehabilitation the confidence to systematically brand supporters of liberal reforms as 'soft' on murderers and drug dealers."[160] With the specter of Watts and the "black menace" in the background, prison policy became an issue in the following year's race for governor, with challengers to Democratic Governor Pat Brown claiming that he "coddled prisoners." Ronald Reagan won the election and took office in 1966, cutting funds for rehabilitative programs and directing monies instead toward police efforts at riot and crowd control.[161] The thinly veiled racial politics of law and order, energized by the Watts uprising and black rebellion more generally, served as a death knell for prison-based democratic therapeutic communities in California and across the country.[162]

Programs developed in the wake of the democratic TC adopted increasingly punitive approaches. In attempting to control the escalating resistance among (often nonwhite) political activists who were disrupting the prison in a variety of ways (ranging from riots to hunger strikes to legal actions), correctional officials began to employ psychiatric drugs such as Prolixin, Thorazine, and other tranquilizers in an effort to maintain control.[163] In other instances, aversion therapy techniques involving the use of electric shock, drugs that induce vomiting, or Anectine (a muscle relaxant that was given in sufficient quantities as to produce paralysis, including an inability to breath properly, for up to two minutes) were administered to prisoners who failed to obey a guard's orders.[164] While these procedures were ruled unconstitutional in 1973 (*Knecht v. Gillman*), other behavioral techniques remained constitutionally viable.[165] The use of long-term segregation during which inmates are kept in small isolated cells for 23 to 23.5 hours per day—now a common practice within maximum security control units across the United States[166]—was first pioneered in 1960 with California's notorious adjustment centers and justified as a form of treatment.[167] Perhaps the best known (and most infamous) of these programs was Project START, established in 1972 at the medical center for federal prisoners in Springfield, Missouri. Project START was designed for "that element of the prison population which has chronically demonstrated inability to effectuate adherence to established regulations"[168] and was intended as a prototype for subsequent programs in the future.[169] Project START worked with a tier system in which "good behavior" was rewarded through promotion to a higher tier; after a hunger strike by inmates, however, a subtier was added that involved chaining inmates' arms and legs to their beds at all times.[170] Conditions within Project START's subtier generated newspaper stories, protests, and lawsuits against the program, and the program was abruptly ended approximately eighteen months after its inception in the midst of Congressional hearings.[171] While the Bureau of Prisons (BoP) claimed it ended START due to financial concerns, this explanation was widely seen as not credible. Speculation circulated that the BoP did not wish to have the practices ruled upon by the Supreme Court and thereby risk having them declared unconstitutional.[172] A week after the BoP cancelled the program, the Law Enforcement Assistance Administration (LEAA) announced that it would no longer support any programs involving behavior modification because it did not have the capacity to properly screen and monitor such projects.[173]

Given these political considerations, Synanon-style therapeutic communities became virtually the only option for those wishing to promote rehabilitation regimes within the prison, the program being hard enough to protect administrators from the charge of coddling prisoners and yet soft enough to pass constitutional muster.[174] Prison administrators now evinced much less enthusiasm for rehabilitative programs directed at prisoners—the famous "nothing works" report by Martinson had concluded that such efforts were pointless[175]—but the federal government and various state projects nevertheless began to offer increasing support for the treatment of drug users. New York State, for example, founded Daytop—originally DATOP, "Drug Addicts Treated on Probation"[176]—in 1963, and others began to receive clients from newly-created diversion programs promoted by the 1966 Narcotic Addiction Rehabilitation Act (NARA).[177] NARA additionally created a series of five hierarchical therapeutic communities within the federal prison system, the first opening in March 1968 in Danbury, Connecticut.[178] In 1972, Nixon's Special Action Office for Drug Abuse Prevention (SAODAP) similarly created Treatment Alternatives to Street Crime (TASC), expanding the growing need for treatment programming in association with the promotion of the drug war.[179] While

NARA had established TC treatment options within the prison system, TASC now began diverting low-level drug offenders into treatment and out of the prison system.[180]

Ronald Reagan's rise to the presidency in 1980 marked an even greater decline in the rehabilitative focus within the prison system, with federal funding dropping dramatically. State-level funding enabled some programs to survive, but a series of changes in the notion of treatment and rehabilitation was nevertheless effected. Democratic TCs had been eliminated within the prison system as a result of appearing too soft on prisoners, while the more punitive practices within hierarchical therapeutic communities proved more politically viable in a political environment fueled by the war on crime. And while the first hierarchical TCs within prisons had aimed at rehabilitating *all* inmates, by 1980 all such rehabilitation efforts for the general prison population had virtually ended (figure 3.6). A few hierarchical TCs continued to exist but only in relation to drug users. Secondly, a shift occurred in relation to the type of prisoner being considered appropriate for treatment. While some early hierarchical TCs and behavioral modification programs such as Project START were designed to deal with the most difficult-to-manage populations within the prison (including, but not limited to, political prisoners), TCs such as Daytop and Phoenix House were established either for probationers and parolees or for nonviolent criminals considered to be low-risk. TASC similarly handled people at the periphery of the criminal justice system (mostly first-time offenders).

By the end of Reagan's presidency, a need to reduce spending in light of skyrocketing imprisonment began to once again generate interest in programs that might lower recidivism and thereby reduce costs.[181] Reagan supported a significant increase in funding for treatment in the 1986 Anti-Drug Abuse Act (ADAA), particularly in relation to hierarchical TCs, whether prison- or community-based.[182] As was the now established formula, these programs were generally directed at low-risk inmates, restoring, for example, federal monies to the TASC program. Even as treatment options began to slowly expand for low-risk drug users, however, higher security inmates were increasingly subjected to techniques of long-term isolation in so-called supermax control units that patterned themselves on California's behaviorist-oriented adjustment centers (as noted above). Thus, through the strategic deployment of drug treatment, a two-track system within the criminal justice system began to develop. Drug use offered a convenient

FIGURE 3.6 Images from the CBS show *The Twentieth Century*, hosted by Walter Cronkite. This 1966 episode, "Synanon in Prison," focused on the program Synanon ran for inmates at the Nevada State Prison located in Carson City. Fewer than one-third of the participants had any involvement with drugs, highlighting the fact that early TC proponents envisioned their programs as reaching far beyond the issue of addiction. Seen above is Candy Latson, who founded and ran the program on Synanon's behalf, and several participants in the program in a room known as "The Cave," a quarry dug by the original inmates at the penitentiary where many of Synanon's sessions were held. Synanon's program at the prison ran from 1962 to 1966, ending when the prison moved from a rehabilitative philosophy to a custodial orientation (Clark, 2017: 55). Latson later helped to establish Phoenix House.

Source: Photos courtesy of CBS News.

means to differentiate between many high- and low-risk prisoners in that, while not all low-risk inmates utilized drugs, many did[183] (meanwhile, violent offenders were excluded from most drug treatment programs within the criminal justice system whether they used drugs or not). Advocates for TCs often argued that they offered an effective means of countering the criminal code (or the prison code), marketing themselves directly to their institutional clientele.[184] As CJ-oriented drug treatment occurring outside of prisons became more common, it was decisively positioned to serve as an auxiliary minimum security adjunct within the prison system, "treating" (as well as monitoring and controlling) inmates, probationers, and parolees. Drug treatment, even before the advent of drug courts, thus operated as a system of *stratified penalization*, as the criminal justice system increasingly created a two-track system, with one path leading to treatment-oriented supervision and the other to long-term segregation.

Regardless of its effectiveness or its value to persons going through it, in lowering costs for this low-risk group, the turn toward treatment has helped to make the ongoing expansion of the criminal justice system's reach into poor, nonwhite communities possible, offering a low-cost means to handle the increased number of prisoners created through a much-widened net. Without drug treatment facilities to ease the cost of this targeted expansion of the criminal justice system, it is conceivable that budgetary concerns would have forced imprisonment rates to hold level as early as 1986 (when the ADAA passed), or even as early as 1982 (when many states began to invest more heavily in drug treatment), rather than being enabled to continue rising for an additional twenty years. In this sense, drug treatment can be said to constitute a "humane" face for a vastly expanded system of criminalization, without which today's system of racialized mass incarceration likely would not have extended as far. I will again address the issue of drug treatment and criminal justice reform at the end of this book, but I now return to the micropolitical nature of control, detailing the ways in which such control operates within contemporary therapeutic communities. In most ways, the model developed at Synanon and its second-generation followers have continued into the present. While the practice of attack therapy has been somewhat marginalized and limited in comparison to the central role it used to hold, many of the "brainwashing" techniques and the overall theory of addiction that were innovated at Synanon continue into the present.

4

Control and Agency in Contemporary Therapeutic Communities

Synanon initially rejected direct government funding due to the many conditions that they feared would be attached;[1] however second-generation therapeutic communities were often founded either as direct expressions of, or in close association with, public policy. As Chuck Dederich feared, this symbiotic relationship has indeed greatly changed the nature of drug treatment within the therapeutic community (TC). As the historian Claire Clark argues, the shift toward state funding also involved a shift away from some of Synanon's model of social experimentation. As she notes, "To politicians, the TC approach for treating addiction proved most acceptable when residents were socialized into appropriate religious and gender roles along with their new abstemious behaviors."[2] Similarly, the idea that TCs might act as change agents within society at large (an approach fostered by David Deitch at Daytop, who began to follow some Black Panthers in describing addiction as a tool of societal oppression)[3] was rapidly abandoned in favor of a closed definition of community.[4] Similarly, due to funding constraints placed by insurance companies and by Medicaid, many TCs have also had to limit the amount of time residents were expected to remain in treatment, typically reducing a program's length from two to three years to twelve to eighteen months, and in some cases to as few as three months.[5] Reliance on state funding sources has also led many TCs to offer vocational training, educational services, and medical services in addition to their ongoing TC programming.[6]

Most critically, however, have been changes in TC staffing and practice. While the vast majority of TC staff positions continue to be filled by individuals who have undergone treatment themselves and who therefore learn the TC method through apprenticeship,[7] state-mandated training offers an indirect means for governmental regulation of therapeutic communities, a process that has slowly led them in more conventional directions. The National Institute of Drug Abuse (NIDA) has been particularly instrumental in promoting what it terms *evidence-based practices* (EBPs) over the past two decades. These therapies are created by researchers and then statistically validated, a procedure that requires standardization of treatment, thereby favoring pharmaceutical and cognitive-behavioral therapy (CBT) interventions over, for example, long-term counseling.[8] Though pharmaceutical approaches have been resisted by most TCs, CBT approaches (e.g., relaxation training, stress management, and relapse prevention [which involves the identification of triggers that might lead to drug use]) have been more readily integrated into many TC programs.[9] A growing number of TCs likewise integrate Motivational Interviewing (MI), an approach that explicitly eschews an "evaluative, hierarchical, or coercive relationship" between client and counselor and that instead seeks to enhance a client's desire to abstain from drugs through a "positive, friendly, collaborative" exploration of their own ambivalences.[10] In some therapeutic communities—including the TC where I conducted the bulk of my ethnographic fieldwork—formally trained social workers, persons with no necessary prior experience with the TC model, have been hired to offer both group and individual counseling sessions for participants. Notably, however, CBT, MI, and formal counseling have been introduced as *adjuncts* to the traditional TC approach; CBT classes are held only once a week at some TCs, for example, whereas MI is often used solely during intake procedures. At the TC where I conducted my fieldwork, participants received counseling sessions once a week, with a second weekly group session, while their day-to-day experience was still governed by a slightly modified version of the totalizing community that was pioneered at Synanon. Taken together, state regulation and trends toward professionalization have nevertheless produced a significant change in the basic tone of the day-to-day practices within contemporary TCs. While I provide a more thoroughgoing discussion regarding all of these factors elsewhere,[11] here I first examine some of the contemporary trends impacting the enforcement of discipline within TCs before returning to an ethnographic lens, ultimately examining the ways in which participants both embrace and resist the still intense pressures exerted by the TC.

Mitigating Abuse Within the TC Environment

First- and second-generation TCs were always controversial due to their reputation for exerting extremely harsh forms of abuse upon participants. As TCs began to professionalize in the 1980s and 1990s, they sought to curb the most severe of these practices in an effort to gain more professional credibility.[12] The trend away from punitive forms of control has been particularly commented on in a European context, where the tradition of democratic TCs holds more sway and has perhaps served to temper the severity of the U.S. hierarchical TC. Writing in 1998, for example, Broekaert et al. describe the rise of a new TC that features "increasing professionalism"[13] and ensures that "learning experiences, such as the wearing of large signs, must never be degrading and dehumanizing."[14] In a later essay, Broekaert et al. similarly point to "an ongoing evolution in encounter group methods from one of harsh confrontation to one of dialogue and discussion."[15] Several researchers pointed to the high rates of dropouts from the first- and second-generation TCs as a reason to make such a shift. As Bracke, an addiction therapist working in a Belgian therapeutic community, suggested:

> [T]he encounter and its hard confrontations strove to "break" the image of the addict. However, it often happened that the person himself [*sic*] felt broken, devalued, humiliated, and without support. Consequently, many stopped their treatment prematurely because they did not get time to experience the support and comprehension that made therapy tolerable.[16]

Because of this, many European researchers have emphasized "the necessity to avoid destructive confrontation" within TCs, particularly at the outset of treatment.[17] Broekaert et al. thus argue that the overall direction within at least European TCs has been "from harsh confrontation to dialogue and discussion."[18]

Within the United States, a similar shift has occurred, though it is by no means clear how complete such a transition has been. George De Leon's canonical text on TCs, *The Therapeutic Community: Theory, Model, and Method* (sometimes called *The Red Book* in reference to its cover), argues for a move away from some of the most extreme practices within the early TCs. Noting, for example, that "provocative tools" such as anger or ridicule "risk personal injury," De Leon recommends that reprimands (aka haircuts) involve only staff members: "Residents alone are prohibited from delivering reprimands as they have not acquired enough self-control and could exploit the reprimand to ventilate their own emotions regarding another individual."[19] De Leon argues that staff-initiated therapeutic confrontation should "focus on specific behaviors and attitudes, not address the unchangeable, nor attack the 'inner' person,"[20] and that confrontational statements be limited to "behaviors not people" (thereby ruling out the earlier use of "cultural and gender pejoratives" as well as personalizing statements such as "You're no good inside. You're evil").[21] While softening the tone of the TC, these recommendations pointedly still allow for negative and derogatory comments regarding traits deemed changeable such as body size, as well as traits such as "laziness" or "sexual promiscuity." Indeed, the entire point of the TC is to change personal features deemed changeable, and personal insults regarding these issues remain deeply integrated into the therapeutic regimen of many contemporary therapeutic communities.

De Leon recommends additional changes in the TC milieu, placing greater emphasis on *pick-ups* (supportive statements) than did an earlier generation of TC practitioners. De Leon here argues that "the effective peer encounter group balances its confrontational and supportive elements,"[22] and highlights the importance of a thirty to forty-five minute period of friendly socializing (with coffee and snacks) after an encounter group. Socializing after encounter groups is meant to offer opportunities for "expressions of support, consolation, humor, and affection, particularly toward those who might have experienced hurt or discomfort during the confrontation," and De Leon recommends that facilitators and staff "offer further resolution and offer encouragement to encountered residents if necessary."[23]

In an interview, De Leon further notes that every national and international association of therapeutic communities (including the World

Federation of Therapeutic Communities, Therapeutic Communities of America, the European Federation of Therapeutic Communities, the Australian Therapeutic Communities Association, the Asian Therapeutic Communities Association, the Federation of TCs of Central & Eastern Europe, and the Latin American Federation of Therapeutic Communities) has taken a stand against abuse and actively works to discourage it amongst federation members, arguing that therapeutic communities have done much more to counter abusive practices than other parts of the mental health field and suggesting that TCs are held to a different standard due to stigma developed during the early years of the institutions.[24] Nevertheless, this leaves open the question as to what constitutes "abuse," particularly in relation to insults hurled toward "behaviors not people."

Punishment Modified? Learning Experiences Within Contemporary TCs

While placing some limits on encounter groups and on the delivery of reprimands and other "provocative tools," the question as to exactly how "provocative" one should be remains an open one. De Leon, for example, continues to recommend the use of stigmatizing signs as a learning experience:

> Signs may be worn by the resident, strung around the neck or pinned to the shirt. These display what the resident must remember concerning an infraction. Typically, the themes center on a social label (e.g., liar, thief, manipulator) and what they must do to change (e.g., speak respectfully, listen, stop reacting or threatening people).[25]

Furthermore, De Leon reasserts the primacy of the disciplinary regime within therapeutic communities, arguing that "in the TC, the process of socialization occurs mainly through *consequential learning experiences*" and that "peer self-management is a critical component of sanctions . . . peers are instructed and expected to detect infractions, confront these, and actively support the implementation of all forms of sanctions."[26] He further recommends utilizing marathon group sessions of twelve to thirty-six hours "in order to dissipate defenses and resistances through the use of a variety of physical, psychological, and social techniques,"[27] indicating a general approach that still seeks to "break down" an addict's defenses.[28]

Even given moderating influences, then, some of the currently existing therapeutic communities continue to rely on punitive elements of the earlier TC model, including the use of humiliating punishments in order to discipline their residents. In my interviews with TC residents, I heard stories concerning a small number of therapeutic communities in which those receiving treatment were required to wear large dunce caps, stigmatizing signs—one, for example, read: "My values and priorities are distorted"—or adult-sized diapers worn over their other clothing as "learning experiences." In another incident, a resident relayed to me how they had been forced to count all the leaves that had fallen to the ground in a courtyard area. De Leon suggests that these practices are most commonly found in the Northeastern United States, where TCs developed a particularly strong presence in the 1960s and 1970s, and where the traditional Synanon model is still followed to a greater extent than elsewhere.[29] Whatever the case, the punitive nature of these so-called learning experiences struck me as highly objectionable, particularly given that individuals are often attending such programs under a criminal justice mandate. One individual, for example, described a learning experience in which they were required to go outside and find a male and a female rock. Confused, but receiving no clarification from the staff member, the person returned with two rocks; "No, you've got two males," came the reply, "Find a female." After bringing back rock after rock for more than two hours, the staff member finally relented and said the person had at last found a female rock. At another TC, a group of residents was forced to literally dig their own graves (outside, on the institution's grounds) in order to drive home the point that they were killing themselves by using drugs. Another facility features extended confrontation sessions held in blacked out rooms (so that the time cannot be known) that last over twenty-four hours without a break. One resident who shared such stories with me said that he still sometimes experienced nightmares from the trauma these "learning experiences" inflicted. Extreme stories such as these, however, were limited to just a few TCs whose names reoccurred several times during the course of my interviews.

In interviewing personnel at the New York State Office of Alcoholism and Substance Abuse Services (OASAS), the agency in charge of regulating such treatment centers, I was informed that practices of this sort were "frowned upon" and considered "abusive," but that they were not considered illegal. The legal office for the agency receives approximately 100 complaints from patients in treatment centers a month (including not just TCs but all manner of drug treatment facilities: hospital-based detox units, methadone clinics, outpatient clinics, and so on), handling incidents such as these on a case-by-case basis, with most decisions favoring the treatment providers. Such practices thus constitute something of a regulatory "gray zone," with very little chance of an actual penalty except in extremely severe cases. One of the district attorneys who worked with the drug court, upon hearing stories detailing these practices from the people they prosecuted, had concern about the constitutionality of such punishments and called OASAS to see their position concerning such potentially cruel and unusual punishments. Upon hearing that OASAS knew about the practices, the district attorney abandoned the issue (offering me a shrug as they relayed the story).[30]

While abusive practices such as the above continue to occur, most therapeutic communities have renounced the prior harshness of the first- and second-generation TCs, many as early as the mid-1980s.[31] As one program director—working at a facility that did not use signs or other intentionally humiliating tactics—noted during an interview:

> I've been working with TCs for more than ten years, and I think the movement has been toward professionalizing the field. The fear concept and the idea of breaking people down before building them up is really moving out. . . . The expectation today is that I'm going to be more of a clinician. You can't come in and curse someone out and expect them to listen to you and say "OK, I'll stop doing drugs." It's not ten, fifteen, twenty years ago when it was good enough to say "You son of a bleep, you need to go clean this, you need to go do that." Now it's "You need to clean that." "Why?" And you have to explain why. . . . So you're coming from a place where you're trying to engage the client more. You're trying to teach the client more, to educate the client more, rather than just trying to intimidate the client. Because you can intimidate the client into being compliant, but that doesn't mean that they're going to internalize anything.

Several commentators have viewed these changes favorably and spoken of a convergence of practice among hierarchical and democratic therapeutic communities, with both a professionalization of hierarchical TCs and an increasing reliance upon staff guidance within democratic TCs.[32] Haigh and Lees go so far as to identify the development of what they call "fusion TCs."[33] To the extent it exists, the shape of this fusion involves both a scaling back of the prior harshness of the hierarchical TC and a diminishment of the extent to which residents actually shape policy within the democratic TCs. Given the historical evolution, I term this new model the *professionalized TC.*[34]

Mandated Clients and the Professionalized TC

Beyond changes that have occurred in relation to regulation from without and professionalization from within, the impact of treating a population that is not only drug involved but mandated to treatment (whether by a drug court, or through probation or parole) greatly changes the atmosphere within the therapeutic communities.[35] The effects of these changes can be seen over time, and significant oscillations that have occurred within criminal justice policy make it possible to see the effects of having larger or smaller numbers of mandated clients in particular. While Daytop began by receiving 100 percent of its clientele from the criminal justice system, for example, this quickly changed; by 1968, only about half of its residents were legally mandated.[36] Phoenix House likewise originated as a direct subsidiary of the criminal justice system, receiving all of its clientele from the court system; by 1970, however, only 40 percent of Phoenix House residents were mandated, a figure that dropped even farther to 20 percent in 1985 (a time when Reagan had eliminated many rehabilitative services and before he reversed course in 1986 and began to support drug treatment).[37] With greater emphasis on diversion and drug courts today, a staff member at Phoenix House estimated that the current figure is closer to 70–75 percent.[38] The rise in criminal justice populations, the staff member noted, has resulted in a younger and less white population as well as a larger percentage of individuals being treated for marijuana and cocaine instead of heroin. The percentage of legally-mandated clients has increased over the last ten years, and—with the passage of New York's 2009 law concerning judicial diversion (Criminal Procedure Law Article 216, which essentially expands the drug court model across the entire state)—that growth continued.[39] Together with changes wrought by regulatory agencies and insurance companies, having a high percentage of their clientele being mandated through the criminal justice system has had a significant impact on TCs, as detailed below.

Dynamics Within the Professionalized Therapeutic Community

The self-described modified therapeutic community (MTC) at which I performed the bulk of my ethnography was reputed to be rather gentle in comparison to some of the other treatment centers to which the drug court and other criminal justice agencies referred clients.[40] Many of the structural elements at the facility indeed made it notably milder than even many other TCs that had significantly toned down their previous practices. There were no mortification practices, for example, that effectively greeted newcomers with a ritual hazing; confrontational encounter groups between peers were virtually eliminated; and a set of licensed social workers offered weekly therapy sessions modeled on more conventional and supportive modes of therapist–client interaction. There were no obviously stigmatizing punishments such as wearing signs, and there were few verbal haircuts in which discipline was enforced by a group ganging up against an individual with angry tones of voice (when this did occur, it did not have a special label; haircuts were no longer marked as a ritualized and named activity). The basic levels of punishment involved *benching* a resident or taking away their privileges. Any resident could bench another for any infraction of the rules, the person benched being required to sit in silence on a seat located in a publicly visible spot near the front desk. Only staff could take away a person's privileges, an action that would leave one without the ability to make phone calls, receive visitors, or use a pass to leave the facility for a short time. This basic repertoire of learning experiences—benching and the removal of privileges—could be augmented by the assignment of early morning duties that required waking up an hour or more before everyone else or special cleaning assignments (very infrequently, these latter could take on a highly punitive quality as when two individuals were made to clean the bathroom floors with toothbrushes, an event that made sufficient impression as to lead several residents to mention the incident to me during our interviews, but that particular form of "learning" was not imposed a second time during my nearly one year of observation).

Despite this clear movement in the direction of a softer disciplinary regime, elements of the older TC model continued to exist. The institution struck me as being significantly oriented toward the daily enforcement of discipline, and as in the past, this was frequently administered in a fairly punitive manner. Sitting in the downstairs office, for example, often involved watching client after client approach the floor staff with issue after issue and request after request. Residents literally lined up outside the door to raise their concerns, and even with rules requiring clients to approach other senior residents first, there were still a number of areas that only staff members could address and for whom no resident was appointed. From my fieldnotes:

Imani, a long-term staffer, was alone in handling the rush. A young black man came in, but Imani reprimanded him before he could get any words out: "Nah, uh-ah [signaling "no"], get that do-rag off your head! You look like a street rat! You need to dress nice in here because you're not out there copping for drugs. Those are clothes that you wear when you're out there copping for drugs." The man took off the do-rag. He seemed to be moving slowly—he was somewhat ill and had been assigned to bedrest. He said he had been told to come down for a house meeting but didn't know if he should. "You don't come down here for that!" said Imani. "You came down here because you wanted to smoke, didn't you?" The man denied the charge. "C'mon, c'mon, you dope-fiend. I haven't heard as big a story all day! Can you believe this guy?" (Imani glanced at me, though the question was rhetorical.) Imani's harangue continued and was quite loud despite the man's proximity. Failing to convince Imani about the smoking, and being told to go back upstairs, the resident eventually walked away, seeming somewhat hurt by the accusation I thought, though he could have simply been moving slowly because he was ill.

Another resident, Antonio, came in, talking quickly as always: "I just want you to know that I benched Marissa, but she's not in trouble. There was a meeting downstairs, and someone kept talking, but I just wasn't sure who it was, so I benched her just to see if the talking continued. I benched Sharna too, but she's not doing it." Imani yelled out the door at one of the other residents standing in line: "Tony! Get Sharna up here!" When Sharna turned up a couple of minutes later, Imani began sternly: "Look, if somebody tells you that you're benched, then you're benched. And if they're wrong, I'll deal with them later. But you don't have a choice. You have to go sit on that bench." "But I wasn't talking!" Sharna protested. "If I had, I would have been the first one sitting there!" "No, now you listen. If somebody tells you you're benched, you are benched. Period. You got it?" Sharna kept protesting: "I've been punished my whole life for things I didn't do." "It wasn't a punishment, sis," piped in Antonio, standing nearby. "Look, here is how it is," continued Imani, "if you're benched, you're benched. That's all there is to it. Now you have to go sit down, like it or not." Sharna did as told, seeming to accept Imani's justification or perhaps simply being resigned to her fate.

Another client approached Imani, this time for something concerning a problem with the heater in their room (for which they were supposed to have approached the resident in charge of maintenance). "Structure! Structure!" shouted Imani. "You never approach staff directly with these kinds of things!" "It's sometimes difficult to know who to approach," began the woman. "Oh no, I'm not buying that! You knew who to approach to get your drugs out on the street, right?" "I'm not talking about copping," replied the woman, "I'm talking about structure. It's apples and oranges." "Look, I'm not going to have any back and forth with you about this. You plug in and you learn. You know what you know, and what you don't know, you're responsible for. How long have you been here?" "Twenty five days" said the woman. "Well you know more than you want to know already," said Imani, dismissing her.

Imani had a reputation for yelling and being more abrasive that any of the other staff—indeed, at times it seemed to me that she yelled at residents more than she talked with them—but she was hardly alone in having an aggressive demeanor. Almost all of the floor staff regularly called residents *dope-fiends* (a term in common use at Synanon) and engaged constantly in a disciplinary harangue that rarely ceased. Staff members similarly treated most resident claims with evident suspicion, making their mistrust clear even when not having direct knowledge of the situation (as seen with the claim that the sick man actually came downstairs in order to smoke). Despite its severity, this type of policing had the full institutional support of the TC as a whole, and the director informed me that the house "nearly fell apart" when Imani once took a two-week vacation.

Not all interactions were disciplinary in nature, of course. Sitting in the staff office on the same day as the above set of incidents, I watched Imani offer another resident heartfelt advice about the resident's future.

Clara approached Imani later in the afternoon, at a quieter time, concerned because another resident had told her that she would not be able to become a beautician because she now had a criminal record. Neither Imani nor I thought this would be a problem, particularly as neither charge she had was a felony. Imani continued: "Look, when you were out on the street, you went through all sorts of stuff to stick with that drug. You did all sorts of degrading things, and you didn't let go of that drug. Now you have to be just as tough with your goals—you can't let go of them just because someone says something like that." Imani's comment struck me as deeply empathetic in nature, and it highlighted the usefulness of having individuals who have lived through profound challenges with drugs act as counselors. It is also the case that the near-constant refrain of *dope-fiends* from the mouths of the floor staff seemed at times to have an identificatory quality to it; though the term was a chastising one, it did not stigmatize to the extent that it might seem to at first, nor did it establish an us-versus-them dynamic as the floor staff were also (former) "dope-fiends."

Nevertheless, residents frequently complained about the way that staff treated them, particularly their yelling. One said to me he had been in a group meeting near the staff office for ninety minutes, overhearing Imani yell practically the entire time. "How can it be that every single person needed to be yelled at for an hour and a half? She means it with love, but still . . ." Many others disliked the entire disciplinary approach. "I'm a man," said one, "I don't like being pushed around all the time." Other residents, however, found benefit in the daily structure, with perhaps a third or more saying they had been helped by the program's disciplinary regimen: "I have to learn that if I want to succeed in life, I'm going to have to do some things that I just don't feel like doing," offered one. "I have five assault charges on a police officer. I've learned that sometimes you can avoid a whole lot of provocation by just taking directions. Although you may not like it, just take it. . . . Now I think before I act and handle the situation." Even residents who were supportive of the harsh discipline, however, noted the challenges of being in such an environment: "Sometimes I hate this program, but I love what it's doing for me."

The MTC had established—unintentionally, it seemed—a new regulatory structure within the facility, one in which the professional social workers generally acted as supportive counselors while the floor staff acted as daily disciplinarians. One of the social workers glossed this new regimen of treatment: "We're here for the nurturing and the floor staff are the ones who handle the behavioral issues and dealing out whatever punishments and restrictions and all that stuff. I mean, without the nurturing side, I think we'd just be sort of abusive to people." Whereas this perspective somewhat dismissed the TC regimen, another counselor offered, "They break 'em; we mend 'em." From this latter frame, the floor staff broke through the psychic defenses of the residents, while the social workers worked in a more nurturing way in utilizing the emotional space thereby created to heal the residents, whether from early life traumas or potentially from the pain and stress of the disciplinary regime itself. Though only one counselor made such a direct comment about the way her work related to that of the floor staff—and no social workers offered an analysis that centered on the therapeutic effects of the daily discipline (the historic raison d'être of the TC)—the social work staff generally sought to bond with clients by offering nurturing support in relation to the stresses of life in the TC. The danger here, as I saw it, was that a semiconscious version of the good cop/bad cop dynamic—good counselor/bad counselor—was being established, creating a set of circumstances in which the therapist's supportive role was constituted directly in contrast to the severe intensity of the other floor staff and the disciplinary regime they put forth.[41] While the social workers saw clients once a week (with a few of the social workers offering weekly group sessions as well), their interactions with residents mostly ended with that weekly session, thereby removing them from any significant disciplinary role. Social workers in fact spent most of their time on a separate floor that residents were not allowed to enter without specific permission, with a full schedule of therapy sessions preventing them from spending too much time on the ground level. As noted above, the original TC model had emphasized minimal differentiation between staff and clients.[42] Given their day-to-day separation from the residents, in a sense the social workers might best be seen as constituting something of an *adjunct* to the therapeutic community model, which continued relatively unaltered—albeit in a milder form—on the floor level while social workers were visited only occasionally in a different (and restricted) section of the building. Though social workers also helped to make decisions about resident requests and advances or demotions in program level (with a resident's level determining what privileges they were entitled to), social workers were not responsible for the daily operation of the facility and generally did not enforce any rules.

Instead, the paraprofessional floor staff continued to operate the MTC, utilizing the same basic disciplinary techniques as at other TCs, albeit relying on less intense methods than in the past (or even at other contemporary facilities). The floor staff had all learned how to run a TC by going through treatment themselves—some in the very same facility—augmenting this informal apprenticeship with the two years of training that the state now required. And while I never heard any of the floor staff state that their goal was to "break" anyone's will, or even to "break through" someone's defenses, their exercise of discipline often (though not always) tended toward a stern and sometimes sharp style of interaction, even when no longer relying on some of the harshest first- and second-generation TC techniques.

Jessie, one of the longer-term staff members—someone who had been through a TC program herself a number of years prior—suggested that a combination of professionalization, regulation, and a changed client population (with a much higher percentage now being mandated through the criminal justice system) had significantly disrupted the ability of the facility to impose discipline on the residents, particularly as staff often relied upon clients to act as their eyes and ears, but also because her own practices had changed in accord with a general trend toward professionalization. I spend some time with Jessie's comments because her perspective was developed in relation to seeing an historical shift from a more traditional TC—one with a high percentage of voluntary clients—to a "modified" one featuring a high percentage of mandated clients. Jessie's comments also reveal a vision of discipline as a therapeutic force, as well as ways in which she modulates her castigations in order to better achieve a therapeutic effect. She reveals significant awareness of the ways in which disciplinary mechanisms have changed as TCs accepted more people who had been mandated through criminal justice:

> Ten years ago, there wasn't so much alternative-to-incarceration business. . . . Most clients were ready for change, and they were willing to go through whatever they had to go through for change. You had people who were mandated, but not the majority like now. The belief systems now are totally different. To get them to buy into honesty, to be their brother's keeper, is very hard. A lot of our clients now have this institutional mentality where "snitches get stitches," so they're not gonna tell.

That's where the professionals come in and get them to more or less surrender, to make them realize that they haven't been arrested, they've been rescued. Here you have a chance to change your life around completely because, obviously, if you're here, your way wasn't the way . . .

Staff is usually the last to know [when someone breaks a rule]. . . . If it's someone they have a conflict with, they don't mind telling staff, but if they're with their homegirl or homeboy or somebody they get along with, they don't want to go to staff and get the client in trouble, they think. What they don't realize is that in reality your worst enemy is your best friend in this setting, because they're going to put your issue out there where it can be addressed and you can get help with it. But believe me, nine times out of ten, they go to each other [they address any conflicts among themselves without informing staff]. . . . Back in the day, you couldn't hide in the cracks. You were going to be exposed. . . . You know, you're only as strong as your weakest link. I would say we now only have ten residents [out of approximately 90] who are really TC. . . . Overall, the treatment worked better before. . . .

Me: How do you reach out to the person who's just here to do their bid [to sit out a legal mandate], and they're like, "I don't need to change."—How do you reach out to that person?

We have one here like that. I more or less try to—not try to—I enforce the rules on them, the compliance, to make them part of it. . . . I'll get on his butt but you know, if you squeeze them too hard you'll choke them and if you hold them too loose they'll fly away, so you've got to be in between and balance it out.

A number of interrelated concerns regarding discipline become clear in Jessie's account. As noted above, changes in professional practice, state regulations, and resident population (particularly in relation to having more mandated clients) served to curtail both the intensity and extent of punishment and surveillance within the facility. Arguably, all three of these changes relate to the rise of drug treatment as an alternative to incarceration, with trends toward regulation and professionalization following a broad need for greater bureaucratization as the state both manages its prison population and pays for an indigent population's treatment through Medicaid. But whatever the case, the result has threatened the integrity of the TC. A second staff member offered a similar set of observations, in his case, however, highlighting the shifting population that has resulted from a rise in criminal justice referrals over the past ten years:

> Ten years ago or longer, most of the clients we saw were either hardcore cocaine or heroin, or some alcoholics. Now we're seeing a lot of marijuana smokers who haven't been dependent necessarily but . . . a lot of drug sellers. So they are clearly not buying into the process as much, particularly the sellers. . . . The younger pot-smoking clients are more apt to try and get over because they don't take anything seriously, much less treatment. The drug dealers don't think they identify with these things. . . . Because if you're trying to facilitate services that were really designed and built for an adult heroin user, and I smoked pot while ditching school, I might not buy in.[43]

Overall, suggested yet another staff member, no more than half of a TC's population can be mandated if the model is to work effectively (the population of mandated clients at the time of my fieldwork ranged between 75–85 percent).[44]

Beyond highlighting the way that too many mandated clients threatened the integrity of the TC model, Jessie's discussion also points toward the way in which disciplinary measures are positioned as therapeutic and a form of help (i.e., as *caring violence*). As similarly seen in relation to the drug court, the therapeutic community works by identifying "out-of-control" subjects who require ready consequences if they are to learn proper boundaries—"you still have to have that weight fall on your head." The frames utilized within both drug court and TC vacillate between one in which drugs create a boundaryless need and one in which a street-criminal culture establishes norms that are entirely self-centered in nature. Whatever the source of this antisocial behavior, however, the drug court/TC vision goes so far as to turn arrest into a benefit, suggesting—if one follows the logic to its ultimate conclusion—that low-income black and brown communities are *aided* by the disproportionate drug war arrests to which they are subject, rather than oppressed by such over-policing.

Furthermore, the TC is explicit in appealing to normative expectations in an effort to shame residents into compliance (comments such as, "Haven't you screwed your kids around enough already?" are common). While I will address the gendered aspects of this shaming in the next chapter, here I simply wish to highlight the ways in which this appeal to normativity invokes standards that residents have presumably internalized, both emphasizing their past failure in these regards and implicitly suggesting that one can stop such failures by following the program's rules. Combined with techniques that are straightforwardly punitive in nature (e.g., yelling at the resident, benching, assigning additional chores, etc.), these petitions for normalization strike what the staff members hope will be an emotionally laden point that might be mobilized in motivating change away from not just drugs but the entire "drugs lifestyle." Arguably, they constitute what Braithwaite might term a form of *reintegrative shaming*, techniques "directed at signifying evil deeds rather than evil persons in the Christian tradition of 'hate the sin and love the sinner.' "[45] The idea is to invoke and mobilize shame in order to provoke a rededication to normative principles, with a promise being made that the program will help one to achieve normative goals that have previously been denied. As Braithwaite comments, "Reintegrative shaming is not necessarily weak; it can be cruel, even vicious. It is not distinguished from stigmatization by its potency, but by (a) a finite rather than open-ended duration which is terminated by forgiveness; and by (b) efforts to maintain bonds of love or respect throughout the finite period of suffering shame."[46]

But while the TC aims to create an environment in which residents are surrounded by "reintegrative shaming," without the ability to force clients to police one another, staff was unable to create the type of panopticonic environment that was the hallmark of the earlier generation of TCs. Members of the floor staff often bemoaned the ways that their disciplinary regime had been disrupted through a combination of factors. In addition to the aforementioned matters of state regulation, professionalization, and additional mandated clients, a rise in the number of treatment centers has resulted in significantly greater competition among facilities. This final factor is exacerbated within the New York City area, where an unusually high concentration of treatment facilities has created what one director referred to as a "buyer's market" for clients. However, such pressures are felt nationally as well. A member of the floor staff blamed both monetary pressures and state regulations for "tying our hands" in the enforcement of discipline:

> When I was in treatment it was much more intense. Today it's all about the numbers. It's sad but true. Before if there was a problem we'd have

> a GM [a general meeting in which those breaking rules would be disciplined in front of the entire community] and he'll [*sic*] handle it, and if he didn't he'd be on his way. That was the treatment. That was the true treatment. That's when you knew that we [staff] weren't for bullshit. Now everything is just so wack. Now advisory staff [the administrators] have to handle the GMs, and they decide what we're going to do. Oh, we're not going to do anything to them [the clients], oh no. . . .
>
> It's because of the numbers. The main office started to say, "What's going on with the numbers? Last week you had X and this week you have *X*–*4*, so what's going on? You gotta stop terminating people for this. You gotta stop terminating people for that." Nobody said it straight out like that. It just gradually happened. But now we can't terminate a client for drinking. We can't terminate a client for using. OK, this is the first time, so you gotta let them stay. We can't even GM them half the time. That's why I say it's not treatment anymore. And it's not hurting me, it's hurting the clients. . . .
>
> Structure and discipline. You have to have it in treatment because that's what's mostly missing in addict's lives. . . . And in order for us to maintain a discipline, we gotta be able to do certain things that we're not allowed to do. Like we're not allowed to keep a client up at certain times anymore. Clients have to have eight hours of sleep. I mean, you would think that would be natural and normal [to get eight hours of sleep], but it's not what they were doing when they were using. They didn't care about sleeping. So we're just here trying to get them to learn, but there's not a lot of consequences anymore.

A second member of the floor staff shared a similar perspective:

> Before they made you walk around with diapers on, a pacifier in your mouth, you know, cry baby. You'd have to walk around with a sign saying "I'm a cry baby." Today you get consequences, but it's like a slap on the wrist. Today you get put on LE [a learning experience, such as doing dishes all day] and it's like two or three weeks. It used to be two or three *months.* We used to have signs that said like "woman beater" or "child neglector," stuff like that. . . . But now our hands are tied.
>
> Instead of giving them [the residents] treatment, they just want to "do no harm" and keep them in there. Every time we have a staff meeting,

> it's all about the numbers. "Oh, my pop is down." So you let them [the residents] have their way so that they'll stay, but they're not getting any treatment. . . . What about the client's treatment? If you think only about treatment, don't say that part about the pop going down because then you're thinking only about the pop. . . .
>
> And mostly now you have clients who are mandated. And that's the sad part about it because they're not taking it seriously because a lot of them just have to be there or go to jail. . . . So it's bad enough that you have clients with that type of attitude and then you have this other thing with the pop on top of it. So it's like you're really fucking stuck because you have the clients who don't want to be there, and they're going to act out, and you just have to deal with them. You have [admin] saying, "No, you can't throw them out because of our pop." Years ago, I terminated somebody and that was the end of it. . . .
>
> It's not a lot about treatment anymore. If you're not already serious about getting your life together, you're kind of lost. I can point you in the right direction, but my hands are tied on so many things. You're kind of on your own.

The shift has obviously been frustrating to many floor staff, particularly in relation to what they see as the inappropriate intrusion of financial concerns into the treatment decision-making process. Nevertheless, these pressures are impossible to avoid and result from a privatized, competitive structure in which the ultimate customer of the TCs are criminal justice (CJ) administrators rather than their clients. An administrator at a TC I visited (at a different facility than the one where I conducted the bulk of my research) explained the pressures he experiences to work with otherwise disruptive clients:

> If you discharge a client because of noncompliance with your program, the legal agency gets mad at you. "Well, we're not going to refer you any more clients because you can't work with them." Sometimes it's subtle and sometimes is real overt. . . . So many programs are under census right now . . . that sometimes you don't want to push the wrong person in the wrong way because that might be 5 or 10 percent of your referrals. So if I piss off Person A who works at probation, who generally refers two or three or four people a week to me, they might decide, "Well, if you're not

> going to work with me, I'm not going to send you these referrals." . . . I mean, if a client is over-the-top, there's no ifs, ands, or buts. But if something is kind of questionable, then you're kind of stuck sometimes, or stuck for a longer period of time.

Though second-generation TCs such as Daytop initially had 100 percent of its clientele referred through the criminal justice system, the exclusive nature of their contracts enabled them to expel noncooperating participants.[47] Today's competitive market pressures make it difficult to expel such individuals, thereby undermining the ability of the TC to establish the disciplinary atmosphere to which it aspires.

Residents experienced the overall breakdown in the disciplinary structure in a strong way. One client pointed to the existence of numerous infractions occurring within the facility—several residents had cell phones in their rooms, there were a number of ongoing sexual relationships, two residents were rumored to be prostituting while on outside passes, and a small number of residents were known to be using drugs within the institution—yet while many clients spoke about these incidents, no one reported what was happening to staff. Even "learning experiences" had been undermined through the lack of peer surveillance, with what were supposed to be silent LEs doing chores in the kitchen becoming playful party scenes due to a lack of policing. The code against snitching remained in effect, even when the violations make other residents more likely to relapse due to the resultant environment, as when Teresa's roommate came back to the facility while noticeably high:

> The little stuff doesn't bother you, but her being high right in front of me and my [other] roommate immediately kicked up my—you know, my heart started pounding out of my chest. And she was right where you want to be, like she loved it. She was like "Oh, you are the best roommate." She's never spoken to me in three months, but now I'm her favorite roommate. You know, exactly that point in the high that you're going for where you love everyone. Everyone's perfect. My other roommate is Sarah, and she's a heroin addict and was really vulnerable right then. Not like all of us aren't, but she was just hanging on. She still wants to use every day. And she's watching this, and I know what's going through her mind. . . . If that girl had dropped a bag on the floor, I would have done it

> in a second. . . . Sarah tells me later "I was getting ready to look through her stuff for the rest of it." So now this isn't just affecting me; now I have to worry about my roommate [Sarah] too. . . .
>
> We both wanted to tell staff, but there's also this sense of not wanting to be the rat. And we still care about Mary [the first roommate]. . . . I was angry when it happened, I really was. Not for getting high but for doing it in front of us and putting us at risk. And I wanted to go to staff and say, "You need to take everyone's urine. All the women." But I didn't. I discussed it with three of the guys here that I'm close with and they said, "What doesn't come out in the wash will come out in the rinse." Like eventually she'll get found out. And you just don't tell when you are using. You know, snitches get stitches. You don't do the right thing. And so we [she and Sarah] spoke about it, and we kept checking in to make sure the other was ok.

Eventually another resident found out about Mary's drug use and told staff, and both Sarah and Teresa were punished for not stepping forward, but the general lack of disciplinary effectiveness within at least this particular MTC sometimes became apparent.

Overall, only a minority of residents (perhaps 15–20 percent) directly complained that the MTC had too little discipline. However, this minority expressed strong opinions that may have reflected sentiments others sometimes felt as well, even if this larger group did not wish for tighter enforcement of the rules. Said one resident who *did* wish for more daily structure:

> The rules aren't followed here. It's not strict enough. There's no coordination and they don't follow through. Example: when people use the mop, they mop in a half-ass way, rinse it out in dirty water, put mop up on its rack, but it's been in dirty water, so it's not clean for the next time. I'll go and say something, but people will say "fuck you" or "I do it my way, you do it yours" or something like that. Everyone is a chief in here. There's no structure really, so nothing gets done.

Others similarly lamented the lack of discipline within the facility, arguing (based on their experiences with other facilities) that strict enforcement of the rules worked to chase away anyone who was not "serious" about their recovery, whereas the gentler system allowed many disruptive individuals to comfortably remain in the program.

At the same time, the disciplinary structure in place within the MTC nevertheless has a considerable impact on residents, even hobbled as it is by the variety of factors explored above. The obligation that residents inform on one another, in particular, was felt very keenly and significantly shaped community life. More than any other policy, this requirement drew the most criticism and resistance from residents, and while many acknowledged that *some* infractions might be serious enough to warrant approaching staff, only one resident I interviewed (out of over fifty) spoke unequivocally in favor of the rule. Instead of informing staff of infractions, residents instead generally dealt with the rule by attempting to isolate themselves from others, so as to avoid being placed in a situation where their knowledge of another's rule-breaking would put them in a compromised position. As put by one resident:

> I try not to pay attention to a lot of stuff that's here. I try to avoid all that negative stuff so that I can do what I gotta do. If I do something negative and get in trouble for it, I paid my consequences. . . . But I'm not here to give nobody pull-ups like that. I'm not here to put no people on no bench.

In a sense, one of the aims of the policy is to make people avoid involving themselves in transgressive networks, so it arguably achieves at least part of its aim. But the policy sometimes works to make all manner of social bonding difficult and a fraught affair:

> I don't feel that they encourage you to really build trust with other people here because it's all Peter Pays for Paul [the phrase often used to explain the policy], so if one person screws up, and you're in the vicinity, you're hit for it. You know, you're expected to go to staff and drop guilt [inform]. . . . In 12-step meetings there's a lot of downtime where you get to talk to other people and you bond with them. Here it's like . . . bonding is almost not conducive to what they're doing here. . . . It makes it hard to feel like you're on the same team. . . . There's a lot of paranoia because of that rule.

Numerous residents offered some version of this sentiment, noting that they avoided others and kept to themselves. Upon viewing an infraction of the rules, most residents either said nothing or, if they felt compromised, approached the person and informally asked them to do the behavior out of their view *without* approaching staff. As one resident said:

> Why I should tell them anything? I'm not here for that. I'm here to get me better. I get ready for out of here. I'm not here for watch who the fuck you're fucking, who you're giving the money. It's not my motherfucking concern. They try to come for me for that, but I gotta keep it real with myself. I can't but work within.

Even one of the residents in a higher position within the facility acknowledged that he handled most issues "on the side. A lot of things I just say 'Just don't do it around me.' "

At the same time, residents who do inform on one another are, unsurprisingly, viewed favorably by staff. Ironically, however, the few who took a strong stance in enforcing the rules against other residents seemed *to me* to be among the most "antisocial" and "self-oriented" that I interviewed. This "selfish" orientation supposedly characterized all drug addicts, yet here the rules of the facility meant that certain actions, behaviors that most residents understood as uncaring, were *rewarded*. This "me-first" attitude was increasingly revealed as the following interview with Elaine progressed:

> If someone does something, they hit us over the head with it. . . . I'm not here to hold your hand. I'm really not. Listen, if someone doesn't listen to me [when given an initial warning or *pull-up*], I'm going to staff. Now it's in *your* hands. I throw the ball right back in your court. Because I'm not going to pay for it. . . . I walk to you and ask you, "What are you doing? . . . Is that what we do?" So I'm giving you a chance, an opportunity, because I don't want to bench you. If I can talk to you, and you back off, it's all well and good. I know why I'm here, I know what I got. . . . If you have a chance to listen, but don't listen? You're not gonna take me down. . . .
>
> Don't tell me nothing [i.e., don't share information about infractions with me], and don't do nothing so that I can see it, because I'm going to go to staff. And they [the other residents] know that. They pretty much call me "Robo-Cop" or what have you, I don't care about that. There's two of us, me and Gene, and we got a compliment the other day. They [staff] said "If it wasn't for you two, this place would be out to lunch" [a phrase

> commonly used within the facility to indicate a lack of disciplinary control]. We're like a tag team. I'm strictly, "Don't do that." Like I said, rules and regulations, I have no problem following them. And if you do something in front of me, I'm going to say something about it, and I'm going to tell staff. I don't care what you say about it. You shouldn't be doing it. When it comes to your ass and my ass, your ass is grass because I'm going to tell. I'm going to get *me* out of that. I never had a problem with that. I'm not holding what they call somebody's guilt. *Don't do it in front of me.* They've known that since day one. I stood up in group and told them all. "You know how I get down." Staff likes that because that's how it should be. I'll pull you up: "What are you doing?" And they back down. . . . That's who I am. I guess I would be an ideal client because I follow all the rules and regulations.

While the staff's praise enabled Elaine to envision herself as "an ideal client," her motivation seemed primarily to derive from a desire to avoid being punished, rather than from a desire to genuinely assist other residents ("You're not gonna take me down"; "When it comes to your ass and mine, your ass is grass"). It also seemed to me that Elaine sometimes took a degree of pleasure in her ability to dominate others and make them "back down" by drawing upon the institution's ability to punish. While the dynamics might operate differently within a facility in which mutual informing became normative and those who refused were regularly dismissed (as within the early TCs), in this modified TC such strict enforcement of the rules was actually quite atypical. I was thus reminded of Gresham Sykes's observation from over sixty years ago:

> It is doubtful if this lack of allegiance to other criminals is a token of ideological commitment to the forces of law and order or that it even represents the bare beginnings of reformation. Rather, it would appear that the reverse is true—that the inmate who is alienated from fellow prisoners to the extent that he exploits and betrays them for his personal aggrandizement is a man who has set his face against all normative demands.[48]

Other residents offered more sympathetic explanations for enforcing the rules. One resident said simply that "Peter pays for Paul in here, and I don't want the house put on restriction. I want to see my daughter." A third similarly added: "My child is first and foremost. I don't give a fuck about anything else. . . . If that's put on the line, I'm totally going to sing, and I've told people that." But at least in some cases, it seemed that antisocial behavior was rewarded when such activity helped to maintain order within the facility. As another resident offered, "The more you tell on people, the better you're treated."

General Meetings: Reinvigorating the Disciplinary TC

Despite the ways in which disciplinary techniques had been displaced or toned down, the institution relied upon periodic harshness when order within the facility was deemed to have broken down. As in the first- and second-generation TCs, periodic General Meetings (GMs) were called in order to instill tighter discipline among the entire group and to force residents to police one another. The one GM I witnessed in my months of intensive fieldwork—a second occurred on a day I was not present and a third was held two months prior to my arrival—helps to highlight some of the sharp differences between a counseling orientation and the behaviorist techniques foregrounded within the TC orientation, as well as to perhaps point toward the ultimate emphasis upon traditional TC methods over those counseling techniques. The incident concerns the most extreme instance of punishment that I witnessed during my ethnographic participation, but it also serves to illuminate the more daily and mundane practices that the institution relied upon as well.

"What are you prepared to do?! What are you prepared to do?!" The assistant director kept playfully but earnestly challenging the rest of a staff with this Sean Connery line from The Untouchables.[49] *The staff as a whole had decided that the house had gotten out of control and that something strong needed to be done in response. "What are you prepared to do?!" One of the residents had broken a cane and then thrown it at another resident, fortunately missing him. Sexually explicit love letters had been found written between another two residents (both of whom were married to other people). Another of the residents had been loaning out small amounts of money to others—a definite transgression—and worse yet, when one of the residents was challenged about being one of the borrowers, he responded*

by asking, "What business is it of yours if I borrow $5?" Two residents had gotten into a yelling match with one another, and there were even reports of gambling downstairs. Residents were refusing to enforce discipline with one another; "How can they report on anything, when they all have secrets to hide?" "What are you prepared to do?!" asked the assistant director again. "I even heard them listening to some hip-hop thing called 'Cocaine on Steroids.'[50] No, no, no—that won't do."

A GM had been called, and all the residents were sitting downstairs in silence—monitored by a staff member—while the rest of the staff sat upstairs and decided on exactly what penalties to dole out to each resident and how to reimpose order more generally. "We want to get tough, not just on the people doing things, but on everyone who is colluding with them," offered one staff member. Having everyone sit in silence for the three or so hours it took to talk about the situation and decide upon all the punishments was only an opening prelude. "I know they're adults, but sometimes we have to play the part of the parents," said another counselor. Most of the staff had worked together for some time and spoke in very jocular and convivial ways, and the meeting resembled something of a working party as the staff shared pizza and informally and more-or-less collectively decided on each resident's fate.

While the residents continued to wait in silence downstairs—a tactic deliberately meant to be not only unpleasant but to make them anxious about what might come next—I walked with the staff as we entered the residents' living quarters. A decision had been made to go through all of the rooms and to essentially trash everything, not in any search for contraband but simply as a disciplinary measure. A carnivalesque mood predominated among the staff as they moved from room to room, stripping the beds and overturning mattresses, removing all clothing from the dressers and throwing them onto the floor, removing pretty much every single possession from its place and putting it into the center of each room. The only room spared was one that contained two residents who had arrived less than a week prior, but everyone else's room was left in rather sad shape (see figure 4.1 below). At first I joined in destruction myself—fearful that I had to if I wished to stay in the confidence of the staff—but I grew so uncomfortable after the first room that the director noticed and kindly suggested that I did not have to participate. One of the other counselors—someone new to the job—ruefully joked, "Oh, this is what I got my MA for," while another of the social workers sympathetically explained that he had also felt guilty the first time he had done this, but that he had come to see the "therapeutic value" and "effectiveness" of doing it. The director—perhaps feeling a bit awkward with me as an outside observer and my

FIGURE 4.1 Ransacked rooms after a TC House meeting. Clients are required to keep their rooms in a very clean and neat condition—beds are to be made with hospital corners, for example — and can be punished if their rooms are too disorderly. These well-kept rooms were much altered after staff deliberately unmade them, as seen above.

Source: Photos taken by author.

obvious discomfort—commented on the gleeful mood of most of the staff, suggesting that they were only human and this was a way they could blow off some steam while doing what needed to be done. After they were finished, the staff shared several pizzas while the residents continued to sit downstairs in silence. The entire experience seemed to bond the staff closer together, fostering a renewed commitment to "get tough" in enforcing the rules. By the time the staff had finished and arrived downstairs, they had altogether changed their emotional tone, entering the room almost growling. The assistant director again took the lead. "Sit up straight! Hands on your knees! You deaf? Put your hands on your knees! A GM is the most important meeting we have! . . . There's some sorry-ass shit been going on here. People gotta step up. Nobody's stepping up. Nobody's taking any responsibility. This is your house, and you gotta run it. But you aren't running it, so this is what happens." The staff then proceeded to call up each of the offending residents one by one to address their infractions. A man who had been loaning out small amounts of money to others while claiming to be a "big-time dealer" was ridiculed for having no changes of clothing; a woman and a man having an affair were both shamed for their behavior, with the woman being called a "home-breaker," among other things; and the woman who had gotten into a shouting match with another resident was forcefully told she obviously did not love her daughter since she was willing to risk having CPS take her custody away for such negative behavior. [I discuss these individual interactions at greater depth in the next chapter.]

The assistant director challenged the entire group: "This is about making you face up to your responsibilities. If you're not here to do the work, leave. You'll make it easier for all of us." A man standing toward the back of the room started laughing a little bit (sitting near the back of the room, I had earlier seen him and another man playfully kicking at a paper napkin that had fallen to the floor, generally doing their utmost to not pay attention to the proceedings). "Oh, you think that's funny?" Called out, the man was suddenly serious. "No." "Maybe you should just pack your bags and leave then. Maybe we'll just have you pack your bags and you can go." After a bit of back and forth, the threat was not carried through, but the man was benched and forced to sit in front of the rest (a punishment that enforced his silence). The assistant director further required that on the subsequent day the man would have to offer a seminar on himself to the rest of the group. "You're going to tell everyone what brought you in here. No jokes allowed. You have to be serious and explain to everyone why you're here."

The meeting finally ended after midnight but with additional punishments for the house. The staff had decided that they needed to apply the "Peter pays for

Paul" principle in order to make people "look at each other's stuff." The "Peter pays for Paul" principle was the way the staff referred to the idea that one is responsible not only for any rule-breaking that one engages in but also for any rule-breaking that one even knows about. Given the more general breakdown of order, staff decided to apply the principle even more broadly, imposing collective punishments on everyone for the wrongdoing. The idea—according to the staff members—was to force people to interact in a new way, to push them from a "subversive" way of relating and "colluding" and to instead establish relations based on rule-abiding behaviors. The entire house was thus placed on restriction: no days out for any entertainment or church purposes, and no family visits, even for one resident being treated for cancer. Residents were now allowed to return to their rooms, only to discover their personal space thoroughly wrecked, the second and more dramatic element of their collective punishment. At that late hour, the residents had to clean everything up before going to sleep.[51]

The fallout from such an event, and from the associated ongoing penalty of having the house placed on restriction, was, unsurprisingly, quite significant. By the next morning, three residents had left the program, including the woman referred to as a "home-breaker" (she returned about ten days later and—after an extended conversation among the staff—was readmitted into the facility). One man who decided not to leave was nevertheless considering it immediately after the event:

> Man, I just can't take this *bullshit* anymore. I'm gone. . . . This place is like a shelter. It's not a treatment center. These people are *street*. I'm not street, I'm voluntary. I've never been in prison. I've never done treatment in order to avoid a bid [a prison sentence]. I was clean for seven years, and I've got a job. I've always had a job. I put myself in here because I needed to chill out and get away from the drugs. But I had a job and I knew I needed to chill out and get my head on straight. But this place is just a shelter.

Another resident unfavorably compared the sanctions in the MTC to the sanctions in jail: "In jail they line you up and turn you around so you can watch while they search your cell. They'd never do it without you looking." At least one resident seemed not offended at all, again comparing the MTC to jail. "Sorry about the rooms," I offered. "Aw, that don't matter. It's just like prison. That don't matter at all."

None of the residents, however, were pleased with the fact of being punished for things that they themselves did not do (i.e., "Peter pays for Paul"): "I don't know why they come out behind the concept of it. You should pay for your own crime, you know what I'm saying? And this makes everyone suffer for what one person did. It's crazy," suggested one. Others felt that the whole incident just revealed the daily sadism that they had to put up with from the staff:

> I don't understand why it seems like they derive pleasure, sometimes, from knocking people down. I mean, the conflict resolution group is like the *Jerry Springer Show*. That's yet another way they get their shits and giggles, the staff. . . . [And in relation to the GM] Oh yeah, stand me up in front of a room and pick six people who absolutely despise me to get up and confront me. Just slamming into you. . . . I would like to think that the people running this place really have good intentions. I would like to think that they would like to help people repair their lives, but sometimes you wonder.

Even Elaine, who seemed to benefit from a system in which she could inform on other residents (quoted above), would not unequivocally endorse the rule penalizing individuals for things they didn't do, saying instead:

> That would affect anybody. Peter paying for Paul, when you have to pay for somebody else's mistakes . . . I just deal with it. You just go through the flow of it. My belly's clean [i.e., "I have no feelings of resentment"]. So in situations like that, what do you do? You gather up the strength to deal with it, and you go through it. You can't change it, you just have to go through it.

This response was, in fact, the least condemnatory I received on the topic of "Peter pays for Paul" in all of my interviews with residents.

Nevertheless, in many ways the GM had the desired result on residents; in other words, the "therapeutic benefit" spoken of by one of the counselors was real. Residents met in small groups to discuss the situation, attempting to negotiate agreements amongst themselves to make sure that the rules were better followed so that the house restriction might be lifted more quickly. As one resident explained to me a bit later:

> Basically, we're just trying to do what we gotta do so that staff ain't coming in and telling us what we gotta do. We take control of the house and make it what it was before it got locked up. So we had to take control and make sure that we did everything right.

This, of course, is precisely the result that TCs seek: pressuring residents to police one another with the idea that such self-policing will help clients to internalize the staff position through the assertion of control over the house.

In the case of the MTC, however, such effects were too short-lived and did not seem to have the sort of sustained impact that might be required to *force* a long-term change of behavior. Whereas approximately half of the residents I interviewed said that they benefited enormously from the program, sometimes in life-saving ways, others felt that "nothing changes; people here just get sneakier about what they do." The facility thus very much retained a custodial feel, with the "code of the streets" still a very present ethic that shaped community interaction. Unable to force clients to impose total control against one another, the GM seemed more like a last-ditch effort designed to maintain basic order rather than a tune-up that forced every resident to continually police all others. The extent to which a custodial focus prevailed was driven home to me during an interview with the director, who was (perhaps somewhat idly) contemplating having closed-circuit cameras installed in the hallways of the facility. Even the fantasy of such staff-oriented surveillance reveals the extent to which the therapeutic orientation toward peer policing, however supervised and enforced, had been somewhat displaced by a new therapeutic modality.

While unable to offer the full benefits of the earlier TCs, which clearly worked for some people, the MTC was unable to entirely eliminate all of the harshest tactics, seeming to need them in order to ensure a modicum of order. At the same time, however, the therapeutic value of the institution as a whole was certainly not eliminated, and the MTC offered many more support-oriented environments (such as individual and group counseling) than its predecessors. I will speak more about the ways in which residents responded to various elements within this particular modified TC below; here, however, I simply point to the way in which discipline operates within the MTC, how that discipline has changed since the early generations of TCs, and highlight the way in which that discipline is or is not experienced as therapeutic. In this sense, only a handful of the residents actively praised the disciplinary regimen as a source of therapeutic value for their own lives. This, of course, may have partially resulted from the fact that such discipline was too unevenly applied in order to achieve its full effect, but it also seems to reflect the fact that sanctions had come to serve a different social role within the MTC than within the TC: as the floor staff themselves noted, a series of factors had displaced "true treatment" (that is to say, *discipline*) and replaced it with supportive modes of counseling. Discipline, while retaining some therapeutic claims and effects, had in many ways become simply custodial in nature.

Cultivating Agency: Dope Fiends and the Coerciveness of Freedom

Given the suffering associated with rehabilitation, as well as the ways in which treatment is involved in controlling those whose social marginality render them subject to vastly intensified policing efforts, there is a need to explain why at least some participants undergoing treatment find it beneficial. At one level, it seemed clear that, beyond providing the state with a depoliticized means of pressing people toward low-wage work, the narrative of addiction also provided residents with a frame that explained their prior difficulties in the labor market, offering them hope for better success upon conquering their past "drugs lifestyle." Said one resident, "I'm not in the streets no more, and I'm trying to better myself. . . . I've been shot at, stabbed, jumped, raped, almost beaten to death. . . . I got arrested that last time and when I was in there I said 'I really got to get help or I'm going to end up dying.' " Desires for class mobility and an escape from the hardships of street life, on the one hand, and for decreased state surveillance, on the other, seemed to be the strongest elements in participants' reasons for appreciating treatment. In this way, treatment is effectively a promise made by the state to those it seeks to rehabilitate: do all this and be "free," not only from drugs, but from poverty, from the chaotic danger of street life, and from the most oppressive of state sanctions (e.g., incarceration and/or removal of one's children).

To some extent, the state makes an effort to live up to its promise. Beyond the disciplinary program, treatment additionally consists of job training and GED classes for those without a diploma. These welfarist benefits—available much more widely outside of the criminal justice system a few short decades ago—were the most highly-praised and sought-after components of the treatment program. Even those who were cynical regarding other aspects of treatment were generally enthusiastic about the prospect of job training in particular. At the facility I examined most closely, vocational counselors worked with residents in assessing what type of job they most wanted and then attempted to get them their desired training.[52] These practical benefits were nearly universally praised, the only exceptions being the small number of middle-class professionals in the program (an engineer and a nurse) for whom the sorts of training available offered nothing.

But while job training and, to a lesser extent, GED assistance explain a good deal of the interest in the program, the effects of the disciplinary regime itself were also sometimes seen as beneficial, particularly for those participants who were successfully nearing the end of their time within the program. One of the small number of voluntary clients spoke to this point directly:

> The things they teach me here, through discipline. I hated being here sometimes and I really wanted to leave a lot. No one said recovery is easy. . . . It's moving from the street to a whole different type of career path. . . . And you gotta clean, and you gotta get up at 6:30, and sometimes you just don't feel like it. But I have to learn that if I want to succeed in life I'm going to have to do some things I don't feel like doing. I'm going to have to get up and go to work sometimes even if I don't feel like it because I have bills to pay, you know. And they're instilling those essential qualities in us. They're helping instill these essential qualities in us that we should have anyway.

Another resident, someone who had been homeless prior to their entry into the program, similarly spoke of their gratitude for the disciplinary aspects of the program, despite the discomforts that came with it:

> Staff is not here chewing my head off twenty-four hours a day because they hate me. It's because they love me. They're trying to help me in some way. There's a method in the madness. . . . And when a staff is an ass, it's because they want to put pressure. Pressure bursts pipes or it fucking

> makes diamonds. And if I can deal with all the pressure and all the stress and all the ins and outs of daily fucking life in this facility, when I get out into the real world, it's going to be a fucking cake. . . . I've been drowning in four feet of water for a long time. This place is helping me stand up.

A third resident who had a basically sympathetic perspective on the disciplinary regime suggested that, "They do want you being as uncomfortable as possible, so that you learn to deal with it. Because my instinct is always just to head right to the bottle. You know, like as soon as I get to that agitation or anxiety, it's like I just want to get rid of it. So I think they're working on keeping me very uncomfortable here."

This lived experience of discomfort, combined with the need of "just having to take it," *is* treatment, "real treatment." Within its own terms, treatment *produces* freedom, not only from drugs, but from the entire so-called drugs lifestyle. It is a social technology that operates primarily through the reconstruction of emotional dispositions and what Pierre Bourdieu calls *habitus*; that is, it operates primarily through the emotionally-sensate body rather than through a cognitively-focused reformulation of self.[53] As Saba Mahmood writes (glossing Foucault), in this regard "the body is not a medium of signification but the substance and the necessary tool through which the embodied subject is formed."[54] In learning to tolerate the extreme discomfort of the disciplinary regime (as well as the discomfort of the regime's failures, including one nonlethal but still disturbing overdose that occurred on site prior to my arrival at the facility), residents develop one of the key capabilities that—it is hoped—will render the rest of what is statistically likely to be a low-wage life as "cake." While conceptual considerations are not ignored within the treatment regime (recall the reconfiguration of punishment as "learning experiences"), these rest squarely upon a field of embodied emotional praxis, creating what Mahmood refers to as "embodied capacities."[55] Treatment indeed inflicts disciplinary distress, and deliberately so, but its cognitive tools ideally work to give that hardship meaning and to direct the emotional fallout toward specific ends: the construction of personal agency (known as *empowerment* in some treatment centers). This is not agency in the abstract but a specific formation of agency centered around a refigured Protestant work ethic that constitutes the core of "right living." The development of this form of agentic self-control may even help when it comes to dealing with cravings for drugs, but this is only a small locus of concern, as treatment practitioners themselves make clear.

The agency constructed through the process of treatment, at least when successful, is genuine; that is to say, new pre-vocational capabilities are developed that enable different types of action than were previously possible. At the same time, it is not at all the case that those enacting a so-called drugs lifestyle have no agency. While their agency has been politically disavowed and made to appear nonexistent—hence the justification for criminal justice intervention—in talking with the approximately 50 percent of residents who rejected the terms of the program, it was immediately clear that an alternate perspective on the program exists, one that does not accept the terms of freedom that are offered and that argues for another sense of agency in its place. One resident offered the following:

> I don't like authority figures. I don't like staff members. I don't like cops. I just have to bide my time. . . . I don't like snitches either. I stay away from them. I got a couple of people that I hang out tough with. Guys who are just trying to do their thing and get out of here, like me. These other robot people, I got no time for that. No time for ratting everyone out. Go try telling everyone off on a train and see what they do to you! This is like a little world within a world in here. I'm looking at the bigger picture. Other people become robots in here, the chief, and this and that. No. Never. I don't like to tell people what to do. . . . I don't dream about it, I don't think about it, or nothing. I just want to do what I gotta do and get outta here.

This critique of the "robot people" (i.e., those whose disciplined rule-following rendered them without agency) and the way they colluded with staff/cops rests upon an awareness that there are large parts of society where the normalized hierarchies promoted by treatment simply do not apply; indeed, it may also stem from a sense that the parts of the world that do operate according to the logic of *right living* are either inaccessible and/or undesirable. Following the rules can thus be seen as subordinating in and of itself, and irrelevant in terms of the development of different types of agentic capacities.[56] Those who resist the subordination of the treatment regime sometimes turned therapeutic rhetoric against itself; one resident, for example, proclaimed, "I don't buy into everything here, because that's not right. Some people seem to think it's better to compromise themselves and kiss butt, being tattle-tales. . . . I don't think they know themselves enough." Ironically, both those who bought into the program and those who criticized it in this way generally did so in reference to "standing up for oneself" and not "compromising themselves."

Alternative forms of agency also came less in direct critique of the program and more in terms of scrutiny of authority figures, searching not for the appropriate way to follow orders, but for ways to circumvent as many of the rules as possible. Early in my ethnographic study, for example, I watched as residents boasted about how to best "work" various staff members. One suggested that the only way to deal with Imani (who had the reputation for being the most difficult) was to utterly submit to everything she said. "Here's what you have to do," he said, quickly putting on something of a wide-eyed "very serious" look and somberly nodding his head *yes*. Others laughed at this, but it was clear that information about how to best "pass"—to mimic the demeanors and behaviors that signaled *right living* without any internalization—was being communicated through this comic enactment. On another occasion, during an interview with a new resident who had only seen me for a couple of weeks, I heard how I myself was being carefully observed and assessed: "I watch you. I watch everything."

Those who were critical of the program generally did the minimum they could within the bounds created by the semi-effective system of peer surveillance that governed the institution. Known by the staff as "getting by," the practice often involved doing as one was told—at least when discovery was probable—but maintaining a critical distance from the program. "Some of these people have been through programs three or four times, so they know the ins and outs of the program, and they know how to dope fiend their way through it," offered one resident who was critical of the practice. "If I skate by, I skate by," suggested another, "but I'm skating by the right way. I'm not doing things I'm not supposed to be doing. I'm staying under the radar." From the perspective of the program, however, it may not matter whether or not those going through the program were true believers or not; while such internalization is ultimately desired, following the daily discipline is understood to have salutary effects in and of itself.

Though I conducted no statistical evaluation, speaking in a loose sense, it seemed that there were two basic groups who bought into the treatment framework and attempted most vigorously to develop a new sort of self-disciplined agency. On the one hand, there were those who had lived extremely unstable lives within the street economy or those whose increasing age made participation in street life less viable. On the other hand, there were those who typically had a job and perhaps a relatively stable family, whose drug use threatened these life anchors but who were caught by the police prior to losing them. Both groups were sometimes described as having "bottomed out"; but while this psychological frame argued that each person has their own "bottom," it struck me that there was some general social patterning involved in the process and that a few different "bottoms" had been established. Those who resisted treatment, meanwhile, were able to more or less manage their involvement with the street economy and to find some degree of success within it.

Whether accepted or not, what is at stake in treatment concerns the reconfiguration of agency, the "habilitation" or capacitation of certain modes of being in the world and the decapacitation of others. Following rules without complaint, tolerating boredom, and being on time are indeed capacities, modes of agency, that bring definite benefits within certain contexts (e.g., a paying job, when such work is available). As Mahmood argues, whereas agency has long been associated with resistance within critical social theory, this is best seen to be an artefact of its relationship with notions of freedom and a desire to use agency as a transhistorical ground for political projects of "emancipation." The example of treatment reveals a difficulty in this formulation in that it becomes impossible to locate true resistance: Is it to be found amongst those who resist poverty and hope that formalized work will enable a different type of life, or is it among those who resist the obvious forms of subordination entailed within treatment itself? Rather than seeking agency—here seen as opposition to imposed structures—as an essential, elemental core of the subject, it perhaps makes more sense to speak of particular formations of agency rather than speaking of agency in the abstract.

Foucault offers possibilities as to what an alternative theory of agency, one not simply limited to a concept of resistance to imposed structures, would look like. Drawing out Foucault's perspective, Mahmood writes that agency is better thought of "in terms of the capacities and skills required to undertake particular kinds of moral actions" and as necessarily embedded in specific, socially-situated disciplines of self.[57] Noting the "paradox of subjectivation," in which "capacity for action is enabled and created by specific relations of subordination," she suggests "we might consider the example of a virtuoso pianist who submits herself to the often painful regime of disciplinary practice, as well as to the hierarchical structures of apprenticeship, in order to acquire the ability—the requisite agency—to play the instrument with mastery."[58] In seeing the ways in which agency, the ability to think and act as one wishes, is itself socially constructed and variable across diverse social contexts, one can make sense of the various sorts of agentic capacities that arise both within *right living* (self-discipline, emotional control, and at least some degree of allegiance to order and duty) and within the so-called drugs lifestyle (which perhaps involves a more improvisational approach that relies upon the mobilization of many diverse emotionalities, sometimes using chemical technologies to achieve this). These diverse forms of agency help make different sorts of choices and actions possible—they enable particular sorts of "freedom"—but only within specific social contexts (one must have actual access to particular types of working-class jobs for *right living* to truly function, for example). As prerequisites for these freedoms, however, they necessarily implicate differing forms of characterlogical formation, involving, among other things, dispositions toward authority and rules, introspective awareness (or a lack thereof), certain types of logical cohesion or abilities to defer such cohesion (e.g., through "denial"), inclinations toward particular types of relationships, and so on.

At the same time, the rhetoric of addiction—particularly when backed by the power of the police—repudiates certain types of agency as unreal (at least for targeted populations) while mandating other sorts of agency that it deems worthwhile.[59] If, as Nic Rose argues, we are "governed through our freedom,"[60] the necessary correlate is a failure to recognize what has sometimes been termed *fugitive agency*.[61] As the political theorist Neil Roberts comments in relation to the slave, the agency of liberalism's Others has long been disavowed, that is, such agency is both recognized and denied.[62] Such disavowal is a critical component within a liberalism that seeks to maintain social inequalities while fostering "freedom."[63] In establishing a para-racial category of "addiction"—a definition that references class and race inequalities more than drug use while simultaneously rendering these references invisible—court-enforced drug treatment naturalizes its own need to exclude and imprison certain categories of people who have already been marginalized. In defining the addict's subjectivity as a form of slavery, liberalism fails to theorize ways subjectivity manifests and choices are made within these margins. The process of dehumanizing or objectifying those who are oppressed is here revealed as a tendency within liberal political culture, rather than a universal requirement of all forms of domination.[64] Not only is "viable citizenship" a necessary prerequisite for "freedom," this formulation automatically understands anyone whose citizenship is not deemed viable as unfree rather than more properly seeing their fugitive status.[65]

Labor and the TC Regime

What then is the disciplinary aim of this new form of agency? Earlier in this chapter, I quoted the director of one of the programs saying that one could no longer simply yell at residents and demand they do something; one has to also explain why. Here is how he explained that "why":

> Well, because it's teaching you a sense of responsibility. You're following directions. If you're working with a crew, you're working on your interpersonal skills, your pre-vocational skills. You're learning time management skills.

More than reporting on one another, the core elements within criminal justice-sponsored treatment programs concern waking up early, following orders (a specific "emotional management skill" noted by De Leon),[66] learning bureaucratic procedures, and doing unpleasant, boring, and repetitive tasks without complaint. Indeed, the need to do these tasks and to obey all rules is emphasized much more than any conventional counseling practice concerning drug use itself. In this vein, De Leon argues that "teaching the work ethic embraces the entire TC perspective,"[67] embracing a wide range of disciplinary foci, including "personal habits, work habits, work relations, self-management, and work values."[68]

> Work in the TC reflects its view of substance abuse as a disorder of the whole person and its reality orientation to recovery. Work has long been

> considered the hallmark of emotional health and a positive lifestyle. Being able to work consistently, responsibly, and effectively requires not only marketable skills, but a psychological level of maturity and adherence to values such as self-reliance and earned achievement (right living). Thus, in the TC, work is both a *goal* and a *means* of recovery.[69]

The pre-vocational training that residents receive thus works "therapeutically" to accustom residents to the pains they are likely to experience in the bottom rungs of formal employment, though this is glossed simply as *right living*. Elsewhere, De Leon offers a table listing all the areas that labor addresses (reproduced as table 2, below).

As argued by Jonathan Simon, the normative ends of the therapeutic community replaced an earlier labor regime (such as that which was present within workhouses and other similar institutions) with a model that emphasized "the adjustment to the norms and rhythms of working life."[70]

TABLE 4.1 Work's therapeutic role within the TC

Typical client characteristics addressed by the work hierarchy

Personal habits	Punctuality, dress, attendance Time and chore management Goal setting
Work habits	Responsibility, consistency, accountability Poor problem solving skills Manipulation or exploitation of people and systems
Work relations	Rebelliousness, problems with authority Cooperativeness and competition with coworkers Accepting and giving supervision, praise, and criticism Interpersonal and communication skills Assertiveness, aggressiveness, and passivity
Work values	Learning work ethic Learning self-reliance, excellence, pride, and ownership of performance Work commitment: making a maximal effort

Source: "Work's Therapeutic Role within the TC" (from De Leon [2000: 139])

> It replaced the intensive focus on disciplining individual bodies with a broader notion of adjustment to working life, for example, getting along with coworkers and feeling positive about one's prospects. Labor in the therapeutic community showed up as an anchor for social life, not the main purpose of it. Finally, the logic of social therapy moved out from a normality defined by labor to a range of practices that could provide their own validation of normality independent of work, for instance, one's attitude in group sessions or how one treats one's spouse and friends.[71]

Even as the TC expanded the therapeutic gaze to a wide variety of aspects of social life, labor remained its central focus, often being straightforwardly positioned as the rehabilitative goal (as seen through a supposed opposition between work and criminality). As Simon notes, work is here framed as a foundation for social life, one which tethers other aspects of the rehabilitative process to its needs.

The conception of work within the TC, however, is a particular one, and it points to the demands of the low-wage labor market within which most residents are confined. De Leon's vision of work, for example, can be seen in the skills it requires, as laid out in this imagined therapeutic encounter:

> "Give me a break" might be heard from a resident to a coordinator or staff person, who replies "If I did, you would be out on the street." This typical exchange in the TC illustrates the clinical relevance of the daily regimen in the recovery process. Routine, in particular, teaches residents that goal attainment occurs one step at a time. Residents typically cannot pursue long-term goals because these require tolerance for repetition and sameness, patience in delaying gratification, and consistency in performance. These characteristics are notably lacking in most residents. . . . The daily schedule helps residents to perform consistently through teaching them to tolerate the boredom of repetitive activity, moderate any extreme behavior, and regulate their affective states. . . . Although the activities of the daily regimen are essentially the same over days, weeks, and months, the individual is on a progressive path of change.[72]

The vision here is not of a generalized *homo oeconomicus* but of a specific laborer who works for others under conditions of routinized labor exploitation. The TC thus "treats" drug abuse by fighting an alleged culture of poverty and replacing it with a habituated accommodation to tedium and rule-following.[73] As pointedly noted by Hackett and Turk:

> Rehabilitation programs largely attempt to teach ex-prisoners how to accommodate themselves to an unjust social order. To graduate from a rehabilitation program has less to do with being changed or rehabilitated and more to do with successfully navigating programmatic norms and developing gestures and performances of remorse, of compliance, of respectability and deservedness that *might* unlock access to the benefits of (lower) middle class life. In a white supremacist capitalist order, advantages are provided to those poor whites and people of color who can successfully disavow vilified categories.[74]

And of course, in a para-racial structure in which race is largely unspoken but loudly heard, this ability to "disavow vilified categories" is much more readily accessible to whites than non-whites.

The basic "skills" of rule-following and the more general imposition of "orderly living" are supplemented by another critical job skill in the low-wage job market: learning to accept abuse from one's superiors without responding. In this regard, residents are frequently instructed to "hold their belly"—to control their anger—and to not respond to insulting behavior. Residents frequently complained about what they perceived to be injustices in the way the program operated, but while their concerns were sometimes addressed, in other instances they were instead informed that the procedures were not meant to be fair, and that they "just have to take it." Learning how to deal with bureaucratic irrationalities and frustrations, to handle unfair treatment and being regularly yelled at by staff, are features that are thus directly incorporated into the treatment regime, and residents are required to learn to offer calm responses in order to demonstrate their recovery from drug abuse.

The residents who were most engaged with job training as a part of treatment clearly had higher aspirations than routinized, abusive work. Men often hoped for jobs in construction, plumbing, car repair, or as truckers (appealing to several because they would not have to deal with a boss), while women often trained for work as paralegals or receptionists. One man was particularly excited to receive training in underwater welding, a highly paid if somewhat risky profession. But even if some were able to truly make good use of the job training, one must nevertheless keep in mind the basic lower-tier occupational vision of *right living* that the TC promotes. And in any event, in the end many needed to seek poorly compensated, dead-end "McDonald's jobs" in order to graduate from the drug court.

From the perspective of at least some of those undergoing treatment, this sort of pre-vocational training may have made sense given both the reality of many jobs in the bottom tier of the postindustrial economy,[75] and their (perhaps accurate) sense of their prospects within that economy, leading several residents to show an openness toward learning such skills (as seen above). But in medicalizing these issues as "addiction" rather than openly speaking about them as a means to adapt to unfair and unjust workplaces, the TC works to normalize its residents, actively condemning those who fail to perform and even working with the criminal justice system to imprison them. At an ethnographic level, it seemed to me that the treatment facility placed people under far greater levels of stress than is usual in most work environments. Its deliberate attempts to induce such stress—and these efforts are indeed deliberate, as acknowledged by De Leon[76]—were often quite successful. The idea that intense stress of this sort might, even in merely some instances, be countertherapeutic—like the idea that work itself might lead some to drug use—was simply unthinkable within the logic of the TC. Instead a simple formula that essentially equated "dope-fiend behaviors" with a supposed culture of poverty prevailed. This is not a new formula but rather an updated version of a civilizational project in which the savage needs either discipline or containment. In this respect, the use of formal labor as an implicit litmus test for psychological health reveals a cunning mode of medicalized social control: those who succeed in the workforce are allowed to go free, while those who do not are deemed to be addicted, as having no agency of their own (or rather, only a "savage" and untutored agency). The savage must become a docile worker, that is to say they must be "made civil," or they must be locked up. In Soss, Fording, and Schram's words, such practices amount to "a racialized political project of market discipline."[77] Yet this disciplinary project is very much a tactic of "freedom," one that ironically reveals itself as resting upon tremendous amounts of force in order to make people free.

5

Gender, Sexuality, and the Drugs Lifestyle

In chapter 4, I discussed the effects of collective punishment as manifested in one of the general meetings (GMs) within the facility. Here I wish to continue discussing that GM and its effects, this time focusing on issues pertaining to the management of sexuality and gender within the facility. As will be seen, gender and sexuality form the nexus through which much of treatment is made personal. While the drug court prided itself on its personalization and the (self-imagined) intimacy held between the judge and drug court participants, in truth, even as those interactions were enormously consequential, they remained relatively distant from the intimate lives of most participants. While drug court judges often spoke "parentally" to participants, sometimes even sharing their own experiences (though in limited ways), the interaction between judges and participants nevertheless retains a great deal of social distance. Within the generally privatized space of the treatment center, however, the state—or the para-state apparatus, more specifically—imposed intimacy upon those it administered. These *intimacies of the state* were often of a violating and intrusive nature, involving tactics designed to shame gendered performances deemed to pertain to the so-called drugs lifestyle. The emotional violence of these interactions was keenly felt, being deliberately meant to impact participants as forcefully as possible and thereby break through any defenses associated with the purported denial of drug addiction. If rule-following and collective surveillance constituted two central components of treatment and "accountability," shaming practices constituted a third critical leg.

As noted in the prior chapter, the GM began when staff had decided that too many rules were being broken in the facility, and that a series of collective punishments—bans on telephone calls and on passes for short trips outside of the facility, as well as the systematic disordering of their rooms—would have to be enforced. As part of the GM, individuals who had broken specific rules were also made to stand in front of the larger group where their particular infractions were addressed:

A man who had claimed to be a big-time dealer was called up first. Despite loaning out money, the staff had noticed that he had been wearing the same clothing literally every day since arriving a week prior. "Why are you loaning out all this money when you're wearing the same clothes every day?" one of the staff members began. "How do you wash those clothes anyway if that's all you have?" Some of the residents chuckled at this. The staff member went for more: "If you've got his money, please pay him back so that he can go buy some clothes." While nearly all laughed at this, I silently wondered what types of therapeutic lessons they were being taught in terms of making fun of others who perhaps made questionable decisions while being down on their luck. Isaac, the man being mocked, attempted to speak back at this point, but he was quickly cut off: "I didn't ask you to say anything! You just listen. You need to <u>hear</u> and <u>understand</u>." The staff then tried to get people to whom this resident had loaned money to confess. "We got the master list," staff members bluffed. "You might as well tell us now, because we know who you are." Three women stood, accepting blame. "All right, Isaac. You need to tell us who you loaned money to, if you're serious about staying here." Staff had talked about Isaac during their meeting and were hoping that the jail sentence that hung over his head should he be kicked out of the program might help convince him to talk. After hesitating a bit, Isaac named one man. "I don't know what he's talking about," came a quick reply from the back. After more hesitation, Isaac named several others who had already left the facility.

A woman having an affair with a man in the facility (both she and he were married to others) was next. Sexually explicit love letters that the woman had written to the man had been found, and a staff member began to read these aloud to the entire group (much to the appreciation of most of the assembled residents). "You're making me look like a fool!" complained the woman. "We're not making you look like a fool. <u>You're</u> making yourself look like a fool." After reading a bit more, one of *the staff members joked: "Hell, if it's the dick, I'll get you a dick. . . . It'll have batteries and it won't talk back." The residents laughed. "It's more than that," offered the woman somewhat meekly. A second staff member continued to press: "Where's your self-esteem? Going with someone who puts you second?" "Well, I ain't got none," responded the woman, "Why do you think I'm here?" "You gotta stand up for yourself," returned the first staff member, " 'cuz that's no way to be. . . . And you got a husband, too?" "Yes." Eyes rolled and staff members shook their heads as nearly all visibly reacted: "Your husband takes care of your kids, and you're cheating on him?" "No, he doesn't! Why don't you ask me this stuff before I'm up here in front of everyone?" came the angry reply. "Because I'm not your case manager," came the reply, with the staff member not backing down. "Well, I'll tell you what he's done," continued the woman. "All he's done is sleep around with whores, taken all my money, and used it for drugs for both of us. And that's all he's ever done." "You know who you sound like?" asked the second staff member. "The wife of the man you just slept with." Several audible "Oooohhhhhs!" rose from the residents, and the woman seemed quite chastised. Near tears, she offered a final defense: "You're making me out to be a home-breaker, and I'm not!" "Yes, you are!" came the quick retort, a claim that met with no further resistance.*

Following this, the married man this woman had slept with was sharply chastised, but in a notably different way; instead of being called a "home wrecker," he was told he "had no respect for the mother of his child." Less time was spent humiliating him in front of the group, though he had all of his "privileges" removed, was demoted to an earlier stage within the program (one with fewer rights to have visits or go outside), and was given an indefinite learning experience (including early morning wake-ups and all-day-long dishwashing, as described in relation to a different incident above). The man did not speak much in response, and he did not attempt to justify his behavior, whether because he accepted the punishment or was merely resigned to it. The man who had thrown his cane—someone who had been in the program for some time—had his supervisory position stripped and all privileges revoked while being blamed for not taking responsibility for his feelings and for setting a bad example.

Meanwhile, one of the women who had gotten into a yelling match—someone who (like nearly half the women in the facility) stood to lose custody of her daughter if she failed at treatment—was told she obviously didn't love her child if she put her at risk in that way. "Why don't you just give your daughter away, if that's how it is?" asked the director. "You could be going home to see your kid, if you wanted to," added the assistant director, "but I guess you don't care. It sure seems like you don't care." "I can go home, take care of my kid. And kiss my kid," chimed in one of the other staff members, loudly and angrily, "and go to sleep and get up the next day, and it's all good because I've done the work." Speaking to the entire group, she added: "None of you have done the work, and just a few of you are going to make it! You know, you-all put yourselves here," the staff member continued, "and if you all don't want to be here, you can just walk out that door. Please do." The woman being confronted began to cry, and the staff member's voice quieted a bit as she turned back to her: "Welcome to the pain. And that pain is just going to keep coming until you decide to get better."

The other woman in the shouting match did not have a child and received a less shaming reprimand. "Amira, get up here" (everyone was made to stand in front of the others during their dress-downs). "So she gets up in your face," said the assistant director, "does that mean you have to respond?" "I gotta do what I gotta do," replied the woman. "You're from the street, and you keep that. You break it out if you need to. But you don't want to be responding like that all the time. What are you going to do out on the street if somebody steps to you like that?" "Well, then I guess we're fightin'." "Is that your only option?" pressed the assistant director, "You need to be smart. You need to walk away. You need to 'woman-up' here. And they can think that you're a punk, but that's on them. And they'll get caught and you'll just walk by them like they're nothing. Like they don't mean nothing to you." She had her privileges to go outside revoked, and was demoted within the program. "But that's not fair!" complained the woman. "She came at me!" "It's not supposed to be fair, you just have to take it," came the curt reply.

It bears repeating that the institution I examined was understood to be mild by residents who had experiences with multiple treatment centers. The use of yelling and peer shaming are not atypical in such facilities, but they are considered to be core elements of treatment. As De Leon writes in his canonical text on therapeutic community (TC) practice:

> Reprimands are designed to focus a recalcitrant resident's attention on hearing what is being said and feeling the seriousness of the impact of his or her behaviors on others. . . . The presence of peers during the reprimand is a critical element in a properly delivered reprimand. It is designed to maximize the vicarious learning concerning community expectations and to discourage negative peer associations. . . . Most importantly, the credibility of the reprimand is enhanced because the confronted resident cannot easily disallow or ignore what was being said in the witness of peers.[1]

De Leon emphasizes that such confrontational approaches must be employed with "responsible concern," and "must always reflect the element of concern for the individuals to whom they are directed."[2] From the perspective of the drug counselors, the verbal reprimands are acts of care, a form of "tough love" (though I did not hear that term used) that hopefully drive home the realities of drug abuse. What struck me, however, was that the "realities" they emphasize all pertain to failed gender norms that are then vaguely linked to drug use. The man who is disgraced and made fun of for being poor, the couple having an affair, the woman who risks losing custody of her daughter due to her drug use: all are made individually responsible for the entirety of their situation, with drug treatment as the proffered solution.

Yet how precisely are drug addiction and having an affair linked? What is the social imaginary that connects the two behaviors? While residents were not always clear as to the logic—this seemed like something that the staff could have made more clear, even in terms of the treatment center's own logic—the link between addiction and sexual affair is precisely what TC proponents refer to as treating "the whole person" rather than simply addressing brain factors or drug effects. As De Leon argues, in addiction, "Thinking may be unrealistic or disorganized; values are confused, nonexistent, or antisocial. . . . Moral and spiritual 'bankruptcy' is evident."[3]

> The prominence of lying, manipulation, and deception may reflect longstanding features of a character or conduct disorder that has been significantly exaggerated by drug use. . . . Teachers, police, physicians, social workers, mental health professionals, and social service bureaucrats are often seen as hypocritical, naïve, or corrupt people. Characteristically, residents have learned to get around and exploit such systems (i.e., "beat the system"), and to disrespect or manipulate (i.e., "get over on") the people who are part of such systems. They often defend their lies with arguments about victimization, entitlement, the necessities of survival, the need to "even the score," and other rationalizations, projections, and excuses. In TCs, residents and staff refer to the strategies pejoratively as "typical dope fiend thinking and behaving." They are seen as socially and interpersonally noxious features that are habitual ways of coping with others, avoiding perceived pressures, and obtaining relief.[4]

Far from seeing such behaviors as at least potentially adaptive within a context of systemic impoverishment and racial domination, TCs work to adjust their clientele to such oppression in the name of drug treatment. But while the staff members were perhaps somewhat errant in carefully explaining the links between drug use and being poor or having an affair, the connections were indeed articulated, at least at times. Beyond general condemnations of *dope-fiend behaviors* or *stinking thinking*, various staff members informed clients that: "If you followed the rules, you wouldn't be here right now," a refrain I heard multiple times while at the facility. Disobedience and addiction are thus seen as tightly linked, and both are placed into a sharply dichotomous relation with *right living*.

In point of fact, however, I never witnessed anyone called to account for having cheated a public bureaucracy of some sort, nor do I suspect that efforts to shame residents for such a reason would be effective (even if not considered ideal, such a behavior might be considered justifiable given the circumstances of need). Instead, closely felt experiences of gender failure—failure to uphold norms to which the residents themselves had some attachment—worked to make real the purported consequences of drug use. Beyond an invocation of obedience there thus lies a more implicit and taken-for-granted framework that links drug use and the shame of gender failure, an assertion that one will obtain a respectable, non-shame-inducing gender identity only by endorsing the therapeutic project that the treatment center enforces. Until a person complies with the rules of the program, staff members see it as their responsibility to drive home the unsustainable and shameful nature of identities linked to the so-called drugs lifestyle by actively embarrassing and discrediting participants as sharply and as intimately as possible.

Just as the staff members entered the (provisionally held) personal space of the residents' rooms and overturned all of their belongings, so too do the staff members seek to enter the intimate psyche of the residents, throwing their identities into disarray in an effort to force reconstruction on a new terrain. The man bragging about his high status on the street is revealed to be a destitute fraud. The woman having an affair is humiliated for her "inappropriate" sexual desires, while only the sexual double standard prevents her male partner from receiving equal treatment. The woman who shouted is not only reminded of the possible consequences of her actions but is emotionally made to feel "the reality" of her situation by being pointedly told that she is an uncaring mother. While shouting at another resident might not have initially seemed terribly consequential, the gender shaming makes it real: as the staff member offered, "Welcome to the pain. And that pain is just going to keep coming until you decide to get better." Treatment thus uses the shame of gender failure to deliberately inflict suffering, and staff actively search for ways to shame and humiliate residents who have transgressed. At least in some instances, women might be more vulnerable than men to this type of therapeutic tactic—such as when the woman having the affair was sexually shamed while the man was merely castigated for "not having respect for the mother of his child"—but this is a feature of wider gendered disparities in discursive susceptibility to shame. I have no doubt that the counselors sought to shame the man as forcefully as possible, but due to the sexual double standard, they had fewer tools they could call upon to do so. In whatever case, however, gender and sexuality are regularly invoked precisely because they are powerfully and intimately felt; their imminence within the construction of self worth makes them useful tools that can inflict psychic distress.

Detailed knowledge pertaining to the values of participants was necessary in order to enact this sort of shaming. In this regard, it was important that the counselors—at least the floor staff who parceled out most of this discipline—were persons who had similar race and class backgrounds as the residents and who had themselves lived through intensive experiences with drugs and impoverishment. These staff members (and not the social workers, who generally had a somewhat more middle-class background) knew from experience where the vulnerabilities lay, where the tensions and contradictions within street identities might be found, where one might encounter inner antagonisms between street life and ongoing attachments to and desires for conventional working-class gender norms. They understood the way these norms had been foreclosed and collapsed by the exigencies of a life oriented toward hustling and "getting by," places where one could hurt, shame, and "break through." Teresa Gowan's ethnographic work with homeless men in San Francisco details (among other issues) the way in which desires for respectability are held in a dynamic tension with the needs of survival. Gowan points to deep ambivalences that appear in inconsistent oscillations these men engage in, between what she refers to as "sick talk" (talk that might excuse homelessness but that implied a denigrated self that denied individual capacity for agency) and "sin talk" (talk that, in it its official form, castigated the "bad behavior" of the homeless, but which in a flipped form worked to address homelessness via a bravura posture that embraced the "wildness of the streets" and the "evil" deeds one had to do to survive, thereby not only asserting one's powerfully masculinized status but also asserting one's capacity for agentic action as well). Vacillations between these two discourses resulted not only from individuals' own uncertainties and inner conflicts but from structural features as well. As Gowan perceptively writes:

> Already in acute personal crisis, they were confronted continuously by forceful iterations of elite sin-talk and sick-talk in the form of rabble management by obligatory medicalization. In these contexts, their actions became highly strategic. People on the street learned fast how to position themselves when quizzed by shelter workers, police officers, welfare officials, nurses, lawyers, or activists.
>
> Yet the men's iterations of dominant discourses ran far deeper than the purely instrumental. Shame, stigma, and isolation kept these ideas twisting and turning in the minds of their objects. Out in the more autonomous spaces of street life—among sidewalk sleepers, corner "bottle gangs," panhandlers, recyclers, and thieves—multiple answers to the ever-implied question, "Why are you homeless?" hung in the air.[5]

When applying Gowan's insights to the TC, we see that drug treatment offers participants a combined promise of gendered respectability and economic ascendency into the lower tiers of the formal labor force in exchange for an acceptance of sick talk and a willingness to work within the program's disciplinary path toward "wellness."[6]

Rethinking Hegemonic Masculinity in the Therapeutic Community

Discussion of a single, hegemonic masculinity does not adequately describe the embedded nuances of the gendered politics of masculinity within TCs. At a general level, the idea of hegemonic masculinity is often taken as a normative contrast for a street-based masculinity, which is itself framed as a derivative and deviant gender formation (variously referred to as protest masculinity, crisis masculinity, hypermasculinity, or even compensatory masculinity).[7] Raewyn Connell's useful advance in developing the notion of hegemonic masculinity[8] here runs the risk of devolving into a singular measure of masculinity, one to which all men presumptively aspire and against which they hide their shame through compensatory practices when they cannot achieve it. While Connell and Messerschmidt emphasize "locally specific constructions of hegemonic masculinity,"[9] too often the concept serves to reify a particular vision of an almost invariably white and middle-class ideal, bolstering the cultural centrality of that ideal.[10] This framing is potentially misleading and offers few tools in illuminating the many entrenched complexities and contradictions within gendered discourse. Culturally prevalent forms of masculinity, for example, feature numerous elements that valorize working-class masculinities over middle-class ones and sometimes position white or middle-class masculinities as compromised or "effeminate" in relation to these more "rugged," "muscular" forms. This contradiction is sometimes noted within the literature,[11] but it is under-theorized, pointing as it does toward a more complex set of power relations than the concept of hegemonic masculinity is capable of capturing, and toward the more general inadequacy of a singular measure of cultural dominance (i.e., hegemony). The long-standing practice in which white, middle-class men draw from subordinated masculinities (ranging from the pursuit of sports and other physical acts of prowess to fandom for black hip-hop artists displaying stylized "street-based" masculinities) would seem to make no sense if these latter forms were indeed completely subordinate. Instead, these innovations elaborate upon continuities, ambiguities, and contradictions within the vision of masculinity itself; they can operate as "compensations" only because the vision of gender is itself fractured and contradictory. Whereas the term *hegemonic masculinity* suggests that a single standard predominates—risking a return of the *male sex role* that the concept was meant to replace[12]—the dominant forms are in fact already mutually imbricated with supposedly subordinated forms, following more closely the logic of an assemblage with many contradictory borrowings.[13]

Gail Bederman's historical analysis of the shift from *manliness* (based on social honor) to *masculinity* (based on physical prowess) at the turn of the nineteenth century points toward ways in which middle-class men's model of "masculinity" has always involved the appropriation of working-class men's cultural practices, existing in a permanent state of unstable compromise. The reason for these contradictions lies precisely in the origins of masculinity that Bederman references: middle-class men have never fully recovered from the economic subservience that the rise of corporate life has entailed, leaving them dependent on working-class men's social practices as a way to restore normativity in the face of this loss of honor. From the perspective of the middle-class men, "real masculinity" is thus a working-class phenomenon, one that they often seek to embody while simultaneously combining it with aspects of "honor."[14]

Street-based masculinities, for their part, lack access to stable work as a source of identity, and thus they tend to intensify a focus more intently on bodily practices (becoming something that middle-class commentators have seen as "hyper" in the process), but they are nevertheless seen as non-normative because they fail at being "socially honorable." Men exhibiting street-based masculinities are instead portrayed as inherently hostile toward women and failing to secure upward mobility. *Hypermasculinity* is seen as *improperly* masculine—its practices so "accelerated" that its very status as masculine requires a modifier—even as it intensifies certain aspects of the form. Even those working-class men who are in more favorable economic circumstances must continue to face both economic subordination and stigmatization regarding their alleged lack of honor (reactionary politics, misogyny, interpersonal brutishness, etc.). Capitalist-class men, meanwhile, constitute only an isolated and idiosyncratic few, existing as a group so small as to be unable to form a coherent cultural alternative. The above schematic points toward a complex situation in which no form of masculinity is uncompromised and in which none is fully hegemonic over the others. If the fault of "hypermasculinity" is that it generates "too much" masculinity, then we are clearly dealing with a cultural structure that cannot be measured by a single standard (unlike, say, wealth, where more is indeed more). Instead, the bodily practices associated with masculinity are placed into a contradictory and unstable relationship with the potentially "effeminizing" expressions of social honor (liberal politics, supposedly egalitarian relations with women, civilized demeanors, etc.), leaving no masculine formation fully hegemonic. A dynamic tension among divergent norms thus shapes social evaluations of men's behaviors, generating cross-class/cross-race patterns that are not explicable within a frame that sees only one standard as straightforwardly hegemonic.[15]

Rather than thinking of a single hegemonic masculinity, I believe we would be better off thinking of a *hegemonic gender order* that rests upon complex alliances among varied gender formations, both "masculine" and "feminine." In this sense, the masculinity of cis-male global capitalists—to the extent that this even exists as a coherent cultural formation—does not need to be seen as being universally aspirational and hegemonic over all men; in fact such capitalists *require* and depend on the existence of other masculinities in order to achieve their societal power. Unlike Gramsci's notion of hegemony as a singular common sense, this hegemonic gender order does not feature a unified formation that is universally dominant and is instead filled with points of both continuity and contestation among its various components. The overall hegemonic gender order can thus be seen as an interlinked conglomerate among an assortment of gendered formations that are themselves related in complex and sometimes contradictory ways.[16]

Within the treatment center, a singular vision of gender is indeed forcefully imposed on residents, and the residents generally hold some level of cultural allegiance toward that vision (hence its effectiveness as a "therapeutic" shaming device). At the same time, however, residents often hold other allegiances to other visions of gender, and these cannot be reduced to mere "compensations" for failure in a more primary realm of gendered performance. The situation of the TC is itself sometimes framed as a competition between the values of the therapeutic community and the "addictive social system."[17] This competition between differently constructed visions of gender—each locally dominant in different ways and in different cultural locales and moments—is a more fruitful way to begin the analysis.[18]

Even the term *competition* is misleading, however, if it connotes two entirely different visions of masculinity in conflict. Part of my suggestion is that there is a significant degree of continuity between the gendered vision of *right living* and of *dope-fiend behavior*. This overlap was made apparent in the general meeting described above. I continue below to narrate another moment from that meeting, describing the treatment received by a young Latino man who had been a drug dealer and a member of a gang prior to being admitted into the treatment facility:

While the attacks on person after person (seven in total) were generally quite sharp in tone, one of the men was shown a good deal of sympathy in his punishment. A twenty-year-old man who had been wearing his gang colors was told sharply that he was not allowed to do that within the facility, but the intervention was done with much more sympathy. "One of my own children is in a gang," said one of the floor staff, "and gangs aren't all bad; there's some good stuff about them, and not everyone in a gang does bad, but you just can't wear that in here." While being very clear that the rule against wearing gang colors was a requirement—"You're going to take that off or you're going to go. It's just that simple"—staff members suggested that he could instead "fly his flag on the inside," offering him a potentially face-saving compromise that might enable him to bridge loyalties to both the gang and the institutional requirements he now faced. "If you're real, you got it in your heart. You don't have to wear it on the outside." "You can yell about it, you can be pissed about it," suggested another staff member, "but you just can't do it. You can walk out the door and do all the gang stuff you want, and I can respect that, but you can't do it here. No matter what. So are you willing to make some adjustments?" After some grumbling, the ultimatums and perhaps the gentler tone and face-saving gestures offered by the staff eventually convinced the man to remove his brightly colored necklace. In fact, during the prior meeting when the staff had decided on what punishments to dole out to each resident, they had decided that this particular resident, who otherwise obeyed the rules and who was deemed one of the "strong ones," needed to show more "leadership" within the house. Rather than being given a learning experience, he was therefore assigned to a supervisory position within the house.

In this instance, the domains of overlap between *dealer* (which, as Philippe Bourgois's ethnography shows, often entails a significant work ethic[19]) and *leader* were significant, as were many other elements of participation in the gang that the staff deemed "positive" (one staff member mentioned values of friendship, loyalty, and even love when I asked her later). Here the connection of the staff to the local communities was again significant; rather than attempting to demonize his involvement in the gang—an effort I suspect would have failed and served only to alienate, if attempted—the "pro-social" aspects of his former life were acknowledged and no effort was made to shame him whatsoever. A decidedly non-middle-class and knowledgeable perspective on gang life was invoked that sought to draw forth constructive aspects from affiliations that are overwhelmingly belittled and disparaged by outsiders. Instead, as one of the "strong ones" who had done well in the program—and perhaps it is not coincidental that he, like some of the other dealers, only smoked marijuana[20]—his life prior to treatment was seen to exhibit many elements that the staff wished to cultivate, albeit in a changed context (the formal, rather than the informal, labor market). Both the heterosexist appeal in the flyer criticizing sagging pants (discussed in chapter 2) and the respect shown for the gang member—whose "deviance" conformed to a certain set of masculine ideals instead of failing at them—highlights the fact that there are definite continuities between the masculinity that the institution seeks to replace and the one it seeks to foster. For men, then, participation in drug treatment often involves a reorientation toward previously learned gender patterns rather than a complete rejection of prior norms.[21]

Navigating Masculinities in the TC

Men undergoing TC treatment often sought to make use of these continuities even as the institution placed them in situations that might otherwise be seen as shamefully "effeminizing." The gendered challenges that the institution presents these men are manifold: there was directly gendered shaming, as seen above, but also a medicalized, "therapeutic" demand for the revelation of embarrassing details in front of others.[22] Such difficulties are commonly compounded by the sense many men experienced that blindly following the institution's rules would be compromising (as seen in chapter 4). Further, at its most general level, the very aims of the TC—pressing people toward (generally low-wage) work involving rule-following, tedium, and the acceptance of abuse from superiors—often stand in opposition to the masculinity many of the men had adopted on the street. In relation to men, the competition that TCs stage between themselves and "drug subcultures" (as De Leon puts it)[23] is very much a struggle between different visions of masculinity; however, the clash between the two models is better seen as being between closely related cousins rather than between polar opposites. The overlap between these apparently conflicting gendered modalities leaves many ways open in which men who have been accustomed to one set of standards might choose to navigate the TC's seemingly rigid impositions.

For example, there were men who complied with the TC's rules while rejecting its logic. One man who had spent ten years in prison (for a manslaughter charge that occurred during a robbery) framed it as simply another challenge that the criminal justice system offered to his sense of gendered dignity, a challenge he could apparently best address through masculinized indifference and bluster: "Hey, there's nothing more personal than some guy having to lean over and ripping open your ass cheeks. There's nothing personal like that, so this is easy after that." While his framing was atypical, other male residents who did not buy into the program found other ways to engage with the TC that did not violate their sense of gendered selfhood. One twenty-three-year-old Latino man who had been sentenced to treatment for a parole violation, for example, simply denied that he had a drug problem (he had smoked marijuana and drank alcohol on a regular basis when he was initially arrested for stealing cars). Like several others, he distanced himself from "sick-talk" and any need for the program, while making use of select parts of it to both cope with the criminal justice system and to advance his economic position:

> I just did what I had to do, you know what I'm sayin'? I needed it just for my parole to get off my back a little bit, see that I'm actually doing something and doing what I got to do. . . . I'm just here to do what I got to do for my family. My son is only two years and eight months. . . . I'm basically here for is to use the program for what it's giving me, which is my schooling, training, and also getting work, you know what I'm sayin'? We already got an apartment, me and my wife . . . and the only thing I basically need is my GED and training for the job. Like a good trade, you know. I wanted to take up plumbing because that right there is a great field and the money actually coming in where I could be able to take care of myself, and not only myself, my family.

In its congruity with a more respectable gendered future, it is not surprising that job training was the component of the program that was most universally praised by residents, both male and female. But in framing drug treatment as a means of "doing what I had to do," residents might also frame their participation in ways that reinforced an anti-institutional sense of masculine self.

While the entire basis of participation within the TC involves the imposition of a diseased identity (as "addicted" and therefore "out of control" in relation to drugs), the institution itself created a variety of tools that mitigate against the feminization of vulnerable forms of self-disclosure and of sick talk. In the facility I examined, for example, group-oriented personal disclosure was established on a relatively infrequent basis, generally once a week (though women were offered a second "women's only" weekly group, to be discussed below). While each resident met one-on-one with a counselor each week, the social workers conducting those sessions generally emphasized that they did not push the clients to disclose too much if they did not wish to do so. Although sitting through the hour-long sessions was mandatory, the nature of one's participation was one of the few areas within the program that was highly negotiable. Beyond this, the types of vulnerable self-disclosure that did occur did not extend into all aspects of life; for example, while two male residents privately shared with me that they had exchanged sex for crack with other men, this never became a point of discussion within any of the groups (one of the two men discussed the issue individually with his counselor, while the other had chosen not to share the information with anyone else in the facility). While the program director was clearly very proud of being one of the few treatment facilities that offered regular counseling sessions—its inclusion required significant financial resources—the daily disciplinary regimen nevertheless struck me as far more central to the TC's de facto model of treatment.[24]

This disciplinary regimen—itself enforced by rough and abrasive interactions with staff—offered residents ready ways in which they could encode a diseased identity and treatment as masculinized, enabling many of the men in particular to relate to the TC in ways that did not violate their sense of gendered selfhood. One male resident, for example, framed discipline as an implicitly masculinized tool in a "fight" against addiction:

> The things they teach me through discipline—there's a lot of discipline, and it's not easy. . . . And the disease talks to you in so many different forms. . . . It puts thoughts in your head that aren't necessarily real and true, just to get you out there, to get you stressed, to get you to use again. It comes at you in so many different ways, it's ridiculous. You gotta keep telling yourself, I'm not going to let the disease win.

Staff members frequently reinforce this framing of recovery as a masculinized accomplishment. During the general meeting referenced above, for example, one staff member sharply challenged the residents: "None of you have done the work, and just a few of you are going to make it! You know, you-all put yourselves here," she continued, "and if you all don't want to be here, you can just walk out that door. Please do." The hostile nature of these confrontations, combined with the "elite" status of recovery for the few, worked to make sobriety—or more saliently, subordination within the lower tiers of the formal labor market (as argued in chapter 4)—a strongly gendered achievement. It turns one's ability to *hold one's belly* (maintaining self-control over one's anger in the face of abuse) into an alternative form of masculinity, one that offers a substitute for other forms of gendered performance—e.g., defending one's reputation at virtually all costs, for example—that are commonly seen a requisites for participation in street life.[25]

While most residents either adopted or distanced themselves from sick talk, others found more creative ways to engage with the discourse. One fifty-two-year-old black man I spoke with, for example, accommodated himself to the gendered regime of the program by subordinating a street-based masculinity via age and maturity, further appropriating masculine parts of the program toward ends that the program would not fully support:

> When you are young, you look at life a certain way. You don't think of certain experiences as catching up to you. When you're young, you think, "I'm gonna get by this," because you're still young. I'm not young like that anymore. So now I have to look at life from a more mature point of view. I have my ups and downs, but even in the midst of that, I keep moving forward. It's at a slower pace, but I have to be realistic with myself. If I have to survive out here, and accomplish something, I have to slow my pace down and take it one step at a time. Some days it's aggravating, sometimes I still have to go hustle out there, but the thing about me now is that I look at the consequences deeper. If I go out there and take chances, and risks, what would happen?
>
> Being here, one thing it has added to is my discipline. . . . It's good up to a point, but I'm not going to be here forever. I'm not going to be in this mode where I'm going to be using it to live my life. What I want it to be is an experience that helps build my character for a certain period of time, keeps me in check, and then as time goes on, it falls back into place. It's a treatment program; it goes no further. . . . The whole purpose of using this program is to use it as a stepping stone, to get what I can out of it while I am here, exercise the discipline that goes with it, and apply it once I go back out into the world, start working, get my own place.

Bruce here identifies himself—not the treatment program—as the agent of change. The program offers him useful resources that he can take or leave, but on *his* terms (this was a common approach among those who saw only the job training as beneficial). For him, however, the program is useful insofar as he has seen a need to "slow down," be "realistic with himself," and "take it one step at a time." It offers him a form of disciplinary control that he recognizes that he does not have, and that he believes will be useful to him, despite his expectation that he will continue to need to hustle in the informal economy once done with treatment. In his case, the program's goals would only be incompletely achieved: instead of moving into the formal economy, Bruce envisions ongoing participation in an informal street economy and arrogates the tools of treatment toward that end. Had he said the above directly to staff members, which he did not, they almost certainly would have told him that memories of "people, places, and things" would bring him back to drug use if he returned to the hustle of street life. However this issue is considered, Bruce's approach to treatment allows him to appropriate these tools through a discourse that valorizes the "maturity" of an alternative outlook that does not simply embrace risk. Instead of utilizing risk and danger to emphasize fearlessness or to otherwise elevate his masculine status, as he had done in the past, Bruce instead suggests that he will carefully consider and evaluate risky activities.[26]

As Wilton, DeVerteuil, and Evans note, drug treatment programs are "places in which men are encouraged to rework performances of masculinity as part of the process of recovery."[27] As a gendered institution,[28] the TC is governed internally by a highly masculinized logic. This logic operates in similar ways to the discursive practices identified by Eamonn Carrabine and Brian Longquist in their study of a Scottish prison: "One of the ways in which hierarchy is established and maintained in prisons . . . is through the use of gendered discourse, around masculinity, in the making of decisions, based in interaction between managers and the managed."[29] As seen in the decision to promote the young man who wore gang colors, gendered comportment helped govern the operation of the TC as well, shaping the way in which individuals were punished or rewarded. In the instance of the TC, gender is even more at stake insofar as the product that the TC is meant to generate pertains directly to gendered discourses and practices. And as seen earlier, the contestation between gendered projects is immediately linked with the classed agenda of the state, managing street poverty through a psychiatric discourse of addiction that effectively turns structural problems into individual acts of gendered failure.

Women Within the Male-Dominated TC

While the gender strategies used to treat men retain significant continuities with the past (in that the criminal justice system has always sought to at least partially denigrate "street" masculinities in favor of "respectable" masculinities), the treatment of women has involved some significant changes, even as significant continuities with earlier histories relating to the enforcement of conventional gender roles for women are also present.[30] The drug court, for example, requires that all participants, both female and male, have at least a GED and find work as conditions of completing the program. The societal demand that women work, however—perhaps most relevantly embodied (for this population) in the establishment of workfare over welfare[31]—has not been met with any diminishment in demands that they handle childcare and all other conventionally feminine demands.[32] Thus, women in male-oriented TCs face a more difficult and complex set of gendered challenges in which they have remained subject to historically feminine demands while being also subject to new historically masculine ones. This effectively constitutes a system of *incommensurate expectation* in which women can be criticized for failures in relation to either idealized notions of "female" or "male" norms of behavior, with no allowances being made to accommodate the additional and often conflicting burdens imposed by the situation.[33] These difficulties, of course, parallel broader trends in normative work and family life that present women with contradictory demands. Here, however, the consequences are greatly heightened, with women who have children in particular being placed in a situation where they must meet both sets of standards or risk losing their children to Child Protective Services (CPS).

Women's relationships to job training within the program helps to highlight the contradictory gendered position they were in and the ways in which they attempted to manage these conflicts. Many of the women I interviewed, for example, found this aspect of the program both helpful and appropriate. Marie, a forty-nine-year-old Latina woman, spoke of the ways in which the program's support with work and education had benefitted her:

> I got a lot from this program. It gave me a sense of purpose and made me believe in myself again when I didn't believe I could accomplish anything. I always started something with the best of intentions, but never followed through with anything. Here I went to school, I finished, I trained, I got a job right away [as a medical assistant], and a lot of good things are happening because I stayed cool. I stayed focused. . . . In the beginning, who wants to be here? But it's a life changing thing for me.

Though women were generally as enthusiastic as men about the possibility of work, the options thereby generated were limited by the gendered nature of the jobs for which they were trained, a fact that limited women's choices and possible incomes. Women were generally trained as paralegals, medical receptionists, and administrative aides, for example, while men typically received training in plumbing, truck driving, welding, carpentry, or automotive repair (with a small number of residents of both sexes also wanting to become drug counselors). This gendered dichotomy was not, however, imposed by fiat from the job counselors (who expressed enthusiasm about the possibility of placing women into programs for conventionally male jobs when I asked them about it), but was instead developed through a consensus-oriented dialogue with the vocational counselors based upon the preferences and goals of the residents themselves. While there may have been many reasons why the women choose predominantly female fields over higher paying masculinized occupations—internalized norms, fear of gendered harassment, etc.—these differences nevertheless furthered pre-existing gendered divides to women's disadvantage, a result that staff members seemed to neither encourage nor to actively counter. While heavy pressure to train for higher-paying, male-dominated jobs would indeed be an added affront to the residents' already limited scope for decision making, in the absence of encouragement to even consider higher-paying alternatives, it seemed that an unequal status quo was perfectly consonant with the program's aims.

Contradictions associated with work were significantly multiplied for women who had children, as perhaps two-thirds of the women in the program did. Several women were in fact required to attend treatment directly by CPS with the threat of having their children removed if they did not complete the program. For these women, the demands of work—enforced in this case by the TC rather than the court—sometimes operated in direct contradiction to the demand that they not neglect their (sometimes very young) children. As the legal scholar Dorothy Roberts notes, given the costs of childcare, and its lack of availability for poor women, "their mothers' employment may actually reduce the amount of money available for their needs and jeopardize their health care; it may deprive them of their only protection against a myriad of environmental hazards."[34] More generally, women with children often expressed ways in which their experience as mothers guided their efforts at recovery, but these connections could also be quite exasperating insofar as the inpatient treatment regimen isolated them from their families. Said one woman, "I just thank God that I got these two kids in my life. They're positive. They keep me positive. I just can't afford to fall right now because if I do, I lose everything. I'll lose everything: my kids, my apartment. I will lose everything, so it's not worth it, not at all." Nevertheless, this same woman expressed frustration at having had visits with her child taken away due to what she viewed as a minor infringements of the rules (smoking in an unauthorized area): "It just seems like the punishment should fit the crime, and it doesn't." Being a good mother thus requires participation in institutions (work and/or treatment) that undercut their ability to be with their children.

Furthermore, women face a double standard in which norms of sexual respectability are enforced much more sharply against them, both in terms of the amount of stigma that is mobilized against them for "whorish" acts, and in terms of a heightened degree of surveillance and policing against "seductiveness" within the facility. The feminization of sexual stigma can be seen in the above encounter in which a woman had her sexually explicit letters read aloud to a chuckling audience. Her adulterous union renders her a "homewrecker" whereas his equally adulterous actions are merely said to show a lack of respect for "the mother of his children." These sexual judgments had implications beyond insult and shame. One female resident felt that women faced a significant amount of discrimination within the institution, both from staff members and from many of the male residents:

> I think socially there's just more of a stigma. I mean, God forbid you do any hardcore drugs as a woman. If you're a man it's ok if you go out and

> get drunk on the weekend, or drink after work, whereas with women it's as if you're a mother [this woman had no children]. You're not supposed to be drinking. How dare you? . . . Women are just looked at differently. And then they get exploited. . . . There are a lot of them who get into the sex trade and you know. . . . For the rest of your life you're kind of marked. And especially here because all the guys here just assume that you're prey. They assume that you're exactly the way you were on the street.

The emphasis upon policing (hetero)sexuality took on institutionalized forms as well. Despite what might seem like significant social distance between compulsive drug-taking and gender expression and sexuality, the program reinforced the importance of these concerns through a strict gendering of the social space within the institution. One floor was established for women's rooms, with others for men. While a separation of sleeping areas and bathrooms might well be expected, it was notable that certain stairwells were similarly set-aside for women and men, respectively, in order to preclude the possibility of mixed-gender encounters within them. Women and men were not allowed to talk to one another unless a third party was present, purportedly in order to prevent sexual or romantic discussions from taking place. Women and men also sat separately during daily house meetings, though many of the facilitated groups were mixed-gender. In many ways, the facility was thus socially divided and even mapped in terms of prohibitions on heterosexuality (an injunction that created a partial homosocialization of the institution). While these injunctions impacted men as well as women, perhaps half of the residents (both male and female) felt that they were more sharply enforced against women. Said one female resident:

> They say "don't objectify women," but they do. The way in which they respond to us is that we're all whores. . . . When men are reacting a certain way to women—which a lot of these men don't know any other way of interacting with women—it's, "What is it in your behavior that allows him to think he can talk to you like that? You were asking for it." So they put a woman on a speaking ban from a certain man; it's blaming her or targeting her. . . . Immediately, if you spend any amount of time with a guy, you're sleeping with him any chance you get. . . . You know, maybe a lot of these women did work in prostitution, did exchange sex for drugs,

> and have a history of molestation. They have a lot of issues with their sexuality . . . but to then reaffirm that by constantly making the comments that they're making . . .
>
> I asked for a telephone call [the response to such requests is shared in front of the entire group via a note that a staff member reads], and the comment I got was, "It's not Halloween yet, so stop tricking." And they read this in front of a crowd of people, you know, in front of the whole family. And I was like, what am I supposed to do with that? Why was the request that they responded that way? For a phone call. They're just getting their shits and giggles off of stuff like that. And it infuriated me. I was like, that's just despicable. Like if I actually thought there was a purpose to it or it was really going to make you open your eyes, ok. Otherwise, just say no. I'll get the point, you know what I mean? I'll get the message that I've done something wrong and I need to change it, but this kind of degrading. I just didn't understand it. . . .

Signs in drug court waiting areas (in which participants must wait while readying themselves to urinate for their drug tests) similarly evince a double standard, policing a distinctly gendered vision of respectability, one that reinforces the notion that while men need pay attention to only desexualized class attributes, women's sexuality forms a part of her classed status and must be policed in order to ensure class respectability.

Ongoing stigmatization regarding "whorish" behaviors was matched by invocations of failed motherhood. Any woman with a child can be subjected to a sharp reminder of motherhood as a primary identity, as well as their failure to measure up to normative standards. The woman who was asked, "Why don't you just give your daughter away, if that's how it is?" after getting into a shouting match with another resident was far from alone in suffering this sort of taunt. Ironically, for example, the woman who had her visits with her son suspended for smoking in a nondesignated area was also told she was a bad mother: "You're full of shit. You want to walk out over a cigarette. You don't give a fuck about your child. You want to just say forget him for a cigarette." The threat of a termination of parental rights is regularly brought up against women who had children, while I never once heard the threat levied against a man (recall that the man who threw his cane was chastised for "setting a bad example"). Given the ways that CPS relies primarily upon a woman's status in making decisions about child removal, such a threat against a man would have made less sense; hence, it is the combination of conventional norms regarding child care plus subsequent legal discrimination that renders women vulnerable to these forms of shaming while leaving men less exposed.

These discrepancies were not simply the result of prejudicial attitudes among the staff. While biased opinion surely played a role, it struck me that the discriminatory dynamic resulted primarily from exogenous factors. In following a punitive logic that required "driving home" the consequences of drug use, staff members reached for the most profoundly cutting imagery they could find. A point that speaks to their success in finding these shameable sites could be seen in the ways residents sometimes use these same insults against one another. One female resident relayed the conflicts that resulted from the lack of trust and support women had with one another:

> [During one of the group sessions,] S. said that she got called a pot whore by C. She looked at C. and told her to go get an HIV test. . . . I just don't understand how they call each other sluts and whores and tear each other down. As soon as one person leaves the room it's, "Oh, you know what she's doing?" and all this kind of stuff. . . . If you've been high a lot, you've gone through enough fucking stuff already. And a lot of us did behave, you know, promiscuously, and we don't need each other throwing that in our face. . . . I hear women telling other women things like, "That's why they took your fucking kids away from you." You get to the point where you're so angry here that you're lashing out at the people that are supposed to be your support.

Notably, this comment came from one of the women with a middle-class background, someone who had some expectation of mutual support (at least among women) and who therefore noticed its absence. More generally, street norms would dictate that one *not* trust others with whom one has not already established long-term contact and interchange with, leading to these types of pointed exchanges. The familiarity that the staff have with these insults—particularly those staff members who have themselves been involved with street culture—enables them to press upon precisely the most vulnerable points, points that are themselves established within a larger context. In this regard, shaming women as whores or as failed mothers is hardly a surprising result. Meanwhile, men are shamed and humiliated as much as possible; however, certain forms of insult—e.g., calling someone a heterosexist or misogynist slur—are rendered out of bounds because they would invoke a requirement to retaliate. In the absence of an explicit commitment to feminism, these types of rhetorical and structural inequalities result in unequal treatment on the parts of those who administer the extended state apparatus.

The Tolerant TC: Queers in Residential Treatment

While staff members no longer overtly discriminate against queer people in a systematic fashion, the way they did in the early TCs,[35] issues pertaining to institutional bias still exist. As seen above, for example, the treatment center regulates its space in relation to the presumptive needs of hetero-identified individuals, ironically creating a homosocial environment that apparently helped the one openly gay male resident to arrange for a series of surreptitious sexual contacts with straight-identified men in the facility (or so it was rumored among some of the other residents).[36] When I asked the director of the program about homosexuality within this context, given the fact that the facility was decidedly not organized in a way that would prevent same-sex contacts, he said that homosexuality did not create the same sort of "disruptions" as heterosexuality. Same-sex contacts were generally discreet in nature, he explained, and thus did not present the same sort of managerial difficulties in relation to community life. Heterosexual contacts, meanwhile, could readily become public, potentially bringing forth explosive arguments between a couple or involving open jealousies and conflict between multiple individuals. While sexuality was seen as a therapeutic issue in relation to both same-sex and differently-sexed relations—insofar as a normative domesticity was aimed for—heterosexual transgressions were seen as being much more disruptive to the community as a whole, with homosexuality being effectively pre-policed by both internalized homophobia and by the negative prejudices that many residents (and a few staff members) held.

The structuring of social space in relation to presumptively hetero persons reveals, however, the ways in which queer needs were systematically neglected in favor of straight ones, or, said another way, the ways in which the purported needs of straight people were directly catered to while queer people were benevolently "tolerated" as interlopers in an institution not oriented toward them. Programming within the institution, for example, did not address any of the concerns that were specific to at least some of their queer clients, such as using drugs as a means to deal with bigotry or internalized shame, or particular community dynamics concerning anonymous sex and the use of drugs. Queers were likewise expected to participate in counseling groups that included openly hostile or simply ignorant individuals. While issues such as these are generally addressed as matters of *cultural competency* within the TC literature—if even this level of awareness is achieved[37]—it is perhaps more accurate to speak of *institutional bias* given the systematic way in which programming and even the architectural space is directed toward a presumptively heterosexual clientele. State-mandated drug treatment thus is best seen as forming a part of what Margot Canaday refers to as "the straight state."[38]

Nevertheless, even as these biases have resulted in lower success rates for queer individuals (however "success" is defined),[39] the relative tolerance that professionalized TCs have come to show for queer individuals has proven significant for some individuals going through the programs, even as the programs have remained oriented toward a straight-identified clientele. The institution I examined, for example, included two out trans individuals (both MtF), two somewhat closeted lesbian women, and one openly gay man as residents within the facility.[40] While the five sometimes complained about prejudice from other residents, they did not complain about the staff, and one of the trans women in particular, Clarissa, credited her experience at the facility for greatly helping her to accept herself as a woman, partly by putting her in contact with a weekly support group of other trans individuals undergoing treatment:

> That had a lot to do with my addiction, the fact that I was scared to be myself for a lot of my life, and once I did become myself I came across an obstacle course. . . . I've been living as a girl since I was eighteen, but there were times that I had to live as a guy to try to find jobs. . . . I got so tired of it, I said to myself I know there's somewhere I can be myself and not have to worry about discrimination. And I found it here. I found a wonderful network of substance abuse counselors and transgender counselors. I found groups I can attend and, yeah, the way it's been here, I've really found some peace within myself to be myself.

The treatment program also helped Clarissa obtain a doctor's prescription for hormone injections, an enormous concrete benefit not otherwise available through the governmental agencies she had been able to access (previously, she had stolen birth control pills from an employer). While many other queer individuals report significant challenges dealing with the heterosexist biases within the treatment system,[41] the *relative* openness of the staff enabled at least *some* individuals to take advantage of the program in ways that would not have been conceivable in the early days of the TC. At the same time, none of the queer residents felt empowered to bring their complaints about heterosexist bigotry on the part of other residents to the attention of staff members (whether because of norms against snitching for such a "petty" offense, due to the idea that telling staff would have revealed them as "weak" and incapable of handling the situation on their own, or due to the possibility that staff shared those sentiments). For my part, I heard an occasional heterosexist comment from a couple of the staff members, as well as from several of the residents; however, staff comments were voiced only away from residents who were presumed to be queer.[42]

However, while overt forms of antiqueer bigotry were generally somewhat restrained, this does not mean that LGBT individuals in treatment had their specific needs met. While the staff seemed to generally support their queer clients overall, and the bigotries that at least a few of them felt were relatively contained, Clarissa's individual success did not occur due to complete parity within the institution, but rather *despite* ongoing heterosexist biases and individual prejudices. In this regard, it must be noted that the TC's agenda in fostering gender and sexual respectability among its clients poses particular challenges for at least some queer individuals. Queer cultures are, of course, not necessarily oriented toward an enforcement of monogamy, domesticity, and nonflamboyant gender expressions in ways considered respectable, and therefore the demand for monogamy and gender normativity often impacts queer subjects more intensely than it does most straight subjects.[43] The vision of domesticity encouraged or rather demanded by the facility was thus open to lesbian, gay, and trans individuals but only if they were homo- and transnormative. To be sure, this normalizing vision of LGBT life offers some queer individuals exactly the type of support they desire. Clarissa, for example, expressed gratitude that the organization "has given me the chance to tone myself down and to be a woman and not be flamboyant." However, this implicit alliance with homonormative frameworks tacitly pathologized nonnormative sexual and gendered expression as elements of the "drugs lifestyle" that needed treatment. These links remained more implicit than explicit within the program, but it is notable that one social worker expressed his presumption that the gay man who was allegedly sleeping with other men in the institution had an issue with "sex addiction." Unfortunately, this incident occurred at the very end of my fieldwork within the institution, and thus I was unable to see how this situation was ultimately addressed, but it highlights the ways in which a homo- and transnormative vision dominated the institution. This monogamous and gender-normative framework of course applied to heterosexual residents as well, limiting their range of gender and sexual expression, but given the history and current standing of nonnormative practices within queer cultures, it cuts queer individuals off from potentially significant elements of LGBT life. Issues pertaining to domesticity and familialism thus remain strong components of antiqueer institutional bias within the TC, even as questions of overt bias are *somewhat* mitigated.[44]

Crafting Femininity in the Contemporary Women's TC

There is a second model of residential drug treatment for female populations that has its own institutional history and practices. While arising out of the male-dominated TC, women's TCs also modify significant aspects of their approach in an effort to create a "gender sensitive" approach to treatment.[45] These institutional features raise questions as to which women are sent to the women's-only TCs, and which are considered viable candidates for participation in the predominantly male TCs.[46] Discussions with case managers at the drug court revealed that they preferentially sent women with sexual abuse histories to the women's-only facilities. The automatic diversion of women who have suffered sexual abuse—while potentially helpful in some cases—points toward a presumptive logic that stigmatizes abuse survivors by automatically treating them as "damaged goods."[47] Less problematically, women who requested such a placement, whether due to having found prior experiences with mixed-gender TCs onerous or any other concern, were also generally accommodated and sent to women's-only programs.

While I did not conduct ethnographic research within contemporary women's TCs, a small collection of studies conducted by other researchers offers a view into their functioning, enabling some possibility for further exploration into the gendering of addiction treatment for populations with a criminal justice mandate. In order to better compare the ways in which these facilities operate in relation to the traditional, male-oriented TCs, I rely primarily upon descriptions and analysis from Lynn Haney (who studied a program she names Visions),[48] Jill McCorkel (who studied Project Habilitate Women, or PHW),[49] and Allison McKim (who examined Women's Treatment Services, or WTS),[50] further supplementing their insights with observations from other scholars doing work on this topic. In general, it has been noted by many scholars that drug use is seen as counter to femininity.[51] While this issue was certainly present within male-dominanted facilities, Haney, McCorkel, and McKim's research shows that questions of normative femininity seem to be heightened within women's-only TCs. Furthermore, "gender-responsive" programming as currently practiced tends to focus on these issues in ways that often neglect the immediate, practical concerns faced by women in these circumstances.

Women's TCs often place significant emphasis on a discourse of "personal empowerment," making their rhetoric sound significantly different from conventional TCs. According to one advocate, Christine Grella, this approach involves "supportive approaches" rather than "confrontational approaches," promoting a greater focus on "identifying and building upon a woman's strengths, such as her nurturing and relational capacities."[52] Yet this model of women's empowerment within mandated treatment programs has also been criticized by feminists as simply a form of penal control.[53] Another difficulty with women's treatment programs is that in practice the supportive elements of the women's TC seem few and far between. As was seen in relation to modified TCs in the prior chapter, the initial Synanon model was so extreme that a program could become significantly less confrontational and still remain very controlling and punitive.

Lynne Haney explores the living conditions within a women's therapeutic community (comparing it to an earlier institution devoted to ending women's dependence on welfare). Haney's ethnography reveals that although the TC's institutional rhetoric proclaimed itself a "real community free of control and force,"[54] in fact the staff instituted many of the same techniques of social control found in other TCs. The TC she describes, for example, featured mutual surveillance among all residents (here known as an element of "sisterhood" instead of as a feature of "responsible concern"), as well as a practice in which all house activities were put on "freeze" (what Haney describes as "collective solitary confinement") when rule-breaking was deemed to have escalated.[55] As at the facility I examined, Haney writes that: "All of these women were fully aware of the rewards of snitching—from feeling like a staff insider to gaining special house privileges to having their own rule violations ignored."[56] Counselors furthermore held enormous power over the residents *and their children*, deciding based upon their progress whether a resident would be returned to jail or if and when they would see their children again.[57] Haney also details the way in which the women's TC turns the effects of social injustice into a personal pathology,[58] and the ways in which therapy is turned into a prison that links therapeutic intervention to a hierarchical exercise of power.[59]

While Haney does not describe counselors yelling at the residents, nor any incident such as the one I witnessed in which the residents' rooms were ransacked, a heightened emphasis on emotional revelation and self-display arguably turned the women's-only facility into a more coercive environment, even as it was perhaps gentler in other ways. While the male-dominant TC that I examined tended to emphasize behavioral controls and "accountability" as being central to recovery, the women's TC demanded significantly more introspective work on the part of its residents, with public confession being a nonnegotiable element. Haney reports that residents complained frequently to her about being forced to participate in therapeutic activities,[60] something I did not hear from any residents at the modified TC I examined, where even those residents who viewed the TC as simply a lighter alternative to prison found that they could participate more or less as they wished in the one-on-one and group counseling sessions. The demand for therapeutic "openness" generated its own problems that the staff members did not sufficiently counter. Haney writes:

> Because of the constant public exposure, the inmates knew a tremendous amount about their sisters' problems and traumas. So when fights broke out, the inmates had a huge psychological arsenal to draw on; they knew exactly what buttons to push and the fastest way to access them. Even the smallest quarrel could escalate into an all-out psychological war,

implicating everything from the combatants' emotional weaknesses to their histories of deception to their criminal behavior.[61]

While conflicts between residents provided justification for the staff's assertion that the women needed treatment, Haney argues that the conflicts were a direct result of the model of "recovery" the institution practiced.[62] I might add that the structure of the TC is explicitly designed to turn residents against one another through "sisterhood" or "responsible concern" (the TC frames this as working for one another, of course, but makes little effort to counter the traumatizing aspects of these attacks).

A similar set of dynamics seemed even more intense at the women's-only facility examined by Jill McCorkel. There, staff members often called residents "crack hos," "lowdown addicts," and "dirty old dogs" who need to "tighten the fuck up."[63] McCorkel's study, which examined a prison-based TC, found a program emphasizing a high level of "shame," "honesty," and "discomfort" in an effort at "breaking down addiction."[64] Encounter groups derived from Synanon's game were considered foundational within the program, a fact that emphasizes the (coercively) emotive focus of the treatment regimen. Aspects of punitiveness were played up rather than down within the facility McCorkel examined, a factor that enabled it to operate within the "get-tough" environment of the prison.[65] Beyond expecting every women to surveil every other, signs were placed around the facility: "Everywhere You Go, Everything You Do, the Eyes Are Always Watching You."[66] As one of inmates said, "Like they say, there are no friends in treatment."[67] Given the fact that emotionality was often as much at issue as the behavioral rules, this surveillance extended into realms often considered "private." As McCorkel comments, "The surveillance networks gave rise to an interaction order in which any and all thoughts, feelings, and behaviors were potentially knowable to everyone within the community."[68] The program similarly worked much harder than did the one I examined to break down all bonds between the inmates "because they regarded the friendship dyad as having the potential to usurp the program's control apparatus."[69]

According to the staff's logic, close relations with peers jeopardize surveillance, since friends will be less likely to report one another for subversive thoughts and behaviors. To prevent the formation of friendships

> and other types of intimate relations, staff went to great lengths to force friends to confront one another for misdeeds. This appeared to be largely successful.[70]

This "prison within a prison," as the inmates often referred to it,[71] thus applied many of the TC's features to its maximum intensity—levels significantly beyond those I witnessed—all in the name of "gender-specific" programming that would address women's "unique" treatment needs.[72]

Though the dynamics of prison certainly exacerbate the TC's coerciveness, the combined focus on emotionality and elements of feminist rhetoric seems to mark the contemporary women's TC. Allison McKim's study of a women's TC with residents mandated through criminal justice further highlights this shared pattern.[73] As in the traditional TC and the TC Haney examined, women were told "you are your sister's keeper" and expected to enforce the facility's rules and to challenge one another when infractions occur. Beyond this, the TC relied on punitive chores, drug testing, confrontational groups, collective punishments, and wearing signs with messages designed to shame, with labels such as "thief" or "liar" (however, while McKim heard about such signs, they were used infrequently enough that she did not herself witness their use).

As with Haney's observations, McKim notes that an emotive focus was a key feature within the facility, with residents facing what McKim describes as a practice of "coerced confession."[74]

> Staff members expected clients to get gut-level in nearly all groups at WTS, including didactic sessions (e.g. the parenting class) and vocational groups. Clients should be ready to disclose at nearly any moment. This constant level of emotional exposure is painful and exhausting, so some women only pretended to get gut-level, and the staff members policed clients' disclosures for authentic emotions. This made confession obligatory, continuous, and public. As I slipped into the back of the "Getting' Honest" group, the crowded room was going over a sheet about family patterns and discussing how families pass on substance abuse. Counselor Linda asked Jenea, a young black woman, to talk. With a set jaw and hostile tone, Jenea mumbled something vague about her mother's death. Linda jumped in and loudly chastised her, "Jenea! Stop being gangsta and *feel* this!" Other women in the group laughed. [75]

Confrontations such as the above sometimes worked—Jenea responded to Linda's challenge by revealing much more about her need to be "tough"—but the combination of being one's sister's keeper and coerced confession also produced opportunities for intensely emotional conflict. Echoing McCorkel's observation about making friends, a counselor at the facility told a resident, "Where did you get the idea you were here to make friends? . . . There are no friends in treatment."[76] McKim continues:

> Because of the pervasive surveillance and the way clients were pitted against each other, living at WTS could be volatile and treacherous. Several clients complained to me about how they didn't trust fellow clients. . . . The complete lack of privacy accentuated the punitive aspects of treatment.[77]

McKim carefully observes that the feeling rules that WTS required were not always clear to participants, a feature that again distinguishes the women's TC from those the one I observed (where the system of peer policing pertained primarily to behavioral infractions). As McKim notes, "it was not always easy to determine what kinds of emotional hurts sufficed and whether clients were confessing every dark part of their past. So counselors often pushed women to raise the stakes of their confessions."[78] Haney notes a similar dynamic:

> With few objective indicators of when an inmate had "gone deep," the audience's reaction to her became critical. So the extent to which a confession provoked tears, shock, or anguish in those hearing it was an indication of its power and depth. Among other things, this resulted in an insidious competition among the inmates: Whose lives were the most shocking? Whose stories were the most lurid? In this competition, the worst outcome was to tell a chapter in one's life to the uninterested faces of the staff and sisters.[79]

While a market for sensationalist stories was thus created, on a different level, the nature of the emotional disclosure in women's programs focused on a rather limited number of topics and seems to have become somewhat scripted. Following what has been termed a "trauma-informed approach,"[80] many women's programs have emphasized the issue of childhood sexual abuse. While creating needed space to discuss these issues, the focus has sometimes overshadowed other issues. As E. Summerson Carr notes in relation to her study of a drug treatment facility working with women in public housing:

> Some clients suggested that in order to meet their therapists' implicit demands, they had to connect their drug use to early sexual abuse, as few other plot lines were considered legitimate. As one former client attested: "You *got* to be abused there, or they start thinkin' there be somethin' wrong with *you*."[81]

Representations of sexual abuse have arguably been a double-edged sword within feminist discourse. While highlighting the violence of (male) power within the family, discussion has also often continued sexist practice in portraying victims of abuse as inherently "broken."[82]

The focus on emotionality within women's-only TCs seems to provoke different types of resistance than those I witnessed at the predominantly male facility where I conducted the bulk of my research. Haney, for example, found that the demand for emotional responsiveness left many clients "emotionally numb," a form of resistance that Haney identifies as originating from a need to expose the self in a frequently hostile environment.[83] Instead of "going deep," Haney found that the women in the program developed premade scripts that they could call upon as needed:

> In groups, I rarely saw an inmate struggle to come to terms with her past. Instead, most seemed to respond to the staff's calls to "go deep" by pushing a button to play a recording of what was expected of them. The recordings even appeared to be catalogued. Some buttons led to specific topics, such as substance abuse, family violence, or sexual assault; others led to an emotion, such as outrage, hurt, or remorse. The repetitive nature of the staff's requests only enhanced the recorded quality of the inmates' responses, forcing the women to replay the tape several times a week. It also led the women to appear numb to some horrific experiences—from gang rapes to suicide attempts to drug overdoses to incest.[84]

Other inmates withdrew into what Haney describes as "a state of semiconsciousness," either using prescribed drugs to medicate themselves, or "using every chance they could to exit into a slumber."[85] The women McCorkel engaged with developed an alternative strategy that was nevertheless focused on this omnipresent and intensely hostile process of emotional confession: "rentin' out your head."[86]

The emotional intimacy of the confrontations within the women's TC rendered it more akin to the older Synanon model, but while Synanon was a voluntary organization that presumably encountered lower levels of resistance, the contemporary TC operates hand-in-hand with the coercive power of the state, generating new forms of both coercion and resistance. The women's TC seems an especially ironic instance of this, given its utilization of some feminist rhetorics. Indeed, none of these outcomes, in which residents were put in situations in which they had to continually present their personal narratives, were apparent at the organization I examined. The masculinist orientation on behavior rather than emotion seemed to mitigate against these types of encounters, creating an organization that was itself "masculinized" in terms of the expectations it maintained and the techniques it deployed. Women at the predominantly male facility I examined did have a weekly women's-only group that focused more on disclosing past hurts, but as a once-a-week event that was run on a voluntary basis (one had to ask to join) the dynamics were far less coercive.[87]

Nevertheless, beyond the emotional intrusiveness of such programs, the "gender sensitivity" of these programs appears as a focus on the attainment of conventional femininity as a mark of recovery, emerging with even greater intensity than in the mixed-sex facility I examined. Issues pertaining to motherhood, sexual respectability, and "co-dependency" were prevalent in various ways at all three of the women's-only facilities.[88] Both Haney and McCorkel, for example, write that accusations of "bad mothering" were both frequent and particularly painful during conflicts between residents.[89] At the same time, Haney found that pleasure in motherhood was rendered as a sign of emotional health and recovery, while "inmates who felt conflicted about their children were told they were acting out their sickness."[90] In a program where three-quarters of the women had children, not only were women frequently criticized as "unfit mothers," but insofar as drug use rendered their parenting illegitimate, motherhood came to be seen as "a contrivance, something done to manipulate others for selfish and ulterior purposes."[91] McCorkel notes that the theme of drug-addicted women abusing their children was raised more than any other, not only in efforts to "break the women down," but also in an effort to justify the need for a women's-only program to prison officials.[92]

While "good mothering" was thus emphasized to participants, its role in treatment was somewhat contradictory. McKim found that the facility she examined both discursively highlighted and heavily regulated the issue: "The belief was that caring for others was not only a trait associated with women's addiction, caring for others while in treatment prevented caring for the self. As a result, mothering, in particular, posed threat to women's recovery."[93] Women in these programs were thus not allowed significant contact with their children until counselors deemed their personal narratives to be adequate, placing an enormous weight upon compliance with this vague and difficult-to-define goal. In this regard, court-supervised drug treatment enacts many of the same contradictions that women face within society more generally where one's own needs are often set against the needs of mothering.[94] Here, however, the needs for "self-development" are externally defined, and the stakes for those who fail to successfully navigate these conflicts involve extended imprisonment and the probable loss of custody over one's children.

While interactions pertaining to LGBT issues were far from perfect within the male-oriented institution I examined, they seem to be even worse within many of the "gender-responsive" institutions that have been studied. The situation in the prison-based TC that McCorkel examined seems particularly oppressive in this regard. As she writes:

> There was no other bit of information about prisoners that drew the attention and focus of the counselors more than reports of sexual relations or romantic overtures between women. In the privacy of staff offices and during get-togethers outside the institution, such information was always met with one or more expressions of disgust and disapproval (e.g., "That's disgusting," "These women are crazy," "Don't leave me alone with her—she may jump me," "It gives me the creeps to know what they're doing").
>
> When staff learned of liaisons or romances between prisoners, they staged fairly lengthy, public confrontations of the sort described previously. Over the course of my participation in the setting, there was no other behavior or rule violation, including violence, that drew so much attention and intervention from staff. During the confrontations,

> counselors cultivated expressions of outrage and condemnation from other prisoners to drive home the point that expressions of same-sex desire were, from the perspective of program ideology, inauthentic and deviant representations of the self.[95]

McCorkel's description perhaps represents an extreme, but Haney similarly notes that program participants were encouraged to report others having illicit sexual encounters with one another,[96] and that at least one woman was ejected from the program because she periodically "hooked up" with new residents.[97] McKim likewise comments on the way that counselors speculated about a woman's "gender identity crisis" and presumed gayness or bisexuality because her clothing style shifted from "butch" to "femme" and back again (a lesbian counselor eventually pointed out to other staff that the woman's clothing choices meant little as they were limited to the options she could find in the facility's donated clothing stash).[98] While the TC I examined produced a relatively "tolerant" (if not fully equal) environment for queer participants, the presumed feminism of women's TCs has not necessarily worked to eliminate their gender normativity and heterosexism.[99]

Very importantly, and in contrast to the facilities oriented toward men, women's institutions also seem to have a much more tenuous connection with programs such as job training and educational aid, precisely because "recovery" is deemed to be psychological in nature, having little to do with such practical considerations. The program that Haney studied, for example, offered no job training nor educational benefits whatsoever. This absence was a point of significant conflict within the facility:

> The inmates complained vociferously about these gaps in the program, claiming that they needed far more "practical help"; or, as Chanel put it, "Give us the shit we'll need in the real world." Whenever the inmates raised these issues, the staff countered that they were receiving longer-lasting help at Visions [the false name Haney gave to the institution she studied]. Jane, the facility director, always responded to such arguments by telling the inmates that if they wanted practical skills, they should have stayed in prison. "You can get education and job training at Valley State," she would remark. "Would you like to go back? We help you to get better, to recover, and to deal with your concerns and stresses."[100]

Similarly, the program offered no legal services despite the fact that many of the residents had questions regarding welfare regulations or concerning their criminal or child protective custody cases. Haney reports that "Whenever the women asked for these services, they were told they had 'deeper' issues to address first."[101]

While the facility McKim studied did offer such programming, like Haney's program, it emphasized introspection and mutual confession in its approach, viewing a job "as something clients were not ready for until they had built up a therapeutic self-understanding."[102] McCorkel similarly notes that "Prisoners were expected to prioritize dealing with their addictions over their education and job training because, as the PHW director put it, 'without habilitation there is nothing. You cannot educate or train an addict and expect that it will pay off in terms of economic independence.' "[103] In this regard, McKim notes that "most studies find that gender-responsive programs deemphasize women's material needs and instead emphasize therapeutic work on the self."[104] The women's-only TCs thus viewed the explication of abuse and the production of a psychologizing account of self as essential work that *must* be accomplished prior to participation in either work or motherhood, a contrast with male-oriented TCs that follow Synanon in emphasizing work (chores) and self-discipline from the outset.

McKim argues that these efforts were ultimately limited in their capacity to effect change for the women. "The process of habilitation actively sought to undermine women's existing identities while replacing it with an identity that had, by definition, no social supports at all—the perfectly autonomous woman. Especially with limited access to careers, pervasive racism, and the stigma of a criminal record, the women at WTS were left with little but introspection, consumption, and makeovers to build a new self."[105] Beyond this, McKim argues that the emphasis on "penal makeovers" and emotional confession led to a significant contradiction to the expectations of drug courts which, as seen above, demand formal labor as a sign of recovery from those it controls. Women at the women's-only facility are thus placed at a systematic disadvantage in relation to getting through drug court insofar as the facility raised additional requirements that had to be met prior to obtaining a job. To be sure, a resident also had to be doing well within the male-oriented programs before those facilities would allow anyone to obtain outside employment; however, the meaning of "doing well" within those predominantly male institutions focuses primarily upon behavioral compliance, whereas the facility McKim examined required both an absence of behavioral infractions *and* particular sorts of emotive performances. Thus, the women's-only facilities that delay or even eliminate such trainings seem to place additional burdens upon residents in such programs before they can graduate from the court and remove the heightened levels of state supervision and control that the drug court entails. However problematic the emphasis on formal labor may be within predominantly male programs, the failure to emphasize it within a context that requires formal labor in order to succeed can put women in these "gender-responsive" institutions at a significant disadvantage. Thus, while women-only facilities may successfully address certain aspects of women's subordination within conventional treatment models, in some areas they can replicate or even exacerbate the gendered disadvantages faced by women.[106]

Gender, Privatization, and the Intimacies of the State

As seen above, issues pertaining to gender and sexuality continue to have great relevance within drug treatment, even as their importance is obscured through a medicalizing rhetoric. While the state mandates that people attend these programs, the role of gender and sexuality remains largely invisible to most state actors. The institutional structure establishes a dynamic that differs slightly from the way that Foucault describes biopolitical action, and it sheds light on both the particularities of these state functions and the stakes of gender and sexuality within governance. Foucault, for example, famously argues that sexuality (and we might add gender) becomes an important topic because it mixes two forms of biopolitical control: those related to control over the population at large and those related to control over individual behavior.[107] Foucault further suggests that these two axes of power "were not to be joined at the level of a speculative discourse, but in the form of concrete arrangements (*agencements concrets*) that would go to make up the great technology of power in the nineteenth century."[108] Drug courts and their associated treatment programs offer a detailed window into one of these *agencements concrets*, further revealing the ways in which neoliberal approaches to privatization shape its relationship to gender and sexuality.

In this regard, the drug court can be said to consist of three distinct components: the court itself, the (generally private) treatment programs to which it refers its participants, and—standing at something of a distance—the social scientists who, working on behalf of the state, evaluate the courts based upon their cost-effectiveness. Of these three branches, only the privatized treatment programs have an explicit focus upon the issues concerning gender and sexuality. The drug court itself focuses primarily on the issue of (a formally degendered notion of) work, using its case managers to perform drug tests and to make sure that participants are fulfilling their mandates, but more generally relying upon the reports of the treatment staff in evaluating people.[109] The social scientists doing cost-benefit analyses, for their part, focus on the issue of recidivism, and as we have seen, go so far as to refer to the process of treatment as a black box about which they know nothing. While a few of the court's case managers had been through drug treatment programs of the sort to which they now referred people, in general it was remarkable how little court professionals knew about the treatment programs they utilized so regularly. And indeed, while the professionals working with the court would undoubtedly hear stories of the programs from participants, it was in fact very difficult to gain a true sense of how the programs worked without going through the program oneself. One of the judges who worked with the drug court, for example, made a point to visit each of the programs to which she assigned participants. Over a period of several years, she had visited more than fifty treatment programs, yet she was nevertheless surprised to hear some points of basic information I offered her about the programs (the ways in which "responsible concern" operated, for example). Despite her good intentions and the amount of time she had devoted to the project, it seemed to me that the many visits she had taken had yielded dozens of tours that all explained the programs from a TC perspective, leaving her without any sense as to what these practices might concretely look like.

So whereas Foucault argues that sexuality becomes an important tool of governance because it mixes two forms of biopolitical control—those related to control over the population at large and those related to control over individual behavior—here those interested in control at the level of the population express no direct interest in gender or sexuality whatsoever. Their one point of evaluation concerns the issue of recidivism and subsequent cost-effectiveness. And yet, in establishing this privatized form, the state creates the opportunity for local groups—moral entrepreneurs who often have deep familiarity with the local community—to innovate ways to deliver that final outcome. In effect, the private groups use the issues of gender and sexuality to sell the state something that it really wants: a population that is more tightly controlled by the labor regime than by a prison regime, even in the absence of decent jobs. These private moral entrepreneurs thus sell a vision of respectable gender and sexuality to participants; meanwhile, the formal parts of the state remain effectively unaware within this arrangement that they are even purchasing something that has to do with gender and sexuality. Discipline is largely managed through the organization of gender and sexuality via privatized channels, while the court merely supervises the disciplinary process (adding its own threats as needed). Biopolitical power at the level of the population remains largely disconnected from both the court and the treatment centers.

In this sense, the privatized structure creates greater opportunities for local groups to use their intimate knowledge of community mores to more effectively inflict psychic costs for behaviors that are disapproved by the state, precisely by attaching those behaviors to more intimate sets of meaning related to gender and sexuality (it is important to remember in this regard that many drug counselors come from the same communities as their clients and are thus able to draw upon a shared vocabulary of norms and aspirations). These privatized programs are thus much more violently intimate at a psychic level than most historical examples of rehabilitative programs that were administered by a centralized state. The process of "making things real" draws upon a discourse of gender and sexuality that is not simply imposed from the outside, but one that elaborates upon the gender and sexed discourses that many of the participants themselves already share.[110]

Not only are these privatized programs better able to effectively shame participants, they also seem to be more effective at appealing to participants in a more positive sense, precisely through their invocation of gender and sexual mores to which the participants themselves have some adherence (e.g., drawing upon the idea that drug abstinence and sexual respectability go together).[111] While the state focuses primarily on work as a sign of proper citizenship, counselors establish ad hoc sets of meaning to bring these work-related behaviors into better alignment with the aims of their clients. Even the women's-only programs do this to an extent, despite their lack of emphasis on formal labor (if they did not accomplish this aim, the courts would cease offering them referrals). As Hannah-Moffat argues in relation to discourses of "women's empowerment" within penal settings, this is an approach that seeks to "make links between the aspirations of individuals and those of government," creating "prudent subjects . . . for whom the ethic of discipline is part of their mental fabric and not a product of external policing,"[112] yet here it does so without even gaining knowledge as to the links it is forming. The formally neutral "know-nothing" state is thus able to establish a treatment regime that is intimately aware of issues of gender and sexuality, even as it appears to be unconcerned with such issues. In this respect, and within this context, privatization facilitates practices that are indeed more responsive to local conditions, just as some politically conservative advocates of privatization argue.[113]

In contrast, the new forms of biopolitical practice—i.e., the "evidence-based practices" that the state develops through statistical measurement—tend to engage the psyche in only superficial ways (think, for example, of the cognitive-behavioral identification of "triggers"). The requirement that procedures be standardized in developing statistical measures of evidence virtually ensures that approaches requiring improvisational engagement with a participant's idiosyncratic and variable senses of self are ruled inadmissible from the outset.[114] Here, in this financialized realm of cost-benefit analyses and statistically evaluated "best practices," *the addict* is essentially degendered and reduced to a number within an equation. Spillers sees a similar process in relation to African Americans, one where domination by a financial regime left slaves ungendered.[115] Within the confines of the treatment center, however, and to a lesser extent within the drug court, participants are very much gendered, however this gender is identified as deviant and in need of correction. Residents are thus placed in a position of forced tutelage, one where nonnormative embodiments of gender are linked to drug use and subjected to discipline and control.[116] The state-NGO apparatus variously treats "addicts" as degendered numbers or as highly gendered in different institutional moments as it sees fit.

While there may be some advantages—if they can be called that (given that what we are talking about is the institution's ability to utilize local mores in order to better shame participants)—in privatized arrangements, this arrangement is far from actual democratic control. This form of public-private partnership remains governed by the needs of the state, which not only regulates the facilities and the types of training that counselors receive but also establishes the definitions for program success (offering ongoing referrals only to programs that achieve the court's ends). The managerial centrality of criminal justice within this particular schema ensures that any welfarist benefits will follow a security-centric logic: as seen earlier, rates of recidivism have become key to state measures of success. The goals and aims of participants are systematically subordinated within this structure precisely due to the coercion of the criminal justice system, leaving them subject not only to tactics (such as shaming) that are problematic at best but to the enforcement of priorities and goals that are not necessarily meaningful to participants. This dynamic was particularly visible in relation to the small handful of middle-class clients within the program, all of whom were consistently critical of the treatment program, both for being overly punitive and for not addressing their perceived needs (via a greater focus on talk therapy and a lesser emphasis upon behavioral control, for example). Even many people who had heavy involvement with the street—arguably the individuals for whom the programs were designed—often had sharp critiques, as we have seen. The situation differs greatly from voluntary programs, even ones dealing with impoverished drug users.[117] What privatization means in the context of a public-private partnership is not a practice that "empowers" participants in the sense of giving them actual power over their situations, but rather an arrangement designed to generate profit from governmental services while maintaining centralized control over essential functions (such as in defining "treatment success").[118]

The argument of privatization advocates is that it creates possibilities for entrepreneurs to meet governmental criteria with potentially greater awareness of local conditions than a heavily bureaucratized governmental institution would be able to manage. While true in a limited sense, such a question evades the more central question, that of power. Instead of providing resources and structures that participants themselves seek, the drug court apparatus maintains state control while distributing public monies on a for-profit basis. In exchange, the state receives a certain amount of flexibility (it can reduce its referral rate without having to concern itself with the possible consequences in terms of lost jobs, effectively dispersing any concerns for the welfare of its indirect labor force to privatized entities). Perhaps more importantly, however, privatization allows the state to redistribute accountability. As seen in chapter 4, drug courts rely on facilities that regularly engage in practices that raise even prosecutors' concerns regarding cruel and unusual punishment. If the state itself engaged in these practices—forcing people to wear signs, keeping them awake for therapeutic sessions that lasted more than twenty-four hours at a stretch, forcing people to dig their own graves, shaming them in front of other participants by reading their diaries—it seems much more likely that scandalous news headlines would erupt.[119] With privatization, the state not only creates a situation in which it can claim little knowledge concerning treatment practice, it also outsources its responsibilities for care, at least to a significant extent. In this respect, privatization involves a redistribution of accountability away from the state.[120] Privatization in this sense is simply a restructuring of bureaucratic state control, rather than its dismantling (as is promised) or its democratization (as is actually needed).

This same restructuring of accountability occurs within the treatment centers themselves. In designing "community as method," the TC does all it can to make residents enforce rules on each other, effectively "deputizing" participants and turning them into agents of the court.[121] Particularly when residents are encouraged to confront one another or to impose penalties on one another, this constitutes a means of imposing punishment for which the state offers little oversight or means of appeal (as such interventions are "therapeutic" in nature, they are not subject to the usual controls). Here again, accountability has been off-loaded from the institution onto the assembled "community," where the institutional rewards arguably push people toward "antisocial" behaviors that favor one's own standing within the program over any sort of genuine assessment concerning the needs of one's peers.

Meanwhile, though the literature on therapeutic jurisprudence pays great attention to the supposedly intimate role of judges within their wards' lives (with the judge allegedly becoming a parental figure, as noted in chapter 2), this seems more like wish fulfillment on the part of at least some commentators than a reality. In fact, I did not hear a single participant—even those enthusiastic about drug court—offer such an analogy. While the literature praises the closeness of drug court judges, and indeed their role is more intimate than in the traditional court, it is nevertheless their distance which is most noticeable. This distance facilitates the drug court's own lack of accountability, its own inability to recognize the harms its version of *caring violence* imposes. But if the court holds its wards at arm's length, the intimacies of the state are forcibly imposed within the privatized rehabilitation complex. Here, the day-to-day shouting and shaming practices of counselors combines with a careful channeling of residents' anger toward one another, bringing participants into a violently intimate relationship with the veiled power of the state. The emotional brutality of this structure is officially frowned upon by state regulators but in practice ignored.

6

Retrenchment and Reform in the War on Drugs

Drug courts and the therapeutic communities that work closely with them raise a series of issues at practical, political, and theoretical levels. Perhaps not surprisingly, I find that both institutions are fundamentally structured by their role in a punitive form of racialized poverty management, and that they therefore offer inadequate approaches to problematic forms of drug use. Such a judgment, however, leaves behind questions pertaining to ways in which we might better address the issues of both criminal justice reform and the many different patterns of problematic—and sometimes not-so-problematic—patterns of drug use misleading referenced through the same term: addiction. Though both drug courts and therapeutic communities (TCs) are far from ideal, I argue that there are elements within each institution that merit engagement rather than outright rejection. Such programs offer genuine opportunities and therefore have many enthusiastic participants, even while others may suffer unnecessarily as a result of numerous shortcomings. Rather than simply rejecting drug courts as seductive yet counterproductive, and TCs as poor therapeutic practice—tempting as those options are—I argue that we might instead comb through the models each institution utilizes to see what elements might be salvageable within a reformulated framework. After detailing these possibilities for reform, I consider what the rise of drug courts and TCs signifies about larger trends related to the governance of racialized poverty. Before doing so, however, it is necessary to examine the somewhat equivocal status of drug courts within even more radical efforts at challenging ongoing systems of racialized mass incarceration.

Judging Drug Courts

In 2009, New York State significantly amended the notorious Rockefeller Drug Laws that had effectively set a nationwide standard regarding the meaning of being tough on drugs since their establishment in 1973. The Drug Law Reform Act (DRLA) of 2009 reduced the sentencing requirements for certain drug crimes and further established a Judicial Diversion Program—drug courts—on a statewide basis. While the *New York Times* reported that this meant the outright repeal of the Rockefeller Laws,[1] activists greeted the news with a mixture of feelings ranging from cautious optimism to cynical dismissal. The Drug Policy Alliance welcomed the change, saying, "New York could actually become a national leader. . . . We're going in a public health direction here. We're making that turn, and that's what's significant."[2] The New York Civil Liberties Union (NYCLU) vacillated as to whether the reform actually constituted "repeal" of the Rockefeller Laws, but nevertheless "applauded" the reform as "a significant step."[3] The advocacy group Drop the Rock also offered an even more guarded appraisal, claiming that: "This is not the end of the Rockefeller Drug Laws, [but] if we have anything to do with it, it will be the beginning of the end."[4] Meanwhile, one of the activists who had been most involved in the struggle to reform the Rockefeller drug laws, Randy Credico, did not greet the news happily, fearing that the change "creates the illusion that the problem has been solved, and makes it that much more difficult to revisit the issue." In his words, "They came up with an agreement to get people to stop complaining. . . . It's not sweeping. It's misleading advertising. These guys may as well be selling used cars."[5] "What remains untouched is the basic punishment structure of the laws," adds the journalist Jennifer Gonnerman. "Selling only one bag of heroin or one vial of crack still qualifies as a B felony."[6]

In the years since New York passed the DLRA of 2009, both the guarded hopes and the doubtful concerns expressed by these groups seem to have been confirmed. As drug courts became a statewide initiative, the number of people being incarcerated for drug crimes has indeed declined; but given that the numbers were already declining prior to the DLRA, it is difficult to know the extent to which the new law impacted the situation.[7] Even prior to the DLRA, New York State already had 170 drug courts operating throughout the state, as well as other sorts of diversion programs, so the change only involved the creation of six new courts.[8] However, as the activists in Drop the Rock point out, many of the mandatory minimums first established by Rockefeller still stand, even if some have been lowered.[9] More generally, as I have argued throughout this book, the ongoing reliance on police and arrest in an effort to control and manage populations that are largely excluded from the labor market indicates that the shift at stake is one of tactics *within* the so-called war on crime, not a cessation of hostilities. While seeming to mitigate these effects by offering drug treatment instead of imprisonment, the particular arrangements involved in most drug courts work to actually intensify punishments for the half of participants who are most marginalized, additionally raising the possibility that even more people will be brought into the criminal justice system's orbit (i.e., *net widening*), particularly in relation to juvenile cases.[10]

While it is understandable that many activist groups welcomed the 2009 reforms (particularly as they involved not only the statewide establishment of *judicial diversion* (i.e., court supervised drug treatment) but also the lowering of mandatory minimums on some drug crimes), greater experience with drug courts has led a number of organizations—including the National Association of Criminal Defense Lawyers, the Justice Policy Institute, the Drug Policy Alliance, the Canadian HIV/AIDS Legal Network, the New York Academy of Medicine, Physicians for Human Rights, and the Open Society Foundation—to issue critical reports concerning their operations.[11] As a strategy of reform, drug courts leave much of the existing criminal justice system intact, including ongoing police intervention (of a sort that targets areas of concentrated racialized poverty), lengthy sentences for nonviolent crimes, and a control-oriented prison system with few services. As position papers from the National Association of Drug Court Professionals (NADCP) make clear, without these three elements, drug courts cannot bring large numbers of people into the criminal justice system, cannot coerce people into treatment, and cannot threaten people as they undergo treatment. Instead of seeking to end the racial- and class-based policing strategies that has led to a five-fold increase in the imprisonment rate since 1973, those advocating drug courts accept heightened levels of policing while trumpeting the idea that those caught up within such oversized nets will benefit from the transaction (in that they will receive benign-sounding *treatment*).

To highlight one of these three critical continuities, the drug court/TC model involves the use of the warehouse prison as a threat (and sometimes an actuality) for use against those who prove recalcitrant to treatment. As discussed in chapter 1, the drug court utilizes this threat in a show of leniency, incarcerating participants for short periods of time as a means of "motivating" them while retaining the power to imprison them for longer periods of time whenever it so desires. The entire therapeutic technique of the court relies on the threat of a punishment that simply should not exist in its current form; people are treated with unnecessary cruelty for brief periods of time as a means of motivating them to avoid further unnecessary cruelty. Rather than critiquing the warehouse prison, the drug court/TC model attempts to deploy the prison to greater effect, giving persons with low-level crimes a taste of the maltreatment they will receive if they do not adopt the personal practices that the court (and the TC) deem necessary. As with the endorsement of ongoing police oppression, the trend toward drug courts signals a move of liberal reformers toward an implicit endorsement of the warehouse prison and an end of efforts to better the treatment of those deemed unredeemable. Drug courts thereby legitimate the creation of an outcaste group, bringing a wide swathe of the mostly poor into its supervisory power, making implicitly racialized assessments as to who constitutes the respectable poor and who constitutes the disrespectable, and locking up the latter. Overall, the use of therapeutic jurisprudence for low-level crimes does more to ensure the continuation of the war on drugs than it does to mitigate the harm caused by that war, hiding the punitive and coercive aspects of its approach behind the promise of beneficent reform.

Though drug courts act in some ways to bring low-level offenders into contact with a variety of services (such as job training) that have otherwise been largely eliminated in the wake of neoliberal restructuring, they do so by relying on and lending legitimacy to more punitive aspects of the criminal justice system. In this regard, the drug court/TC model significantly alters the meaning of therapy, reconstituting punishments as "learning experiences" and transforming the warehouse prison into a therapeutic instrument. While the therapeutic model of introspection and explication of an inner psyche forms its own logic of control, therapeutic process within neoliberal criminal justice places practices of "accountability" at its core, introducing a rhetoric of morality and accounting where one balances transgressions with an equal proportion of punishment. While the new models of treatment have softened the TC to an extent, they have also legitimized coercion within the treatment environment and converted the deliberate infliction of suffering into a therapeutic act. Although the drug courts and their associated TCs do represent something of a shift away from a totalizing punitiveness, the conditions under which drug courts fuse the medical with the penal favor securitization over support. This is rather precisely indicated by David Wexler's term *therapeutic jurisprudence*, in which the *therapeutic* is positioned as an adjective while *jurisprudence* forms the substantive noun. In medicalizing criminal justice, penalty becomes a form of assistance, blotting out the many ways in which the system serves as an instrument of raced and classed oppression. In many ways, this is indeed carceral humanism at its worst.

The claims drug courts make regarding the benign nature of the criminal justice system are therefore intensely problematic at the critical level of political vision. While the precise effects upon activism are debatable, drug courts have the potential to direct attention away from other approaches that better address issues of both racialized mass incarceration and drug misuse, siphoning off energies for criminal justice reform into programs that in fact deepen race- and class-based inequalities. In this sense, the rise of drug courts represents the political entrenchment of conservative approaches to punishment into liberal political culture, a hegemonification of neoliberal securitization. A more genuine alternative in relation to drug policy, on the other hand, would necessarily begin with a thoroughgoing restructuring of the laws that sentence people for drug crimes. Vigorous efforts focused on harm reduction and the development of a more robust public health orientation to the control of currently banned substances—treatment on demand, not treatment when demanded—remain essential, not only in order to better address problematic drug use but as a critical reform within the criminal justice system as a whole.[12] For these reasons, the most appropriate position toward drug courts is to call for their elimination, together with the rest of the war on drugs.

It is thus important to oppose specialty courts for low-level offenses—including other sorts of problem-solving courts as well as drug courts—even as we consider if there are ways in which their model of jurisprudence might be reformulated and redeployed. Overall, perhaps half of the drug court participants I spoke with felt they had benefitted from the program at some level, and a significant minority—perhaps 10 percent of those with whom I spoke—credited the court and its affiliated treatment programs for profoundly positive transformations in their lives, with some saying they would be dead if not for the court and thanking God for their arrests. Even those participants who approached the TC as simply an easier way to do their time saw it as just that: *an easier way to do their time.* While there were a small number of individuals who left residential treatment in favor of prison (due to the "head games" that the TC played), such decisions were relatively few. These favorable assessments of the drug courts and TCs are not to be dismissed, and they challenge those who are critical of the courts to carefully exhume the drug court model for elements that can perhaps be brought forward in a different context.

Penal Welfarism and Penal Abolition

If the central danger of drug courts concerns the way in which they envision drug users as "savage" and necessarily outside of the social community (i.e., inherently criminal and in need of confinement), the chief benefit of drug courts concerns the way in which they offer possibilities for social integration, even if these possibilities are conditional. While drug use and other low-level crimes should ideally be moved out of the criminal justice system entirely, there will continue to be areas in which the court system will remain involved, at least into the foreseeable future. Most relevant to the drug court model is perhaps the issue of drunk driving, where regulatory and adjudication procedures of some sort seem necessary. In this instance, the drug court model might be utilized as an option for someone who agrees to state supervision over treatment in exchange for the right to drive. Key to this effort, however, must be administrative changes within the drug court model to ensure that participants will not be additionally punished for failing to accomplish the court's goals. If drug courts indeed represent a devil's bargain in which the fine print contains qualifiers that render their effects much more harmful than they first appear, then any revival of those models must involve careful attention to such details. Judicial supervision might indeed provide a structure that aids at least some people, but individuals must not be forced to plead guilty in order to participate, nor should penalties for "failure" be assessed. And with some jurisdictions creating "truancy courts" and other innovations that rely on the state system of punishment in order to address mundane social issues, one must ensure that any such innovations do not expand the domain of the criminal justice system, instead channeling offenses away from the court system to whatever extent practicable and toward less controlling modalities (e.g., fines based on a sliding scale, mediation, or complete decriminalization). With these stipulations in mind, however, a less punitive model of drug courts in which participation is more incentivized than coerced might be offered to those who commit a variety of more serious crimes that remain within the scope of the criminal justice system, at least until more thoroughgoing changes can be made.[13]

At a concrete level, the promise of social incorporation has involved the provision of services of various sorts (job training, GED courses, drug treatment, etc.) and implies a return to some version of penal welfarism. In the contemporary moment, the rise of drug courts represents a shift not simply from the punitive to a situation of stratifed punishment that includes penal welfarism for low-level crimes, but toward a condition in which the therapeutic has been thoroughly subordinated to the penal. Carceral welfare and the "corrective" aspects of social control rely heavily on the methodologies of the punitive, retain the carceral close at hand for "corrective failures," and exist only insofar as they can be shown (even if only tenuously) to offer economic efficiencies over and against the purely penal, a logic leading to the disturbing conclusion that only those who would otherwise cost the state money in the form of a prison cell are able to induce the state's assistance. Furthermore, therapeutic jurisprudence programs are presently directed only toward the "non-non-nons" (nonviolent, nonserious, and nonsexual offenders), while an ongoing outside of nondeserving others remains. In this regard, drug courts represent the rise of a new structure of *neoliberal penal welfarism* in which the penal maintains primacy over any welfarist elements. While a more progressive system of carceral welfare should not act as a substitute for a more comprehensive antipoverty policy (occupational, educational, and drug treatment programming should be available on a no-cost basis at any time), voluntary services should be expanded and established on a system-wide basis in an effort to transform the warehouse prison.

Beyond this, there are a number of reforms that, while even more politically difficult to implement, would nevertheless help to respond to the issues that drug courts purportedly address but which are not raised even as long-term goals within the rhetoric proffered by drug court and TC advocates. Part of the issue concerns the way in which the medicalizing language of addiction obscures the social realities that are being addressed, instead framing them solely as individual personality disorders, a lack of self-discipline, or insatiable cravings caused by drugs themselves. In isolating problematic forms of intensive drug use from their social context, the discourse of addiction makes it difficult to think of alternative approaches. At one's boldest, for example, one could envision restructuring economic policy in a way that would produce greater equality amongst the entire population rather than promoting elite wealth. While most drug users do not follow a pathway in which poverty leads to compulsive forms of drug use, an effective jobs program would nevertheless address many of the needs of the poor and would indirectly address some of the problems that can lead to destructive patterns of drug use. Most particularly, a more just economic structure would address many of the concerns raised by drug use in poor and mostly nonwhite communities, the types of drug use that the criminal justice system addresses most regularly. Keeping such politically ambitious possibilities in mind not only reminds us of the fundamentally social nature of "addiction"—in this case, as the medicalization of adaptive responses to poverty as a "drugs lifestyle"—but can also help to generate alternative interventions. Harm reduction activists, for example, have created a housing-first model that significantly reduces the harms associated with drug use, despite the fact that research has been mixed when determining whether housing helps to reduce drug use itself.[14] Other broader efforts to provide jobs and housing would no doubt similarly reduce the social and physical harms of drug use. Indeed, it may be the drug court's link to formal labor and other services—rather than any inspiration offered by the bench or its oft-touted model of predictable, swift, and certain sanctions—that is most central in helping it to generate the favorable outcomes it sometimes achieves.

Therapeutic Practice and the Hierarchical TC

To these suggestions must be added others pertaining to the status of therapeutic communities. While I was often distressed to see the levels of what I considered abuse within the TC, I was also struck by the ways in which many people responded favorably to the institution (as well as the ways in which many others reacted negatively). Another complex combination of positives and negatives, the TC model presents many challenges in finding ways in which its strengths might be taken advantage of and augmented while attempting to minimize the harms that it also clearly inflicts. Here it seems worthwhile to rethink the basic nature of the institution. While TCs are today seen in relation to drug treatment, perhaps their more authentic role could be in assisting individuals to develop the pre-vocational forms of self-discipline that formal-sector work requires. In a context in which work often forms a critical component of social identity, further existing as the only legitimized means through which poor persons can gain the resources they need to survive, it makes sense that many people would wish to become "productive members of society"—however problematic that notion is. If the TC were stripped of its governing ideology concerning drug use (keeping in mind that many early therapeutic communities operated in order to "rehabilitate" inmates more generally, not only drug users, as do some contemporary TCs in the UK),[15] one might find elements of a valuable social mechanism through which these prevocational aptitudes could indeed be taught. As Allison McKim argues:

> Cultural capital can help people succeed, especially in formal settings like courts and job interviews, and therefore such unstated rules of behavior reproduce privilege. The education scholar Lisa Delpit argues that people from marginalized communities benefit from being taught these rules explicitly.[16]

Demystifying the TC in favor of an approach that explicitly acknowledges its class dimensions would help to both contextualize and to depathologize the norms of various street cultures that are at stake in the so-called drugs lifestyle.[17] McKim further shows that this is far from the case within contemporary TCs: "at WTS, women's problematic self-presentation was not seen as deriving from their social disadvantages. Nor did WTS pitch changes in appearance and language as strategies for successfully playing the mainstream game. Staff members approached women's self-presentation as a sign of psychological issues."[18] Such an approach also recognizes that TCs have much less to offer middle-class drug users who already possess these pre-vocational aptitudes (a fact that led virtually every single middle-class participant in the TC I studied to sharply criticize the program, as noted previously). Lastly, acknowledging the actual orientation of TCs toward formal labor in this way might emphasize the need to build in additional components of therapeutic practice in order to better deal with the specific issues of intensive drug use as such (e.g., CBT techniques, insight-oriented therapy, or whatever else).[19]

To be clear, therapeutic communities feature enormous reactionary elements, being akin to other institutions aimed at effecting a "civilizing process."[20] Like missionary schools, TCs take those deemed too "savage" and attempt to inculcate them with the values, norms, and dispositions required of "civilized society." In this sense, we must ask critical questions not only about who is excluded from society but how the terms of inclusion operate as a form of disciplinary power in and of themselves. Samera Esmeir's work reminds us that people continue to live in terms that exceed those recognized by the law. As she argues, "these alternatives highlight juridical humanity as excluding nonjuridical forms of life, as refusing to register ways in which subjects in this world go about living with or without the thought of being human."[21] One aspect of our political vision must thus involve a rejection of "the civil" and an embrace of "fugitive life" (as Dillon puts it),[22] an effort designed toward the creation of greater opportunities for people to live undisciplined (or less disciplined) by formal labor.[23] In this sense, the "reintegrative shaming" practiced by drug courts and TCs becomes simply another form of supposedly civilizing violence enacted against dehumanized others in an effort to make them "human." As a theoretical perspective, reintegrative shaming risks justifying any and all manner of purportedly caring violence without any critique regarding (a) the initial violence of the dehumanization, (b) the criteria for inclusion (replete as they are with correlating criteria for exclusion), or (c) the potential injury done in the process of effecting a violent mode of integration. Violence done in the name of enabling and ennobling others—arresting people, imprisoning them, humiliating them in front of their peers—often simply enables and ennobles the violence itself. The reason that humanizing violence generally fails to "humanize" is not necessarily because its enactment of violent care is not sufficiently caring; at a deeper level, the political formation that includes is the same one that excludes in other cases. "Reintegration" rests on top of prior projects of removal, with the necropolitical often working in close proximity to the biopolitical; humanizing violence works directly with an earlier dehumanizing violence. Indeed, in the case of TCs working with a criminal justice clientele, the technique used to enforce biopolitical discipline involves the very real possibility of having previously existing necropolitical forces aimed at the subject. The biopolitical and the necropolitical—the reintegrative and the stigmatizing—work hand-in-glove.[24]

While these considerations weigh heavily against the TC, it is important to consider that many forms of violence operate simultaneously in the lives of those undergoing "treatment" within the criminal justice system, and one cannot automatically presume which of those forms should be prioritized. In this case, given the relative lack of viable, sustainable alternatives to "civil society"—which, in this case, involve only various forms of "street hustling"—an ideologically demystified and voluntarily chosen version of the TC might be worthy of support (though with many caveats). Here one must ask difficult questions regarding agency and normalization: Is a disciplinary environment designed to counter the "drugs lifestyle" and create "productive citizens" (or "normal, ordinary, responsible persons") always a negative? If we are to valorize only resistance, how are we to account for the strongly normalizing desires expressed by at least some participants? And which precise forms of resistance do we wish to valorize: resistance to the state and its disciplinary treatment regime, or resistance to ongoing economic exclusion in the form of a determination to achieve some level of class ascendance and stability? With multiple forms of oppression impacting a given person's social situation, at which level is resistance to be defined? Which forms of resistance are to be valorized and which disparaged? Does not *any* evaluation of this sort on the part of outside observers become yet another effort at violent care?

Given that therapeutic communities generate such an intensive and emotionally abrasive environment for residents, my own solution to this knot is not to completely reject TCs—its appeals are real enough, if not suited for everyone—but to recommend that participation in such communities be made genuinely voluntary, with no incentives offered beyond those that are inherent in the program itself. Alternatively, given a context in which criminal justice punishments are diminished in order to encourage participation in drug treatment (the basic drug court model), and in which many people will participate only because of those incentives, the only way to make participation in TCs more voluntary is to diversify the treatment options that are available. This is not an easy task, particularly in many rural areas where treatment options are already few and far between. Nevertheless, programs that do not rely on the intense confrontational strategies, shaming tactics, and peer-policing strategies of the hierarchical TC must be developed. Techniques might instead build upon ideas present in motivational interviewing (which allows participants to define goals for themselves), strengths-based counseling (which works to further develop positive coping skills that a client already utilizes), harm reduction psychotherapies (which do not demand a complete cessation of drug use), and other approaches that do not aim to "break down" participants.[25] To the extent that treatment programs continue to deal with drug users, they might usefully incorporate more elements from their harm reduction-oriented peers rather than continuing to frame the issue solely in terms of abstinence. The idea of a harm reduction TC is almost unthinkable, but it would offer a genuinely novel approach to problematic drug use, one that might enable less punitive approaches to problems of daily living than currently exist. Instead of pressing participants into this single approach, any criminal justice program that relies on rehabilitation programs should offer participants a variety of treatment models and create conditions that better enable informed choices to be made.

By providing alternatives and making participation in the TC genuinely voluntary, the therapeutic community model can come more into its own: the forms of peer surveillance involved with *responsible concern* could actually come to feel like a form of mutual support, with no need to pretend that the job market is fair or that one's success is solely determined by one's individual effort. While I found many of the tactics of the TC to be offensive, some participants insisted on their beneficial aspects. As the situation now stands, however, therapeutic communities—by their own standards—are rapidly becoming low-cost houses of detention with a veneer of treatment that is becoming thinner and thinner. The fact that some 50 percent of TC participants bought into the program even as things stood is testimony to the fact that TCs offer something perceived to be both real and valuable. My own sense was that support for the TC primary revolved around desires to leave the street economy and to achieve some measure of both economic stability and social respectability.

The fact that some 50 percent of its participants do *not* want to be there and merely go through the motions, however, marks a significant problem that undermines the entire approach. Making participation in the TC more voluntary—by creating genuine treatment alternatives—is necessary if *community-as-method* is to remain a viable model.[26]

At the same time, although the therapeutic community has moved somewhat away from the most extreme of Synanon's practices, clearly much more movement is necessary if TCs are to escape their abusive origins. Digging one's own grave, wearing signs or dunce caps, and so on, are practices that indeed might not survive a constitutional challenge, were one somehow raised, and they should be prohibited. Better and more well-funded efforts at state regulation—or even better and more well-funded administrative monitoring on the part of drug court case managers and probation/parole officers (who can readily stop referrals to any programs with a reputation for abuse)—would go a long way toward achieving this aim. This said, moves toward the professionalized TC and a model of talk therapy threaten to undercut what has been a truly unique and potential benefit of the therapeutic community model: its ability to create a disciplinary community and to instill particular types of pre-vocational agency. Though professionalism has indeed helped to curb some of the most significant abuses within the TC, and while it makes sense to introduce traditional counseling or CBT techniques as *adjuncts* within the TC, the fundamental benefits of the TC model should not be lost. Even more threatening to the therapeutic community's institutional integrity in this regard is its increasingly narrow reliance on clients who do not actively wish to be there. The imposition of discipline need not be as onerous as it currently is if it is more freely chosen and directed toward aims that participants themselves desire. However, with a deepening dependence on criminal justice system clientele, the TC indeed risks becoming simply a containment center.

Beyond rethinking the ways in which it engages with and solicits clientele, the therapeutic community must reexamine its understanding of problematic drug use which, far from being "holistic," is actually profoundly narrow. TCs continue to see only one pattern of addiction that affects everyone (users who take drugs without disastrous effects upon their lives are seen as simply not having reached rock bottom *yet*). Ironically, for an approach emphasizing community, TCs promote an individualistic pull-yourself-up-by-the-bootstraps model, in which each person is solely responsible for their fate and no social dynamics (such as racism, poverty, sexism, heterosexism, etc.) are recognized, evaluated, or discussed. Yet as many scholars have argued, drug use—including very destructive forms of drug use—must be seen as being socially specific, both in the patterns of use that occur and in the nature of any harms that are understood to result.[27] In rethinking the issue of drug use within a more socially-defined frame, it becomes possible to focus upon the truly damaging patterns of drug use without equating all use with catastrophe.

The monolithic approach TCs take toward addiction has resulted in a very punitive stance in relation to those who use drugs within the program, not only kicking such persons out but providing them with no follow-up services and no aid in finding other types of services upon dismissal. Clients who have not been immediately returned to imprisonment have found themselves left on the street with no place to go, bereft of housing and other basic needs, as a result of "their" failure.[28] Even if TCs maintained the same decision-making process when deciding whether to continue working with a particular client or not, they should be required to do more to assist those whom they dismiss, connecting them with other types of services rather than relating to them as a form of social trash. In a therapeutic system aimed at fostering "accountability," the TCs' irresponsibility for those within their care seems infuriatingly hypocritical. By creating institutional links to harm reduction services, for example, TCs might instead constructively build upon the strengths of each model, not only assisting those whom its model fails to help but also establishing greater aftercare services for those who successfully graduate from the TC.

Cooptation and Non-Reformist Reforms

Both drug courts and TCs could thus be significantly improved. The question, however, remains: What are we to make of a reform that has both positives and negatives? A reform that offers real benefits to participants (e.g., job training and access to GED programs) while extending the capacities of the criminal justice system? That shames participants and forces them to police one another, but which, nevertheless, sometimes succeeds in gaining their active consent? That intensifies the basic dynamics of racist and capitalist exclusion for some while mitigating them for others? The New York Civil

Liberties Union and other drug policy activists strongly supported the adoption of the 2009 Drug Law Reform Act: Was this a meaningful reform?

Efforts at reform within the criminal justice system have a long history of playing into the hands of those who wish to strengthen punishment. In the 1970s, liberal reformers criticized rehabilitative approaches that were then long-standing for many of the same reasons that I offer here.[29] As a result, progressive organizations such as the American Friends Service Committee advocated against coerced models of rehabilitation and in favor of determinate sentencing. This effort was famously coopted to conservative ends, with the discriminatory practices of indeterminate sentencing replaced by a punitive approach in which ever more people were incarcerated for ever longer times. And as Murakawa has shown, other liberal reforms enacted in the name of civil rights were also coopted by a growing carceral state, reinforcing punitive approaches precisely by making them appear more bureaucratic and race-neutral.[30] How then are we to conceive of reform in ways that lead to prison abolition or at least the most minimal use of policing and imprisonment possible?

Groups and individuals seeking to change the criminal justice system have made a number of proposals concerning how they might consider their approach to reform. For example, the 1970 report from the American Friends Service Committee (AFSC), *Struggle for Justice*, distinguished between reforms that strengthen the criminal justice system and reforms that benefit those negatively impacted by that system. The AFSC Working Group argued that fundamental changes could only be achieved by "plac[ing] power in the hands of the heretofore powerless," identifying this as their primary criteria in assessing any reforms.[31] Pressing further, in her 1973 exposé of conditions within prison, *Kind and Usual Punishment*, journalist and activist Jessica Mitford distinguished between "two types of reform proposals: those which will result in strengthening the prison bureaucracy, designed to perpetuate and reinforce the system, and those which to one degree or another challenge the whole premise of prison and move in the direction of its eventual abolition."[32] Judah Schept's more recent contribution on *progressive punishment* follows in a similar vein, saying that the dilemma for activists has centered upon distinguishing between "alternatives that broadened the scope of carceral intervention from those that actually provided some measure of autonomy from supervision."[33] All of these framings make general use of André Gorz's suggestion for nonreformist reforms, reforms that give more power to those oppressed within a given system, thereby making further change more possible.[34]

In practice, however, these issues are sometimes difficult to resolve. Angela Y. Davis and other prison abolitionists have commented on the complexity of these issues, noting both the way in which efforts at penal reform have time and again been captured by prison administrators but also the ways in which the prison industrial complex leaves activists having to make challenging decisions regarding the immediate needs of inmates and longer-term strategic goals that seek to undo racialized mass incarceration. Davis argues:

> The seemingly unbreakable link between prison reform and prison development—referred to by Foucault in his analysis of prison history—has created a situation in which progress in prison reform has tended to render the prison more impermeable to change and has resulted in bigger, and what are considered "better," prisons. The most difficult question for advocates of prison abolition is how to establish a balance between reforms that are clearly necessary to safeguard the lives of prisoners and those strategies designed to promote the eventual abolition of prisons as the dominant mode of punishment. In other words, I do not think that there is a strict dividing line between reform and abolition.[35]

Drug courts might seem to present just such a dilemma for abolitionists. While drug courts were established with the explicit intent of perpetuating a court system that was otherwise overwhelmed with low-level drug cases, building the institutional capacity of the criminal justice system, they also provide some useful services and move toward at least *possible* civic incorporation of those who are otherwise completely excluded. The ways in which drug courts work to intensify imprisonment for half of its participants should make them easy to reject, but when other elements are added to a legislative mix (as when reduced sentencing guidelines were included with New York's 2009 reform), it can become challenging to see where the overall balance lies. It may be impossible to fully unravel these contradictions; however, a focus on the effects of reforms on those who are already the most negatively impacted by the criminal justice system helps to make the situation more clear. Though some individuals certainly benefit from the services they receive in drug courts, no reform that surreptitiously lengthens prison terms on the most marginalized half—condemning them to even deeper and more prolonged forms of misery than before—can possibly qualify as a progressive reform. When the perspective shifts from simply the judicial arena toward the myriad forms of both ideological and material support that drug courts offer for the racist forms of policing associated with the drug war, the decision seems even more obvious: more than anything, drug courts are "an effective, efficient weapon in the war on drugs," an opinion coming from the judiciary itself.[36]

But while these criteria make drug courts themselves easy to evaluate—and reject—the situation becomes less clear when examining the institutions through which drug treatment is offered (or could be offered) within the criminal justice system. While treatment programs housed within prisons may be of benefit, particularly if they are undertaken on a more voluntary basis, requiring that parolees and probationers attend such programs may simply extend the capacity of the criminal justice system to monitor its charges in ever more intimate detail. When residential facilities become mini-jails that offer low-cost forms of incarceration, these problems are greatly amplified. Even as the educational and occupational services sometimes offered as part of drug treatment are desperately needed, and *could* be part of a nonreformist reform, a guarded attitude toward the neoliberal fusion of medicalization and penalization—"authoritarian medicalization" in Teresa Gowan's words[37]—is clearly warranted. Particularly in a context in which levels of incarceration remain near the highest peak ever reached by any society in history (as they do in the United States today), the key priority remains decarceration. As Schept argues, "Keeping people out of jail and prison, rather than reconfiguring jail and prison to be slightly more comfortable or humane (if this is even possible), should be a central goal of community organizing to combat poverty, racism, violence, addiction, or crime."[38] Activists must carefully assess the details of any potential arrangement before simply embracing the "help" that such programs promise.[39]

Drug Courts and the Enforcement of Freedom

Beyond the concrete policy-oriented considerations that I have just addressed, I wish to offer a few comments on the new forms of social control that drug courts initiate and the position of the courts within a broader system of governmentality. What do the rise of therapeutic jurisprudence and the reemergence of rehabilitative schemes (carceral welfare) within the criminal justice system imply about the changing nature of social domination more generally? A note of caution is in order, however, before proceeding to answer this question. One of the most insightful commentators on criminological trends during the late 1970s, Stanley Cohen, made a number of extrapolations concerning intermediate punishments and community corrections based on tendencies that then seemed ascendant. Cohen argued that the rise of community-based systems of incarceration (halfway houses and the like) would inevitably displace the prison as the central feature within criminal justice, leading to a much more widely dispersed system of criminal penality that—while offering smaller, community-based punishments—would simultaneously widen the net and impact more people. Cohen warned that compulsory treatment, a hallmark of community corrections, signaled a trend in which members of "the community" would increasingly become agents of social control themselves, creating a "correctional continuum" that operated through a "carceral archipelago" of diffusely located institutions, effectively blurring the lines between public and private in the process.[40]

In some ways, Cohen's remarks sound uncommonly relevant to today's situation, yet they were expressed nearly forty years ago, just as the United States was turning away from the rehabilitative ideal and embarking on the greatest increase in the prison population in world history. Far from being displaced, of course, the expanded prison became even more dominant, replacing Cohen's dystopian vision of pervasive community corrections with an arguably even more dystopian reality. Cohen happened to draw from the wrong trends in his extrapolations, inadvertently highlighting patterns that seemed exciting and new at the time while being unaware of the still imperceptible shifts that signaled a radical turn away from community-based institutions and toward a newly *non*-rehabilitative prison. The political upheaval following Trump's surprising rise to the presidency similarly highlights the need for social theorists to tread with caution as they attempt to periodize the present and, implicitly, to predict the future.

In today's criminological literature, the new directions taken by the criminal justice system have been referred to under the rubric of the *new penology*. As discussed in chapter 1, Malcolm Feeley and Jonathan Simon, the originators of this much commented upon framework, have suggested that the new penology is characterized by the use of aggregate statistics rather than a focus upon recalcitrant individuals.[41] Similar to some versions of *risk society*, Feeley and Simon use their framework to explain trends toward broken-windows policing and similar efforts which target offenders as a statistical population rather than as individuals.[42] Drug courts, from this perspective, would seem to represent an intriguing hybrid: individual attention is given to inmates only when statistical analysis shows that such attention will result in positive outcomes at an aggregate level. David Garland adds to Feeley and Simon's observations, suggesting that any rehabilitative efforts attempted within the new penology will be oriented toward the "efficient enhancement of social control" rather than toward the promotion of social welfare.[43] "Public safety" and economic rationalities now assume primacy as means through which any treatment programs must prove themselves, a fact that rules out all but the least serious offenders—"non-non-nons"—from the outset. Within this context, recidivism becomes the gold standard in evaluating rehabilitation, while measures of social justice or assessments by participants are distinctly sidelined. Broadly speaking, drug courts and TCs seem to conform well to Garland's assessment.

While it is unspoken in their formulation, the trends identified by Feeley, Simon, and Garland all indicate that the neoliberal state is committed to the use of the criminal justice system as a tool against nonwhite communities dealing with both social marginalization and economic impoverishment. While prognostication is inherently uncertain, the *punishment imperative*[44] seems to have become a relatively permanent feature within the neoliberal moment. Within this general pattern, however, the rise of drug courts and other specialty courts (mental health courts, prostitution courts, truancy courts, etc.) indicates that the state is open to some degree of innovation in terms of how it controls these populations. While globalization and the movement of industries overseas since the 1970s effectively turned such communities into a large "surplus population," setting the stage for state repression, the means of such repression appears to be somewhat open and amenable to change. While advocates of drug courts, re-entry programs, and other carceral welfarist schemes being introduced into the criminal justice system attempt to insulate themselves from criticism through the use of studies showing reduced recidivism and budgetary savings, the state seems perfectly capable of eliminating these programs if reactionary trends toward racism, class-based prejudices, and political conservatism again gain strength. Cohen's failure as a prognosticator (despite his outstanding analytic talents) suggests that one should not mistake shifting tactics within an emphatically fixed governing strategy for actual structural change. Beyond a seemingly deep structural continuity in terms of the populations being policed, it is perhaps sufficient to note that the state seems willing to innovate within this broad constant. While theorists of governmentality have suggested that responsibilization is a key theme in neoliberal governance, it is difficult to suggest that this is a deep trend within the criminal justice system as a whole. The only constant at this point appears to be an overall need to continue the war on crime and thereby control what Malthus disparagingly referred to as a "redundant population."[45]

Yet let us consider the more likely possibility that despite the rise of Trump and a renewed push for so-called law and order, drug courts and other welfarist approaches within the criminal justice system will expand further, bounded only by the need to show effects that can be said to measurably improve "the public's" safety (i.e., the safety of those deemed to constitute the nation *proper*, not the poor communities whose existence poses a threat to these middle-class and elite populations). In this case, "freedom" will be enforced in a way that makes its preconditions ever more apparent, generating images of the "criminal savage" as a counterpoint while simultaneously offering the appearance of civilized benevolence toward those in low-risk populations who are deemed statistically viable. These contemporary versions of the requirement that one be a white, male property-owner in order to vote will be administered through para-racial criteria—seemingly race-neutral formulations such as the court-defined notion of addiction that incorporate and yet extend beyond race—establishing a form of conditional citizenship that has the potential to impose a version of *homo oeconomicus* upon entire probationary populations. Cohen's carceral archipelago may come to exist through this process, but it will be linked to a continent-sized regime of ongoing racialized mass incarceration within the warehouse prison. Meanwhile, the individualized sorting process enabled by drug courts and other similar programs could facilitate a slight downward trend within the overall numbers of those incarcerated, enabling many to feel that the problems of criminal justice have been resolved while the institution actually becomes more pervasive and deeply embedded. Drug courts not only provide ideological cover for such possibilities, but they generate new levels of intrusion into the lives of marginalized individuals (e.g., deciding who people can live with or be friends with, forcing people to utilize birth control, or to attend particular cultural events, etc.). These intimacies of the state are imposed through force and evoke further dystopic potentials, yet given widespread ideological commitments to social respectability—Elijah Anderson's "decent" people who view themselves in opposition to the "street"[46]—it is possible that such innovations would garner the support of even many of those who are themselves part of the increasingly policed probationary population.

Drug courts offer the promise of social inclusion for those who have been excluded, yet it is important to recognize their political limitations. Even during Democratic administrations, drug courts have only achieved political viability by appealing to conservative interest groups within the criminal justice system, working to ensure that no violent offenders ever receive the benefits of carceral welfare and doing nothing to counter the overall legitimacy of racist/classist policing practices. Given the social catastrophe that our current criminal justice system represents in the lives of the racialized poor, drug courts hold some forms of promise. Yet, considering the additional damages that they currently inflict and could inflict in the future, they are far from a benign presence. For every person who feels drug courts have saved their life, or who has at least benefited from their time with the court, there is another individual who languishes in prison for an even longer time for a crime that could have readily been dealt with as a public health issue rather than a criminal one. Moreover, drug courts have a much better record "saving" white lives than black and brown ones, further lending ideological and concrete institutional support to racist forms of policing associated with the war on drugs. Even if these "details" were somehow addressed with an alternative administrative agreement—if, indeed, such elements are not foundational to the basic approach—it is clear that the model of therapeutic justice that drug courts exemplify must be engaged with the utmost caution.

Notes

1. Policing Addiction in a New Era of Therapeutic Jurisprudence

1. Berman and Feinblatt (2005: 3).
2. Marlowe, Hardin, and Fox (2016). U.S.-style drug treatment courts have also been adopted internationally. See materials from the International Association of Drug Treatment Courts (www.iadtc.com).
3. On earlier liberal involvement in the war on crime, see Murakawa (2014).
4. Kerlikowske (2013).
5. Ethan Nadelmann of the Drug Policy Alliance originated the "dinosaur" moniker (in Sullum, 2016).
6. ABC News (2018).
7. See figures from HHS (2017); USDoJ (2017); White House (2016, 2017a).
8. White House (2017b). The current Attorney General, William Barr, similarly pledged to support the expansion of drug courts during testimony in relation to his confirmation hearings (Committee on the Judiciary, 2019: 52).
9. U.S. Congress (2001: 6).
10. Goldkamp (2000: 925).
11. Abramsky (2010).
12. From the Sentencing Project, see Mauer and King (2007) and King and Pasquarella (2009). From the NLADA, see Ward (2000) and ACCD (2004); see also NLADA (2010). Both organizations, it should be noted, added some significant caveats.
13. Overall results showed more of a rural-urban divide than a traditional conservative-liberal one. See county level results at, "2000 Initiative General Election Results—California," U.S. Election Atlas, www.uselectionatlas.org/RESULTS/state.php?fips=6&year=2000&f=0&off=68&elect=0 (accessed February 9, 2019). Differences

between the program created by Proposition 36 and drug courts, as well as the reaction of drug court advocates to the measure, will be discussed below.

14. Thompson (2006).
15. Some conservatives have also claimed that drug courts essentially legalize drug use insofar as a positive drug test will not automatically result in prison time (Armstrong [2003]). In terms of cost, direct outlays for residential drug treatment with drug court supervision typically run between half and two-thirds of those associated with an ordinary prison (Belenko [2001: 41–44]). Costs for treatment programming within prison, meanwhile, typically add to overall expenses (Lipton, Falkin, and Wexler [1992: 22]).
16. Fears (2009).
17. Nolan (2001: 5, 41–42).
18. Maron (2009).
19. In recent years, a small but growing number of organizations advocating for criminal justice reform have been developing a progressive critique of drug courts. Prominent among these are the National Association of Criminal Defense Lawyers (NACDL) (2009), the Justice Policy Institute (Walsh [2011]), the Drug Policy Alliance (DPA [2011, 2014]), the New York Academy of Medicine (Pugh et al. [2013]), and Physicians for Human Rights (Møllman and Mehta [2017]). A wide variety of legal scholars and other academics have also raised objections. These criticisms, however, have thus far remained at the margins of policy making.
20. Murphy (1997), quoted in Goldkamp (2000: 925n10).
21. Fox and Wolf (2004: 7).
22. The NADCP further noted that "if marijuana becomes decriminalized or legalized within a given jurisdiction, this does not necessarily require Drug Court practitioners to abide its usage by their participants" (Marlowe [2010a: 4–5]). On opposition to the decriminalization of marijuana, see NADCP (2012).
23. While a number of scholars have rightly argued that the war on drugs has not been a primary cause of mass incarceration—other proximate causes include the rise of determinate sentencing with longer sentences, "zero tolerance" policies within probation and parole, three-strikes laws, and the rise of prosecutorial power (Jacobson [2005]; Gottschalk [2015]; among others)—it nevertheless remains the case that the drug war has been primarily responsible for the heightened level of racial disparities in prison admissions, generating effects Michelle Alexander has pointedly termed "the New Jim Crow" (Alexander [2010]). The war on drugs, in other words, has greatly expanded the breadth of those caught in the prison system, particularly African Americans, even as it has not as greatly impacted the depth of that involvement (i.e., the length of time in prison). See Mauer (2006, 2009); Oliver (2008); HRW (2008); among others.
24. *USA Today*, 2008.
25. Tiger (2013: 88).
26. Tiger (2008, 2013); Paik (2011); Murphy (2015). Boldt similarly refers to "rehabilitative punishment" (1998), while Moore notes the ways in which "care and control

are neither easily not helpfully distinguished from each other" within a system of "therapeutic surveillance" (2011: 257). The term *therapeutic punishment* seems to derive from earlier behavior modification techniques pioneered by psychiatric facilities in the 1960s as a means to control those who had been institutionalized (Simmons and Reed [1969], cited in Murphy [2015: 152]). It should be carefully noted, however, that earlier techniques of therapeutic punishment—which included slapping and electric shock via a "shock stick"—were derived from behaviorist principles that are distinct from the framework used in most treatment programs today.

27. Tauber (2000: 1).
28. Peters and Wexler (2005: 140). See also Berman and Feinblatt (2002: 10–11; 2005: 107–8).
29. On "guiltless justice," see Nolan (2001: 140, 169–70). See also Satel and Goodwin (1998). On the need for sanctions within drug courts, see Tauber (2000).
30. Turner et al. (2002: 1491–2).
31. Tiger (2013: 113). James Nolan similarly writes of the ways in which therapeutic logics facilitate the intrusion of the state into domains otherwise deemed personal (1998, 2001). In a different context, Stanley Cohen similarly notes that community corrections programs often result in an expanded terrain of intervention, a process he termed "net thinning" or "thinning the mesh" (1979, 1985; see also Jensen, Parsons, and Mosher [2007], who refer to this process as "mesh tightening").
32. *Productive incoherence* is a term developed by Eve Sedgwick (1993: xii) who uses it to refer to the ways in which contradictory models (of gender and sexuality, in her case) are combined in order to generate outcomes that would be unattainable through a singular institutional or ideological arrangement.
33. Irwin (2005). See also Simon's discussion of the "Waste Management Prison" (2007).
34. A 2013 report from the Bureau of Justice Assistance showed a national graduation rate of 46.5 percent from drug courts receiving implementation grants (Steyee [2013]). A 2014 survey revealed a national graduation rate of 58 percent (Marlowe, Hardin, and Fox [2016]).
35. Only 6 percent of drug courts process participants on a preplea basis (Marlowe, Hardin, and Fox [2016: 40]).
36. Marlowe, Hardin, and Fox's 2016 review of the data shows that while a national sample of drug courts demonstrated a 58 percent graduation rate overall, only 39 percent of blacks graduated. A different national sample in the same study revealed a 57 percent graduation rate overall while only 32 percent of Latinos graduated. Although the figure is not provided in the report, given the national rates of racial participation they found (62 percent white, 17 percent black, 10 percent Latino), a simple calculation suggests that approximately two-thirds of whites graduate from drug courts, nearly double the overall rate for blacks and Latinos (36 percent). While not all studies find racial disparities, and a small number of studies actually find higher graduation rates for blacks than whites (Marlowe, [2013]), in general the finding that blacks graduate at significantly lower rates

than whites is exceedingly common within most of the drug court literature (see Belenko [2001]; Murphy [2015: 51]).

37. In a study of Baltimore drug courts, it was found that participants who fail drug court receive sentences that are six to nine months longer than those given to a nondrug court control group (time which is typically added to time spent under drug court supervision). In New York, drug court failures are given sentences that are two to five times as long as if they had not gone through drug court. For both studies, see Bowers (2008: 782–94). See also Belenko (2001: 36); Miller (2004); NACDL (2009: 29); and Murphy (2015: 51).
38. Rempel et al. (2003).
39. Fluellen and Trone (2000: 6).
40. For example, Butzin, Saum, and Scarpitti (2002) and Dannerbeck et al. (2006). On racial disadvantages in drug treatment, see also Brown (1985); Murphy (2015: 51); and Kerrison (2017).
41. Butzin, Saum, and Scarpitti (2002: 1629). Other factors sometimes shown to positively impact drug court success include: being male, having greater wealth, living in a nonpoor community, having less prior criminal involvement, being older, being married, and using drugs other than crack (though this last fact has not been disentangled from the effects of race and other socio-economic variables). Butts and Roman provide a very useful description of this literature (2004: 280–353).
42. A finding directly noted by both Harrison, Patrick, and English (2001: 2) and Bowers (2008: 808, 821–22).
43. Steyee's survey of drug courts showed that approximately 68 percent of those screened for drug court, but 79 percent of those admitted, were white (2013: 5).
44. Alexander (2010).
45. Middle- and upper-class whites generally do not face punishment for drug offenses within the criminal justice system whatsoever—a fact that extends the notion of stratified penalization to ways in which certain groups are not frequently penalized at all.
46. Petersilia (2003).
47. Garland (2001).
48. The term *net widening* is also used to refer to situations in which drug courts accept participants who are not included in the original mission of the court (e.g., people with very little drug involvement; see Edwards [2000] and Miller [2004]). This issue is particularly relevant in relation to juvenile drug courts—representing nearly 30 percent of all drug courts (Butts and Roman [2004: 2])—where some 80 to 90 percent of participants were judged to be nondependent users of either alcohol or marijuana (16). The two senses of the term interrelate in that when more people are arrested, it is likely that many are being arrested for low levels of drug use; however, it seems helpful to keep the two meanings of the term analytically distinct.
49. Miller (2004: 1561).
50. Rossman et al. (2004: 92).

51. Berman and Feinblatt (2001: 128–29; 2005: 23–30); Thompson (2002: 67–70); Armstrong (2008: 273).
52. See Cohen (1979); Morris and Tonry (1990); and Feeley and Simon (1992: 465). The idea that drug courts mark a transition from punishment and to treatment is also challenged as drug courts enter other national jurisdictions. Canadian scholar Dawn Moore points out that drug courts became policy in that country at the same moment that the conservative Harper administration dramatically raised penalties on drug crimes (personal communication [August 2018]). As drug court advocates themselves have argued, these intensified penalties were necessary if drug courts were going to successfully coerce individuals into participating.
53. On therapeutic jurisprudence, see Wexler (1990, 2000); Wexler and Winick (1991); Hora, Schma, and Rosenthal (1999); Hora (2002); Winick, (2003); Winick and Wexler (2003); Wexler et al. (2016); among others. Previously, Wexler used the term *therapeutic justice* (1972).
54. Fischer (2003: 240).
55. Kuhn (1962).
56. The term *administrative research* was coined by the sociologist Paul Lazarsfeld (1941), who advocated such studies. Theodor Adorno (1945) and C. Wright Mills (1959) both famously criticized Lazarsfeld's approach. More recently, Jock Young has offered the term *administrative criminology* in describing a similar set of problems within criminology (1986; see also 2011: 15).
57. One of the most interesting theoretical debates to take place within this literature concerns a discussion as to how to best measure the efficacy of the courts. A 2008 document from the National Center for State Courts compiles a list of sixty-one measures that have been used to evaluate drug courts, including retention rates, the percentage of positive drug tests, the postprogram recidivism rate, the amount of child support collected, graduation rates, employment status two years after exiting the program, and the percentage of babies that are born drug-free (Rubio, Cheesman, and Federspiel [2008]). The question as to what one should measure has an implicit connection to the types of information that administrators and policymakers find valuable, and by implication, what types they do not. In some cases, this data serves the immediate interest of monitoring the program and perhaps making alterations within its structure (e.g., Cissner and Rempel [2005]). In other cases, the data serves to evaluate the effectiveness of the courts (as gauged by certain criteria) or even to promote lobbying efforts on behalf of the courts. A 2006 monograph prepared for the Bureau of Justice Assistance by the National Drug Court Institute noted the political problems that had been created by a lack of uniform data collection between drug courts serving different jurisdictions (Heck [2006: 1], see also USGAO [2002]). In 2008, the Bureau of Justice began to require that courts receiving federal grants report standardized data concerning key performance measures (USDoJ [2007] and USGAO [2011: 3–4]). To the extent that conventional, managerial evaluations of drug court often take rates of recidivism as a primary measure of their success, I here offer overall length of time served

as a more politically significant metric. The Bureau of Justice does not, however, require that courts maintain data on this key measure for the receipt of U.S. government grants.

58. The idea that cost is the determining factor, however, is somewhat misleading and requires a number of caveats—primarily because the studies done in this regard have systematically failed to include all costs. Many early studies, for example, failed to include costs associated with flash incarceration utilized by the court. Similarly, early studies often compared the recidivism rates of drug court graduates to nonparticipants while neglecting the half of drug court participants who failed at treatment and faced extended periods of incarceration (thereby adding significantly to costs). This statistical creaming—looking only at socially privileged populations that help to make the case for the desired program while ignoring those at the bottom—continues in more recent analyses through other means. Most of the problems identified in an early report from the USGAO, for example, pointed toward accounting procedures that favored drug courts (2002; see also USGAO [1995, 1997, 2005]; Fluellen and Trone [2000]; and Murphy [2015: 51]). Even today, no cost-benefit analysis that I am of aware considers costs associated with lengthened incarceration times that result from the lost opportunity to plea bargain that most "failed" drug court participants must confront. Cost-benefit analyses thus cannot be said to accurately reflect all costs and benefits, even when considering only state outlays. When the costs of extended prison terms are added in, it seems probable that many drug courts actually cost the state more money than they save.

    Equally important are the comparisons that are made in these cost-benefit analyses. I am aware of no cost-benefit analysis, for example, that compares drug courts to harm reduction and other public health approaches. Nor do existing cost-benefit comparisons typically examine the costs involved in other policy options, such as reducing drug-related penalties. Instead, current cost-benefit analysis only compare drug courts to existing systems of imprisonment and fail to examine other possibilities. In this way, cost-benefit analyses might best be seen as performing an ideological trick, defining the field of reasonable policy options and excluding others through a systematic process of constructed ignorance.

    All of which is to say that while the rhetoric of cost effectiveness has been a significant factor in winning support for drug courts, their rise to prominence may have in fact occurred *despite* actual costs. If, as the GAO reports suggest, there has been some level of bias in favor of drug courts in the assessment of cost, the more fundamental bias pertains to the routine exclusion of costs and benefits experienced by program participants, families (legally recognized and not), and communities, on the one hand, and to the exclusion of public health alternatives that do not rely primarily upon criminal justice, on the other.

59. A number of scholars have addressed this issue through a variety of different lenses. Most useful to me has been the discussion by Wendy Brown (2015). More generally, see also material on the "New Public Management," "managerialism" or the "new managerialism," "entrepreneurial governance," "quality assurance," "performance

management," and "the audit society." With variations, these new managerial forms seek to centralize control through the creation of measurable indicators, replacing previous evaluative methods based upon professionalized standards with quantifiable benchmarks established by a smaller cadre of experts. Within the field of criminal justice, this approach is found in what Feeley and Simon have variously termed "the new penology" (1992) and "actuarial justice" (1994), ways of approaching crime and punishment through considerations of the aggregate rather than through a focus on individual criminals. Within human services, the new emphasis upon evidence-based practices constitutes a counterpart. Numerous other scholars have also relied upon a Foucauldian frame in commenting upon the use of statistically-determined "risk" in shaping policy (e.g., Castel [1991]; O'Malley [1998]; Peterson and Lupton [1996]; among others). Beyond generating a managerial rhetoric that centers the value of expertise and minimizes democratic challenge, the financialization of public policy seeks to constrain bureaucratic options (as discussed in note 58 above).

60. Wacquant (2008, 2009a). Beckett and Western (2001: 44) and Soss, Fording, and Schram (2011: 6) reach a similar conclusion.
61. As usefully noted by Tiger (2013).
62. In their discussion of *carceral citizenship*, Miller and Stuart have commented upon the ways in which "carceral citizens have access to alternate systems of benefits that are unaccounted for in the literature" (2017: 542; see also Comfort [2007, 2012]; Schept [2015, on *carceral welfare*]; Miller and Alexander [2016]; and Sufrin [2017]). While in no way making up for the pains of imprisonment and surveillance and control in the community, and clearly failing to replace the state benefits that are lost upon receiving a felony conviction, these services nevertheless constitute a significant and underanalyzed substratum. This issue has been particularly important in relation to drug treatment, where access for those without their own funds has often been very restrictive. All of this adds an extremely important asterisk to Wacquant's generally useful notion of a straightforward transition from Keynesian social state to post-Fordist penal state (2009b).
63. Wacquant (2009a: 12), see also Wacquant (2009b).
64. Though as noted above (see note 58), given the poor quality of these assessments, political factors may well be more of a factor than cost as such.
65. As discussed by Brown (2015).
66. For discussions of treatment programming as a black box, see Belenko (2001) and Bouffard and Taxman (2004). On drug courts themselves as a "black box," see Goldkamp et al. (2001).
67. Overall, 33.7 percent of all people who enter drug treatment are referred through the criminal justice system (including 44.4 percent of all adolescents). The largest percentage of these individuals (coincidentally, 33.7 percent) are referred not by drug courts but by probation or parole (SAMHSA [2015: 65, 80]). Given the way data is collected, it is impossible to know how many individuals are referred directly through drug treatment courts. Of the 14,399 drug treatment programs in the

country, 4,854 (also 33.7 percent) feature special programming for criminal justice clients (SAMHSA [2016: 130]). In practice, clients who are referred through criminal justice channels tend to be clustered in these programs.

68. Goffman (1961).
69. Gowan and Whetstone (2012: 87).
70. In a study of the referral process within New York City drug courts, Farley, Rempel, and Picard-Fritsche (2016) perform a statistical analysis on inpatient versus outpatient placements, arguing that race does not play a direct role in these decisions. Nonetheless, other factors that are systematically linked to race, such as employment status, residential stability, educational achievement, and probation/parole status, clearly do play a role (the extent of a participant's drug use is also a factor, but far from the only one). These nonracial factors have a tremendous racial impact. For example, the Brooklyn Treatment Court—where only 9 percent of participants are white—refers 71 percent of its participants to residential treatment, while the Staten Island Treatment Court (where 78 percent are white) refers only 17 percent to similar programs (Edwards [2015]; on racial disparities in Wisconsin's drug court system, see also Chase [2014]).

    It should also be noted that many of the most populous cities in the United States—all with disproportionately nonwhite populations within their criminal justice systems—either regularly refer drug court participants to residential treatment or require such referrals for all participants. A brief survey that I conducted found this pattern to be true in New York City, Los Angeles, Chicago, Houston, Washington D.C., and Boston (the first, second, third, seventh, eighth, and tenth most populous cities in the United States, respectively; data from the other four cities in the top ten was not readily available). So while a national survey suggested that only 32 percent of drug court participants are referred to residential treatment overall (Rossman et al. [2011: v.3, p.65]), the available evidence strongly suggests that urban drug courts rely upon residential facilities far more than the national average, and that rural (and suburban) courts rely upon them far less (see also v.2, p.49).
71. See Hansen and Netherland (2017); Tiger (2017); and Mendoza, Rivera, and Hansen (2018).
72. Some critics have also noted that drug courts tend to include a disproportionately white set of participants overall (e.g., O'Hear [2009]; see also Tiger [2013: 146] and Murphy [2015: 52]).
73. See Netherland (2012); Roberts (2012); Garriott and Raikhel (2015); and Granfield and Reinarman (2015).
74. Nationally, nearly 25 percent of all criminal justice referrals to drug treatment cite marijuana as the primary drug (SAMHSA [2017: 76]). An examination of drug courts in New York City revealed that 67 percent of participants facing felonies were charged with drug sales and that 54 percent of these felony-level participants listed marijuana as their "drug of choice" (Cissner et al. [2013: 28–29]). See also Murphy (2015: 52, 80). The inclusion of marijuana-only drug dealers within drug court will be discussed further below.

75. Murphy similarly found that practitioners at the drug court she examined focused on the "drug lifestyle" in their approach to addiction (2011, 2012, 2015; see also Kaye [2010, 2013]). The term *drug lifestyle* has been in circulation among drug treatment professionals since at least the mid-1970s (Smith, Linda, and Loomis [1974]; Smith [1976]; Cleckner [1976]; and Smith [1977]). Similar terms are also in circulation, such as the *drug-using lifestyle* (Deangelis [1973]), the *addict lifestyle* (Lewis and Glaser [1974]), and the *street addict lifestyle* (Stephens [1985]). In the 1990s, Glenn Walters published extensively upon the *drug lifestyle*, culminating in the creation of a diagnostic tool, the Drug Lifestyle Screening Interview (1995). The term *drug lifestyle* seems to derive from earlier discussions of a *criminal lifestyle* (e.g., Burchard [1955] and Moore [1973]). The court professionals I spoke with referred to a *drugs lifestyle*, and this pluralized form is also commonly used in literature on the topic (e.g., Grapendaal [1992] and Gowing and Ali [2006]).
76. Lewis (1966). Murphy also notes a strong parallel between the drug lifestyle and the culture of poverty, arguing that the "mission of resocialization" engaged in by the court "fits into the culture of poverty arguments popular in the 1960s" (2015: 79, see also Kaye [2010]).
77. Whetstone and Gowan (2011).
78. For example, Stack (1974) and Wilson (1996).
79. Wilson (1996: 73).
80. de Certeau (1984: 31).
81. In which time is precisely measured and time discipline governs the behavior of individuals. See Thompson (1967).
82. Wacquant (1998: 3).
83. Anderson (1999).
84. Hays (2003).
85. Wacquant (1998).
86. Callon (1984).
87. Moore (2007a: 3, 136).
88. Unsurprisingly, this focus on employment has a strongly gendered dimension; one that works to the disadvantage of many women, particularly those in women's programs (an issue that will be addressed in chapter five).
89. In which features related to impoverishment are diagnosed as medical or psychiatric problems. See Harding (1986); Blackwell (1999); Schram (2000); Hansen et al. (2014); and Mills (2015).
90. As noted by Schram (2000: 100).
91. Macpherson (2011).
92. Winnubst (2006: 26).
93. Locke (2012 [1689]: book II, chapter 27, section xxvi).
94. Strawson (2011: 22).
95. Judith Failer similarly notes the way that Locke excludes "lunaticks" and "ideots" from rights based on the fact that they are unable to understand the rules established by "Reason": "[I]f through defects that may happen out of the ordinary

course of Nature, any one comes not to such a degree of Reason, wherein he might be supposed capable of knowing the Law, and so living within the Rules of it, he is *never capable of being a Free Man*" (2012 [1689]: book II, chapter 6, section vx; quoted in Failer [2002: 31]).

96. Wynter (2003, among others). My understanding of Wynter owes a debt to the discussion in Weheliye (2014).
97. Wynter (2015).
98. Wynter likewise suggests that those excluded from the status of *homo oeconomicus* includes a broad grouping, pointing toward "the now institutionalized *Welfare Mom/Ghetto 'Black' Others* (including their *Trailer-Park Trash, Wigger 'White' counterparts*) as the extreme expression of the category of the *non-Breadwinning* 'Planet of Slums' *Jobless* Poor and, at the world-systemic level, of the category of the '*Underdeveloped*' " (2015: 216, emphasis in original). As seen most obviously in relation to the figure of the "wigger," tropes originally conceived in relation to black bodies come to define white counterparts.
99. Toby Seddon's work takes an alternate track, analyzing a variety of drug regimes which have occurred within liberalism, dividing the field temporally into *classical liberalism* (late eighteenth century until late nineteenth century), *welfare liberalism* (end of nineteenth century until 1970s), and *neo-liberalism* (1980s to the present) (2010: 11–12). While appreciating the usefulness of Seddon's approach, here I focus on the overall dynamic of "freedom" generated by liberal governance.
100. Esmeir (2012: 145).
101. Esmeir (2012: 287).
102. Esmeir (2012: 4).
103. Garland (1996: 461).
104. As Scott Vrecko notes, "the term 'ad*dict*' derives from a process in Roman law in which a court would decree, or *dict*ate, that an individual is to be given over to (*ad-*), or enslaved by, another (free) individual. The addicted was a slave, unable to take part in the civilization of free men" (2010: 45). Though the term could be used in other contexts, an *addictus* was typically someone who was temporarily enslaved as a means of paying off a debt (Lewis [1890: 17]). To be an addict, then, was to be temporarily enslaved so that one could again become free.
105. The reality of brainwashing was the subject of much debate and controversy among psychiatrists and academic psychologists following the Korean War. While the influence of ideas related to brainwashing upon the earliest stages of Synanon is uncertain—Chuck Dederich, the founder of Synanon, was perhaps more directly influenced by Thoreau and B. F. Skinner at that time—it is known that he read Robert Lifton's 1961 book *Thought Reform and the Psychology of Totalism: A Study of "Brainwashing" in China* sometime shortly after its release (Morantz [2014: 34, 86]). Dederich himself often made jokes concerning brainwashing, arguing that most people, especially drug addicts, *needed* to have their "brains washed out" every so often, just as the body needed to be bathed (Janzen [2001: 18]; see also Yablonsky [1965: 102] and Gerstel [1982: 76]). David Deitch—who acted as director of one of

Synanon's intake operations before becoming the cofounder of Daytop and later senior vice president and chief clinical officer at Phoenix House (and later, a professor of clinical psychiatry)—also argues that, "consciously or unconsciously, there is the possibility that this widely advertised technique influenced Synanon's Charles Dederich" (1973: 168).

There are other possible sources for Dederich's approach within Synanon, including theories that shaped the way in which Chinese brainwashing was understood in the West. Kurt Lewin, the originator of social psychology, argued that change occurred in a three stage process: freezing, moving, and refreezing, with resistance to change occurring during frozen moments. Lewin writes that "to *overcome this initial resistance*, an additional force seems to be required, a force sufficient to 'break the habit,' to 'unfreeze' the custom" (1947: 32) and that change is easier to accomplish if the entire group to which an individual belongs is changed rather than simply the individual. The sociologist Edgar Schein later compared Lewin's approach to "brainwashing" (1999: 62). It is unclear if Dederich had any direct knowledge of Lewin's ideas; however, Deitch, who was also at Synanon, favorably discusses his work (1973). Whatever the case, such perspectives serve to usefully contextualize Dederich's flippant remarks on brainwashing and further place the notion of needing to "break down the addict" into greater perspective. On Lewin and Schein's borrowings from communist sources, see Cooke (1999).

106. While it has often been presumed that the concept of brainwashing originated in response to Chinese interrogation of U.S. prisoners of war (POWs) during the Korean War, Timothy Melley (2011) notes that the term *brainwashing* appeared in CIA documents in January 1950, six months prior to the Korean War. Melley also notes that the journalist credited with coining the term, Edward Hunter (Hunter [1951, among others]), was a former member of the Office of Strategic Services (the precursor to the CIA) and a specialist in what came to be termed *PsyOps* (psychological operations), including propaganda. Melley therefore argues that: "The term *brainwashing* thus preceded the publication of Hunter's 'groundbreaking' article on the subject, suggesting that the CIA later disseminated the term to fuel public anxiety about Communist methods" (2011: 28; though see Holmes [2017] for a competing explanation).

As noted above, the CIA began investigations into the use of drugs and hypnosis in order to coerce confessions and extract information shortly after the end of World War II, greatly accelerating their program after the 1949 trial of Hungarian cardinal József Mindszenty, during which he confessed to treason and other charges. In October 1950, three months after initial tests, and only four months after the start of the Korean War, the CIA conducted "advanced" interrogation tests on North Korean POWs being held in Japan (two full years before public panic concerning brainwashing began in earnest). Fears that the Soviet and Chinese Communists had developed effective techniques of brainwashing led to apparently genuine concerns within the CIA of a "mind control gap" (Melley suggests that the "propaganda fiction" created within one arm of the CIA "proved so effective that the CIA's operations directorate believed it" [2011: 30]). In response to this purported gap,

CIA Director Allen Dulles consolidated earlier programs (Project Bluebird, Project Artichoke, MK-NAOMI) into MK-ULTRA, which was officially established in 1953. With a budget of some billion dollars annually (McCoy [2006: 7]), this "Manhattan Project of the mind" (7) utilized LSD, electroshock, and hypnosis against unsuspecting U.S. citizens in order to develop techniques that might be used against captured enemies. One program within MK-ULTRA, Operation Midnight Climax, relied on women working in prostitution in order to lure men to a CIA safehouse whereupon they were surreptitiously given drugs (usually a liquid form of marijuana, though LSD was also sometimes used), observed during sex, and sometimes blackmailed in relation to these sexual liaisons. Another MK-ULTRA project involved testing LSD and other hallucinogens on semiwilling patients at the Addiction Research Center of the U.S. Narcotic Farm in Lexington, KY, including one experiment in which seven individuals—all black men—were subjected to LSD for seventy-seven consecutive days (tolerance to the drug began to develop after a few days; see Isball et al. [1956: 475–76]). In a 1986 interview, the director of the Narcotic Farm, Harris Isbell, acknowledged that he had undertaken the experiments at the request of the CIA; see Senechal (2003: 19).

MK-ULTRA was scaled back in 1964 and then again in 1968 before apparently being terminated in 1973 (Marks [1991]; on CIA behavioral research during this period in general, see Price [2016]). The actual practices of Chinese interrogators, which were significantly distinct from the methods utilized by the CIA, are discussed by Smith (2012).

107. Techniques developed through MK-ULTRA were relied upon in creating the 1963 *KUBARK Counterintelligence Interrogation* manual (utilized during the Vietnam War) and the *Human Resource Exploitation Training Manual* of 1983 (see U.S. Government [2014]). Contemporary CIA practices of enhanced interrogation utilized in the war on terror also directly rely upon investigations of brainwashing conducted under MK-ULTRA. A 2008 report in the *New York Times*, for example, details the use of a 1957 Air Force study of Chinese brainwashing techniques in order to train U.S. interrogators. A chart initially entitled "Communist Coercive Methods for Eliciting Individual Compliance" had the title removed but was otherwise unchanged before being presented to interrogator-trainees (Shane [2008]). The two psychologists who created these techniques, James Elmer Mitchell and Bruce Jessen, both worked in a classified military program—SERE (Survival, Evasion, Resistance, and Escape)—that subjected participants to these brainwashing techniques in order to teach U.S. soldiers how to resist interrogation if captured. Allegedly, Mitchell and Jessen reverse engineered these techniques, further combining them with ideas concerning learned helplessness, in order to create a contemporary program for use in the war on terror. Mitchell and Jessen received $81 million for their work (Melechi [2016]).

108. In his 1961 book, Schein argued that the Chinese techniques used against POWs could be utilized in beneficial ways, and that "coercive persuasion has some good features to recommend it" (1961: 269–70). Schein made this same point at a panel convened by the U.S. Bureau of Prisons (BoP) at which he was invited to speak:

"These same techniques in the service of different goals . . . may be quite acceptable to us" (1962: 92). In the conversation that occurred after Schein presented this material—in a panel led by James Bennett, the long-serving director of the U.S. Bureau of Prisons, and with many wardens in attendance—discussion quickly turned to the question "How shall we manage the [black] Muslims?" (98). Further discussion questioned how to deal with conscientious objectors (who were referred to as "non-violent coercionists") (101).

Following criticism in *Harper's* (Mitford [1973b]), Schein denied that he had advised wardens to engage in these practices, saying: "The fact is that I had been asked to *describe* how the Chinese Communists managed their prison camps" (emphasis in original; 1973: 128; cited in Opton [1974]). However Schein's comments were clearly offered in the spirit of advice, with Schein writing that the papers presented were "expanding the potentialities of correctional endeavor" (1962a: 58), and that the symposium introduced "New Horizons for Correctional Therapy" (ibid). The long-serving director of the Bureau of Prisons, James Bennett, acting as chair of Schein's panel, described the prison system as "a tremendous opportunity . . . to carry on some of the experimenting in which the various panelists have alluded," and directly encouraged the wardens in attendance to "undertake a little experiment of what you can do with the [black] Muslims, what you can do with some of the sociopath individuals" (in Schein [1962b: 103]). Schein's book (*Coercive Persuasion*) made similar recommendations, citing such techniques as "morally neutral" and specifically discussing some of the challenges that might arise in applying the methodology in a prison context (1961: 269, 273, 279). Nevertheless, under attack in 1973, Schein minimized his role, saying that "the notion that social scientists were in any way teaching prison wardens these new techniques is naïve in the extreme" (1973: 128). On the defensive, he now took "a clear stand *against* their use as a technique of prison management" (emphasis in original, *idem*). In yet another twist, Schein's research and the writing of his 1961 book were funded by the CIA, which—Schein speculates—became interested in brainwashing "because they realized that what we could learn by what had happened to Americans might teach us something (about) how we could deal with enemy captives" (in Greenfield [1977]).

In later work, Schein recommended a much less coercive (if perhaps no less insidious) version of these attitudinal adjustment techniques, describing a minimally threatening environment in which corporate managers might develop greater identification with the organizations they managed (Schein and Ott [1962]; this followed from earlier work on "training groups," also known as "t-groups" or "sensitivity training"). It seems likely that these techniques influenced the 1971 development of EST—initially referred to as Erhard Sensitivity Training—as well as later spinoffs. On Schein's work and its overall relationship to studies on using such programs to effect change upon prison populations, see Guenther (2013).

109. As discussed by Weinberg (2005), treatment has long followed two tracks: a relatively gentle privatized system for those who are able to afford it and a more punitive, state-funded system for those who are impoverished (see also Hansen and

Roberts [2012] and Whetstone and Gowan [2017]). Allison McKim's work (2008, 2014, 2017) directly compares facilities of these two types, revealing significant differences in the way drug treatment programs are run based on the class background and referral context of their clients. Unsurprisingly, McKim's study reveals that programs that receive a high percentage of their clients from criminal justice sources tend to be significantly more coercive in form than programs serving voluntary clients (Whetstone and Gowan [2017] similarly make comparisons between different types of programs, as do Iacobucci and Frieh [2018]). The work of other scholars reinforces this deduction.

Weinberg's study of two treatment centers working with dually-diagnosed homeless individuals who were seen voluntarily revealed programs in which "fostering trust among residents was a central component of treatment" and where "clients were themselves integral players in the work of defining what in their lives was and was not an appropriate focus of therapy" (2005: 137, 155; see also 1996, 2000). This process through which the content of "addiction" was "socially negotiated" (2005: 127) is considerably less present within scholarly descriptions of criminal justice oriented programs. Likewise, Carr's study (2011) of a program for women in public housing who were required to attend drug treatment in order to maintain their housing benefits does not reveal anything similar to the shaming practices and abrasive interactions with staff that are commonly found in descriptions of CJ-oriented programs. The only apparent exceptions to this general principle, which tend to link the nature of therapeutic practice within drug treatment to the class background and referral context of its clients. The first pertains to some of the religiously-oriented evangelical programs, which at times feature practices that are even more coercive in nature than the state-regulated CJ programs (e.g., see Hansen [2012, 2018] and Upegui-Hernández and Torruella [2015]). Practices within these evangelical facilities vary, however, and are not always more abrasive than in CJ-oriented programs (e.g., see Williams [2016] and Whetstone and Gowan [2017]). A second exception concerns therapeutic communities that focus on juvenile clients. As Szalavitz documents, these facilities have perhaps been even more prone to abuse than CJ-oriented facilities (2006, see also USGAO [2007]).

110. Valverde (1996: 361).
111. Valverde (1996: 370). In regards to the links between childrearing practices and the management of savage Others, it is useful to mark a distinction in that while a certain amount of "despotism" and antidemocratic practice is involved in raising a child, the management of what might be termed *probationary populations* involves the mobilization of necropolitical power and the threat of its use.
112. Norbert Elias similarly argued that violence and fear were essential to "the civilizing process" (1939: 443; cited in Wacquant [1997]).
113. Valverde (1998). Such "diseases" enjoy a foundational status within the history of liberalism, forming one way in which to address otherwise unresolvable paradoxes within its conceptual apparatus. For example, Rousseau, one of the originators of liberal political theory, argues: "In the civil state a man acquires moral liberty,

which alone makes him truly master of himself; for the drive of sheer appetite is slavery, while obedience to a law that we prescribe to ourselves is liberty" (1992 [1762]: I, viii, 2).

114. Hartman (1997: 126).
115. Valverde (1998: 17). See also Rose on the "powers of freedom" (1999a).
116. Rousseau (1992 [1762]: I, vii, 8). The precise meaning of Rousseau's comment has been subject to a wide range of interpretations, and I will make no effort to adjudicate. I introduce the comment merely to note ways in which political freedom is predicated upon force directed against those who either refuse or are incapable of "freedom."
117. There are exceptions to this rule, and Synanon itself was voluntary in nature. Nevertheless, criminal justice institutions represent the primary sites where contemporary therapeutic communities are located.
118. Many of Synanon's spinoff organizations have also been accused of being cults. As noted above (see note 109), treatment practices vary greatly by the social class of participant and the source of referral. Other models of residential drug treatment, such as the Minnesota Model, have a different institutional history than the TC.
119. All done in the name of creating "non-criminal" citizens who can rationally obey the rules of the social contract. See Berlin (2002 [1958]).
120. Willhelm and Powell (1964). See also Boggs and Boggs (1966). I thank Nikhil Singh and Lester Spence for calling this work to my attention.
121. See Camp (2016) and Kurashige (2017). For a parallel analysis set in the UK, see Hall et al. (1978). As early as the mid-1970s, some left-wing groups advanced an analysis linking economic shifts to the growing "disposability" of nonwhite populations and the rise of the prison "warehousing" (as noted by Dillon [2018: 3–4]).
122. Garland (2001).
123. Goldkamp (1994: 3). See also Inciardi (1988) and Belenko (2000a, 2000b) for brief but useful historical overviews of treatment programs within the criminal justice system.
124. Aviram (2010, 2015).
125. For criticisms, see Incite! (2007); Bumiller (2008); Bernstein (2007, 2010, 2018); Spade (2011); and Hanhardt (2013).
126. Bernstein (2007, 2010, 2018).
127. Kilgore (2014).
128. Hall et al. (1978: 322).
129. Hall et al. (310, 323).
130. Fassin (2012: 3).
131. Boltanksi (1999), cited in Grewal (2017b).
132. Fassin (2012: 5). See also Hall et al.'s comments on "liberal reformism" (1978: 176).
133. Simon (2007).
134. Inderpal Grewal's term denoting a government that continually invokes emergency powers "necessitated" by perpetual war (2017a).
135. Italics in original. Peck and Tickell (2002: 384).

136. Peck and Tickell (2002: 391–92 [citing Piven and Cloward (1998)]).
137. While it is still too early to determine exactly what impact Trump will have, it seems clear that his policies are oriented toward even further privatization and a sharp reassertion of roll-back modes of neoliberalization. This seems to be combined with a new formation reemphasizing a particularly racialized type of law and order. Despite this, there appears to be ongoing support for both drug courts and drug treatment more generally. Thus it seems likely that humanitarian approaches to drug control will remain as a consolidating form of roll-out neoliberalization, even as other parts of the criminal justice system are pushed toward a decided roll-back of the mild reforms that had recently been achieved.
138. Phelps (2011).
139. See Marlowe (2012).
140. BJA (2017).
141. Additional criteria of course exist. Drug tests are administered and must be regularly passed, administrative rules must be followed, and so on. Nevertheless, as will be seen in the chapters that follow, formal labor stands at the center of these efforts while even the cessation of drug use—while necessary—is taken as something of a symptomatic issue that the practices of work challenge (by undercutting the "drugs lifestyle"). Thus, in most of the CJ-oriented treatment programs, preparation for work is the means through which drug addiction is addressed. This issue will be discussed at greater length in chapter four.

    For an alternative study in which courts decide upon the necessary prerequisites of freedom in a different context, see Failer's study of civil commitment in relation to homelessness and mental illness (2002). Failer finds that laws regarding civil commitment change over time and involve a wider variety of criteria than I discuss here (she identifies six primary narratives that lead one to be declared sufficiently insane as to be held against one's will, including being an "imminent threat to self or others," for example, and suffering greatly due to their independent living status). The differences between my study and Failer's highlight the historical and institutional specificity of "freedom" as it is enacted with diverse populations and in diverse situations.
142. Drug courts have made graduation ceremonies an important part of their programs. Featuring speeches from selected graduates, the judge, district attorney, and program manager who has been in charge of their case (and often an invited guest); certificates of accomplishment signed by the judge; and with friends, families, and other guests in attendance, these events offer an opportunity to examine the social imaginaries of success deployed by both drug court participants and practitioners. I detail a graduation ceremony at the beginning of the next chapter.
143. Rempel et al. (2003: 38). It is also worth noting that all persons pay regressive sales and excise taxes no matter their employment status. One might also point out that 4.2 percent of drug tests administered to employees in 2016 showed positive evidence of drug use (data represents only one of the testing companies; Quest Diagnostics [2017]). The widespread use of drugs within the finance sector (Granahan

[2008]), together with its invisibility within the context of this criminalized discourse, is also quite remarkable.

144. Murphy finds a similar pattern in the drug court she examined (2015: 100–101; see also 154–55).
145. Despite the fact that no one in the DA's office had any training concerning drug treatment, their recommendations concerning placement (inpatient versus outpatient) were almost always followed by the court—even over and against the recommendations of case managers who had been trained in evaluating drug use—because the court could not function without the cooperation of the DA's office.
146. Niv, Hamilton, and Hser similarly note that questions regarding risk to society have often overridden assessments of clinical need in the placement of participants (2009: 509, 514).
147. I provide a fuller discussion of the impact that criminal justice referrals have on treatment in chapter 4.
148. I thank one of my reviewers at Columbia University Press for this phrasing.
149. I only interviewed eight participants in this manner, however, as I quickly found that the interviews I conducted at the TC, where I had established a connection with many individuals and was a regular, visible presence even for those with whom I interacted little, yielded deeper and more personal reflection than those that occurred during these "cold call" interviews. Individuals in both cases were paid $20 as an incentive to participate.
150. Introducing myself to the community involved participating in a ritual that I did not know about until it was suddenly revealed to me. After I had said a few words about myself and told everyone about the research (including options for opting out, which no one took), the director of the facility asked me to sing a song a cappella in front of the entire group of nearly 100 residents. After panicking for a few moments and struggling to think of a song for which I knew the lyrics, I chose "Let It Be," and the assembled group gamely joined in after I had sung the first few lines. All new staff members are introduced in this same manner.
151. The facility held nearly 100 residents at any given moment, and approximately 200 individuals passed through the facility during my months there.
152. Marlowe, Hardin, and Fox (2016) found that 62 percent of drug court participants were white, while Steyee's survey found the figure to be 79 percent (2013).

2. Drug Court Paternalism and the Management of Threat

1. See Willse for a critical analysis (2015).
2. The NADCP established the "All Rise Ambassadorship" program in 2008, with Sheen its first ambassador (www.nadcp.org/All_Rise_Ambassadors). The 2008 measure was Proposition 5, the Nonviolent Offender Rehabilitation Act (NORA). For a detailed criticism and analysis of the NADCP campaign against NORA, see NORA

Campaign (2008) and CADPAAC (2008). In the end, NORA was defeated 59.5 percent to 40.5 percent.

3. Quoted in Szalavitz (2015).
4. Here I refer to California's Proposition 36, the Substance Abuse and Crime Prevention Act of 2000, which as noted in chapter one was passed by 61 percent of the electorate. Proposition 36 created a diversion program for first- and second-time nonviolent drug offenders that, like drug court, permitted users to attend treatment instead of going to jail. Unlike drug courts, however, Proposition 36 sentences offenders to probation rather than jail, making participation in a treatment program a condition of ongoing probation. Drug court advocates noted that Proposition 36 limited the actions a judge could take in sanctioning participants, particularly in restricting their ability to place someone in jail for brief periods (e.g., after a failed drug test). While the NADCP presented reasons to favor full drug courts over what was proposed in Proposition 36 (citing evidence that persons with greater judicial supervision were more frequently successful in graduating from the treatment program), it is telling that when presented with an option to reduce penalties in a way that—from their perspective—was not sufficiently restrictive, or to maintain a status quo that involved ongoing incarceration and no therapeutic option whatsoever, they chose the latter. For discussions from drug court advocates on the alleged deficiencies of Proposition 36, more properly known as the Substance Abuse and Crime Prevention Act of 2000, see Sheen (2000); Marlowe (2002); Marlowe et al. (2003); Lieupo and Weinstein (2004); Hora and Stalcup (2008); as well as ONDCP (2008). Despite ongoing criticisms, many drug court advocates have reevaluated their position since the establishment of Proposition 36, finding ways to adapt to and even expand drug court programming within the legislative environment Prop 36 created (e.g., Fox and Wolf [2004: 13]; Farole [2006: 11–13]; and Burns and Peyrot [2008]). Nevertheless, in 2008 the NADCP again criticized Proposition 36, calling it "disastrous" (2008: 1). While the law remains, funding for treatment programs associated with Proposition 36 were cut 83 percent in the 2008 fiscal year, and completely eliminated in by 2010 (Richman, 2011), effectively gutting the program.

   More recently, the NADCP criticized another California ballot initiative (Proposition 47, which reduced a number of drug-related crimes to misdemeanors that carried no more than a one year penalty; see NADCP [2014]). Since the passage of Proposition 47 in 2014 (when it won with just under 60 percent of the vote), many have claimed that participation in drug courts have declined dramatically because the courts lack the ability to impose a significant penalty, particularly in areas such as Los Angeles where individuals are often released after serving only 10 percent of their sentence due to overcrowding in the county jail system. Not only are fewer people willing to sign up for a months-long drug court program when they have the option to serve a shorter sentence in jail, but many of the drug courts in the state are structured only for those with felonies (see Woods [2016]). It is not clear, however, what percentage of these declines have occurred because individuals now have a disincentive to participate versus the percentage who are now prohibited from enrolling due to the program rules. Moreover, declines in California drug court enrollments have been occurring since at least 2008–2009 (Hunter et al. [2017: 47]), making it unclear to what extent the declines may simply represent ongoing trends that were already in effect. Whatever the case, Proposition 47 cannot be considered as a shift toward a public health approach to drug issues as little money has been made available for voluntary treatment programs for those who wish to participate (see Castellano et al. [2016] and Michaels [2016]).

5. See Marlowe (2010a) and NADCP (2012).
6. Kluger and Rempel (2013). A more detailed examination of changes since repeal of the Rockefeller Laws found that new participants often consisted of individuals with more serious charges who previously would have been sent directly to prison (see Parsons et al. [2015: 47]). It is possible, then, that a greater proportion of lower-level offenders indeed refused the program, as the DA suggested, but that a larger number of others became eligible.
7. Approximately 97 percent of federal felony cases are decided by plea bargain. With intense pressures to plead guilty, many researchers argue that innocent people are often convicted (HRW, 2013).
8. Feeley and Simon (1992) and Armstrong (2008).
9. Hora and Stalcup (2008: 746). See also Tauber (1994: 2, 4) and Hora (2002: 1473).
10. NIJ (1996: 10), quoted in Hora, Schma, and Rosenthal (1999: 468).
11. Emphasis added. Dorf and Sabel (2000: 841–42).
12. NADCP (1997: 5). See also Murphy, who notes that courts often attempt to force participants to "hit bottom" (2015: 156).
13. Klein (2007). See especially chapter 1.
14. The term *shock incarceration* is common but not ubiquitous within drug courts (though the practice itself is universal). The term is more regularly used in describing penal programs that are structured as boot camps.
15. See also the NADCP document—created with support from the Department of Justice—listing ten "key components" that define a drug court (1997). Also of note is another New York state program variously referred to as DTAP (Drug Treatment Alternative to Prison) or STEPS (Structured Treatment to Enhance Public Safety). DTAP/STEPS is effectively another type of drug court; however, unlike most drug courts, DTAP/STEPS is prosecutor lead, which means that case managers act as employees of the district attorney's (DA's) office rather than of the court, and all decisions are made by the DA. This eliminates much of the haggling I witnessed within the precourt sessions at the drug court, where the court's case managers often recommended a more lenient approach than the prosecuting attorneys. Some of those whom I interviewed (both treatment providers from traditional therapeutic communities and district attorneys) felt that DTAP/STEPS enabled greater accountability than the conventional drug court and was actually more therapeutic (see Young, Fluellen, and Belenko [2004]).

    DTAP began in 1990 in response to the same capacity issues driving the establishment of drug courts in the wake of the expanded drug war. It has been less successful than drug courts in garnering federal support, perhaps in part due to the lower profile taken by judges in the program (a feature that seems to attract attention among both judges and the general public). For more information concerning DTAP, see Sung and Belenko (2006), among others.

16. For example, Hora, Schma, and Rosenthal (1999: 528), among others.
17. Herrick et al. (2008: 31).
18. Cissner and Rempel (2005: 12–13).
19. Rempel et al. (2003).
20. Hora and Stalcup (2008: 786–87). The New York State Adult Drug Treatment Court's set of recommended practices similarly attempts to speak to both needs in suggesting that "Judicial responses may be individualized but the overall approach to participants should be constant. When judges customize their sanctions and incentives to the individual, care should be taken to explain the rationale for different responses to other participants in the courtroom" (Herrick et al. [2008: 30]).
21. Taxman, Soule, and Gelb (1999: 186).
22. NADCP (1997). See also Marlowe and Kirby (1999); Taxman, Soule, and Gelb (1999); Marlowe (2002).
23. Hora, Schma, and Rosenthal (1999: 470).
24. Boldt (1998: 1209).
25. Marlowe and Kirby (1999: 10).
26. Hora, Schma, and Rosenthal (1999: 132).
27. Simon (2007).
28. Numerous scholars have enunciated the idea that the criminal justice system moved away from its "correctional" emphasis in the 1970s toward a punitive emphasis on creating penal harm (Clear [1994]). More recently, this assessment has been contested by some scholars who argue, on the one hand, that rehabilitation was only very weakly rooted in the South (Lynch [2010] and Perkinson [2010]), and on the other, that institutional inertia helped leave many rehabilitative programs in place until the 1990s, and that the overall changes were often more rhetorical than real (e.g., Robinson [1999] and Phelps [2011, 2012]). But while there is clearly a need for greater nuance in characterizing the punitive turn, some significant changes at the level of practice did occur, ultimately pushing rehabilitative programs out of the prison and into the realm of new forms of probationary services and surveillance (including both drug courts and other sorts of problem-solving courts as well as reentry programs). Furthermore, while some consequences of the punitive turn did not manifest until the 1990s, others had immediate consequences as early as the mid-1960s, particularly in terms of the nature of drug treatment within the criminal justice system (as will be discussed at the end of chapter 3).
29. Alternatively, and in contradiction to the image of the criminal as a rational actor, neoliberal penology simultaneously advanced an image of the psychotic monster, a person so psychologically deranged that no amount of rehabilitation would have any effect and for whom only imprisonment provided any solution (see Wacquant [2009a] on sex offenders). Though less directly addressed within Feeley and

Simon's actuarial frame of the new penology, this image of the psychopathic criminal formed a critical component within the new penology, justifying, for example, the increasing use of supermax prisons for the worst of the worst (Rhodes [2002, 2004]). For those who demonstrated their "irrationality" by continuing to commit crimes, incapacitation (in the form of incarceration with few or no services) thus became the order of the day.

30. NADCP (1997).
31. Nolan (2001: 178–84).
32. Nolan bases his analysis upon observations of drug court practitioners—primarily judges—who suggest that participants need to improve self-esteem, need to be in touch with their emotions, and so forth. While such language can indeed be found amongst drug court practitioners, it forms a minor subtheme to the behaviorist and cognitive-behavioral discourses and practices that essentially structure the court's approach to rehabilitation. Far from seeing a self-actualizing ethos as key, I would argue that such comments represent relatively isolated instances in which middle-class professionals introduce elements of their own therapeutic understandings into discussions of the court and the therapeutic process. While this more middle-class therapeutic culture undoubtedly influences interactions between court professionals and participants, these effects seem comparatively minor and should in no way be mistaken for the basic structure of the drug court. Such terms rarely appear within the written literature produced by drug court practitioners or within the evaluative literature, for example, nor does an emphasis upon therapeutic practices oriented toward self-liberation significantly shape practices within the court's affiliated treatment programs (as will be seen in chapters four and five). The criminal justice system overwhelmingly engages with poor and nonwhite populations, and the methods it utilizes to control and rehabilitate this population diverge sharply from the "self-actualizing" approaches utilized within middle-class culture.
33. Taxman, Soule, and Gelb (1999: 185–86).
34. Marlowe and Kirby (1999: 4–5).
35. Recounted in Murphy (2015: 78).
36. Reentry courts and other forms of problem solving justice, for example, follow a similar model. Attempts to incorporate graduated punishments into more conventional probation and parole programs have also been attempted, but they face legal barriers discussed later in this chapter.
37. For an example, see Armstrong (2003).
38. Dorf and Sabel (2000: 841). See also Tauber (1994: 6, 7).
39. Maruna and LeBel (2003). Rhine (1997) makes a similar point in relation to probation and parole.
40. In point of fact, use of many cough syrups (including Vicks) can cause false positives on alcohol detection tests, as can ingestion of herbal or flavoring extracts, inhalation of solvents, or even the use of many hygiene products or hand sanitizers (Massachusetts Medical Society, 2011).

41. DTAP (Drug Treatment Alternative to Prison) is a prosecutor-led program similar to drug court but generally even more restrictive. See note 15 in this chapter.
42. In court, the man was in fact released with a strong warning. The judge spoke sternly: "It is your responsibility to make sure you answer the curfew calls. Your mother also has to speak on the phone, so we can know you're at home. You'll have to wake her up, if necessary. . . . You have to have a job in one month. You quit a job because you couldn't get a day off. That's not how we do things in the real world. You have one month to get a job or it's a year in jail. And if you have one more missed curfew call, it's a year in jail. . . . You're being given a lot of leeway here. That ends now."
43. Garland (2001: 176).
44. Despite the aforementioned legal challenges that arise in incorporating graduated punishments into more conventional probation and parole programs, many states have attempted to do so. The National Institute of Corrections, an agency within the U.S. Federal Bureau of Prisons, has strongly encouraged states to adopt this shift since the late 1980s, when their technical assistance program on the subject began (Burke [1997: 8]). Notably, this innovation has been developed from within the criminal justice system by policymakers responding to the same conditions—overcrowding in the prisons and an overburdened legal system—that lead to the establishment of drug courts. Despite these shifts, a 1999 estimate suggested that no more than 10 percent of probationers and parolees were subject to some sort of intermediate sanction (Petersilia [1998: 21]).
45. O'Hear (2009: 118).
46. The cost of probation varies widely depending upon how it is administered, with annual costs estimated at anywhere from $1,250 to $2,750 per person (Pew Center on the States, 2009). The average costs of drug courts similarly vary but are generally higher, ranging from an annual cost of $1,000 to $17,000 per person, with an average of $6,000 per person (Marlowe, Hardin, and Fox [2016]). As argued in chapter 1 (see note 58), cost-benefit analyses might also usefully compare drug courts to more genuine public health approaches, but thus far they have not done so.
47. Goldkamp (2000: 934), quoted in Fischer (2003: 241).
48. See, e.g., Clear and Cole (2003: 182–211) and Champion (2007). Parole operates in much the same way, except that a parole board rather than a judge is capable of making decisions regarding revocation.
49. Moore (2007b: 42). Josh Bowers similarly notes that the therapeutic turn in drug courts has allowed judges to act in ways that "are unconstrained by customary procedural rules. Thus, judges can impose sanction—sometimes of individual invention—without hearings, and based on potentially flimsy, inadmissible evidence" (2008: 819–20).
50. Tiger (2013: 103–14).
51. As noted by Spillers (1987). See also Hartman who notes that the early black domestic sphere "was a threshold between the public and private rather than a fortified private sphere . . . [T]he fragility of the private . . . was exemplified by the intrusion of strangers and 'friends of the race' who policed the management of household affairs. . . .

Nineteenth-century social reformers considered the home visit essential to eradicating slothful habits and enhancing the moral dignity of the poor" (1997: 160).

52. The notion of the para-racial will be discussed at greater length below.
53. In a 1999 survey, slightly more than half of drug courts reported relying upon probation officers rather than their own case managers (Peyton and Gossweiler [2001: 38]). My presumption would be that this occurs more frequently in rural courts that are smaller and less well funded.
54. Reentry court is another attempt to resolve some of the legal barriers to graduated sanctions through the creation of judicially-monitored parole. As with the drug court model, reentry courts monitor a parolee's behavior, make decisions regarding the need for any outside therapeutic treatment and oversee compliance with those programs, and enforce a series of graduated sanctions—ultimately culminating in the revocation of parole—for any infractions. The idea of a reentry court was first proposed by Attorney General Janet Reno (who, as mentioned above, also developed the first drug court) and Jeremy Travis, director of the National Institute of Justice (Thompson [2008: 155]). As with the rise of drug courts, reentry courts were initiated in relation to fiscal and bureaucratic crises generated in large part by the drug war. A series of nine pilot reentry courts were established in 2000 under the guidance of the federal Office of Justice Program's Reentry Court Initiative (Thompson [2008: 163]; see also Petersilia [2003], among others).

    A similar innovation that several states have attempted relates to a model of judicially-supervised probation that was first created in Hawaii (known as Project HOPE, or Hawaii's Opportunity Probation with Enforcement; see Kleiman [2009]). As with drug courts, the idea is to impose small but increasing sanctions for minor infractions rather than waiting for a series of violations to occur and then revoking probation or parole entirely. While initially presented as a way of ensuring more effective punishment, this structure of swift, certain, and fair (SCF) sanctioning has been criticized as a form of "zero-tolerance supervision" that, moreover, has not proven its effectiveness (see the special issue collected by Nagin [2016, among others]).
55. A report from Physicians for Human Rights (Møllman and Mehta [2017]) notes that this issue can sometimes arise in relation to other psychiatric drugs or medications for ADHD as well. In one instance, the judge enforced the prohibition a treatment provider had issued against the use of antianxiety medications. In other cases I witnessed, judges and treatment providers insisted that participants take drugs that had been proscribed in relation to psychiatric diagnosis (such as bipolar disorder). Drug court judges also have to sometimes adjudicate when the expert advice they receive is contradictory, as in one case I witnessed in which different psychiatrists offered different diagnoses for a participant (in this case, the judge ordered a new evaluation).
56. This fact that has led some to charge that drug court judges are "practicing medicine without a license" (e.g., Szalavitz [2015] and Varney [2015]). Both the NADCP and the federal government have come to support the use of medication assisted treatment (MAT), and the federal government imposed a new rule in 2015 specifying that any courts that receive federal support must allow the use of MATs. Prior to

this rule, 50 percent of drug courts surveyed featured prohibitions against the use of methadone and buprenorphine (Matusow et al. [2013]). See also Csete and Catania (2013); Marlowe and Nordstrom (2016); and Møllman and Mehta (2017).

57. The district attorney supervising a "Vivitrol Court" in Ohio—a name created by that court's presiding judge—offers the following: "We're not forcing anyone into Vivitrol that doesn't want it—it's just one of our options," adding however that "I'm a little more comfortable probably not sentencing someone to prison that wants to go on Vivitrol" (MacGillis [2017]; see also Dissell [2017] and Harper [2017]).
58. See Glass (2011). Harris and Walter report on drug courts that send people to treatment programs that are operated as work camps. One, for example, made participants work on a commercial chicken processing plant, while another placed participants in a Coca-Cola bottling plant—both for no pay (2017a, 2017b, 2019; see also Sforza [2017]). While these instances highlight the potential abuses that arise with the judicial enforcement of a nebulous "therapeutic," I wish to emphasize the more mundane and accepted powers which accrue to the court.
59. In general, probation officers average somewhere between 100 and 150 cases at a time (Petersilia [1998] and DeMichele [2007: 44]), however, some jurisdictions feature caseloads as high as 1,000 to 1 (Jacobson [2005: 49]). Meanwhile, the NADCP recommends caution when drug court caseloads exceed thirty individuals per case manager, and they specify that in no circumstance should caseloads exceed fifty to one (NADCP [2015]). In part, this lowered caseload reflects the fact that drug court participants are defined as high need in terms of probationary work, and their probation officers are therefore given reduced caseloads; however, it seems likely that the additional resources drug courts have been able to mobilize also feature strongly in the discrepancy.
60. Not only does the therapeutic turn erase the ordinary legal protections that defendants maintain in court (see text associated with notes 49 and 50, above), but these punishments are also administered without legal due process within court-ordered treatment programs, not only by counselors but by peers (who are routinely required to enforce rules against one another within the residential facilities). Residents within the programs are thus effectively deputized by the court, giving noncourt officials significant power to informally take on the roles of judge, jury, and executioner, all with only the most limited forms of oversight. Drug courts thus subject participants to the authority not only of the judge but to the enlisted authority of a wide variety of therapeutic professionals and even to other drug court participants—a structure that vastly increases the court's capacity to monitor and sanction. In this same way, participants themselves are required to become the court's agents if they wish to successfully graduate. I will deal with these dynamics at greater length in chapter 4, but suffice it to note here that even when participants feel that the court itself has treated them fairly, they do not necessarily hold this same feeling toward either the treatment providers or their peers.
61. ISP programs were initially developed in the 1960s as part of law-and-order campaigns to make probation more strenuous; however, they became dramatically

more popular as mass incarceration began in earnest in the 1980s (Clear and Hardyman [1990] and Tonry [1998]).

62. See Morris and Tonry (1990). Stanley Cohen's analysis of community corrections has also proven to be quite prescient in these respects (1979).
63. Jacobson (2005: 40).
64. Coto and Sanchez (2014).
65. For example, see Paparozzi and Gendreau (2005), among others. Most ISP programs were introduced at a time of deep skepticism and political opposition to the idea of rehabilitation, and therefore their focus has been upon unearthing infractions.
66. Fluellen and Trone (2000: 6).
67. As noted in chapter 1, note 37.
68. Advocates of drug courts often argue that individuals stay in treatment longer when facing the threat of imprisonment. Marlowe et al., for example, suggest that while 80 percent of those without legal coercion drop out of drug treatment programs prior to twelve months of attendance, approximately 60 percent of those facing the legal pressure supplied by drug court attend for at least a year (2003). But while advocates routinely suggest that longer stays in drug courts result in better outcomes, a recent meta-analysis of studies on coerced treatment shows it as having little positive effect (Werb et al. [2016]). Murphy suggests that contradictory results across various studies suggest a complex reality: "Coercion may be effective, but only for some groups, such as those with less serious drug problems" (2015: 48). My point here is not to resolve this dispute but simply to emphasize that an acknowledgement of the suffering caused by coercion—including both the suffering directly inflicted by the court and the costs to those who fail and are ultimately imprisoned—must necessarily be included in any assessment of its efficacy. Drug court advocates have systematically ignored these issues, preferring to emphasize only the court's success stories and failing to include the costs of the longer sentences that drug courts routinely produce.
69. Domosławski (2011).
70. Some estimates suggest service-oriented ISP programs achieve a greater reduction in recidivism than drug courts, though at a greater cost. In their careful meta-analysis, Drake, Aos, and Miller found the average drug court to reduce recidivism by 8.7 percent while service-oriented ISP programs reduced recidivism by an average of 17.9 percent (2009: Table 1). In a document prepared for the National Drug Court Institute, Marlowe, Hardin, and Fox report lowered recidivism rates from drug courts of anywhere from 8–32 percent (2016: 16). Service-oriented ISPs report similar reductions of 10–30 percent (Paparozzi and Gendreau [2005]). Meanwhile, Marlowe, Hardin, and Fox estimate the cost per drug participant to average $6,000 (though ranging from $1,200 to $17,000), while Drake, Aos, and Miller suggest that the cost for ISP averages $7,356 per individual (Drake, Aos, and Miller also suggest a lower cost for drug courts of $4,474 per participant).
71. The parallel nature of drug courts and probation/parole is further emphasized by the fact that the courts draw readily from approaches developed within those

programs, as indicated by the National Drug Court Institute brochure entitled "Tips for Transferring Probation Practices to Drug Court Programs to Enhance Participant and Program Outcomes" (Cobb [2016]).

72. Skinner (1971: 67).
73. Skinner (1953: 182, 345, 190).
74. Skinner (1953: 192, 345, 406).
75. For an example, see Taxman, Soule, and Gelb (1999: 185).
76. Taxman, Soule, and Gelb (1999: 185).
77. Young (2002: 50).
78. In Herrick et al. (2006: Appendix 1, 8). Also published separately as Meyer (2006: 8). The line originally appears in Marlowe and Kirby (1999).
79. NADCP (1997).
80. Rempel et al. (2003: 243).
81. Marlowe and Meyer (2011: 154).
82. Marlowe and Meyer (2011: 153, 154).
83. Tauber (1994: 16).
84. McColl (1996), quoted in Berman and Feinblatt (2002: 12).
85. Porter (2000: 21).
86. Tauber (1994: 15).
87. Porter (2001: 24).
88. Herrick et al. (2008: 33).
89. Tauber (1994: 15).
90. During the graduation ceremony discussed in the introductory vignette to this chapter, the courtroom architecture sometimes worked against the informal conviviality the drug court team was attempting to establish, with closely-spaced rows orienting bodies toward the front of the court, thereby facilitating passive spectatorship but making face-to-face interaction more difficult. On courtroom architecture, see Mulcahy (2007). On judicial robing, see Woodcock (2003).
91. Weitzman (1995), quoted in Nolan (2001: 61).
92. Tauber (1994: 16).
93. Herrick et al. (2008: 34–5).
94. Farole and Cissner (2005: 15). See also Goldkamp et al. (2001).
95. Berman and Feinblatt (2005: 35).
96. Berman and Feinblatt (2005: 110). This judge did not preside over a drug court but rather over a similarly organized problem-solving court.
97. Goldkamp (2000: 934), quoted in Fischer (2003: 241).
98. Taxman, Soule, and Gelb (1999: 186).
99. Hora, Schma, and Rosenthal (1999: 173).
100. Lewis (1968: 53).
101. Moynihan (1965: 29, 39).
102. In the case of the black and Latino case managers, for example, the "drugs lifestyle" operates more in relation to class prejudices rather than racist ones as such. W.E.B. DuBois commented upon similar patterns of class bigotry and internalized racism

decades ago (see Anderson [2000]). Fortner (2015) and Forman (2017) highlight similar patterns of class prejudice within the Black community in relation to drug policy.

103. In a related vein, Wacquant refers to "the proto-racialization of judicial stigma" in which criminality is framed in biological, semi-racial terms (2001: 101–2). The issue I raise here, however, is not the biologicization of crime but rather the broader ways in which racial discourses shape "post-racial" discourses more generally.

104. Gowan and Whetstone (2012: 69). Gowan and Whetstone's work points toward the new effects that the contemporary image of "addiction" has within the context of drug court and treatment. As they argue:

> In the process of "habilitating" the addict, the strong-arm process [of rehabilitation] is re-mapping our understandings of race, class, and urban marginality, its "disease model" operating as a "neutral," biological, and supposedly universal construct that reduces poverty and racial exclusion to a product of addict psychopathology. (2012: 87; see also Whetstone and Gowan, 2011).

In developing the concept of the para-racial, I aim to call attention to precisely these sorts of remappings as well as to point toward their imbrication with continuing forms of racial oppression.

105. Bonilla-Silva's analysis of a new racism in the post-civil rights period—"racism without racists"—articulates some of these points (2010). His analysis points toward the ways that contemporary racism not only operates in less overt ways (though this has of course changed with the rise of Trump) but also toward some of the remappings that this change has wrought: enlisting the aid of prominent nonwhite elites (e.g., Obama), calling upon nonwhites to endorse an allegedly race-neutral form of liberal politics, and facilitating new formations of race that include a growing category of "honorary whites." In developing the concept of the para-racial, I place additional emphasis on both the social invisibility of many racialized assemblages (even to many nonwhites), and on the partial pluralization of social exclusion at the bottom. The para-racial thus incorporates and points toward links between a variety of different dynamics that require ongoing analysis on their own terms: respectability politics within various nonwhite communities, colorblind racism, the use of racialized metaphors to target class-marginalized white populations, and new racial patterns creating both "honorary whites" and "symbolic blacks," among others. Far from signaling "the declining significance of race," the territory of the para-racial encompasses and is animated by the dynamics of white supremacy.

Yet if the idea of the para-racial serves to inflect contemporary understandings of race, it perhaps even more radically alters prevailing ideas pertaining to class, pointing toward the imbrication of class (in the Durkheimian/Bourdieusian sense) with ideas, affects, and imageries that have been developed within the terrain of race. In other words, the category of class is itself constituted by ideas about race, and vice versa, even as these categories can be usefully taken on their own terms. More than an intersectional crossing of distinct and discrete lines, the categories themselves are thoroughly entangled (as argued in various ways by numerous scholars; see DuBois [1935]; Combahee River Collective [1979]; Robinson [1983]; Hall [1986]; Crenshaw [1989]; Wynter [2003]; Puar [2007]; Roediger [2017]; among others). The notion of the para-racial thus insists upon a genealogical link between race and class that is reciprocal and ongoing, rejecting a frame that sees race as simply derivative of class.

106. Wynter (1996)
107. More precisely, on the infrequent occasions when the possibility of a link between the stresses of work and drug use is acknowledged, it is argued that such users are especially difficult to treat due to their vocational success (e.g., De Leon [2000: 135–36]). By its own estimations, then, drug treatment within the contemporary therapeutic community is thus best addressed to those without these capacities.
108. Again, it is useful to recall that many drug court participants are dealers whose personal consumption of drugs is limited. It is also important to acknowledge that many people who use drugs intensively indeed feel that their drug use has damaged their humanity. As suggested in chapter 1, intensive drug use of this sort often follows from prior forms of violence and harm that render "ordinary humanity" impossible and that generate "inhuman" forms of life. The nature of these harms, of course, are very much subject to interpretation and contestation. In this volume, I focus primarily on the ways that state and para-state institutions define the harm of drugs, a move that effectively turns the category of addiction into a tool of governance. To foreshadow an argument that I will make at greater length in chapter 5, however, links between the understandings of some drug users and state frameworks regarding the nature of "ordinary humanity" help to facilitate "treatment."
109. Callon (1984).
110. Bourgois (1996: 155).
111. Bourgois (1996: 142). See also Anderson (1999).
112. Wilson (1996: 142).
113. Court pamphlet, italics in original.
114. Ironically, given the court's insistence upon employment as a prerequisite for graduation, the burdens associated with drug court appointments sometimes interfere with work (as noted by Murphy [2015: 86]).
115. Copies of the various pamphlets given to participants at each of the New York City drug courts are available online at: www.courts.state.ny.us/courts/nyc/drug_treatment/index.shtml.
116. Moore et al. likewise point toward the ways drug courts (at least in Canada) place entire neighborhoods off-limits due to "therapeutic concerns" (2011).
117. Tiger provides examples of courts that have ordered clients to obtain birth control, refused to allow a parent with a positive urinalysis test to meet with their child, and required participants to attend church or cultural events (such as the ballet). While these are exceptional cases, they point toward the power that the court potentially wields over activities otherwise considered private (2013: 105–6).
118. Hartman (1997: 115).
119. Hartman (1997: 119).

120. Hartman (1997: 122).
121. Hartman (1997: 118).
122. Hartman (1997: 102).
123. Though here it is useful to recall again that many drug court participants only smoke marijuana and cannot be said to face significant issues pertaining to drug addiction.
124. Poor and working-class whites caught up in the war on drugs are thus not "collateral damage," as argued by Michelle Alexander (2010: 199) but are instead ensnared by a remapping of racial logics, establishing a para-racial domain that actively includes them as secondary targets while still focusing primarily on impoverished nonwhites. There are of course several dynamics within whiteness that limit the ways in which whites are brought into para-racial categories. Most notably, as documented by Willoughby-Herard in her work on the Carnegie Foundation's promotion of white supremacy within South Africa, a significant racial divide has been built into the domain of the para-racial, with nonwhites generally positioned for social exclusion and whites often positioned for "civilizing" efforts aimed at social inclusion (2015). But if the white poor are generally targeted for normalizing efforts aimed at social inclusion (the "deserving poor"), some are punished upon failing to meet these expectations (the "undeserving poor"). The history of forced sterilization and other eugenic efforts aimed at those whites deemed undeserving (as targeted, for example, in Richard Dugdale's infamous study of the Juke family in New York [1877]), points toward ways in which white supremacy also necessarily targets some whites in order to enforce its overall logic of racial dominance. Nevertheless, the existence of racial divides within the para-racial generates significant discrepancies at both structural and cultural levels, producing divergent effects based upon a more general linkage between whiteness and political notions of freedom, ethical evaluations of virtue, and economic patterns of success. These patterns are on full display within the U.S. response to drugs, both in the obvious ways in which race has shaped a societal response to drug abuse (see chapter 1, note 71 above), and within drug courts, which work structurally to the advantage of whites (see chapter 1, note 36 and associated text), even as these race-privileged/class-disadvantaged subjects become entrapped within the machinations of the criminal justice system.
125. Lewis (1966: 25).
126. Locke (2012 [1689]: book II, chapter 2, section xi). This section owes a debt to Nikhil Singh's discussion of policing (2017: 35–53). See also Mills (1997: 81–89).

3. Today Is the First Day of the Rest of Your Life: Therapeutic Practice within Therapeutic Communities and the History of Synanon

1. According to the online Urban Dictionary, the term is derived from the television series, *Hawaii Five-O*, a 1970s police drama that originally ran from 1968 to 1980 (the title referencing Hawaii's status as fiftieth state). A reboot of the show began in 2010 (after the time of this fieldwork).

2. The other major inpatient treatment modality in the United States is the Minnesota Model (MM), most prominently identified with the Hazelden Foundation. The differences between TCs and the MM are significant, though both draw in part from the twelve-step tradition, see addiction as a disease, and profess a holistic approach to treatment. The differences become immediately apparent, however, when looking ethnographically at the treatment practices themselves (see McKim [2010] and Whetstone and Gowan [2017]). Generally speaking, whereas TCs utilize techniques of social surveillance, daily discipline, and "accountability" (i.e., punishment for transgressions of any rules), MM programs emphasize self-reflection in peer-oriented groups. Not surprisingly, criminal justice clients tend to be sent to TCs while middle-class and even many voluntary working-class clients tend to go to programs featuring the Minnesota Model (as noted by McKim).
3. See, for example, Perfas (2004: 19–22).
4. Perfas (2004: 21).
5. Perfas (2004: 20–21).
6. Perfas (2004: 23).
7. As Perfas argues, "They [drug addicts] manifest difficulties in appropriately coping with, experiencing, identifying, and expressing feelings. They have low tolerance for discomforts and great difficulty in delaying sensual gratifications. . . . They have unrealistic expectations concerning the satisfaction of their need and wants and a warped sense of entitlement. They are generally irresponsible and lacking consistency and accountability. Their social relationships and manner of relating with people are characterized by a lack of trust or honesty, and an inclination for lying and manipulation to gain an unfair advantage over others" (2004: 21).
8. De Leon (1983: 255).
9. De Leon (1983: 255).
10. De Leon (1983: 252).
11. De Leon (1983: 252).
12. See Parsons (1952) and Skinner (1953).
13. Perfas (2004: 19).
14. Perfas (2004: 22–23).
15. Of course, it is entirely possible that Julia consciously or unconsciously wished to have an excuse so as to not see her daughter. While one could never rule out such an interpretation, I detected only distress and saw no sense of relief from her in speaking about the incident.
16. Perfas (2004: 26).
17. Taxman, Perdoni, and Harrison (2007: 245). This amounts to approximately 1.5 percent of the entire prison population.
18. De Leon (1983: 251).
19. Perfas (2004: 19).
20. De Leon (1983: 256). Such comments recall Barbara Cruikshank's analysis in *The Will to Empower* (1999) in which she argues that the new welfare state works to maximize and activate a particular vision of the will, "to act upon others by getting

them to act in their own interests" (66). Yet as she crucially notes, "those interests must be constituted in order to be acted upon" (66). In this regard the therapeutic community shows no hesitation in insisting on its own vision of right living as opposed to allowing participants to develop their own vision. See also Cruikshank (1996) and Hannah-Moffit (2001: 173).

21. De Leon (1983: 256).
22. In contrast to this perspective, one of the counselors working in the program I studied observed that "if I don't make my bed every day, I'm still allowed to go to work. I'm still allowed to see my friends. So there's a bit of a clash there."
23. Perfas (2004: 22).
24. Nash (1974: 42).
25. In Yablonsky (1965: 212).
26. Yablonsky (1965: 213).
27. Yablonsky (1965: 211). Waldorf reports that the attitude at Phoenix House, another early therapeutic community, was also that "the ex-addict knows better than the addict what is best for him [*sic*]" (1971: 36).
28. A 1960 description of Synanon listed both Dederich and Adaline Ainley—his then girlfriend—as cofounders (Winslow [1960: 12]). Ainley's relationship with Dederich ended and she left Synanon in 1960, with Dederich proclaiming that the split occurred both for "reasons of health" and because she had never been an addict and identified as a "guest" (Morantz [2014: 74]).
29. Janzen (2001: 18).
30. Yablonsky (1965: 102).
31. Gerstel (1982: 76).
32. As noted in chapter 1, it is entirely possible that Dederich developed some of Synanon's practices based on media reports concerning Chinese brainwashing during the Korean War. One final irony of Dederich's endorsement of brainwashing concerns the fact that he attributed his ability to begin Synanon to an experience with LSD he took as part of a UCLA experiment led by Drs. Keith Ditman and Sidney Cohen, and that this research may have received funding through the CIA's MK-ULTRA program, which sought to discover methods to better interrogate or possibly even brainwash people. (Ditman and Cohen's research was funded by the National Institute for Mental Health, one of many channels through which the CIA funneled MK-ULTRA monies for research into LSD, though it is unclear if indeed CIA monies were directed to these particular experiments.) Dederich said of the experience that it gave him a feeling of omnipotence and omniscience which continued for nearly six months and which altered his personality permanently (Winslow [1961]). Walker Winslow, who wrote supportively of the organization and who lived at Synanon in the early 1960s, said of Dederich's experience: "He believes that LSD was responsible for the personal clarity and drive from which Synanon emerged" (1961: 2). Ditman and Cohen's research was directed toward examining the possibilities of LSD for use in rehabilitating alcoholics (Novak [1997, 2004]; Dyck [2006]). Participants in their research also included Bill Wilson, founder of Alcoholics

Anonymous (AA). Wilson similarly credited LSD for helping to inspire the development of AA (AA [1984: 370–71]). On the CIA's MK-ULTRA program and its relationship to LSD research, see Cockburn and St. Clair (1998); Talbot (2015); among others.

33. Janzen (2001: 25). Synanon provided aid to both the Black Panthers and the UFW, sending food to the Panthers' breakfast program, and loaning a bus to the UFW when one the union's buses had been bombed (see Janzen [2001: 29–30] and Clark [2017: 68]). Chávez introduced attack therapy practices into the UFW, directly adopting "the Game" through his contact with Dederich (del Castillo [1996], Janzen [2001: 173–74], Shaw [2010: 249–67], and Bardacke [2011]; see also Coplon [1984]; Pawel [2006]).
34. In Yablonsky (2002: 330).
35. van Gelder (1997).
36. *Time* (1977), quoted in Olin (1980: 275).
37. Szalavitz (2006: 32).
38. Janzen (2001: 123–25).
39. White (1998: 244). See also *New York Times* (1980). On violence at Synanon, see Janzen (2001: 113–40) and Morantz (2014). Morantz has also collected a monologue by Dederich in which he speaks about moving Synanon into a "new religious posture" involving the use of violence, including references to beating people up, throwing people down stairs, and wanting to possess a human ear in a glass of alcohol on his desk. See Morantz (2017).
40. Fredersdorf (2000). See also www.synanon-aktuell.de. On Synanon's legal difficulties, see *New York Times* (1981a, 1981b, 1982a, 1982b).
41. van Gelder (1997). For favorable early accounts of Synanon, see Casriel (1963); Yablonsky (1965); and Endore (1968). More critical accounts of the organization's later years can be found in Olin (1980); Mitchell, Mitchell, and Ofshe (1980); Gerstel (1982); Tourish and Wohlforth (2000); and Morantz (2014). Accounts tracing the evolution of the group can be found in White (1998); Janzen (2001); and Clark (2017).
42. Sugarman (1974: vii).
43. Schecter, Alksne, and Kaufman (1978).
44. Gates and Bourdette (1975: 237–38) and Janzen (2001: 114–21).
45. Sugarman (1974: 8) and White and Miller (2007).
46. Szalavitz (2007: 20).
47. Morantz (2009).
48. Though I have found no evidence that Erhard knew directly of Synanon, by the time he established EST in 1971 Synanon's practices were widely distributed. The intellectual foundations for attack therapy were developed by Dr. Harry Tiebout, a psychiatrist who treated Bill Wilson (founder of Alcoholics Anonymous) for depression and who later acted as a Trustee of AA from 1957 to 1966 as well as the chair of the National Council on Alcoholism in 1950. Tiebout argued that alcoholics were characterized by "egocentricity, rebellion against restrictions, a search for pleasure, a demand for special consideration, a peculiar twisted logic, and finally a

marked irresponsibility and immaturity" (in White [1998: 142]), and that they must therefore be "cut down to size" (Tiebout [1953]).

49. Sugarman (1974: 8).
50. Goffman (1961).
51. Sugarman was not the only advocate of total institutions. The director of the California Department of Corrections, Richard McGee, similarly referenced Goffman in suggesting that total institutions could be used as instruments of positive change (in Kassebaum, Ward, and Wilner [1963: 3]).
52. Sugarman (1974: 14, 17).
53. Goffman used the term *processes of mortification* in describing one of the features of the total institution (1961: 43).
54. Sugarman (1974: 17).
55. Yablonsky (1989: 56).
56. Yablonsky (1989: 52).
57. Sugarman (1974: 14).
58. Yablonsky (1989: 52).
59. Yablonsky (1989: 52)
60. Yablonsky (1989: 51).
61. Yablonsky (1965: 194–213; 1989: 51–52)
62. Sugarman (1974: 13–14).
63. Yablonsky (1989: 52).
64. For example, Sugarman (1974: 88).
65. Sugarman (1974: 88).
66. Ellipses and emphasis in original. Sugarman (1974: 13).
67. Sugarman (1970: 79).
68. Sugarman (1970: 79). I will have more to say about gender within the TC in chapter 5, including the ways in which female addicts have been understood differently than the prototypical male addict, and the types of specific therapeutic practices that were directed at them as a result (see also Kaye [2010]). While noting that such gendered differences existed, here I wish to mark the way in which TC practitioners overwhelmingly focused upon the figure of the male addict, using this constructed image as a prototype for all drug users.
69. Lennard and Allen (1974: 202).
70. Sugarman (1974: 16).
71. Sugarman (1974: 51).
72. Sugarman (1974: 52).
73. "Privileges" at the early Daytop were typically granted in a particular order:

> Letters home are allowed before a visit home, an escorted visit (accompanied by an older resident) before a solo visit, and a day visit before a whole weekend. Other privileges which can often be earned in the first six months [or taken away in the case of noncompliance] include the following: possession of some items of personal clothing brought in the house

> when a resident entered or possession of other personal items (not including watches or jewelry yet), permission to grow sideburns for males, permission to go out on house movie trips or other pleasure excursions for limited groups, and permission to read, watch occasional television, or play a musical instrument. (Sugarman [1974: 53])

New male residents at Daytop did not even have initial access to a bed, being forced to sleep on a sofa in the living room for a period lasting from a few days to a couple of weeks, thus making the point that "one *earns* everything in Daytop—even one's bed" (Sugarman [1974: 53]).

74. Morantz (2014: 56). See also Winslow (1961: 3).
75. Waldorf (1971: 35–36). See also Lennard and Allen (1974: 206–7) and Sugarman, (1974: 21–22).
76. Sugarman (1974: 51–52).
77. Rosenthal (1974: 14).
78. Foucault (1975).
79. Waldorf (1971: 36).
80. Sugarman (1974: 22–23), emphasis in original.
81. Olin (1980: 94).
82. Sugarman (1974: 58–59). He adds:

> Perhaps the most severe form of learning experience, applied only to male residents, is the *shaved head*. For females the equivalent sanction is to be made to wear a stocking cap which covers all the hair, while they are forbidden to wear makeup. A shaved head is normally given to a resident who splits from the house and then seeks to return. . . . Along with the bald head or stocking cap, a person is normally sent into the "dishpan," which means that he spends all his time cleaning pots and utensils in the kitchen or "spare parts" which means that he is at the disposal of any senior resident and will be given a series of heavy, monotonous tasks and required to work until late at night." (1974: 58–59)

83. Nash (1974: 53).
84. Nash (1974: 53).
85. Warren-Holland (2006: 22–23).
86. Sugarman (1970: 83–84).
87. Sugarman (1974: 56).
88. Sugarman (1974: 57).
89. Yablonsky (1989: 134).
90. Aron and Daily (1976: 3).
91. Nash (1974: 45). Waldorf notes: "That is not to say that there is never any criticism of the program, for there is, but criticism must be made in a spirit of constructive change and is generally only allowed from older members of the community" (1971: 36).

92. Freud (1961 [1930]: 72).
93. Sugarman (1974: 57).
94. Sugarman (1974: 63).
95. Waldorf (1971: 35).
96. Waldorf (1971: 35).
97. Sugarman (1974: 57–58).
98. Lennard and Allen (1974: 203, 207), emphasis in original.
99. Yablonsky (1989: 136).
100. Sugarman (1974: 58).
101. Sugarman (1974: v, 30, 104). Lipton reports an even higher figure, with 60–80 percent leaving within the first three months and 70–90 percent leaving within the first year (1998: 217, 219). A more recent study by Keen et al. (2001), performed at Phoenix House, showed 75 percent of residents leaving within ninety days, and only 13 percent successfully graduating from the program. In an earlier study conducted at several "traditional" therapeutic communities, De Leon and Schwartz (1984) found 30 percent of the clients leaving within fourteen days, and 63.8 percent within ninety days. In response to these figures, and as a defense of the TC model, De Leon and Schwartz note that retention is a challenging issue amongst all drug treatment modalities. In 1997, Simpson et al. found significant differences in retention between various types of long-term residential programs, and statistical evaluation suggested that these differences were due to more than simply different populations being treated (1997). Despite the fact that retention has been identified as being key to "successful" treatment outcomes, studies examining how program differences might relate to retention have not been much forthcoming.

    It might be added, however, that the focus on retention has led many researchers to the conclusion that legal force is a useful intervention for drug users insofar as it allegedly increases the time they spend within treatment programs (see Farabee, Predergast and Anglilin [1998], among many others; see also Klag, O'Callaghan, and Creed [2010] and Urbanoski [2010] for critical reviews of this literature, pointing toward difficulties in defining coercion and noticeable differences among various drug using populations and the ways in which they respond to varying kinds of external pressure). These studies often fail to consider that findings showing a correlation between retention and treatment outcome may have been highly reliant upon client characteristics that led to both higher retention and treatment outcome. Furthermore, I am aware of no study which addresses the fate of those who "fail" at mandated treatment (especially increased imprisonment) and which carefully weighs these negative effects against purported benefits. The case for mandated treatment is thus based upon a potentially spurious link between treatment retention and outcome, and systematically fails to consider other more harmful consequences of legal coercion. See also chapter 2, note 68.
102. Sugarman (1974: 65–66).
103. Sugarman (1974: 66).

104. Sugarman (1974: 67; see also Gerstel [1982: 75–76]).
105. Sugarman (1974: 17).
106. De Leon (1974: 17–18).
107. Yablonsky (1989: 145).
108. Yablonsky (1989: 11).
109. van Gelder (1997).
110. Tourish and Wohlforth (2000: 128).
111. Yablonsky (1965: 138).
112. Yablonsky (1965: 330; see also 1989: 134–35).
113. Yablonsky (1965: 192).
114. Sugarman (1974: 111).
115. Sugarman (1974: 111).
116. While I here emphasize the centrality of discipline in the workings of the first- and second-generation TCs, practitioners themselves would often highlight the importance of "the Game" to therapeutic effectiveness (e.g., Yablonsky [1965: 137] and Endore [1968: 164]). On acting "as if," see also Morantz (2014: 113–17).
117. TCs aim at something grander than envisioned by Goffman's notion of the *total institution*. While embodying Goffman's vision in numerous respects (TCs certainly qualify as total institutions), they seek to involve the participation of residents in ways that Goffman did not envision. Similarly, Foucault's panopticon fails to account for the ways in which therapeutic communities operate through forced participation.
118. Sugarman (1974: 82–83).
119. Sugarman (1974: 83). Perhaps unsurprisingly, the management techniques within the early TCs also emphasized obedience and hierarchy over any task orientation, particularly in cases in which the resident/staff division was indistinct (such as at Synanon, where all residents were told that they were effectively staff members). Olin (1980) details the managerial philosophy of one director who was considered "a role model Synanon manager" and who gave courses on the topic to others within Synanon. Describing some useful techniques he had learned directly from Dederich, the director suggests that:

> First and foremost, a Synanon executive must establish himself [*sic*] as *The Boss*. This can be done in much the same way as a Trip Guide [a leader within an extended Game session] sets himself apart from his Trippers: Shake things up, move people and objects around, start morning meetings in the evening, move the second floor to the third, fire, demote, and promote a few people. Don't be afraid. Once you've made a decision, it's a good one. . . . Say "no" to every fourth request that came up, no matter how reasonable it was. In fact, the more reasonable, the greater the effect. This elicits awe from subordinates and may very well launch the myth that you are a deep and charismatic cat. (123–24)

The manager went on to discuss how underlings resist their superiors, and "how to effectively and—heh, heh, heh—creatively deal with them" (Olin [1980:

123–24]). Synanon, of course, represents something of an extreme case, but it bears attention as it was the model program which defined and shaped the field.

120. Weppner (1983: 145–67). Severe abuses have also been documented at other spin-off groups, including very prominent ones. The Seed, for example, received a $1 million grant from the federal government for their work in 1971, yet by 1974 a Senate investigation specifically cited The Seed when comparing TC techniques to practices utilized within North Korean "brainwashing" programs (U.S. Congress [1974b: 15]). Despite being discredited, members of The Seed went on to found a similar organization, Straight Inc. Allegations of beatings and unlawful detention followed Straight as well, and the group was disbanded in 1993 (Fager [2000]; Trebach [2005]; and Szalavitz [2006]). Both The Seed and Straight Inc. found a friendly reception from high-level members within the Republican Party. Straight Inc. in particular was declared by Nancy Reagan to be her favorite drug abuse program, and George Bush Sr., when president, made a commercial for the organization (available online at: www.youtube.com/watch?v=cU34naEp7A0). In 1995, the founders of Straight Inc. created the Drug Free America Foundation, but they currently do not run a rehabilitation program.

    Similar abuses continue in the present. At OASAS—New York State's Office of Alcoholism and Substance Abuse Services, the agency that regulates drug treatment programs—I was informed of a facility for adolescents that was ordered to stop chaining the teen patients together in a group and making them utilize bathroom facilities while chained. The facility stopped the practice but was not fined and continues to operate. In other cases, particularly in cases of Medicaid fraud (e.g., requiring clients to show up at an outpatient facility every day when their case required only a weekly session, thereby enabling the facility to bill Medicaid for the additional sessions), facilities were *encouraged* to close—with threats of lawsuits if they did not—however, no charges were pressed or fines levied. With little interstate cooperation regarding such matters, and no actual penalties enacted, each state regulatory agency would confront the individuals running these groups anew, thereby making it possible for the persons in question to simply move to another state and establish another facility.

121. U.S. Congress (1974b: 15).
122. Yablonsky (1965: 385–86).
123. I have reordered these quotes for clarity; Friedenberg (1965: 258, 259).
124. Sugarman (1974: 60).
125. It is perhaps useful to point out that "Studies of defense mechanisms among people in alcohol treatment have found no characteristic defense structure" (White and Miller [2007]). In other words, there is no singular addict in need of a single form of treatment (see also Kaye [2012]).
126. Yablonsky (1965: 379–82).
127. Similarly, a person's brutal physical attacks based upon jealousy may express love or concern for the future of the relationship while nevertheless remaining a harmful form of abuse.

128. Deitch and Solit (1993: 306–7).
129. Additional favorable discussion of confrontation within TCs can be found within Bratter et al. (1985) and Bratter and Sinsheimer (2008).
130. Fisher (1971).
131. Fisher (1971: 204–5).
132. The term *serious play* was first popularized in a book by Michael Schrage, *Serious Play: How the World's Best Companies Simulate to Innovate* (2000), and the technique he describes, particularly a form known as Lego Serious Play, has been disseminated through the corporate world. I use the term here in a very different sense, simply to gesture toward the intensity and high emotional stakes involved in *the game.*
133. It is difficult to estimate, for example, the effect that permitting the open expression of racism and other bigotries within *the game* might have had on the group, particularly in comparison to a more normative liberal pattern of racial interaction in which such sentiments are experienced and subtly enacted but outwardly rendered mute. Liberal forms of silent racism—advocates for *the game* might argue—actively disable opportunities to openly recognize and confront prejudices within the group.

    Both the content and the context of these interactions matter in this regard. No stranger to self-aggrandizement, in 1962 Dederich proclaimed Synanon "the most successful experiment in integrated living in a segregated area in the world" (in Clark, 2017: 67). In the following year, Dederich married Betty Coleman, a black woman, and she took on a strong leadership role within Synanon. The organization also received favorable coverage in the black press, and *the game* was credited with addressing racial "hangups" among its members, approximately 10 percent of whom were black (Clark, 2017: 67). Carina Ray, an historian of colonialism and the Black Atlantic who grew up within Synanon, suggests that given its "intimate and confrontational" nature, "the game allowed people from all walks of life, and especially whites and blacks, to encounter each other in ways that would have been unimaginable elsewhere" (2012). Synanon also moderated game sessions for the Black Panthers (Clark, 2017: 68), and offered aid to the United Farm Workers (as noted above; note 33). Nevertheless, while Synanon featured women-only games designed to challenge the "feminine mystique" (69), there is no indication that it ran ongoing groups specifically designed to challenge racism, and some prominent members—including David Deitch, who later served as the chief clinical director at Phoenix House and later co-founded Delancy Street, and John Maher, the other co-founder of Delancy Street—did not believe the organization was sufficiently aware of the specific issues facing non-white addicts (68). As race was not directly addressed in a sustained way by those who evaluated and wrote about Synanon, however, it is difficult to gain a more complete picture concerning the issues that might have arisen within the community and the way in which these issues were (or were not) addressed. The fact that race was not directly addressed by most advocates, however, speaks to an ongoing failure, particularly when combined with "para-racial" stereotyping of drug users.
134. For an example, see Gates and Bourdette (1975: 236)

135. Tourish and Wohlforth (2000: 127–28).
136. Endore (1968: 169).
137. Gates and Bourdette (1975: 236). See also Olin (1980: 93).
138. Maslow (1967: 28–29).
139. Maslow (1967: 29).
140. Waldorf writes of his experiences at Phoenix House (1971: 34).
141. Yablonsky (1965: 383).
142. Yablonsky (1965: 383).
143. Yablonsky (1965: 385).
144. Gerstel (1982: 60).
145. Yablonsky (1965: 384).
146. Yablonsky (1965: 385).
147. Yablonsky (1965: 381).
148. Yablonsky (1965: 381).
149. Warren-Holland (2006: 20).
150. Sugarman (1974: 60).
151. The jazz guitarist Joe Pass resided at Synanon and helped to record the highly respected album *Sounds of Synanon* in 1962.
152. Yablonsky (1962: 53).
153. For example, see Sugarman (1974: 23).
154. The rules at Synanon changed greatly over time. In its early days, Dederich had less power over participants in the organization and allowed sex to be used as a sort of incentive to stay with the program. As he later commented: "Sex was all over the place. . . . In a way I felt I was merchandising. I had to allow them to have something quickly that they could understand and stay with. I tried to allow them to have fun in any manner as long as they didn't get drunk, shoot dope, or hurt anybody" (in Casriel [1963: 24]). By the late 1960s, however, more restrictions were placed on sex between residents in order to encourage longer-term romantic unions over short-term sexual ones (including chaperoned courtship periods and warnings that "any pregnancy would result in instant marriage" (see Fisher [1971: 209–10] and Morantz [2014: 122]). The vision of proper sexuality also sometimes included heterosexist understandings of homosexuality. Nash, for example, writes about rules regarding sex during the early days at Phoenix House, noting that "The program is extremely moralistic in that neither heterosexual promiscuity nor any sort of homosexual encounter are allowed in the house" (1974: 51). At some point, however, Phoenix House altered its policy and prohibited sex entirely (I have been unable to ascertain exactly when this occurred, nor the circumstances that might have led to the change).
155. Stine, Patrick, and Molina (1982: 389).
156. Kaye (2010: chapter 4). See also Cummins (1994); Vandevelde et al. (2004); and Janssen (2007).
157. Alternatively, the programs were sometimes referred to as *milieu therapy*.
158. Jones (1953: 40).

159. The U.S. military also created a number of TCs based on the "democratic" model, using them to deal with soldiers who had gone AWOL or committed other civil crimes rendering them unsuitable for combat (see Abrahams and McCorkle [1946, 1947]; Sheehy [2002]; and Abrahams [2006, 2014]).
160. Janssen (2007: 132).
161. Janssen (2007: 133).
162. Perhaps not surprisingly, the democratic TC model has fared somewhat better in Europe than in the United States (Vandevelde et al. [2004: 69]).
163. Opton (1974: 639–40).
164. Opton (1974: 625–27); Mitford (1973a: 139–40).
165. Given the extensive use of pharmaceuticals within prisons today—with more than 10 percent of all inmates receiving psychotropic medications (Beck and Maruschak [2001]; Wilper et al. [2009]; Fabris [2011]), a figure that rises to approximately 40 percent of inmates in some prisons (Hatch [2019: 39, 55, 56]; see also Hatch and Bradley [2016]; Hatch et al. [2016])—one may question why correctional institutions of the 1960s did not move toward more the pervasive medication of inmates, as did psychiatry in relation to its wards. But while there were indeed several instances in which psycho-pharmaceuticals were used in a widespread manner against inmate populations (Mitford [1973a: 18]; Opton [1974]; Whitehead [1985]; Sommers and Baskin [1990]; Hatch [2019: 14]), the use of pharmaceuticals has never been openly acknowledged as a control mechanism, instead being administered either as part of a clinical trial or as a mental health treatment for inmates. Following a series of exposés and congressional hearings, clinical testing on inmates were stopped in 1980 (Hatch [2019: 82]), and psychiatric drugs became useable only as a "service" for inmates, not as an overt control mechanism (though, as Hatch points out, psychotropic drugs may be used when an inmate is deemed a "threat"; 2019: 16–17). In the context of the 1960s, however, both political and legal pressure would have made it very difficult for prison administrators to utilize these medications on a universal or near-universal basis (Hatch points out, however, that there is no good data showing how often these drugs were used on inmate populations at the time, and suggests that it could have been as high or higher than today; personal communication, February 2019).
166. Rhodes (2004).
167. Hollander (1971); Mitford (1973a: 145–48); Kurki and Morris (2001); and Cummins (1994: 270–71).
168. In Moya and Achtenberg (1974: 242).
169. Oelsner (1974).
170. Moya and Achtenberg (1974: 243).
171. U.S. Congress (1974a, 1974b). See also USDoJ (1975).
172. Menzel (1974: 42). See also Geller et al. (1977: 30).
173. Trotter and Warren (1974: 180).
174. Furthermore, though administrative concerns were not as central as political ones, most democratic TCs required an open atmosphere with "some degree of

permissiveness and freedom to make mistakes" (Williams [1996: 28]; see also Briggs [1973: 101, 166–67]). They were also deemed somewhat counterproductive as they "legitimized the search by prisoners for their own community and inadvertently fostered a political sense of self among prisoners that proved central to the crisis in American prison in the late 1960s" (Janssen [2007: 117], see also Cummins [1994: 19–20]), thereby disrupting the punitive security regime. In contrast, Synanon's hierarchical TC promised to achieve change without disrupting—and perhaps even reinforcing—a security-oriented approach.

175. Martinson (1974). See also Lipton, Wilks, and Martinson (1975).
176. Deitch et al. (2002: 131) and O'Brien and Henican (1993: 52). In an earlier essay, Deitch specifies that the acronym initially stood for "Drug Addiction Treatment for Probationers" (1973: 168).
177. It was only at this point that hierarchical TCs began to refer to themselves as "therapeutic communities." DATOP originally referred to itself as a *humanizing community*; however, the psychiatrist Dr. Efran Ramirez, acting as the first Commissioner of New York City's Addiction Services Agency, urged that the organization use the term *therapeutic community* "because of its greater acceptance in the health and mental health communities" (thanks to the prior existence of democratic therapeutic communities). See Deitch et al. (2002: 131). Later organizations institutionalized this rebranding.
178. Wallace et al. (1990: 23). In his text, *The Untherapeutic Community* (1983), Weppner offers a mixed but ultimately unflattering portrayal of one of these programs based upon time he spent there as a researcher.
179. Mecca (1978). Now known as Treatment Accountability for Safer Communities, TASC continues to operate today in more than 125 local jurisdictions.
180. None of this is to say that hierarchical TCs would not have existed were it not for the interest of criminal justice entities—the rapid expansion of Synanon and of other later-generation TCs belies this possibility—but it is to say that criminal justice institutions offered key supports in the expansion of the model, helping at first to promote it over other competitors (notably the democratic TC model) and, over time, working to shape it to meet its own institutional needs.
181. Wexler and Lipton (1993: 215).
182. Wexler, Blackmore, and Lipton (1991); Wexler and Lipton (1993); and Wexler (1995).
183. Slightly more than 50 percent of inmates meet the American Psychiatric Association's *Diagnostic and Statistical Manual* criteria for drug abuse or dependence, as opposed to 13 percent of men and 5 percent of women in the adult population more generally (the prison population is 93 percent male, making the relevant comparison figure approximately 12.5 percent). See Belenko, Hiller, and Hamilton (2013: 414).
184. Waldorf writes that "the concept 'responsibility and concern' is a conscious attempt to overcome the code of the streets" (1971: 36; see also Sugarman [1974: 21]). The positioning of drug treatment as an anticrime measure sometimes led to extreme emphasis upon the criminality of the addict offender. The founders of Daytop, for example, Shelly and Bassin, suggested that "an addict constitutes

a one-man crime wave" and that addicts "pillage and plunder the community . . . deteriorate neighborhoods, impoverish families, and demoralize parents, wives and children" (1965: 186). Odyssey House, another of the early second-generation TCs, similarly framed itself as treating "criminal antisocial" individuals, adding that "one of the major factors in the rehabilitation is the acceptance of authority and the ability to rationally structure one's life" (Imhof [1974: 450–51]). See also Wilson and Snodgrass (1969).

4. Control and Agency in Contemporary Therapeutic Communities

1. Brown (1985: 205). At one point, the King's County (Brooklyn, NY) Probation Department asked Synanon if they would be willing to take charge of the program. Monsignor William O'Brien, one of the founders of Daytop, reports that when Dederich was offered the possibility, he refused to accept unless all monies were entirely under his control and that "no one would ever question how a single penny was spent" (O'Brien and Henican [1993: 50]). O'Brien and Henican suggest that Brooklyn's probation commissioner (Joseph Shelly) saw no way to move forward under these conditions and let the matter drop. Endore tells a slightly different story, suggesting that Shelly moved forward with Dederich's proposal, but that the National Institute for Mental Health (NIMH)—which eventually provided some of the start-up money for DATOP—blocked the move (Endore [1968: 307]).
2. Clark (2017: 112–13).
3. Clark (2017: 99).
4. Clark (2017: 113).
5. De Leon (2000: 3). See also De Leon (1995: 1633–34). Niv, Hamilton, and Hser report that some outpatient treatment facilities have shifted from a one-on-one approach toward group practice as a result of the influx of criminal justice clients and a need to obtain the "biggest bang for the buck" (2009: 513).
6. In some TCs, the addition of these ancillary services was readily embraced and occurred quite early (De Leon [1985: 825]).
7. De Leon (2000: 5).
8. Evidence for the efficacy of TCs has been slow to develop, but many supporters argue that therapeutic communities have a research base that verifies their effectiveness as well (De Leon [2010], NIDA [2015]). Belenko, Hiller, and Hamilton, however, point toward methodological issues in these studies and argue that the evidentiary base remains thin (2013: 217).
9. Egelko and Galanter (1993).
10. Wagner and Conners (2003).
11. Kaye (2010; see esp. chapter 6).
12. To some extent, claims to moderate the TC have been present in all post-Synanon TCs. Daniel Casriel, the psychiatric supervisor at Daytop, asserted as early as 1969 that the organization had achieved an "amalgamation of the hostile

confrontations developed by places like Synanon and the supportive emotional understanding approach that has been classically used by psychiatrists" and that this "new dynamic" was "extremely effective" (Casriel et al. [1969], cited in Clark [2017]).

13. Broekaert, Kooyman, and Ottenberg (1998: 596)
14. Broekaert, Kooyman, and Ottenberg (1998: 597).
15. Broekaert et al. (2004: 232).
16. Bracke (1996), quoted in Broakaert et al. (2004: 233).
17. van der Meer (1997), quoted in Broakaert et al. (2004: 234).
18. Broekaert et al. (2004: 231).
19. De Leon (2000: 220).
20. De Leon (2000: 273)
21. De Leon (2000: 290).
22. De Leon (2000: 297).
23. De Leon (2000: 298).
24. Personal communication with the author (June 2010).
25. De Leon (2000: 226).
26. Emphasis in original. De Leon (2000: 226; see also De Leon [1995: 1624]).
27. De Leon (2000: 279).
28. Writing in 1971, Waldorf notes that:

> During marathons most individuals' defenses are eroded under the intensity and long duration of the confrontations, and considerable behavior, feelings and attitudes (both present and past) not otherwise discovered get out into the open. Marathons are used consciously at Hart Island to tighten the structure of the house and the program. (1971: 35)

Phoenix House's program at Hart Island operated from 1966 to 1976, initially receiving people sent from NYC's jail at Riker's Island, and later expanding to include individuals referred through probation and parole or admitted voluntarily (Deitch [1973: 171] and Nash [1974: 44]). De Leon's experiences with TCs were shaped by his many years as research director for Phoenix House.

29. Personal communication with the author (May 2010). Based on his extensive experience as an international consultant and trainer for those developing therapeutic communities, De Leon suggests that TCs in Europe and Australia, as well as in other parts of the United States, are significantly less beholden to this tradition and offer a significantly less punitive environment. Be that as it may, other ethnographers have nevertheless noted the abusive practices they have encountered in other U.S. locales such as California (Haney [2010]) and Minnesota (Gowan and Whetstone [2012], Whetstone and Gowan [2017]).
30. On these issues, see also chapter 2 (note 58) and chapter 3 (note 120). Concerns about abusive conditions at TCs continue to exist, particularly in relation to institutions working with teenagers (Szalavitz [2006] and USGAO [2007]). Beyond this, a lack of significant regulation continues to allow significant abuses to exist. One

staff member who worked at a TC that I did not directly examine, for example, specified that other staff members sold drugs within the facility, and that the directors knew about and condoned this behavior. Likewise, Rafael Torruella's research (2010) reveals the existence of several drug treatment programs located in New York City that are not certified by the state and that feature many practices (ranging from extreme overcrowding to the lack of an accredited staff) that would render them ineligible for certification were they to attempt to obtain it. These programs often receive clients who are strongly urged to leave Puerto Rico and to attend these New York City-based programs by both small-town mayors and police authorities. As Torruella documents, elected officials sometimes pay for the trip to New York, telling the individuals that treatment services are much better and more widely available in the U.S. mainland than in Puerto Rico, and the residents are sometimes escorted to the airport by police officers. Upon arrival, the inductees often have their papers taken from them by the program, as well as all of their personal funds, only to find that there is in fact no structured treatment program beyond work and prayer. Individuals are also required to apply for all welfare benefits to which they might be entitled (food stamps, Medicaid, etc.), with all of the monies going directly to the facility. As Torruella writes, "Many of the individuals leave the program in haste because of the treatment/living conditions and most have problems attaining their identification materials and moneys back from the treatment center's owner. Many are unsuccessful and when they step out to homeless New York, they do so with no money and no identification" (Torruella [2010: 37–38]). On these issues, see also Sanjurjo (2014); Upegui-Hernández and Torruella (2015); Cardona-Maguigad (2015a, 2015b); and U.S. Congress (2017).

31. White and Miller (2007).
32. Broekaert et al. (2000) and Vandevelde et al. (2004). See also De Leon (1983, 1985) and several additional articles described in Rawlings and Yates (2001).
33. Haigh and Lees (2008).
34. While it would be impossible to study the full range of programs, and my own work was confined to the (potentially atypical) Northeastern U.S., the descriptions in the literature suggest that some generalizations—however tentative and problematic—can be made based upon the existence of roughly comparable environments found by multiple researchers in diverse regions. A significant amount of variation continues to exist even within the frame of the professionalized TC, of course, based upon client population, program location (urban or rural), the presence or absence of licensed social workers, program history, and so on.
35. As noted in chapter 1 (note 67), probation and parole are the primary referral sources within the criminal justice system (SAMHSA [2015: 65, 80]). Nevertheless, drug courts have formed the ideological edge of coerced treatment, having attracted much more media attention than any other legal program.
36. Sugarman (1974: 104).
37. De Leon, 1988: 161, cited by Kooyman (1994: 155).
38. Personal communication with the author (August 2010).

39. The rate of people arrested for drug crimes who were sent to treatment facilities increased by 35 percent following passage of the law (Parsons et al. [2015: 8]). Prior to the law's passage, the state regulatory board of drug treatment facilities, OASAS, helped fund several new drug treatment facilities in expectation of greater need; however, according to staff members at three different facilities, the net increase (from 292 to 495 individuals) still resulted in some crowding within the facilities (personal communications with the author, December 2011).
40. The term *modified therapeutic community* or *MTC* is a commonly used descriptor for this third generation of TCs; however, it has no precise meaning. The term is often used, for example, to refer to institutions that have applied the TC model for specific client populations (e.g., TCs that focus on women, homeless persons, prison inmates, or dually-diagnosed individuals). Alternatively, some outpatient programs have adopted a TC approach and have been called *modified therapeutic communities*. The program I most closely examined worked with a traditional client population (primarily male, often nonwhite, and generally referred to treatment through the criminal justice system) but utilized this term in referring to themselves because of the presence of licensed social workers who offered both individual and group counseling sessions with residents.
41. On the use of "emotional contrast strategies," see Rafaeli and Sutton (1991) and Brodt and Tuchinsky (2000).
42. Stine, Patrick, and Molina, for example, suggested that "Distancing tactics on the part of the staff (whether by physical barriers such as desks or tables or by emotional ones such as excessive formality) are contraindicated" (1982: 379).
43. As noted in chapter 1 (note 74), more than half of individuals who seek treatment for marijuana use are coerced to do so by the criminal justice system, while fewer than 20 percent do so voluntarily (SAMHSA [2016: 77]).
44. Rinella (1976) discusses an earlier moment when TCs were also shifting from voluntary to mandated clients, noting many of the same effects. As he writes:

    > Many new residents entering Eagleville [the name of the TC where he worked] through the criminal justice system viewed Eagleville as simply another phase of incarceration. The initial attitude affected not only treatment possibilities for the individual involved, but also had a profound impact on staff attitude and the structure of the entire community. Despite the absence of formal physical restraints, the tone of community life became more custodial. (54–56)

    Following this early period with many residents referred from criminal justice, most TCs returned to a base of voluntary clients, only to cycle back toward mandated clients in the late 1980s and 1990s.
45. Braithwaite (1989: 101).
46. Braithwaite (1989: 101).
47. Waldorf, for example, casually mentions the possibility of expelling residents from Phoenix House for infringement of the rules (1971: 31, 32).

48. Skyes (1956: 135).
49. The line ("What are you prepared to do?") concerns a moment in the movie in which Elliot Ness (played by Kevin Costner) is being challenged by Malone, one of his squad members (played by Sean Connery), to take extra-legal measures in capturing the Mafia boss Al Capone. Later, when Malone has been mortally wounded by one of Capone's men, he repeats the question to Ness just before dying: "What are you prepared to do?" Ness eventually finds and captures Malone's murderer, only to have the murderer brag about how he is protected and will never have to go to prison. Ness throws him off a roof.

    The use of this phrase, then, calls forth a metaphor in which one must go beyond normative structures such as the law in order to do what needs to be done in order to obtain "justice." In this case, the normative structures being broken seem to concern the fact that the counselors were taking on a directly punitive role in relation to the residents, rather than relying upon a more narrowly supportive disposition.
50. A song by N.O.R.E.
51. As with yelling and name-calling, the practice of collective punishment—in which innocent persons are punished for others' rule-breaking—was considered "abusive" and "therapeutically ill-advised" by the state regulatory board, no matter how gently the punishment was enforced. As with cases of abusive punishments, the administrator responsible for handling such complaints said that he would call up a facility and *advise* them to change their practice; however, he stated he would be unable to impose any sort of fine or to force the facility to change their policy.
52. It is not entirely clear how widespread such benefits are, however. Whetstone and Gowan, for example, examine a "strong-arm rehab" center that did not provide employment and educational programming and that instead simply focused on "the modification and erasure of street culture" (2017: 93).
53. Bourdieu (1977).
54. Mahmood (2005: 29).
55. Mahmood (2005: 7); see also Foucault (1982a: 786–88; also available in 1982b: 217–19).
56. As noted by Kerrison (2017: 579).
57. Mahmood (2005: 29).
58. Mahmood (2005: 29).
59. Hannah-Moffat (2001: 173).
60. Rose (1999b: 62).
61. Meyers (2002), among others.
62. Roberts (2015: 27–49).
63. I draw here from Roberts's argument regarding Hannah Arendt and "Black slavery as the *ultimate Blob*" (or the ultimate threat from the realm of "the social" to the integrity of what Arendt termed the *political sphere*; 2015: 37).
64. Together with others, Collins argues that "racist and sexist ideologies both share the common feature of treating dominated groups—the 'others'—as objects lacking full human subjectivity" (1986: S18). The link of "dehumanization" to liberal political

culture suggests that other modes of oppression exist, modes which oppress *without* dehumanization. Butler offers a parallel though slightly different analysis, suggesting that "to be oppressed you must first become intelligible. To find that you are fundamentally unintelligible (indeed, that the laws of culture and of language find you to be an impossibility) is to find that you have not yet achieved access to the human" (2004: 30).

65. In saying this, I do not mean to valorize the fugitive. As will be seen in the next chapter, questions of agency and resistance proceed on multiple lines and cannot be reduced to a single factor. What I emphasize here is the disavowal of agency as a necessary tactic implied by the use of freedom as a normative project.
66. De Leon (2000: 141).
67. De Leon (2000: 78).
68. De Leon (2000: 138).
69. Emphasis in original; De Leon (2000: 144–45).
70. Simon (1993: 74).
71. Simon (1993: 74). Simon speaks here of the earlier model of democratic therapeutic communities, but his observations pertain equally to the regime developed in later hierarchical TCs.
72. Simon (1993: 130–31). De Leon cites Levy, Faltico, and Bratter (1977: 45).
73. Many TC professionals indeed differentiate between residents who have basic capacities for work and those who do not, enshrining this distinction between those in need of "rehabilitation" and those who never experienced what they term *orderly living* (and who therefore might be said to have been living a supposed drugs lifestyle their entire lives!). For the residents in this latter group, "recovery . . . involves *habilitation*, or learning the behavioral skills, attitudes, and values associated with socialized living for the first time" (Levy, Faltico, and Bratter [1977: 66], emphasis added).
74. Emphasis in original. Hackett and Turk (2018: 42).
75. Kalleberg (2011); Doussard (2013); Tan Chen (2015); among others.
76. De Leon, for example, notes that "Therapeutic goals are not easily achieved if job functions are relatively routine, easy to perform, or even master. . . . Thus, *changing* the resident's job function is a continuously used clinical intervention" (italics in original; 2000: 147). See also Casriel (1963: 39–40, 73–74) and Sugarman (1974: 38).
77. Soss, Fording, and Schram (2011: 174).

5. Gender, Sexuality, and the Drugs Lifestyle

1. De Leon (2000: 221).
2. De Leon (2000: 275–76, 297n).
3. De Leon (2000: 38–39).
4. De Leon (2000: 61).
5. Gowan (2010: 105).

6. Irwin noted that many inmates in California's treatment regime of the 1960s resented the "sickness image of themselves that underpins the treatment ideal" (1970: 53):

   > This view that they are emotionally disturbed has proven to be less dignified and more humiliating than that of moral unworthiness. At least the morally depraved are responsible for their own actions, whereas the emotionally disturbed are considered incapable of willful acts. (Irwin [1970: 53])

   It may be that the idea of drug addiction helps to facilitate adoption of sick talk as opposed to a framing that includes all inmates as ill simply by virtue of their criminality.
7. In relation to crime committed by men, for example, James Messerschmidt argues that "crime by men is a form of social practice invoked as a resource, when other resources are unavailable, for accomplishing masculinity" (1993: 85). Similarly, in speaking of male crack dealers, Philippe Bourgois argues that such men are "Unable to replicate the rural-based models of masculinity and family structure of their grandfathers' generation," and that therefore "a growing cohort of marginalized men in the de-industrialized urban economy takes refuge in the drug economy and celebrates a misogynist predatory street culture that normalizes gang rape, sexual conquest, and paternal abandonment" (1996: 412).
8. Connell (1982, 1983, 1987, 2005 [1995]), Connell and Messerschmidt, (2005); first presented in Kessler et al. (1982).
9. Connell and Messerschmidt (2005: 849).
10. Connell and Messerschmidt put useful emphasis upon "diversity in masculinities" here, and they note that many local varieties of hegemonic masculinity have been discussed within the academic literature, ranging from "patterns of resistance and bullying among boys . . . studies of specific crimes by boys and men, such as rape in Switzerland, murder in Australia, football 'hooliganism' and white-collar crime in England, and assaultive violence in the United States" (2005: 833–34). However, referring to all of these various masculinities through the same term (hegemonic masculinity) risks conceptual slips that would once again position these diverse enactments simply as variations of a singular gender configuration. In this regard, Connell and Messerschmidt suggest that "there is nothing surprising about the idea of diverse practices being generated from common cultural templates," and that therefore, "there is nothing conceptually universalizing in the idea of hegemonic masculinity" (2005: 841). Yet there is definitely a risk that the concept of hegemonic masculinity will here devolve from an analysis pertaining to the specificities of local cultural dominance toward a simplistic and over-generalized assertion of uniform hegemony, one that necessarily elides the many contradictions that exist within and between different forms of masculinity.
11. For example, Messerschmidt (1993: 92–97) and Reeser (2011: 15).
12. Connell (1979, 1987: 47–54).

13. Connell and Messerschmidt acknowledge the inconsistency of adherence to singular masculine goals by individual men, arguing that such aberrations "may . . . represent compromise formations between contradictory desires or emotions, or the results of uncertain calculations about the costs and benefits of different gender strategies" (2005: 852). Yet these compromise formations seem to point precisely toward the ambiguity and instability of hegemonic masculinity within even local environments.
14. See Bederman (1995; especially chapter 3).
15. Beyond this, and perhaps more importantly for my purposes, the word *hegemony* fails to capture the partiality of the relationship between, for example, cis-male drug court judges and the disciplinary punishments they often inflict upon working-class cis-men. Even those participants who accept such judgments as remediation do not necessarily internalize the idea that professional-class masculinities are themselves superior. The hegemony that (cis-male) judges possess, to the extent that they have it, is not totalizing in all social spheres, even as gender is relevant within all of those spheres. Hegemony must be considered in terms of specific aspects of symbolic domination, and this domination cannot be automatically presumed to exist at all levels. In other words, the effort to reconceptualize the notion of hegemonic masculinity must involve questions regarding the nature of power as much as it raises questions pertaining to gender.
16. Part of the reason such an analysis has not been considered in the past concerns the way in which theorists have often framed hegemonic masculinity in relation to nonintersectional understandings of men's dominance over women, a frame that necessitates that femininities cannot be hegemonic because of their subordinate status (hence the development of the term *emphasized femininities*; Connell [1987: 183–88]). Yet I argue that gender as a system cannot be understood in nonintersectional terms and that attempting to do so has led to many of the difficulties inherent in a femininity that is "emphasized" and yet somehow not "hegemonic" at any level. Once one adds elements of race, class, age, caste, disability, etc., the positioning of certain femininities within a broader hegemonic gender order—a multifaceted complex where no single gender enjoys complete centrality and universalizing power over all others—becomes thinkable in novel and more comprehensive ways. Within this frame, men's domination over similarly situated women is best thought of as a point of relative continuity among many diverse masculinities.
17. Lennard and Allen (1974: 202). Alternatively, this is sometimes framed as a competition between the TC and a "drug subculture" (De Leon, 2000: 102).
18. Notably, neither of the cultural forms at stake, a working-class masculinity and a "street-based" masculinity, can be said to be hegemonic in the sense meant by Connell and Messerschmidt due to the fact that they both are located within subordinated class positions. The term they offer to address such a situation, "locally specific constructions of hegemonic masculinity" (2005: 849), would need to represent a formation that is sharply distinguished from society-wide constructions of

hegemonic masculinity; however, this is a distinction that is rarely carried out in practice, once again revealing the way in which the theoretical nuances intended by hegemonic masculinity can suddenly collapse into a singular "male sex role." For parallel critiques of the reification of hegemonic masculinity, see Donaldson (1993) and Rogoff and Van Leer (1993). For additional discussions regarding the various ways in which hegemonic masculinity has been deployed, see Martin (1998); Beasley (2008); Messerschmidt (2008, 2018); Elias and Beasley (2009); and Messerschmidt and Messner (2018).

19. Bourgois (1996).
20. As discussed in chapter 1, drug dealers are often placed in residential treatment facilities even if their drug use patterns are comparatively mild.
21. These observations echo Connell and Messerschmidt's observation that: "A degree of overlap or blurring between hegemonic and complicit masculinities is extremely likely if hegemony is effective" (2005: 839).
22. In Teresa Gowan's analysis of *sick talk* within the lives of the homeless, she notes that: "The self-examination required by sick-talk is a highly feminized and middle-class cultural form, a requirement to investigate and expose dirty laundry in public, to demonstrate honesty through self-revelation. It is not surprising that those most attracted by the disease discourse were far more likely to be female, white, gay, or from more middle-class backgrounds" (2010: 194). And as she notes, these sorts of revelations have racial implication: "African Americans and Latinos in particular were often fiercely loyal to their families of origin and extremely resistant to the idea that their problems might stem from neglectful or abusive child rearing" (194).
23. De Leon (2000: 102).
24. Some therapeutic communities also continue on with the tradition of gaming (discussed in relation to Synanon in chapter 3). In a study of a male-dominated therapeutic community in the southeastern United States, for example, Ezzell (2012) notes that the confrontational encounter groups or games that the TC established between the residents created an environment in which a masculinized identity could be created, establishing spaces in which one could launch aggressive verbal attacks and denigrate others, or, alternatively, where one could display a cool and controlled response while under attack. While these types of encounter groups have been discontinued in many settings, including the facility that I examined, they were referenced in several of the interviews I conducted with residents who had previously undergone treatment at other facilities. Interestingly, variously named gaming practices were also present in many of the women's TCs that have been studied (e.g., Haney [2010]; McCorkel [2003, 2013]; and McKim [2008, 2010, 2014, 2017]).
25. Anderson (1999).
26. In this regard, Moore and Hirai (2014) identify three typical identities that arise in relation to the responsibilization practices of drug courts: *outcastes* (who reject or are excluded from responsibilization), *performers* (who go through the motions),

and *true believers*. Those who appropriate and repurpose responsibilization schemes might be usefully seen as a fourth group.

27. Wilton, DeVerteuil, and Evans (2013: 294). The facility Wilton and colleagues examined, however, featured many more middle-class individuals among the residents and does not appear to have been run as a therapeutic community. In their case, middle-class therapeutic practices involved "careful attention to one's own feelings" and "(feminized) emotional expression in a nurturing, witnessing space" (298), approaches that were not entirely absent from the TC I studied, but which, as noted above, were infrequent at best.

    In a different context, Hansen describes yet another approach to masculinity within a religiously-oriented evangelical drug treatment center, one where participants are encouraged to draw upon a discourse of "maturity" in order to justify new power as "responsible family men" within the domestic sphere. In a Puerto Rican context in which formal labor is often unavailable, "adopting the 'new masculinity' of addiction ministries . . . might be seen as a strategy for ex-addicts to insert themselves on a track to middle-class respectability by pursuing a spiritually-based, rather than economically-based patriarchy" (Hansen, 2012 1724; see also 2018).

    Differences such as these highlight the necessity of specificity when examining gender projects within drug treatment. The centrality of work within U.S.-based programs that cater to criminal justice populations has to do precisely with the emphasis that criminal justice has long placed upon formal labor as an opposite to criminality (Simon [1993]).
28. Acker and van Houten (1974); Acker (1990, 1992); and Britton (2003).
29. Carrabine and Longhurst (1998: 165).
30. I discuss this history at length elsewhere (Kaye [2010; see esp. chapter 6]).
31. Roberts (1993–1994).
32. Hays (2003).
33. Women's participation in the drug court system could also be considered an issue of "equality with a vengeance" or "vengeful equity" (Chesney-Lind and Pollack [1995] and Chesney-Lind [2006], respectively) insofar as women—particularly black women—have been increasingly targeted through the war on drugs (Chesney-Lind [1995]; Bush-Baskette [1998, 2000]; and Boyd [2004]).
34. Roberts (1993–1994: 876). See also Minow (1994: 828–30)
35. Waldorf reports, for example, that: "Phoenix Houses view homosexuality as being part of the addict's general character disorder and it is behavior not to be tolerated" (1971: 33). The issue is *somewhat* more complex than simple bigotry, as this position was understood as protecting gay men from sexual exploitation in this prison-like environment (32–33), however the automatic presumption that all such sex was exploitative is clearly more than problematic.
36. The incidents were never proven, so it is possible that the rumors represented forms of homophobic prejudice among the other residents. When he and I spoke about the topic directly, he acknowledged that other straight-identified men in facility had

approached him, but then playfully refused to say whether he had taken them up on the offer. I was left with the impression that he had, but I could be mistaken.

37. De Leon writes, for example, that "the management of sexual conduct in the TC is the same for homosexuality as it is for heterosexuality" (2000: 185), a framing that ignores the possibility of unique needs based on cultural difference (including a distinct culture of drug use), dissimilar sets of experiences, and the harms of bigotry and institutionalized oppression.
38. Canaday (2009). On issues pertaining to discrimination and bias against LGBT individuals within drug treatment, see Graham, Carney, and Kluck (2012); Stevens (2012); and Rowan, Jenkins, and Parks (2013), among others. On the particular treatment needs of heterosexually-identified men who have had sex with men, sometimes in the context of prostitution, see Senreich (2015).
39. Senreich (2009); Hicks (2000).
40. No staff members, however, were openly queer, nor did I learn of any who were closeted or otherwise discreet.
41. Matthews and Selvidge (2005); Lombardi (2007).
42. On the pervasiveness of heterosexist bias amongst drug counselors more generally, see Eliason and Hughes (2004) and Cochran, Peavy, and Cauce (2007). I myself identify as queer, though I made no special attempt to highlight this fact to the staff (nor, however, did I hide it).
43. Warner (2000).
44. On a different level, it is interesting to note that many of the Christian conversion programs that attempt to "cure" homosexuality appear to have adopted program elements from the hierarchical therapeutic community model (see, e.g., Erzen [2006]). With many Christian groups thinking of homosexuality as an addiction, and with TC's historic orientation toward the instillation of normative values, the model of treatment offered by the therapeutic community perhaps seemed an appropriate form to draw upon in creating these programs.
45. I discuss the institutional history of women's TCs elsewhere (Kaye [2010; see esp. chapter 6]).
46. There are also male-only facilities, however interviews with staff at these facilities and with residents who had received treatment there revealed that they operate on essentially the same principles as the mixed-gender (yet invariably male-dominant) facilities.
47. Lamb (1999); Kitzinger (2004); and Kaye (2005), among others.
48. Haney (2010).
49. McCorkel (2013).
50. McKim (2008, 2014, 2017).
51. For example, Kandall (1996); Campbell (2000); and Rotskoff (2002).
52. Grella (2008: 333). For parallel perspectives offering positive rationales for women's TCs, see also Covington and Bloom (2007).
53. For example, Pollack (2005), among others. It should be noted that the original movement for women's treatment facilities had an ambivalent and often

conflictual relationship with the organized women's movement (see Kaye [2010; esp. chapter 6]). The feminism embraced by women's-only TCs today seems to generally embrace a logic of "cultural feminism" (Alcoff [1988])—as well as "carceral feminism" (Bernstein [2007, 2010, 2018])—more than other possible versions.

54. Haney (2010:157).
55. Haney (2010: 140).
56. Haney (2010: 161).
57. Haney (2010: 158).
58. Haney (2010: 129, 168, 176–77).
59. Haney (2010: see esp. 205–6). As at the facility I most closely examined, Haney notes that many participants did not have serious drug problems. They were instead deemed to be addicted to money or destructive relationships. "Most generally," she writes, "there were those who were addicted to a way of life—to the energy, sounds, and sensations of street, or 'gangsta life' " (2010: 128; see also Murphy [2015: 74]). The link to the so-called drugs lifestyle discussed in the drug court I examined seems quite direct.
60. Haney (2010: 153).
61. Haney (2010: 162; see also 189).
62. Haney (2010: 181).
63. McCorkel (2013: 122).
64. McCorkel (2013: 127, 123).
65. McCorkel (2013: 59).
66. McCorkel (2013: 107).
67. McCorkel (2013: 107).
68. McCorkel (2013: 108).
69. McCorkel (2013: 112).
70. McCorkel (2013: 112).
71. McCorkel (2013: 126).
72. McCorkel (2013: 61).
73. McKim looks at two women's treatment communities, highlighting the differences in approach between a working class program with voluntary clients and a TC oriented toward those with a criminal justice mandate (2008, 2014, 2017). I limit my discussion here to the institution she refers to as "WTS," which predominantly accepted clients through the criminal justice system.
74. McKim (2017: 146).
75. McKim (2017: 120)
76. McKim (2017: 106)
77. McKim (2017: 106–7).
78. McKim (2017: 117–18).
79. Haney (2010: 193).
80. Covington (2008).
81. Carr (2011: 115; emphases in original).
82. As discussed earlier (see text associated with note 47, above).

83. Haney (2010: 136–37, 158, 191–92).
84. Haney (2010: 193).
85. Haney (2010: 192).
86. McCorkel (2013: 162–63; see also 181–211).
87. From the perspective of TC practice, this failure to force participants to expose their "intimate" selves would likely be perceived as a weakness of the program I examined.
88. Discourse on women and crime often presumes that it is women's choices in relationships that lead to crime (see Pollack [2007] and Turnbull and Hannah-Moffitt [2009]).
89. Haney (2010: 162) and McCorkel (2013: 127).
90. Haney (2010: 145).
91. Haney (2010: 134).
92. Haney (2010: 127).
93. McKim (2017: 128).
94. For example, Crittenden (2001).
95. McCorkel (2013: 137–38).
96. Haney (2010: 139).
97. Haney (2010: 255, note 24).
98. McKim (2014: 441; 2017: 136).
99. It is unclear if women's programs are systematically worse on this issue than most men's programs or if other factors resulted in this preliminary finding. With so few studies on these issues, particularly within men's-only and predominantly male facilities, further research must be conducted in order to better delineate the patterns of heterosexism within the drug treatment system.
100. Haney (2010: 167).
101. Haney (2010: 132).
102. McKim (2017: 17).
103. McCorkel (2013: 140).
104. McKim (2014: 438). See also Morash, Haarr, and Rucker (1994) for a discussion of disparities in vocational opportunities available to women in prison during the 1980s (disparities that continue to this day; Morash, Haarr, and Rucker [1994]; Pollack-Byrne [2002 {1990}]; and Schram and Morash [2002]).
105. McKim (2017: 145).
106. I did not attempt to gather any data examining graduation rates or times for women attending women's-only TCs versus male-dominated, mixed-gender TCs, nor am I aware of any other studies that have done so. Any such study, of course, would have a significant confound in terms of comparing women who for some reason were selectively sent to one or the other type of TC.
107. As Foucault writes:

> This is the background that enables us to understand the importance assumed by sex as a political issue. It was at the pivot of the two axes along

> which developed the entire political technology of life. On the one hand it was tied to disciplines of the body: the harnessing, intensification, and distribution of forces, the adjustment of economy and energies. On the other hand, it was applied to the regulation of populations, through all the far-reaching effects of its activity. It fitted both categories at once. . . . Sex was a means of access to the life of the body and the life of the species. . . . That is why in the nineteenth century sexuality was sought out in the smallest details of individual existences . . . But one also sees it becoming the theme of political operations, economic interventions . . . and ideological campaigns. (1978: 145–46)

108. Foucault (1978: 140)
109. The notion of a "good worker" is of course heavily gendered at an implicit level, and *economic man* in general makes implicit reference to reproductive labor of various sorts that are to be accomplished invisibly by women (see Eisenstein [1978]; Hansen and Philipson [1989]; Hochschild [1993]; Duggan [2003]; and Fineman and Dougherty [2005]). Here I mean only to suggest that these implicit assumptions remain essentially invisible to court actors and that even more direct uses of gender (detailed above in this chapter) remain similarly unknown.
110. I mean to suggest that the forms of shaming that such programs utilize require an intimate knowledge of their participants and are therefore drawing to some extent upon a shared set of values. I do not mean that state practices are not violent in their effects; as seen in the final section of chapter 3, the state has experimented with the harshest forms of behaviorist punishment, and currently utilizes solitary confinement to an excessive degree. However, these forms of psychic assault are less personal and less intimate in their capacity to actively draw upon a participant's own hopes and fears. It may also be the case that earlier forms of state organization—those seen within early women's reformatories, for example (Freedman [1984])—may have been able to draw upon local sets of gendered meaning in ways that were similarly intimate.
111. Murphy, for example, cites one male graduate of drug court: "I came into this program as a little boy and I'm walking out as a man" (2015: 87). See also Fader (2013), especially chapter 6, aptly entitled "I Just Want to See a Part of Me That's Never Been Bad."
112. Hannah-Moffit (2001: 169).
113. More generally, it is perhaps helpful to introduce Geiger and Wolch's notion of a *shadow state* (1986; see also Wolch [1990]) formed by nongovernmental organizations (NGOs) in the wake of neoliberal devolution and a "hollowing out" of state functions (Jessop [1994]). Fairbanks similarly argues that what he terms a "shadow welfare state" is characterized by "new forms of statecraft" that can engage the poor in more intimate and involving ways than prior formations (2009: 18; on these dynamics, see also Cruikshank [1999]; Haney [2010: 86–111]; and Schram [2015: 109–33]). In effect, this shadow state often takes on dynamics more associated with

what Hasenfeld referred to as "people changing institutions" rather than "people processing institutions" (1972, cited in Miller [2014: 317]). Many scholars point to ways in which privatization and its associated reliance on actuarial performance measures nevertheless create a series of "perverse organizational responses" for NGOs delivering services (e.g., Soss, Fording, and Schram [2011: 208]). See also Lake and Newman (2002) for a discussion of race in the shadow state. See Morris (2004) for a discussion of the early history of NGOs in the war on poverty.

114. Unsurprisingly, advocates for TCs nevertheless attempt to make favorable claims regarding the evidentiary base of TC practice (e.g., De Leon [2010]). See also chapter 4, note 8.
115. Spillers (1987: 68, 72).
116. Writing in relation to white supremacist constructions of gender within the system of Jim Crow, Sarah Haley argues that black women were subjected to a "forced proximity to masculinity" that turned them into "queer colonial subjects" (2016: 253, 40). This "forced queering" (2013: 73, note 55) removed black women from the category of womanhood altogether: "They were situated in opposition to the normative gender position, and produced outside of binary oppositional gender categories as something else altogether; that 'else' was contradictory and ambiguous but in black women's lives it fundamentally meant exposure to violence" (2016: 88).

    In relation to drug courts, I suggest that degendered and gendered modes of domination operate in close association with one another, articulating across diverse sites of interlinked surveillance and control. While the degendered cost-benefit analysis or recidivism statistic is decisive in some respects, it does not in and of itself form a disciplinary technology. Although the biopolitical elements of ungendered statistical evaluation are crucial to governance, disciplinary techniques require a non-normative *human* who must be corrected, necessarily gendering their subjects in intimate ways (insofar as a recognizable gender remains part of what it means to be "human"; see Butler [2004: 30, 42, 57, 74, 104, 206, 218]). Whereas the women Haley references were institutionally targeted for exclusion (via the chain gang) rather than "rehabilitation"—and thus were perhaps never gendered within white supremacist logics at the time—the correctional logics of the drug court necessitate that a potentially normative subject be targeted. See also Dillon (2018: 14–16).
117. As noted in chapter 1 (note 109).
118. A parallel though differently structured process of governmental linkage with local organizations can be seen in the Community Action Programs (CAPs) established through President Johnson's "war on poverty" (particularly as it was enacted from 1964–1967, during which time CAPs were designed to facilitate the "maximum feasible participation" of poor people themselves). For a diverse range of perspectives on the possibilities and dangers of the CAP model, see Cruikshank (1999: 67–86); Cazenave (2007); and Orleck and Hazirijan (2011).
119. To be sure, state-run prisons frequently maintain living conditions that are extremely brutal without attracting much outside comment, so it is possible that

harsh conditions within state-run drug treatment programs would not garner attention. My assertion, nevertheless, is that direct state control over these facilities would make such attention more likely, if not automatic.

120. Soss, Fording, and Schram similarly find that privatization of welfare services results in a significantly less accountable structure (2011: 42, 189–90). Significantly, they also find that privatization creates pressures that lead to more punitive forms of case management (226–30), and that for-profit welfare institutions in particular are 25 percent more likely to sanction clients than non-profit ones (218). More generally, they suggest, the need to meet narrowly defined numerical goals leads to efforts at "reshaping the client rather than serving them more effectively" (214). Soss, Fording, and Schram's findings suggest that more state involvement leads to greater oversight and less severe forms of discipline for both welfare programs and TCs.
121. As noted in chapter 2 (note 60).

6. Retrenchment and Reform in the War on Drugs

1. Peters (2009).
2. Peters (2009).
3. Lieberman (2009) and NYCLU (2009).
4. Common Sense for Drug Policy (2009).
5. In Gonnerman (2009).
6. Gonnerman (2009).
7. Kellam and Bates (2014).
8. Kellam and Bates (2014: 9).
9. See Arnold (2009).
10. As noted in chapter 1 (note 48).
11. NACDL (2009); JPI (2011); DPA (2011, 2014); Allard, Lyons, and Elliot (2011); Pugh et al. (2013); Csete and Tomasini-Joshi (2015); and Møllman and Mehta (2017). For responses defending drug courts, see NADCP (2009); Marlowe (2010b, 2011, 2013); and Sanders (2011).
12. For similar arguments, see Boldt (1998); Fischer (2003); Miller (2004); Bowers (2008); and Tiger (2013).
13. In considering such a reformist possibility, I perhaps step outside the abolitionist frame and toward what might be more closely affiliated with a *left realist* position (Lea and Young [1984]; Young [1986, 1992, 2002]). As critics of left realism have pointed out, however, there is a danger that this tendency simply amounts to what has been termed a "Left Campaign for Law and Order" (Steinert [1985]), a turn that positions left realism as a sort of loyal opposition within mainstream criminology (Ferrell [1997]), an opposition that remains too closely situated to the punitive turn associated with right realism. At the same time, like at least some abolitionists, I do see a need to address concrete reforms within the current structures and to think of approaches that can make things better in the immediate moment, while

attempting to make sure that these efforts support and do not undermine more utopian possibilities. Without resolving these conflicts, I draw from both tendencies in an effort to avoid some of the potential pitfalls of each approach.

14. Tsemberis, Gulcur, and Nakae (2004) found no reduction in drug use while TSS&HA (2007) did find a significant reduction; see also Atherton and McNaughton (2008).
15. See Brookes (2010); Shuker and Sullivan (2010); Stevens (2013); among others.
16. McKim (2017: 95, see also 2014: 446). Referencing Delpit (1988).
17. Indeed, many of these soft skills are taught in reentry programs, where efforts are made to counter the *carceral habitus* developed by many inmates in favor of a attitudes and demeanors that are desired by employers. "Students practice walking, smiling, shaking hands, and making small talk. Staff members deliberately engineer situations in an attempt to observe and test the students' reactions" (Caputo-Levine [2012: 174]).
18. McKim (2017: 95).
19. In her discussion of treatment options associated with drug courts in Canada, which focus on cognitive-behavioral therapy, Dawn Moore points to the ways in which this approach limits therapy to targeted interventions that the state identifies (2007a: 39; citing Hannah-Moffit [2001]). Despite such problematics, these difficulties seem to improve upon the challenges posed by the "holistic" treatment offered within therapeutic communities.
20. Elias (1939).
21. Esmeir (2012: 286).
22. Dillon (2018)
23. For example, by reducing the work week and increasing pay, making housing more affordable, and providing free access to health care.
24. I do not mean to suggest that all efforts at reintegrative shaming automatically fall into this trap, merely that the theoretical perspective invoked by this frame fails to adequately address these issues.
25. For alternatives to *tough love* within community and familial contexts, see also SMART Recovery and CRAFT (Kirby et al. [2015]). For a popular treatment, see also Maté (2008).
26. A point made by some TC practitioners (as seen above; see also Zelvin and Mallow [2005: 94]).
27. See Kaye (2012); Garriot and Raikhel (2015); among others.
28. Indeed, one of the voluntary clients whom I became close to as a resident contacted me at the TC after she was released. Having given up her job in order to live in the facility for several months, she now found herself without a home and on the street. Seeing her desperation, an emergency psychiatric facility had generously loosened its diagnostic criteria in order to briefly admit her and provide housing for a couple of days. I visited her in the facility, bringing her a few items she had left behind at the TC, and spent a few hours with her listening to her current plight and trying to strategize ways to move forward. She eventually was able to find both

housing and work, but the incident put an exclamation mark on the TC's irresponsibility for care of its clients.

29. For example, Greenberg and Humphries (1980: 208), among others.
30. Murakawa (2014). See also Schept on the failures of progressive reform (2015).
31. AFSC Working Group (1970: 158).
32. Mitford (1973a: 319).
33. Schept (2015: 64).
34. Gorz (1967).
35. In Davis and Rodriguez (2002: 216).
36. From the Honorable Sheila Murphy, writing as the presiding judge of the Circuit Court of Cook County, Illinois (Murphy [1997]).
37. Gowan (2010: 272).
38. Schept (2015: 236).
39. This same caution applies to all forms of problem-solving courts, though each must be examined on its own terms.
40. Cohen (1979: 353, 360; see also Sommer [1976]). Cohen adopts the term *carceral archipelago* from Foucault (1975).
41. Feeley and Simon (1992).
42. Feeley and Simon (1992: 450).
43. Garland (2001: 176).
44. Clear and Frost (2014).
45. See Hill (2014).
46. Anderson (1999).

References

AA (Alcoholics Anonymous). 1984. " 'Pass It On': The Story of Bill Wilson and how the A.A. Message Reached the World." New York: Alcoholics Anonymous World Services.

ABC News. 2018. "President Trump Delivers Remarks on Combating Drug and Opioid Crisis in Manchester, NH." YouTube Video, 55:08, March 19, 2018. www.youtube.com/watch?v=4kkf01bDyzA.

Abrahams, Joseph. 2006. *Turning Lives Around: Wartime Treatment of Military Prisoners*. Bloomington, IN: AuthorHouse.

——. 2014. *Terra Incognita: A Psychoanalyst Explores the Human Soul*. Lanham, MD: University Press of America.

Abrahams, Joseph, and Lloyd McCorkle. 1946. "Group Psychotherapy of Military Offenders." *American Journal of Sociology* 51 (5): 455–64.

——. 1947. "Group Psychotherapy at an Army Rehabilitation Center." *Diseases of the Nervous System* 8 (2): 50–62.

Abramsky, Sasha. 2010. "Is This the End of the War on Crime?" *The Nation*, June 16. www.thenation.com/article/end-war-crime.

ACCD (American Council of Chief Defenders). 2004. "Ten Tenets of Fair and Effective Problem Solving Courts." Washington, D.C.: National Legal Aid & Defender Association. https://c.ymcdn.com/sites/nysda.site-ym.com/resource/resmgr/Docs/10TenetsFairProbSlvCtsACCD.pdf.

Acker, Joan. 1990. "Hierarchies, Jobs, Bodies: A Theory of Gendered Organizations." *Gender and Society* 4 (2): 139–58.

——. 1992. "From Sex Roles to Gendered Institutions." *Contemporary Sociology* 21: 565–69.

Acker, Joan, and Donald Van Houten. 1974. "Differential Recruitment and Control: The Sex Structuring of Organizations." *Administrative Science Quarterly* 19 (2): 152–63.

Adorno, Theodor. 1945. "A Social Critique of Radio Music." *Kenyon Review* 7 (2): 208–17.

AFSC (American Friends Service Committee Working Group). 1971. *Struggle for Justice: A Report on Crime and Punishment in America*. New York: Hill and Wang.

Agamben, Giorgio. 1998 (1995). *Homo Sacer: Sovereign Power and Bare Life*. Translated by Daniel Heller-Roazen. Stanford, CA: Stanford University Press.

Alcoff, Linda. 1988. "Cultural Feminism Versus Post-Structuralism: The Identity Crisis in Feminist Theory." *Signs: Journal of Women in Culture and Society* 13 (3): 405–36.

Alexander, Michelle. 2010. *The New Jim Crow: Mass Incarceration in the Age of Colorblindness*. New York: New Press.

Allard, Patricia, Tara Lyons, and Richard Elliot. 2011. "Impaired Judgment: Assessing the Appropriateness of Drug Treatment Courts as a Response to Drug Use in Canada." Toronto: Canadian HIV/AIDS Legal Network. www.aidslaw.ca/site/wp-content/uploads/2013/09/DTCs-Oct11-E.pdf.

Anderson, Elijah. 1999. *Code of the Street: Decency, Violence, and the Moral Life of the Inner City*. New York: Norton.

——. 2000. "The Emerging Philadelphia African American Class Structure." *Annals of the American Academy of Political and Social Science* 568 (1): 54–77.

Armstrong, Andrew. 2003. "Drug Courts and the De Facto Legalization of Drug Use for Participants in Residential Treatment Facilities." *Journal of Criminal Law and Criminology* 94 (1): 133–68.

Armstrong, Edward. 2008. "The Drug Court as Postmodern Justice." *Critical Criminology* 16: 271–84.

Armstrong, Elizabeth. 2003. *Conceiving Risk, Bearing Responsibility: Fetal Alcohol Syndrome and the Diagnosis of Moral Disorder*. Baltimore, MD: The Johns Hopkins University Press.

Arnold, Sarah. 2009. "Rockefeller Drug Laws: Ripe for Reform." *The Nation*, January 23. www.thenation.com/article/rockefeller-drugs-laws-ripe-reform.

Aron, William, and Douglas Daily. 1976. "Graduates and Splitees from Therapeutic Community Drug Treatment Programs: A Comparison." *International Journal of the Addictions* 11 (1): 1–18.

Atherton, Iain, and Nicholls McNaughton. 2008. " 'Housing First' as a Means of Addressing Multiple Needs and Homelessness." *European Journal of Homelessness* 2: 289–303.

Aviram, Hadar. 2010. "Humonetarianism: The New Correctional Discourse of Scarcity." *Hastings Race and Poverty Law Journal* 7 (1): 1–52.

——. 2015. *Cheap on Crime: Recession-Era Politics and the Transformation of American Punishment*: Oakland: University of California Press.

Bardacke, Frank. 2011. *Trampling Out the Vintage: Cesar Chavez and the Two Souls of the United Farm Workers*. New York: Verso Press.

Beasley, Christine. 2008. "Rethinking Hegemonic Masculinity in a Globalizing World." *Men and Masculinities* 11 (1): 86–103.

Beck, Allen, and Laura Maruschak. 2001. *Mental Health Treatment in State Prisons, 2000*. Bureau of Justice Statistics Special Report, ed. Office of Justice Programs. Washington, D.C.: U.S. Department of Justice.

Beckett, Katherine, and Bruce Western. 2001. "Governing Social Marginality: Welfare, Incarceration, and the Transformation of State Policy." *Punishment & Society* 3 (1): 43–59.

Bederman, Gail. 1995. *Manliness & Civilization: A Cultural History of Gender and Race in the United States, 1880–1917*. Chicago: University of Chicago Press.

Belenko, Steven. 2000a. *Drugs and Drug Policy in America: A Documentary History*. Westport, CT: Greenwood Press.

—. 2000b. "The Challenges of Integrating Drug Treatment into the Criminal Justice Process." *Albany Law Review* 63: 833–76.

—. 2001. *Research on Drug Courts: A Critical Review, 2001 Update*. New York: National Center on Addiction and Substance Abuse at Columbia University.

Belenko, Steven, Matthew Hiller, and Leah Hamilton. 2013. "Treating Substance Use Disorders in the Criminal Justice System." *Current Psychiatry Reports* 15 (11): 414–24.

Berlin, Isaiah. 2002 [1958]. *Liberty: Incorporating Four Essays on Liberty*, ed. Henry Hardy. Oxford: Oxford University Press.

Berman, Greg, and John Feinblatt. 2001. "Problem-Solving Courts: A Brief Primer." *Law and Policy* 23 (2): 125–40.

—. 2002. *Judges and Problem-Solving Courts*. New York: Center for Court Innovation. www.courtinnovation.org/sites/default/files/JudgesProblemSolvingCourts1.pdf.

—. 2005. *Good Courts: The Case for Problem-Solving Justice*. New York: The New Press.

Bernstein, Elizabeth. 2007. "The Sexual Politics of the 'New Abolitionism.' " *differences* 18 (5): 128–51.

—. 2010. "Militarized Humanitarianism Meets Carceral Feminism: The Politics of Sex, Rights, and Freedom in Contemporary Antitrafficking Campaigns." *Signs: Journal of Women in Culture and Society* 36 (1): 45–70.

—. 2018. *Brokered Subjects: Sex, Trafficking, and the Politics of Freedom*. Chicago: University of Chicago Press.

BJA (Bureau of Justice Assistance). 2017. *Adult Drug Court Discretionary Grant Program FY 2017 Competitive Grant Announcement*. United States Department of Justice, Bureau of Justice Assistance. www.bja.gov/funding/DrugCourts17.pdf.

Blackwell, Marilyn. 1999. "The Deserving Sick: Poor Women and the Medicalization of Poverty in Brattleboro, Vermont." *Journal of Women's History* 11 (1): 53–74.

Boggs, James, and Grace Lee Boggs. 1966. "The City Is the Black Man's Land." *Monthly Review* 17 (11): 35–45.

Boldt, Richard. 1998. "Rehabilitative Punishment and the Drug Treatment Court." *Washington University Law Quarterly* 76: 1206–306.

Boltanski, Luc. 1999. *Distant Suffering: Morality, Media and Politics*. Cambridge: Cambridge University Press.

Bonilla-Silva, Eduardo. 2010. *Racism without Racists: Color-Blind Racism & Racial Inequality in Contemporary America*. 3rd ed. Lanham, MD: Rowman & Littlefield.

Bouffard, Jeff, and Faye Taxman. 2004. "Looking Inside the 'Black Box' of Drug Court Treatment Services Using Direct Observations." *Journal of Drug Issues* 34 (1): 195–218.

Bourdieu, Pierre. 1977. *Outline of a Theory of Practice*. Cambridge: Cambridge University Press.

Bourgois, Philippe. 1996. *In Search of Respect: Selling Crack in El Barrio*. New York: Cambridge University Press.

Bowers, Josh. 2008. "Contraindicated Drug Courts." *UCLA Law Review* 55: 783–835.

Boyd, Susan. 2004. *From Witches to Crack Moms: Women, Drug Law, and Policy*. Durham, NC: Carolina Academic Press.

Bracke, Rudy. 1996. "De encounter, het hart van de therapeutische gemeenschap (The Encounter, the Heart of the Therapeutic Community)." In *De nieuwe therapeutische gemeenschap*, ed. Eric Broekaert, Rudy Bracke, Dirk Calle, Anita Cogo, Georges van der Straten, and Hilde Bradt, 65–70. Leuven, Belgium: Garant.

Braithwaite, John. 1989. *Crime, Shame and Reintegration*. Cambridge: Cambridge University Press.

Bratter, Thomas, Ernest Collabolletta, Allen Fossbender, Matthew Pennacchia, and John Rubel. 1985. "The American Self-Help Residential Therapeutic Community: A Pragmatic Treatment Approach for Addicted Character-Disordered Individuals." In *Emotions in Social Life: Critical Themes and Contemporary Issues*, ed. Gilliam Bendelow and Simon Williams. New York: Routledge.

Bratter, Thomas, and Lisa Sinsheimer. 2008. "Confrontation—A Potent Psychotherapeutic Approach with Difficult Adolescents." *Adolescent Psychiatry* 30: 103–116.

Briggs, Dennie. 1973. "Chino, California." In *Dealing with Deviants: The Treatment of Antisocial Behavior*, ed. Dennie Briggs, Stuart Whiteley, and Merfyn Turner, 95–171. London: Hogarth Press.

Britton, Dana. 2003. *At Work in the Iron Cage: The Prison as Gendered Organization*. New York: New York University Press.

Brodt, Susan, and Marla Tuchinsky. 2000. "Working Together but in Opposition: An Examination of the 'Good Cop/Bad Cop' Negotiating Team Tactic." *Organizational Behavior and Human Decision Processes* 81: 155–77.

Broekaert, Eric, Martien Kooyman, and Donald Ottenberg. 1998. "The 'New' Drug-Free Therapeutic Community: Challenging Encounter of Classic and Open Therapeutic Communities." *Journal of Substance Abuse Treatment* 15 (6): 595–97.

Broekaert, Eric, Wouter Vanderplasschen, Ingrid Temmerman, Donald Ottenberg, and Charles Kaplan. 2000. "Retrospective Study of Similarities and Relations Between American Drug-Free and European Therapeutic Communities for Children and Adults." *Journal of Psychoactive Drugs* 32 (4): 407–17.

Broekaert, Eric, Stijn Vandevelde, Gilberte Schuyten, Kris Erauw, and Rudy Bracke. 2004. "Evolution of Encounter Group Methods in Therapeutic Communities for Substance Abusers." *Addictive Behaviors* 29: 231–44.

Brookes, Michael. 2010. "The Impact of Grendon on Changing Lives: Prisoner Perspectives." *Howard Journal of Criminal Justice* 49 (5): 478–90.

Brown, Barry. 1985. "Federal Drug Abuse Policy and Minority Group Issues: Reflections of a Participant-Observer." *International Journal of the Addictions* 20 (1): 203–15.

Brown, Wendy. 2015. *Undoing the Demos: Neoliberalism's Stealth Revolution*. New York: Zone Books.

Bumiller, Kristin. 2008. *In an Abusive State*. Durham, NC: Duke University Press.

Burchard, Max. 1955. "Mature Criminal as Hypothetical Type: An Evaluation." ETD Collection for University of Nebraska. http://digitalcommons.unl.edu/dissertations/AAI0014348.

Burke, Peggy. 1997. *Policy-Driven Responses to Probation and Parole Violations*. Silver Spring, MD: Center for Effective Public Policy.

Burns, Stacy Lee, and Mark Peyrot. 2008. "Reclaiming Discretion: Judicial Sanctioning Strategy in Court-Supervised Drug Treatment." *Journal of Contemporary Ethnography* 37 (6): 720–44.

Bush-Baskette, Stephanie. 1998. "The War on Drugs as a War Against Black Women." In *Crime Control and Women: Feminist Implications of Criminal Justice Policy*, ed. Susan L. Miller, 113–29. Thousand Oaks, CA: Sage Publications.

——. 2000. "The War on Drugs and the Black Female: Testing the Impact of the Sentencing Policies for Crack Cocaine on Black Females in the Federal System." *Journal of Drug Issues* 30 (4): 919–28.

Butler, Judith. 2004. *Undoing Gender*. New York: Routledge.

Butts, Jeffrey, and John Roman. 2004. "Drug Courts in the Juvenile Justice System." In *Juvenile Drug Courts and Teen Substance Abuse*, ed. Jeffrey Butts and John Roman, 1–26. Washington, D.C.: Urban Institute Press.

Butzin, Clifford, Christine Saum, and Frank Scarpitti. 2002. "Factors Associated with Completion of a Drug Treatment Court Diversion Program." *Substance Use & Misuse* 37 (12–13): 1615–33.

CADPAAC (County Alcohol and Drug Program Administrators Association of California). 2008. [untitled letter]. Sacramento, CA: County Alcohol and Drug Program Administrators Association of California. www.prop5yes.com/cadpaac-response-to-nadcp.

Callon, Michael. 1984. "Some Elements of a Sociology of Translation: Domestication of the Scallops and the Fishermen of St. Brieuc Bay." *Sociological Review* 32: 196–233.

Camp, Jordan. 2016. *Incarcerating the Crisis: Freedom Struggles and the Rise of the Neoliberal State*. Oakland: University of California Press.

Campbell, Nancy. 2000. *Using Women: Gender, Drug Policy, and Social Justice*. New York: Routledge.

Canaday, Margot. 2009. *The Straight State: Sexuality and Citizenship in Twentieth-Century America*. Princeton, NJ: Princeton University Press.

Caputo-Levine, Deirdre. 2012. "The Yard Face: The Contributions of Inmate Interpersonal Violence to the Carceral Habitus." *Ethnography* 14 (2): 165–85.

Cardona-Maguigad, Adriana. 2015a. "Puerto Rico Exports its Drug Addicts to Chicago." *WBEZ News* (Chicago), produced by Jesse Dukes, April 10. http://interactive.wbez.org/puertoricochicagopipeline.

——. 2015b. "This American Life: *Como se Dice 'Not It'?*" WBEZ News (Chicago), *This American Life*, April 10. https://www.thisamericanlife.org/554/not-it#act-1.

Carr, E. Summerson. 2011. *Scripting Addiction: The Politics of Therapeutic Talk and American Sobriety*. Princeton, NJ: Princeton University Press.

Carrabine, Eamonn, and Brian Longhurst. 1998. "Gender and Prison Organization: Some Comments on Masculinities and Prison Management." *Howard Journal of Crime and Justice* 37 (2): 161–76.

Casriel, Daniel. 1963. *So Fair a House: The Story of Synanon*. New York: Prentice-Hall.

Casriel, Daniel, Jerome Jaffe, and Frances Gearing. 1969. *Concepts and Controversies in Modern Medicine*. Transcript of video T-1701. Washington, DC: U.S. Department of Health, Education and Welfare, Public Health Service. https://collections.nlm.nih.gov/catalog/nlm:nlmuid-8600251A-vid.

Castel, Robert. 1991. "From Dangerousness to Risk." In *The Foucault Effect: Studies in Governmentality*, ed. Colin Gordon Graham Burchill and Peter Miller, 281–98. Chicago: University of Chicago Press.

Castellano, Jill, Brett Kelman, Kristen Hwang, Cheri Carlson, Amy Wu, and Jenny Espino. 2016. "Two Years After Prop 47, Addicts Walk Free with Nowhere to Go." *Desert Sun*, December 14. www.desertsun.com/story/news/crime_courts/2016/12/14/prop-47-california-addiction/94083338.

Cazenave, Noel. 2007. *Impossible Democracy: The Unlikely Success of the War on Poverty Community Action Programs*. Albany: State University of New York Press.

Champion, Dean. 2007. *Probation, Parole and Community Corrections*. 6th ed. New York: Pearson.

Chase, Taylor. 2014. "Wisconsin Drug Courts Grow, but Racial Disparities Exist." Wisconsin Center for Investigative Journalism, August 17. www.wisconsinwatch.org/2014/08/wisconsin-drug-courts-grow-but-racial-disparities-persist.

Chesney-Lind, Meda. 1995. "Rethinking Women's Imprisonment: A Critical Examination of Trends in Female Incarceration." In *The Criminal Justice System and Women*, ed. Raffel Price and Natalie Skoloff, 99–121. New York: McGraw-Hill.

——. 2006. "Patriarchy, Crime, and Justice: Feminist Criminology in an Era of Backlash." *Feminist Criminology* 1 (1): 6–26.

Chesney-Lind, Meda, and Joycelyn Pollock. 1995. "Women's Prisons: Equality with a Vengeance." In *Women, Law, and Social Control*, ed. Alida Merlo and Joycelyn Pollock, 155–76. Boston: Allyn & Bacon.

Christian, Margena. 2007. "The Facts Behind the Saggin' Pants Craze." *Jet*, May 7: 16, 18, 52.

Cissner, Amanda, and Michael Rempel. 2005. *The State of Drug Court Research: Moving Beyond "Do They Work?"* New York: Center for Court Innovation.

Cissner, Amanda, Michael Rempel, Allyson Franklin, John Roman, Samuel Bieler, Robyn Cohen, and Carolyn Cadoret. 2013. *A Statewide Evaluation of New York's Adult Drug Courts: Identifying Which Policies Work Best*. New York: Center for Court Innovation.

Clark, Claire. 2017. *The Recovery Revolution: The Battle Over Addiction Treatment in the United States*. New York: Columbia University Press.

Clear, Todd. 1994. *Harm in American Penology: Offenders, Victims, and Their Communities*. Albany: State University of New York Press.

Clear, Todd, and George Cole. 2003. *American Corrections*. New York: Wadsworth/Thomson Learning.

Clear, Todd, and Natasha Frost. 2014. *The Punishment Imperative: The Rise and Failure of Mass Incarceration in America*. New York: New York University Press.

Clear, Todd, and Patricia Hardyman. 1990. "The New Intensive Supervision Movement." *Crime and Deliquency* 36 (1): 42–60.

Cleckner, Patricia. 1976. "Blowing Some Lines: Intracultural Variation Among Miami Cocaine Users." *Journal of Psychedelic Drugs* 8 (1): 37–42.

Cobb, Kimberly. 2016. "Tips for Transferring Probation Practices to Drug Court Programs to Enhance Participant and Program Outcomes." National Criminal Justice Reference Service, NCJ 251667, December. www.ncjrs.gov/App/Publications/abstract.aspx?ID=273881.

Cochran, Bryan, Michelle Peavy, and Ana Mari Cauce. 2007. "Substance Abuse Treatment Providers' Explicit and Implicit Attitudes Regarding Sexual Minorities." *Journal of Homosexuality* 53 (3): 181–207.

Cockburn, Alexander, and Jeffrey St. Clair. 1998. *Whiteout: The CIA, Drugs and the Press*. New York: Verso Publishing.

Cohen, Stanley. 1979. "The Punitive City: Notes on the Dispersal of Social Control." *Contemporary Crises* 3: 339–63.

——. 1985. *Visions of Social Control: Crime, Punishment and Classification*. New York: Polity Press.

Collins, Patricia Hill. 1986. "Learning from the Outsider Within: The Sociological Significance of Black Feminist Thought." *Social Problems* 33 (6): S14–32.

Combahee River Collective. 1977. "A Black Feminist Statement." *WSQ: Women's Studies Quarterly* 42 (3–4): 271–80.

Comfort, Megan. 2007. *Doing Time Together: Love and Family in the Shadow of the Prison*. Chicago: University of Chicago Press.

——. 2012. "'It Was Basically College to Us': Poverty, Prison, and Emerging Adulthood." *Journal of Poverty* 16: 308–22.

Committee on the Judiciary. 2019. "Questions for the Record, William P. Barr, Nominee to be United States Attorney General: Questions from Senator Feinstein." www.judiciary.senate.gov/imo/media/doc/Barr%20Responses%20to%20Feinstein%20QFRs1.pdf.

Common Sense for Drug Policy. 2009. "New York State Reforms Harsh Rockefeller Laws: Civil Rights Groups, Community Organizers, Political Leaders Join to 'Drop the Rock.'" www.csdp.org/news/news/newyork.htm.

Connell, Raewyn. 1979. "The Concept of Role and What to Do with It." *Australian and New Zealand Journal of Sociology* 15 (3): 7–17.

——. 1982. "Class, Patriarchy, and Sartre's Theory of Practice." *Theory and Practice* 11 (35): 305–20.

——. 1983. *Which Way is Up? Essays on Sex, Class and Culture*. Sydney, Australia: Allen and Unwin.

——. 1987. *Gender and Power: Society, the Person, and Sexual Politics*. Stanford, CA: Stanford University Press.

——. 2005 [1995]. *Masculinities*. Berkeley: University of California Press.

Connell, Raewyn. and James Messerschmidt. 2005. "Hegemonic Masculinity: Rethinking the Concept." *Gender and Society* 19 (6): 829–59.

Coplon, Jeff. 1984. "César Chávez's Fall from Grace." *Village Voice*, August 14 and 21.

Cooke, Bill. 1999. "Writing the Left out of Management Theory: The Historiography of the Management of Change." *Organization* 6 (1): 81–105.

Coto, Guillermo, and Marcelina Sanchez. 2014. "Intensive Supervision Programs." In *Wiley Series of Encyclopedias in Criminology and Criminal Justice: The Encyclopedia of Criminology and Criminal Justice*, ed. Jay Albanese. Hoboken: Wiley.

Covington, Stephanie. 2008. "Women and Addiction: A Trauma-Informed Approach." SARC Supplement 5, *Journal of Psychoactive Drugs* (November): 377–85.

Covington, Stephanie, and Barbara Bloom 2007. "Gender Responsive Treatment and Services in Correctional Settings." *Women & Therapy* 29 (3–4): 9–33.

Crenshaw, Kimberle. 1989. "Demarginalizing the Intersection of Race and Sex: A Black Feminist Critique of Antidiscrimination Doctrine, Feminist Theory and Antiracist Politics." *University of Chicago Legal Forum* 1: 139–67.

Crittenden, Ann. 2001. *The Price of Motherhood: Why the Most Important Job in the World is Still the Least Valued.* New York: Henry Holt and Company.

Cruikshank, Barbara. 1996. "Revolutions Within: Self-Government and Self-Esteem." In *Foucault and Political Reason: Liberalism, Neo-Liberalism and Rationalities of Government*, ed. Andrew Barry, Thomas Osborne, and Nikolas Rose, 231–51. Chicago: University of Chicago Press.

——. 1999. *The Will to Empower: Democratic Citizens and Other Subjects.* Ithaca, NY: Cornell University Press.

Csete, Joanne, and Holly Catania. 2013. "Methadone Treatment Providers; Views of Drug Court Policy and Practice: A Case Study of New York State." *Harm Reduction Journal* 10 (1): 35–43.

Csete, Joanne and Denise Tomasini-Joshi. 2015. "Drug Courts: Equivocal Evidence on a Popular Intervention." New York: Open Society Foundation. www.opensocietyfoundations.org/reports/drug-courts-equivocal-evidence-popular-intervention.

Cummins, Eric. 1994. *The Rise and Fall of California's Radical Prison Movement.* Stanford, CA: Stanford University Press.

Dannerbeck, Anne, Gardenia Harris, Paul Sundet, and Kathy Lloyd. 2006. "Understanding and Responding to Racial Differences in Drug Court Outcomes." *Journal of Ethnicity in Substance Abuse* 5 (2): 1–22.

Davis, Angela, and Dylan Rodriguez. 2002. "The Challenge of Prison Abolition: A Conversation." *Social Justice* 27 (3): 212–18.

Deangelis, Gerald. 1973. "Treatment and Rehabilitation of the Young Drug Abuser." *Pediatric Annals* 2 (2): 62–79.

de Certeau, Michel. 1984. *The Practice of Everyday Life.* Berkeley: University of California Press.

Deitch, David. 1973. "Treatment of Drug Abuse in the Therapeutic Community: Historical Influences, Current Considerations, and Future Outlook." In *National Commission on Marijuana and Drug Abuse. Report to Congress and the President*, 158–75. Washington, D.C.: U.S. Government Printing Office.

Deitch, David, Susie Carleton, Igor Koutsenok, and Karin Marsolais. 2002. "Therapeutic Community Treatment in Prisons." In *Treatment of Drug Offenders: Policies and Issues*, ed. Carl Leukefeld, Frank Tims, and David Farabee, 127–37. New York: Springer Publishing Co.

Deitch, David, and Robin Solit. 1993. "Training Drug Abuse Treatment Personnel in Therapeutic Community Methodologies." *Psychotherapy: Theory, Research, Practice, Training* 30 (2): 305–16.

De Leon, George, ed. 1974. *Phoenix House: Studies in a Therapeutic Community (1968-1973)*. New York: MSS Information Corporation.

——. 1983. "The Next Therapeutic Community: Autocracy and Other Notes Toward Integrating Old and New Therapeutic Communities." *International Journal of Therapeutic Communities* 4 (4): 249–61.

——. 1985. "The Therapeutic Community: Status and Evolution." *International Journal of the Addictions* 20 (6–7): 823–44.

——. 1988. "Legal Pressure in Therapeutic Communities." *Journal of Drug Issues* 18 (4): 625–41. Also included in *Compulsory Treatment of Drug Abuse: Research and Clinical Practice*, ed. Carl Leukefeld and Frank Tims, 160–77. Washington D.C.: U.S. Department of Health and Human Services.

——. 1993. "Training Drug Abuse Treatment Personnel in Therapeutic Community Methodologies." *Psychotherapy: Theory, Research, Practice, Training* 30 (2): 305–16.

——. 1995. "Therapeutic Communities for Addictions: A Theoretical Framework." *International Journal of the Addictions* 30 (12): 1603–45.

——. 2000. *The Therapeutic Community: Theory, Model, and Method*. New York: Springer Publishing.

——. 2010. "Is the Therapeutic Community an Evidence-Based Treatment? What the Evidence Says." *Therapeutic Communities* 31 (2): 104–28.

De Leon, George, and Steven Schwartz. 1984. "Therapeutic Communities: What Are the Retention Rates?" *American Journal of Drug and Alcohol Abuse* 10 (2): 267–84.

del Castillo, Richard. 1996. "César Estrada Chávez: The Final Struggle." *Southern California Quarterly* 78 (2): 199–214.

Delpit, Lisa. 1988. "The Silenced Dialogue: Power and Pedagogy in Educating Other People's Children." *Harvard Educational Review* 58 (3): 280–99.

DeMichele, Matthew T. 2007. *Probation and Parole's Growing Caseloads and Workload Allocation: Strategies for Managerial Decision Making*. The American Probation and Parole Association, May 4. www.appa-net.org/eweb/docs/appa/pubs/SMDM.pdf.

Dillon, Stephen. 2018. *Fugitive Life: The Queer Politics of the Prison State*. Durham, NC: Duke University Press.

Dissell, Rachel. 2017. "Ohio's Spending on Opioid Addiction Treatment Drugs Vivitrol and Suboxone Spikes, Spurs Debate on What Treatments Work." Cleveland.com, April 30. www.cleveland.com/metro/index.ssf/2017/04/ohios_spending_on_opioid_addiction_treatment_drugs_like_vivitrol_and_suboxone_spikes_spurs_debate_what_treatments_work.html.

Domoslawski, Artur. 2011. "Drug Policy in Portugal: The Benefits of Decriminalizing Drug Use." In *Lessons for Drug Policy* series, June. Warsaw, Poland: Global Drug

Policy Program, Open Society Foundations. www.opensocietyfoundations.org/sites/default/files/drug-policy-in-portugal-english-20120814.pdf.

Donaldson, Mike. 1993. "What is Hegemonic Masculinity?" *Theory and Society* 22 (5): 643–57.

Dorf, Michael and Charles Sabel. 2000. "Drug Treatment Courts and Emergent Experimentalist Government." *Vanderbilt Law Review* 53 (3): 829–83.

Doussard, Marc. 2013. *Degraded Work: The Struggle at the Bottom of the Labor Market*. Minneapolis: University of Minnesota Press.

DPA (Drug Policy Alliance). 2011. "*Drug Courts Are Not the Answer: Toward a Health-Centered Approach to Drug Use*. March. www.drugpolicy.org/sites/default/files/Drug%20Courts%20Are%20Not%20the%20Answer_Final2.pdf.

——. 2014. "*Moving Away from Drug Courts: Toward a Health-Centered Approach to Drug Use*. May. www.drugpolicy.org/sites/default/files/Fact_sheet_Moving_Away_from_Drug_Courts_Toward_Health_Approach_May2014.pdf.

Drake, Elizabeth K., Steve Aos, and Marna Miller. 2009. "Evidence-Based Public Policy Options to Reduce Crime and Criminal Justice Costs: Implications in Washington State." *Victims & Offenders* 4 (2): 170–96.

DuBois, W.E.B. 1935. *Black Reconstruction in America, 1860–1880*. New York: Atheneum Publishers.

Dugdale, Richard. 1877. *The Jukes: A Study of Crime, Pauperism, Disease and Heredity*. New York: Putnam.

Duggan, Lisa. 2003. *The Twilight of Equality? Neoliberalism, Cultural Politics, and the Attack on Democracy*. Boston: Beacon Press.

Dyck, Erica. 2006. " 'Hitting Highs at Rock Bottom': LSD Treatment for Alcoholism, 1950–1970." *Social History of Medicine* 19 (2): 313–29.

Edwards, Darren. 2015. *Drug Court Initiative, 2014 Annual Report*. Ed. Lisa Lindsay. New York: Criminal Court of the City of New York. www.nycourts.gov/courts/nyc/drug_treatment/publications_pdf/2014_drug_court_annual_report.pdf.

Edwards, Timothy. 2000. "The Theory and Practice of Compulsory Drug Treatment in the Criminal Justice System: The Wisconsin Experiment." *Wisconsin Law Review* 2: 283–368.

Egelko, Susan, and Marc Galanter. 1993. "Introducing Cognitive-Behavioral Training into a Self-Help Drug Treatment Program." *Psychotherapy: Theory, Research, Practice, Training* 30 (2): 214–21.

Eisenstein, Zillah, ed. 1978. *Capitalist Patriarchy and the Case for Socialist Feminism*. New York: Monthly Review Press.

Elias, Juanita, and Christine Beasley. 2009. "Hegemonic Masculinity and Globalization: 'Transnational Business Masculinities' and Beyond." *Globalizations* 6 (2): 281–96.

Elias, Norbert. 1939. *The Civilizing Process*. Oxford: Basil Blackwell.

Eliason, Michele, and Tonda Hughes. 2004. "Treatment Counselor's Attitudes About Lesbian, Gay, Bisexual, and Transgendered Clients: Urban vs. Rural Settings." *Substance Use & Misuse* 39 (4): 625–44.

Endore, Guy. 1968. *Synanon*. Garden City, NY: Doubleday & Co.

Erzen, Tanya. 2006. *Straight to Jesus: Sexual and Christian Conversions in the Ex-Gay Movement.* Berkeley: University of California Press.

Esmeir, Samera. 2012. *Juridical Humanity: A Colonial History.* Stanford, CA: Stanford University Press.

Ezzell, Matthew. 2012. " 'I'm in Control': Compensatory Manhood in a Therapeutic Community." *Gender and Society* 26 (2): 190–215.

Fabris, Erick. 2011. *Tranquil Prisons: Chemical Incarceration Under Community Treatment Orders.* Toronto: University of Toronto Press.

Fader, Jamie. 2013. *Falling Back: Incarceration and Transitions to Adulthood among Urban Youth.* New Brunswick, NJ: Rutgers University Press.

Fager, Wes. 2000. "A Clockwork Straight." Straight (website). www.thestraights.net /book/.

Failer, Judith Lynn. 2002. *Who Qualifies for Rights? Homelessness, Mental Illness, and Civil Commitment.* Ithaca, NY: Cornell University Press.

Fairbanks II, Robert. 2009. *How It Works: Recovering Citizens in Post-Welfare Philadelphia.* Chicago: The University of Chicago Press.

Farabee, David, Michael Prendergast, and Douglas Anglin. 1998. "The Effectiveness of Coerced Treatment for Drug-Abusing Offenders." *Federal Probation* 62 (1): 3–10.

Farley, Erin, Michael Rempel, and Sarah Picard-Fritsche. 2016. *Assessment and Treatment Matching: A Case Study of Traditional Practices in Three New York City Drug Courts.* New York: Center for Court Innovation.

Farole, Donald. 2006. "The Challenges of Going to Scale: Lessons from Other Disciplines for Problem Solving Courts." New York: Center for Court Innovation.

Farole, Donald, and Amanda Cissner. 2005. *Seeing Eye to Eye? Participant and Staff Perspectives on Drug Courts.* New York: Center for Court Innovation.

Fassin, Didier. 2012. *Humanitarian Reason: A Moral History of the Present.* Berkeley: University of California Press.

Fears, Darryl. 2009. "A Racial Shift in Drug-Crime Prisoners: Fewer Blacks and More Whites, Says Sentencing Project." *Washington Post*, April 15.

Feeley, Malcolm, and Jonathan Simon. 1992. "The New Penology: Notes on the Emerging Strategy of Corrections and Its Implications." *Criminology* 30 (4): 449–74.

——. 1994. "Actuarial Justice: The Emerging New Criminal Law." In *The Futures of Criminology*, ed. David Nelkin, 173–201. London: Sage Publications.

Ferrell, Jeff. 1997. "Against the Law: Anarchist Criminology." In *Thinking Critically About Crime*, ed. Brian MacLean and Dragan Milovanovic, 136–54. Vancouver, BC: Collective Press.

Fineman, Martha, and Terence Dougherty, eds. 2005. *Feminism Confronts Homo Economicus: Gender, Law, and Society.* Ithaca: Cornell University Press.

Fischer, Benedikt. 2003. " 'Doing Good with a Vengeance': A Critical Assessment of the Practices, Effects and Implications of Drug Treatment Courts in North America." *Criminal Justice* 3 (3): 227–48.

Fisher, Florrie. 1971. *The Lonely Trip Back.* New York: Doubleday.

Fluellen, Reginald, and Jennifer Trone. 2000. "Do Drug Courts Save Jail and Prison Beds?" In *Issues in Brief.* New York: Vera Institute of Justice.

Forman, James. 2018. *Locking Up Our Own: Crime and Punishment in Black America.* New York: Farrar, Straus and Giroux.

Fortner, Michael. 2015. *Black Silent Majority: The Rockefeller Drug Laws and the Politics of Punishment.* Cambridge, MA: Harvard University Press.

Foucault, Michel. 1975. *Discipline and Punish: The Birth of the Modern Prison.* New York: Random House.

—. 1978. *The History of Sexuality.* New York: Pantheon.

—. 1982a. "The Subject and Power." *Critical Inquiry* 8 (4): 777–95.

—. 1982b. "The Subject and Power." In *Michel Foucault: Beyond Structuralism· and Hermeneutic,* ed. Hubert Dreyfus and Paul Rabinow, 208–26. Chicago: University of Chicago Press.

Fox, Aubrey, and Robert Wolf. 2004. *The Future of Drug Courts: How States Are Mainstreaming the Drug Court Model.* New York: Center for Court Innovation.

Fredersdorf, Frederic. 1999. "Synanon in Germany: An Example of a Residential Self-Help Organization for Drug Dependent Individuals." *International Journal of Self-Help & Self-Care* 1 (2): 131–43.

Freedman, Estelle. 1984. *Their Sisters' Keepers: Women's Prison Reform in America, 1830–1930.* Ann Arbor: The University of Michigan Press.

Freud, Sigmund. 1961 [1930]. *Civilization and Its Discontents.* New York: Norton.

Friedenberg, Edgar. 1965. "The Synanon Solution," review of *The Tunnel Back,* by Lewis Yablonsky. *The Nation* 200 (10 [March 8]): 256–60.

Garland, David. 1996. "The Limits of the Sovereign State: Strategies of Crime Control in Contemporary Society." *British Journal of Criminology* 36 (4): 445–71.

—. 2001. *The Culture of Control: Crime and Social Order in Contemporary Society.* Chicago: University of Chicago Press.

Garriott, William, and Eugene Raikhel. 2015. "Addiction in the Making." *Annual Review of Anthropology* 44: 477–91.

Gates, Eileen, and Philip Bourdette. 1975. "The Synanon Alternative to the Criminal Justice System." *Journal of Drug Issues* 5 (Summer): 233–41.

Geiger, Raymond, and Jennifer Wolch. 1986. "A Shadow State? Voluntarism in Metropolitan Los Angeles." *Environment and Planning D: Society and Space* 4 (3): 351–66.

Geller, Scott, Daniel Johnson, Paul Hamlin, and Thomas Kennedy. 1977. "Behavior Modification in a Prison: Issues, Problems, and Compromises." *Criminal Justice and Behavior* 4 (11): 11–43.

Gerstein, Dean, and Henrick Harwood, eds. 1990. *Treating Drug Problems: A Study of the Evolution, Effectiveness, and Financing of Public and Private Drug Treatment Systems,* v.1. Committee for the Substance Abuse Coverage Study, Division of Health Care Services, Institute of Medicine. Washington, D.C.: National Academy Press.

Gerstel, David. *Paradise Incorporated: Synanon.* 1982. Novato: Presidio Press.

Gilroy, Paul. 1987. *"There Ain't No Black in the Union Jack": The Cultural Politics of Race and Nation.* Chicago: University of Chicago Press.

Glass, Ira. 2011. "Very Tough Love," March 25. In *This American Life,* produced in collaboration with WBEZ Chicago and PRX The Public Radio Exchange. www.thisamericanlife.org/430/very-tough-love.

Goffman, Erving. 1961. *Asylums: Essays on the Social Situation of Mental Patients and Other Inmates.* Garden City, NJ: Anchor Books.

Goldkamp, John. 1994. *Justice and Treatment Innovation: The Drug Court Movement.* Washington D.C.: National Institute for Justice. www.ncjrs.gov/pdffiles1/Digitization/149260NCJRS.pdf.

—. 2000. "The Drug Court Response: Issues and Implications for Justice Change." *Albany Law Review* 63: 923–61.

Goldkamp, John, Michael White, and Jennifer Robinson. 2001. "Do Drug Courts Work? Getting Inside the Drug Court Black Box." *Journal of Drug Issues* 31 (1): 27–72.

Gonnerman, Jennifer. 2009. "Addicted: The Myth of the Rockefeller-Drug-Laws Repeal." *New York Magazine*, March 29.

Goodwyn, Wade. 2007. "In Dallas, a Hip-Hop Plea: Pull Your Pants Up." Washington, D.C.: National Public Radio, October 24.

Gorz, André. 1967. *Strategy for Labor: A Radical Proposal.* Boston: Beacon Press.

Gottschalk, Marie. 2015. *Caught: The Prison State and the Lockdown of American Politics.* Princeton, NJ: Princeton University Press.

Gowan, Teresa. 2010. *Hobos, Hustlers, and Backsliders: Homeless in San Francisco.* Minneapolis: University of Minnesota Press.

Gowan, Teresa, and Sarah Whetstone. 2012. "Making the Criminal Addict: Subjectivity and Social Control in a Strong-Arm Rehab." *Punishment & Society* 14 (1): 69–93.

Gowing, Linda, and Robert Ali. 2006. "The Place of Detoxification in Treatment of Opioid Dependence." *Current Opinion in Psychiatry* 19 (3): 266–70.

Graham, Stepanic, Jamie Carney, and Annette Kluck. 2012. "Perceived Competency in Working with LGB Clients: Where Are We Now?" *Counselor Education and Supervision* 51 (1): 2–16.

Granahan, Thomas. 2008. "High Finance: Long Hours, Plenty of Money and Loads of Ambition Can Be a Recipe for Substance Abuse on Wall Street." *Investment Dealers' Digest* 74 (1): 12–18.

Granfield, Robert, and Craig Reinarman, eds. 2015. *Expanding Addiction: Critical Essays.* New York: Routledge.

Grapendaal, Martin. 1992. "Cutting Their Coat According to Their Cloth: Economic Behavior of Amsterdam Opiate Users." *International Journal of the Addictions* 27 (4): 487–501.

Greenberg, David, and Drew Humphries. 1980. "The Cooptation of Fixed Sentencing Reform." *Crime & Delinquency* 26 (2): 206–25.

Greenfield, Patricia. 1977. "CIA's Behavior Caper." *APA Monitor* 8: 1, 10–11.

Grella, Christine. 2008. "From Generic to Gender-Responsive Treatment: Changes in Social Policies, Treatment Services, and Outcomes of Women in Substance Abuse Treatment." SARC Supplement 5, *Journal of Psychoactive Drugs* (November): 327–43.

Grewal, Inderpal. 2017a. *Saving the Security State.* Durham, NC: Duke University Press.

—. 2017b. "Drone Imaginaries: The Technopolitics of Visuality in Postcolony and Empire." In *Life in the Age of Drone Warfare*, ed. Caren Kaplan and Lisa Parks. Durham, NC: Duke University Press.

Guenther, Lisa. 2013. *Solitary Confinement: Social Death and Its Afterlives*. Minneapolis: University of Minnesota Press.

Hackett, Colleen, and Ben Turk. 2018. "Shifting Carceral Landscapes: Decarceration and the Reconfiguration of White Supremacy." In *Abolishing Carceral Society*, ed. Abolition Collective, 23–54. Brooklyn: Common Notions.

Haigh, Rex, and Jan Lees. 2008. " 'Fusion TCs': Divergent Histories, Converging Challenges." *Therapeutic Communities* 29 (4): 347–74.

Haley, Sarah. 2013. " 'Like I Was a Man': Chain Gangs, Gender, and the Domestic Carceral Sphere in Jim Crow Georgia." *Signs*, 39 (1): 53–77.

——. 2016. *No Mercy Here: Gender, Punishment, and the Making of Jim Crow Modernity*. Chapel Hill: University of North Carolina Press.

Hall, Stuart. 1986. "Gramsci's Relevance for the Study of Race and Ethnicity." *Journal of Communication Inquiry* 10 (2): 5–27.

Hall, Stuart, Chas Critcher, Tony Jefferson, John Clarke, and Brian Roberts. 1978. *Policing the Crisis: Mugging, the State, and Law and Order*. New York: Holmes & Meier.

Haney, Lynne. 2010. *Offending Women: Power, Punishment, and the Regulation of Desire*. Berkeley: University of California Press.

Hanhardt, Christina. 2013. *Safe Space: Gay Neighborhood History and the Politics of Violence*. Durham, NC: Duke University Press.

Hannah-Moffat, Kelly. 2001. *Punishment in Disguise: Penal Governance and Federal Imprisonment of Women in Canada*. Toronto: University of Toronto Press.

Hansen, Helena. 2012. "The 'New Masculinity': Addiction Treatment as a Reconstruction of Gender in Puerto Rican Evangelist Street Ministries." *Social Science and Medicine* 74: 1721–8.

——. 2018. *Addicted to Christ: Remaking Men in Puerto Rican Pentecostal Drug Ministries*. Oakland: University of California Press.

Hansen, Helena, Philippe Bourgois, and Ernest Drucker. 2014. "Pathologizing Poverty: New Forms of Diagnosis, Disability, and Structural Stigma under Welfare Reform." *Social Science & Medicine* 103 (February): 76–83.

Hansen, Helena, and Jules Netherland. 2017. "White Opioids: Pharmaceutical Race and the War on Drugs That Wasn't." *BioSocieties* 12 (2): 217–38.

Hansen, Helena, and Samuel Roberts. 2012. "Two Tiers of Biomedicalization: Methadone, Buprenorphrine, and the Racial Politics of Addiction Treatment." In *Critical Perspectives on Addiction*, ed. Julie Netherland, 79–102. Bingley, UK: Emerald Group Publishing.

Hansen, Karen, and Ilene Philipson, eds. 1989. *Women, Class, and the Feminist Imagination*. Philadelphia: Temple University Press.

Harding, J. 1986. "Mood Modifiers and Elderly Women in Canada: The Medicalization of Poverty." In *Adverse Effects: Women and the Pharmaceutical Industry*, ed. Kathleen McDonnell, 51–86. Penang, Malaysia: International Organization of Consumer Unions.

Harper, Jake. 2017. "To Grow Market Share, a Drugmaker Pitches Its Product to Judges." NPR, August 3. www.npr.org/sections/health-shots/2017/08/03/540029500/to-grow-market-share-a-drugmaker-pitches-its-product-to-judges.

Harris, Amy Julia, and Shoshana Walter. 2017a. "They Thought They Were Going to Rehab. They Ended Up in Chicken Plants." *Reveal News*, Center for Investigative Reporting, Emeryville, October 4. www.revealnews.org/article/they-thought-they-were-going-to-rehab-they-ended-up-in-chicken-plants.

——. 2017b. "Inside a Judge's Rehab: Unpaid Work at a Local Coca-Cola Plant." *Reveal News*. The Center for Investigative Reporting, Emeryville, December 4.

——. 2019. "They Worked in Sweltering Heat for Exxon, Shell and Walmart. They Didn't Get Paid a Dime." *Reveal News*, Center for Investigative Reporting, Emeryville, April 24. www.revealnews.org/article/they-worked-in-sweltering-heat-for-exxon-shell-and-walmart-they-didnt-get-paid-a-dime.

Harrison, Linda, Diane Patrick, and Kim English. 2001. *Evaluation of the Denver Drug Court: The Early Years, 1995–1996*. For Division of Criminal Justice Office of Research and Statistics. Denver: Colorado Department of Public Safety.

Hartman, Saidiya. 1997. *Scenes of Subjection: Terror, Slavery, and Self-Making in Nineteenth-Century America*. New York: Oxford University Press.

Hasenfeld, Yeheskel. 1972. "People Processing Organizations: An Exchange Approach." *American Sociological Review* 37 (3): 256–63.

Hatch, Anthony. 2019. *Silent Cells: The Secret Drugging of Captive America*. Minneapolis: University of Minnesota Press.

Hatch, Anthony, and Bradley Kym. 2016. "Prisons Matter: Psychotropics and the Trope of Silence in Technocorrections." In *Mattering: Feminism, Science, and Materialism*, ed. Victoria Pitts-Taylor, 224–44. New York: New York University Press.

Hatch, Anthony, Marik Xavier-Brier, Brandon Atell, and Eryn Viscarra. 2016. "Soldier, Elder, Prisoner, Ward: Psychotropics in the Era of Transinstitutionalization." In *50 Years after Deinstitutionalization: Mental Illness in Contemporary Communities*, vol. 17 of *Advances in Medical Sociology*, ed. Brea Perry, 291–317. Bingley, UK: Emerald Group Publishing.

Hays, Sharon. 2003. *Flat Broke with Children: Women in the Age of Welfare Reform*. New York: Oxford University Press.

Heck, Cary. 2006. *Local Drug Court Research: Navigating Performance Measures and Process Evaluations*. Alexandria, VA: National Drug Court Institute.

Herrick, Stephen, Gerianne Abriano, Linda Baldwin, Justin Barry, Steve Hanson, Cindy Heady-Marsh, Deborah Kaplan, Leslie Leach, Robert Lonski, James McCarthy, Michael Magnani, Edward Nowak, Kenneth Perez, Valerie Raine, and Laura Ward. 2008. *New York State Adult Treatment Courts: Recommended Practices*. New York State Unified Court System. Albany: New York State Unified Court System. www.courtinnovation.org/sites/default/files/Recommended_Practices_10.pdf.

HHS (U. S. Department of Health and Human Services). 2017. "HHS announces $80.8 million in grants for Adult and Family Treatment Drug Courts, and Adult Tribal Healing to Wellness Courts." July 14. www.hhs.gov/about/news/2017/07/14/hhs-announces-808-million-grants-adult-and-family-treatment-drug-courts-and-adult-tribal-healing.html.

Hicks, Daniel. 2000. "The Importance of Specialized Treatment Programs for Lesbian and Gay Patients." *Journal of Gay & Lesbian Psychotherapy* 3 (3–4): 81–94.

Hill, Ian. 2014. "The Rhetorical Transformation of the Masses from Malthus's 'Redundant Population' into Marx's 'Industrial Reserve Army.'" *Advances in the History of Rhetoric* 17 (1): 88–97.

Hochschild, Arlie. 1993. "Inside the Clockwork of Male Careers with a 1990s Postscript." In *Gender and the Academic Experience: Berkeley Women, 1952–1972*, ed. Ruth Wallace, Kathryn Meadow-Orlans, 125–39. Lincoln: University of Nebraska Press.

Hollander, Lynne. 1971. "The 'Adjustment Center': California's Prisons within Prisons." *Black Law Journal* 1 (Summer): 152–59.

Holmes, Marcia. 2017. "Edward Hunter and the Origins of 'Brainwashing.'" The Hidden Persuader's Project, May 26. http://www.bbk.ac.uk/hiddenpersuaders/blog/hunter-origins-of-brainwashing.

Hora, Peggy. 2002. "A Dozen Years of Drug Courts: Uncovering Our Theoretical Foundation and the Construction of a Mainstream Paradigm." *Substance Use and Misuse* 37: 1469–88.

Hora, Peggy, William Schma, and John Rosenthal. 1999. "Therapeutic Jurisprudence and the Drug Treatment Court Movement: Revolutionizing the Criminal Justice System's Response to Drug Abuse in America." *Notre Dame Law Review* 74 (2): 439–538.

Hora, Peggy, and Theodore Stalcup. 2008. "Drug Treatment Courts in the Twenty-First Century: The Evolution of the Revolution in Problem-Solving Courts." *Georgia Law Review* 42: 717–811.

Howard, Jane. 1970. *Please Touch: A Guided Tour of the Human Potential Movement*. New York: McGraw-Hill.

HRW (Human Rights Watch). 2008. *Targeting Blacks: Drug Law Enforcement and Race in the United States*. New York: Human Rights Watch. www.hrw.org/sites/default/files/reports/us0508_1.pdf.

——. 2013. *An Offer You Can't Refuse: How US Federal Prosecutors Force Drug Defendants to Plead Guilty*. New York: Human Rights Watch. www.hrw.org/report/2013/12/05/offer-you-cant-refuse/how-us-federal-prosecutors-force-drug-defendants-plead.

Hunter, Edward. 1951. *Brainwashing in Red China: The Calculated Destruction of Men's Minds*. New York: Vanguard Press.

Hunter, Sarah, Lois Davis, Rosanna Smart, and Susan Turner. 2017. *Impact of Proposition 47 on Los Angeles County Operations and Budget*. Santa Monica: RAND Corporation. www.rand.org/content/dam/rand/pubs/research_reports/RR1700/RR1754/RAND_RR1754.pdf.

Iacobucci, Alaina, and Emma Frieh. 2018. "(In)dependence and Addictions: Governmentality Across Public and Private Treatment Discourses." *Theoretical Criminology* 22 (1): 83–98.

Imhof, John. 1974. "Is Odyssey House the Tiffany of TCs?" *Contemporary Drug Problems* 3 (4): 443–56.

Inciardi, James. 1988. "Some Considerations on the Clinical Efficacy of Compulsory Treatment: Reviewing the New York Experience." National Institute on Drug Abuse (NIDA). Rockville, MD: U.S. Department of Health and Human Services, National Institutes of Health.

Incite! 2007. *The Revolution Will Not Be Funded: Beyond the Non-Profit Industrial Complex.* Durham, NC: Duke University Press.

Irwin, John. 1970. *The Felon.* Berkeley: University of California Press.

——. 2005. *The Warehouse Prison: Disposal of the New Dangerous Class.* New York: Oxford University Press.

Isbell, Harris, R.E. Belleville, Havelock Fraser, Abraham Wilker, and C.R. Logan. 1956. "Studies on Lysergic Acid Diethylamide (LSD-25)." *A.M.A. Archives of Neurology and Psychiatry*, no. 76 (November): 468–78.

Jacobson, Michael. 2005. *Downsizing Prisons: How to Reduce Crime and End Mass Incarceration.* New York: New York University Press.

Janssen, Volker. 2007. "From the Inside Out: Therapeutic Penology and Political Liberalism in Postwar California." *Osiris* 22 (1): 116–34.

Janzen, Rod. 2001. *The Rise and Fall of Synanon: A California Utopia.* Baltimore, MD: Johns Hopkins University Press.

Jensen, Eric, Nicholas Parsons, and Clayton Mosher. 2007. "Adult Drug Treatment Courts: A Review." *Sociology Compass* 1–2: 552–71.

Jessop, Bob. 1994. "Post-Fordism and the State." In *Post-Fordism: A Reader*, ed. Ash Amin. Oxford: Blackwell Publishers.

Jones, Maxwell. 1953. *The Therapeutic Community.* New York: Basic Books.

JPI (Justice Policy Institute). 2011. "Addicted to Courts: How a Growing Dependence on Drug Courts Impacts People and Communities." Washington, D.C.: Justice Policy Institute. www.justicepolicy.org/research/2217.

Kalleberg, Arne. 2011. *Good Jobs, Bad Jobs: The Rise of Polarized and Precarious Employment Systems in the United States, 1970s to 2000s.* New York: Russell Sage Foundation.

Kandall, Stephen. 1996. *Substance and Shadow: Women and Addiction in the United States.* Cambridge, MA: Harvard University Press.

Kassebaum, Gene, David Ward, and Daniel Wilner. 1963. *Group Treatment by Correctional Personnel: A Survey of the California Department of Corrections.* Sacramento: State of California, Youth and Adult Corrections Agency.

Kaye, Kerwin. 2005. "Sexual Abuse Victims and the Wholesome Family: Feminist, Psychological, and State Discourses." In *Regulating Sex: The Politics of Intimacy and Identity*, ed. Elizabeth Bernstein and Laurie Schaffner. New York: Routledge.

——. 2010. "Drug Courts and the Treatment of Addiction: Therapeutic Jurisprudence and Neoliberal Governance." PhD diss., New York University.

——. 2012. "De-Medicalizing Addiction: Toward Biocultural Understandings." In *Critical Perspectives on Addiction*, vol. 14 of *Advances in Medical Sociology*, ed. Julie Netherland, 27–51. Bingley, UK: Emerald Group Publishing.

——. 2013. "Rehabilitating the 'Drugs Lifestyle': Criminal Justice, Social Control, and the Cultivation of Agency." *Ethnography* 14 (2): 207–32.

Keen, Jenny, Phillip Oliver, Georgina Rowse, and Nigel Mathers. 2001. "Residential Rehabilitation for Drug Users: A Review of 13 Months' Intake to a Therapeutic Community." *Family Practice* 18 (5): 545–8.

Kellam, Leslie, and Leigh Bates. 2014. "2009 Drug Law Changes: 2014 Update." In *Drug Law Series*, Report number 5 (May). New York: Division of Criminal Justice Services. www.criminaljustice.ny.gov/drug-law-reform/documents/dlr-update-report-may-2014.pdf.

Kerlikowske, Gil. 2013. "What Drug Policy Reform Looks Like." Director's Remarks at the National Press Club, Washington D.C., April 17. https://obamawhitehouse.archives.gov/ondcp/news-releases-remarks/what-drug-policy-reform-looks-like.

Kerrison, Erin. 2017. "An Historical Review of Racial Bias in Prison-Based Substance Abuse Treatment Design." *Journal of Offender Rehabilitation* 56 (8): 567–92.

Kessler, Sandra, Dean Ashenden, Raewyn Connell, and Gary Dowsett. 1982. *Ockers and Disco Maniacs: Sex, Gender, and Secondary Schooling*. Sydney, Australia: Inner City Education Centre.

Kilgore, James. 2014. "Repackaging Mass Incarceration." *Counterpunch*, June 6. www.counterpunch.org/2014/06/06/repackaging-mass-incarceration.

Kilmer, Beau, Gregory Midgette, and Clinton Saloga. 2016. "Back in the National Spotlight: An Assessment of Recent Changes in Drug Use and Drug Policies in the United States." Center for 21st Century Security and Intelligence: Foreign Policy at Brookings, July. www.brookings.edu/wp-content/uploads/2016/07/Kilmer-United-States-final-2.pdf.

King, Ryan, and Jill Pasquarella. 2009. "Drug Courts: A Review of the Evidence." The Sentencing Project, April 1. www.sentencingproject.org/publications/drug-courts-a-review-of-the-evidence.

King, Wayne. 1981. "Synanon Members Accused in Beating." *New York Times*, March 1. www.nytimes.com/1981/03/01/us/synanon-members-accused-in-beating.html.

Kirby, Kimberly, Brian Versek, MaryLouise Kerwin, Kathleen Meyers, Lois Benishek, Elena Bresani, Yukiko Washio, Amelia Arria, and Robert Meyers. 2015. "Developing Community Reinforcement and Family Training (CRAFT) for Parents of Treatment-Resistant Adolescents." *Journal of Child & Adolescent Substance Abuse* 24 (3): 155–65.

Kitzinger, Jenny. 2004. *Framing Abuse: Media Influence and Public Understanding of Sexual Violence Against Children*. Ann Arbor, MI: Pluto Press.

Klag, Stephanie, Francis O'Callaghan, and Peter Creed. "The Use of Legal Coercion in the Treatment of Substance Abusers: An Overview and Critical Analysis of Thurty Years of Research." *Substance Use & Misuse* 40: 1777–95.

Kleiman, Mark. 2009. *When Brute Force Fails: How to Have Less Crime and Less Punishment*. Princeton, NJ: Princeton University Press.

Klein, Naomi. 2007. *The Shock Doctrine: The Rise of Disaster Capitalism*. New York: Henry Holt and Company.

Kluger, Judy, and Michael Rempel. 2013. "Reform of the Rockefeller Drug Laws and the Impact on Criminal Justice." In *NADCP Conference*, July. www.nadcp.org/sites/default/files/nadcp/Cybercafe/2013/handouts/D/D-17.pdf.

Kooyman, Martien. 1994. *The Therapeutic Community for Addicts: Intimacy, Parent Involvement, and Treatment Success*. Amsterdam: Swets & Zeitlinger.

Kuhn, Thomas S. 1962. *The Structure of Scientific Revolutions*. Chicago: University of Chicago Press.

Kurashige, Scott. 2017. *The Fifty Year Rebellion: How the U.S. Political Crisis Began in Detroit.* Oakland: University of California Press.

Kurki, Leena, and Norval Morris. 2001. "Supermax Prisons." In *Crime and Justice: A Review of Research*, ed. Michael Tonry, 385–424. Chicago: University of Chicago Press.

Lamb, Sharon. 1999. "Constructing the Victim: Popular Images and Lasting Labels." In *New Versions of Victims: Feminists Struggle with the Concept*, ed. Sharon Lamb, 108–38. New York: New York University Press.

Lake, Robert, and Kathe Newman. 2002. "Differential Citizenship in the Shadow State." *GeoJournal* 58 (2/3): 109–20.

Lazarsfeld, Paul. 1941. "Remarks on Administrative and Critical Communications Research." *Studies in Philosophy and Social Science* 9: 2–16.

Lea, John, and Jock Young. 1984. *What Is to Be Done About Law and Order?* New York: Penguin Books.

Lee, Laura. 2002. "Changing Selves, Changing Society: Human Relations Experts and the Invention of T Groups, Sensitivity Training, and Encounter in the United States, 1938–1980." PhD Diss., University of California, Los Angeles.

Lennard, Henry, and Steven Allen. 1974. "The Treatment of Drug Addiction: Toward New Models." In *Phoenix House: Studies in a Therapeutic Community (1968–1973)*, ed. Gerorge De Leon, 199–214. New York: MSS Information Corporation.

Levy, E. S., G. J. Faltico, and T. E. Bratter. 1977. "The Development and Structure of the Drug Free Therapeutic Community." *Addiction Therapist* 2 (2): 40–52.

Lewin, Kurt. 1947. "Frontiers in Group Dynamics: Concept, Method and Reality in Social Science; Social Equilibria and Social Change." *Human Relations* 1 (1): 5–41.

Lewis, Charlton. 1890. *An Elementary Latin Dictionary*. Wadsworth, GA: American Book Company.

Lewis, Oscar. 1966. "The Culture of Poverty." *Scientific American* 215 (4): 19–25.

——. 1968. *La Vida: A Puerto Rican Family in the Culture of Poverty—San Juan and New York.* London: Panther.

Lewis, Virginia, and Daniel Glaser. 1974. "Lifestyles Among Heroin Users." *Federal Probation* 38 (21): 21–28.

Lieberman, Donna. 2009. "Column: Let's Repeal Rockefeller." *New York Metro*, March 17.

Lieupo, Kelly, and Susan Weinstein. 2004. "Ballot Initiatives—Wolves in Sheep's Clothing." *Drug Court Review* 41 (4): 49–66.

Lipton, Douglas. 1998. "Therapeutic Community Treatment Programming in Corrections." *Psychology, Crime & Law* 4: 213–263.

Lipton, Douglas, Gregory Falkin and Harry Wexler. 1992. "Correctional Drug Abuse Treatment in the United States: An Overview." In *Drug Abuse Treatment in Prisons and Jails*, ed. Carl Leukefeld and Frank Tims, 8–30. NIDA Research Monograph 118. Washington, D.C.: U.S. Department of Health and Human Services.

Lipton, Douglas, Judith Wilks, and Robert Martinson. 1975. *The Effectiveness of Correctional Treatment: A Survey of Treatment Evaluation Studies*. New York. Praeger.

Locke, John. 2013 [1689]. *Two Treatises Concerning Government*. Ed. Peter Laslett. Cambridge: Cambridge University Press.

Lombardi, Emilia. 2007. "Public Health and Trans-People: Barriers to Care and Strategies to Improve Treatment." In *The Health of Sexual Minorities: Public Health Perspectives on Lesbian, Gay, Bisexual and Transgender Populations*, ed. Ilan Meyer and Mary Northridge, 638–52. Boston: Springer.

Los Angeles Times. 1966. "Synanon Methods Being Used to Aid Collegians with Lost Feeling." April 3.

——. 1968. "The Synanon House of Cards: Deck Is Stacked for Recovery." October 6.

Lynch, Mona. 2010. *Sunbelt Justice: Arizona and the Transformation of American Punishment*. Stanford, CA: Stanford University Press.

MacGillis, Alec. 2017. "The Last Shot." *ProPublica*, June 27. www.propublica.org/article/vivitrol-opiate-crisis-and-criminal-justice.

Macpherson, C. B. 2011. *The Political Theory of Possessive Individualism: Hobbes to Locke*. New York: Oxford University Press.

Mahmood, Saba. 2005. *Politics of Piety: The Islamic Revival and the Feminist Subject*. Princeton, NJ: Princeton University Press.

Marks, John. 1991. *The Search for the Manchurian Candidate: The CIA and Mind Control: The Secret History of the Behavioral Sciences*. New York: Norton.

Marlowe, Douglas. 2002. "Effective Strategies for Intervening with Drug Abusing Offenders." *Villanova Law Review* 47 (May): 989–1026.

——. 2010a. "Need to Know: The Facts on Marijuana." Alexandria, VA: National Association of Drug Court Professionals. www.ndci.org/resources/the-facts-on-marijuana.

——. 2010b. "Research Update on Adult Drug Courts." Alexandria, VA: National Association of Drug Court Professionals. www.ncjrs.gov/App/Publications/abstract.aspx?ID=256232.

——. 2011. "The Verdict on Drug Courts and Other Problem-Solving Courts." *Chapman Journal of Criminal Justice* 2 (1): 53–92.

——. 2012. "Behavior Modification 101 for Drug Courts: Making the Most of Incentives and Sanctions." *Drug Court Practitioner Fact Sheet*. Washington, D.C.: National Drug Court Institute, September. www.ndci.org/wp-content/uploads/BehaviorModification101forDrugCourts.pdf.

——. 2013. "Achieving Racial and Ethnic Fairness in Drug Courts." *Court Review* 49: 40–47.

Marlowe, Douglas, Amiram Elwork, David Festinger, and A. Thomas McLellan. 2003. "Drug Policy by Popular Referendum: This Too, Shall Pass." *Journal of Substance Abuse Treatment* 25: 213–23.

Marlowe, Douglas, Carolyn Hardin, and Carson Fox. 2016. *Painting the Current Picture: A National Report on Drug Courts and Other Problem-Solving Courts in the United States*. Washington, D.C.: National Drug Court Institute. www.ndci.org/wp-content/uploads/2016/05/Painting-the-Current-Picture-2016.pdf.

Marlowe, Douglas, and Kimberly Kirby. 1999. "Effective Use of Sanctions in Drug Courts: Lessons from Behavioral Research." *National Drug Court Institute Review* 2 (1): 1–31.

Marlowe, Douglas, and William Meyer. 2011. "The Drug Court Judicial Benchbook." Washington, D.C.: National Drug Court Institute. www.ndci.org/wp-content/uploads/14146_NDCI_Benchbook_v6.pdf.

Marlowe, Douglas, and Benjamin Nordstrom. 2016. "Medication-Assisted Treatment for Opioid Use Disorders." *National Drug Court Institute Drug Court Practitioner Fact Sheet* 11 (2): 1–15.

Maron, Dina Fine. 2009. "Drug Courts Appeal to Democrats and Republicans." *Newsweek*, October 6. www.newsweek.com/drug-courts-appeal-democrats-and-republicans-81225.

Martin, Patricia Yancey. 1998. "Why Can't a Man Be More Like a Woman? Reflections on Connell's Masculinities." *Gender & Society* 12 (4): 472–74.

Martinson, Robert. 1974. "What Works? Questions and Answers about Prison Reform." *The Public Interest* 35 (Spring): 22–54.

Maruna, Shadd, and Thomas LeBel. 2003. "Welcome Home? Examining the 'Reentry Court' Concept from a Strengths-Based Perspective." *Western Criminological Review* 4 (2): 91–107.

Maslow, Abraham. 1967. "Synanon and Eupsychia." *Journal of Humanistic Psychology* 7 (Spring): 28–35.

Massachusetts Medical Society. 2011. "Urine Abstinence Testing and Incidental Alcohol Exposure." www.massmed.org/uploadedFiles/Physician_Health_Service/Clients_and_Monitors/10-20-11_Incidental_Alcohol_Exposure.pdf.

Maté, Gabor. 2008. *In the Realm of Hungry Ghosts: Close Encounters with Addiction*. New York: Random House.

Matthews, Connie, and Mary Selvidge. 2005. "Lesbian, Gay, and Bisexual Clients' Experiences in Treatment for Addiction." *Journal of Lesbian Studies* 9 (3): 79–90.

Matusow, Harlan, Samuel Dickman, Josiah Rich, Chunki Fong, Dora Dumont, Carolyn Hardin, Douglas Marlowe, and Andrew Rosenblum. 2013. "Medication Assisted Treatment in US Drug Courts: Results from a Nationwide Survey of Availability, Barriers and Attitudes." *Journal of Substance Abuse Treatment* 44 (5): 473–80.

Mauer, Marc. 2006. *Race to Incarcerate, Revised and Updated*. New York: The New Press.

—. 2009. *The Changing Racial Dynamics of the War on Drugs*. Washington D.C.: The Sentencing Project. www.sentencingproject.org/wp-content/uploads/2016/01/The-Changing-Racial-Dynamics-of-the-War-on-Drugs.pdf.

Mauer, Marc, and Ryan King. 2007. *Uneven Justice: State Rates of Incarceration By Race and Ethnicity*. Washington, D.C.: The Sentencing Project. www.sentencingproject.org/publications/uneven-justice-state-rates-of-incarceration-by-race-and-ethnicity.

McColl, William. 1996. "Baltimore City's Drug Treatment Court: Theory and Practice in an Emerging Field," *Maryland Law Review* 55 (2): 467–518.

McCorkel, Jill. 2003. "Embodied Surveillance and the Gendering of Punishment." *Journal of Contemporary Ethnography Journal of Contemporary Ethnography* 32 (1): 41–76.

—. 2013. *Breaking Women: Gender, Race, and the New Politics of Imprisonment*. New York: New York University Press.

McCoy, Alfred. 2006. *A Question of Torture: CIA Interrogation, from the Cold War to the War on Terror*. New York: Owl Books.

McKim, Allison. 2008. " 'Getting Gut-Level': Punishment, Gender, and Therapeutic Governance." *Gender & Society* 22 (3): 303–23.

——. 2010. "Transforming the Self: Patients, Prisoners, and Therapeutic Governance." PhD diss., New York University.

——. 2014. "Roxanne's Dress: Governing Gender and Marginality Through Addiction Treatment." *Signs* 39 (2): 433–58.

——. 2017. *Addicted to Rehab: Race, Gender, and Drugs in the Era of Mass Incarceration*. New Brunswick, NJ: Rutgers University Press.

Mecca, Andrew. 1978. "TASC (Treatment Alternatives to Street Crime): Historical Perspective and Future Implications." *Offender Rehabilitation* 2 (3): 279–94.

Melechi, Antonio. 2016 "Bodies of Evidence: Psychologists and the CIA Torture Scandal." *Times Higher Education*, September 29.

Melley, Timothy. 2011. "Brain Warfare: The Covert Sphere, Terrorism, and the Legacy of the Cold War." *Grey Room* 45: 19–41.

Mendoza, Sonia, Allyssa Rivera, and Helena Hansen. 2018. "Re-Racialization of Addiction and the Redistribution of Blame in the White Opioid Epidemic." *Medical Anthropology Quarterly* 32 (3): 1–21.

Menzel, Carol. 1974. "Coercive Psychology: Capitalism's Monster Science." *The Campaigner* 7 (4–5): 33–54.

Messerschmidt, James. 1993. *Masculinities and Crime: Critique and Reconceptualization of Theory*. Lanham, MD: Rowman & Littlefield.

——. 2008. "And Now, the Rest of the Story: A Commentary on Christine Beasley's 'Rethinking Hegemonic Masculinity in a Globalizing World.' " *Men and Masculinities* 11 (1): 104–108.

——. 2018. *Hegemonic Masculinity: Formulation, Reformulation, and Amplification*. Boulder, CO: Rowman & Littlefield.

Messerschmidt, James, and Michael Messner. 2018. "Hegemonic, Nonhegemonic, and 'New' Masculinities." In *Gender Reckonings: New Social Theory and Research*, ed. James Messerschmidt, Patricia Yancy Martin, Michael Messner, and Raewyn Connell, 35–56. New York: New York University Press.

Meyer, William. 2006. "Ten Science-Based Principles of Changing Behavior Through the Use of Reinforcement and Punishment." Alexandria, VA: National Drug Court Institute.

Meyers, Diana. 2002. *Gender in the Mirror: Cultural Imagery & Women's Agency*. Oxford: Oxford University Press.

Michaels, Samantha. "California Set a Bunch of Drug Offenders Free—and Then Left Them Hanging." *Mother Jones*, December 16. www.motherjones.com/politics/2016/12/california-proposition-47-former-prisoners-drug-rehab-addiction-investigation.

Miller, Eric. 2004. "Embracing Addiction: Drug Courts and the False Promise of Judicial Interventionism." *Ohio State Law Journal* 65: 1479–576.

Miller, Reuben. 2014. "Devolving the Carceral State: Race, Prisoner Reentry, and the Micro-Politics of Urban Poverty Management." *Punishment & Society* 16 (3): 305–35.

Miller, Reuben, and Amanda Alexander. 2016. "The Price of Carceral Citizenship: Punishment, Surveillance, and Social Welfare Policy in an Age of Carceral Expansion." *Michigan Journal of Race and Law* 21: 291–314.

Miller, Reuben, and Forrest Stuart. 2017. "Carceral Citizenship: Race, Rights and Responsibility in the Age of Mass Supervision." *Theoretical Criminology* 21 (4): 532–48.

Mills, Charles. 1997. *The Racial Contract*. Ithaca: Cornell University Press.

Mills, China. 2015. "The Psychiatrization of Poverty: Rethinking the Mental Health-Poverty Nexus." *SPC3 Social and Personality Psychology Compass* 9 (5): 213–22.

Mills, C. Wright. 1959. *The Sociological Imagination*. New York: Oxford University Press.

Minow, Martha. 1994. "The Welfare of Single Mothers and Their Children." *Connecticut Law Review* 26 (3): 817–842.

Mitchell, Dave, Cathy Mitchell, and Richard Ofshe. 1980. *The Light on Synanon: How a Country Weekly Exposed a Corporate Cult—and Won the Pulitzer Prize*. New York: Seaview Books.

Mitford, Jessica. 1973a. *Kind and Usual Punishment: The Prison Business*. New York: Knopf.

——. 1973b. "The Torture Cure." *Harper's Magazine*, August: 16, 18, 24–6, 28, 30.

Møllman, Marianne, and Christine Mehta. 2017. *Neither Justice nor Treatment: Drug Courts in the United States*. Boston: Physicians for Human Rights, June. http://fileserver.idpc.net/library/PHR_DrugCourts_Report.pdf.

Moore, Dawn. 2007. *Criminal Artifacts: Governing Drugs and Users*. Vancouver: University of British Columbia Press.

——. 2011. "The Benevolent Watch: Therapeutic Surveillance in Drug Treatment Court." *Theoretical Criminology* 15 (3): 255–68.

Moore, Dawn, and Hideyuki Hirai. 2014. "Outcasts, Performers and True Believers: Responsibilized Subjects of Criminal Justice." *Theoretical Criminology* 18 (1): 5–19.

Moore, James. 1973. "Drugs and Crime: A Bad Connection?" *Yale Review of Law and Social Action* 3 (3): 1–18.

Morantz, Paul. 2009. "The History of Synanon and Charles Dederich." www.paulmorantz.com/cult/the-history-of-synanon-and-charles-dederich.

——. 2014. *From Miracle to Madness: The True Story of Charles Dederich and Synanon*. Pacific Palisides, CA: Cresta Publications.

——. 2017. "Claire Clark's 2017 Recovery Revolution: The Speech Charles Dederich of Synanon She Will Not Tell You." www.paulmorantz.com/cult/claire-clarks-recovery-revolution-the-speech-charles-dederich-she-will-not-tell-you.

Morash, Merry, Robin Haarr, and Lila Rucker. 1994. "A Comparison of Programming for Women and Men in U.S. Prisons in the 1980s." *Crime & Delinquency* 40: 197–221.

Morris, Norval, and Michael Tonry. 1990. *Between Prison and Probation: Intermediate Punishments in a Rational Sentencing System*. New York: Oxford University Press.

Moya, C. Benjamin, and Roberta Achtenberg. 1974. "Behavior Modification: Legal Limits on Methods and Goals." *Notre Dame Lawyer* 50 (2): 230–50.

Moynihan, Daniel. 1965. *The Negro Family: The Case for National Action*, ed. U.S. Department of Labor Office of Planning and Research. Washington, D.C.: Office of Planning and Research, U.S. Department of Labor.

Mulcahy, Linda. 2007. "Architects of Justice: The Politics of Courtroom Design." *Social Legal Studies* 16 (3): 383–403.

Murakawa, Naomi. 2014. *The First Civil Right: How Liberals Built Prison America*. New York: Oxford University Press.

Murphy, Jennifer, 2011. "Drug Court as Both a Legal and Medical Authority." *Deviant Behavior* 32 (3): 257–91.

—. 2012. "The Continuing Expansion of Drug Courts: Is That All There Is?" *Deviant Behavior* 33 (7): 582–88.

—. 2015. *Illness or Deviance: Drug Courts, Drug Treatment, and the Ambiguity of Addiction*. Philadelphia: Temple University Press.

Murphy, Sheila. 1997. "Drug Courts: An Effective, Efficient Weapon in the War on Drugs." *Illinois Bar Journal* 85: 474–87.

NACDL (National Association of Criminal Defense Lawyers). 2009. *America's Problem Solving Courts: The Criminal Costs of Treatment and the Case for Reform*. Washington, D.C.: National Association of Criminal Defense Lawyers. www.nacdl.org/drugcourts.

NADCP (National Association of Drug Court Professionals). 1997. *Defining Drug Courts: The Key Components*, ed. Department of Justice Office of Justice Programs. Washington, D.C.: Bureau of Justice Assistance.

—. 2008. *Position Statement on the Nonviolent Offender Rehabilitation Act (NORA)*. Alexandria, VA: NADCP.

—. 2009. *Response to the Report of the National Association of Criminal Defense Lawyers (NADCL): America's Problem-Solving Courts: The Criminal Costs of Treatment and the Case for Reform*. Alexandria, VA: NADCP.

—. 2010. *Resolution of the Board of Directors on the Equivalent Treatment of Racial and Ethnic Minority Participants in Drug Courts*. Alexandria, VA: NADCP.

—. 2012. *Position Statement on Marijuana*. Alexandria, VA: NADCP.

—. 2014. *National Association of Drug Courts Professionals Statement in Opposition of California's Proposition 47 Ballot Measure*. Alexandria, VA: NADCP.

—. 2015. *Adult Drug Court Best Practice Standards*. Volume 2, ed. Douglas Marlowe and Carson Fox Jr. Alexandria, VA: NADCP.

Nagin, Daniel. 2016. "Project HOPE: Does it Work?" *Criminology & Public Policy* 15 (4): 1005–7.

Nash, George. 1974. "The Sociology of Phoenix House—A Therapeutic Community for the Resocialization of Narcotic Addicts." In *Phoenix House: Studies in a Therapeutic Community (1968–1973)*, ed. George De Leon, 42–62. New York: MSS Information Corporation.

Netherland, Julie, ed. 2012. *Critical Perspectives on Addiction*. Vol. 14 of *Advances in Medical Sociology*. Bingley, UK: Emerald Group Publishing Limited.

Nevada State Journal (Reno). 1966. "'Squares' Getting in on 'Synanon Game.'" May 22. www.newspapers.com/newspage/79011460.

New York Times. 1966. "Synanon to Help Nonaddicts Here." May 29. https://timesmachine.nytimes.com/timesmachine/1966/05/29/139998332.html.

—. 1980. "Synanon Founder Gets Probation in Snake Attack." September 4. www.nytimes.com/1980/09/04/archives/synanon-founder-gets-probation-in-snake-attack.html.

——. 1981a. "AROUND THE NATION; 18 Indicted in Kidnapping Tied to Synanon Members." January 22. www.nytimes.com/1981/01/22/us/around-the-nation-18-indicted-in-kidnapping-tied-to-synanon-members.html.

——. 1981b. "Synanon Members Accused in Beating." March 1. www.nytimes.com/1981/03/01/us/synanon-members-accused-in-beating.html

——. 1982a. "Synanon Founder Advocated Violence Against Opponents." March 9. www.nytimes.com/1982/03/09/us/synanon-founder-advocated-violence-against-opponents.html.

——. 1982b. "AROUND THE NATION; Founder of Synanon and 12 Others Indicted." December 16. www.nytimes.com/1982/12/16/us/around-the-nation-founder-of-synanon-and-12-others-indicted.html.

NIDA (National Institute on Drug Abuse). 2015. *Therapeutic Communities*, ed. U.S. Department of Health and Human Services. NIH Publication Number: 15-4877.

NIJ (National Institute of Justice). 1996. *1995 Drug Use Forecasting: Annual Report on Adult and Juvenile Arestees*, ed. U.S. Department of Justice. Rockville, MD: National Criminal Justice Reference Service.

NIMH (National Institute of Mental Health). 1970. *Here's Help*. Washington, D.C.: National Audiovisual Center.

Niv, Noosha, Alison Hamilton, and Yih-Ing Hser. 2009. "Impact of Court-Mandated Substance Abuse Treatment on Clinical Decision Making." *Journal of Behavioral Health Services & Research* 36 (4): 505–16.

NLADA (National Legal Aid & Defender Association). 2010. *Defender Participation in Treatment Courts, Draft*. Washington, D.C.: NLADA, American Council of Chief Defenders. www.nlada.net/library/documents/accdbestpraccomm_treatmentcts_04-07-2010draft.

Nolan, James. 1998. *The Therapeutic State: Justifying Government at Century's End*. New York: New York University Press.

——. 2001. *Reinventing Justice: The American Drug Court Movement*. Princeton, NJ: Princeton University Press.

NORA Campaign. 2008. "Response to the NADCP Position Paper on NORA (Prop. 5)." Sacramento, CA: Campaign for New Drug Policies and Drug Policy Alliance Network.

Novak, Steven. 1997. "LSD before Leary: Sidney Cohen's Critique of 1950s Psychedelic Research." *Isis* 88 (1): 87–110.

——. 2004. "LSD Before Leary: Sidney Cohen's Critique of 1950s Psychedelic Drug Research." In *Altering American Consciousness: The History of Alcohol and Drugs Use in the United States, 1800–2000*, ed. Sarah Tracy and Caroline Jean Acker, 353–82. Boston: University of Massachusetts Press.

NYCLU (New York Civil Liberties Union). 2009. "Rockefeller Drug Law Reform." Press release. www.nyclu.org/en/issues/racial-justice/rockefeller-drug-law-reform.

O'Brien, William, and Ellis Henican. 1993. *You Can't Do It Alone: The Daytop Way to Make Your Child Drug Free*. New York: Simon & Schuster.

O'Hear, Michael. 2009. "Rethinking Drug Courts: Restorative Justice as a Response to Racial Injustice." *Stanford Law & Policy Review* 20 (2): 463–99.

O'Malley, Pat, ed. 1998. *Crime and the Risk Society*. Aldershot: Ashgate Publishing.

Oelsner, Lesley. 1974. "House Panel Schedules Hearings on Behavior Modification in Federal Prisons." *New York Times*, February 26.

Olin, William. 1980. *Escape from Utopia: My Ten Years in Synanon*. Santa Cruz: Unity Press.

Oliver, Pamela. 2008. *Racial Patterns in State Trends in Prison Admissions 1983–2003: Drug and Non-Drug Sentences and Revocations: Introduction and National Graphs*. University of Wisconsin-Madison, Department of Sociology. www.ssc.wisc.edu/~oliver/RACIAL/StateTrends/RacialPatternsNCRPintroduction.pdf.

ONDCP (Office of National Drug Control Policy). 1994. *National Drug Control Strategy*. Washington, D.C.: Office of National Drug Control Policy, Executive Office of the President.

——. 2000. *National Drug Control Strategy: FY 2001 Budget Summary*. Washington, D.C.: ONDCP.

——. 2003. *Drug Policy Information Clearinghouse Fact Sheet*. Ed. John P. Walters. Washington, D.C.: U.S. Government Printing Office.

——. 2008. *National Drug Control Strategy: 2008 Annual Report*. Executive Office of the President, ed. Washington D.C.: U.S. Government Printing Office.

——. 2015. *National Drug Control Budget: FY 2016 Funding Highlights*. Washington, D.C.: U.S. Government Printing Office.

——. 2017. *National Drug Control Budget: FY 2018 Funding Highlights*. Washington, D.C.: U.S. Government Printing Office.

Opton, Edward. 1974. "Psychiatric Violence Against Prisoners: When Therapy is Punishment." *Mississippi Law Journal* 45: 605–44.

Orleck, Annelise, and Lisa Gayle Hazirjian, eds. 2011. *The War on Poverty: A New Grassroots History, 1964–1980*. Athens: University of Georgia Press.

Paik, Leslie. 2011. *Discretionary Justice: Looking Inside a Juvenile Drug Court*. New Brunswick, NJ: Rutgers University Press.

Paparozzi, Mario, and Paul Gendreau. 2005. "An Intensive Supervision Program That Worked: Service Delivery, Professional Orientation, and Organizational Supportiveness." *Prison Journal* 85 (4): 445–66.

Parsons, Jim, Qing Wei, Joshua Rinaldi, Christian Henrichson, Talia Sandwick, Travis Wendel, Ernest Drucker, Michael Ostermann, Samuel DeWitt, and Todd Clear. 2015. *A Natural Experiment in Reform: Analyzing Drug Policy Change in New York City, Final Report*. New York: Vera Institute of Justice.

Parsons, Talcott. 1952. "The Superego and the Theory of Social Systems." *Psychiatry* 15 (1): 15–25.

Pawel, Miriam. 2006. "Decisions of Long Ago Shape the Union Today." *Los Angeles Times*, January 10. www.latimes.com/local/la-me-history10jan10-story.html.

Peck, Jamie, and Adam Tickell. 2002. "Neoliberalizing Space." *Antipode* 34 (3): 380–404.

Perfas, Fernando. 2004. *Therapeutic Community: Social Systems Perspective*. Lincoln, NE: iUniverse.

Perkinson, Robert. 2010. *Texas Tough: The Rise of America's Prison Empire*. New York: Metropolitan Books.

Peters, Jeremy. 2009. "Albany Reaches Deal to Repeal '70s Drug Laws." *New York Times*, March 25. www.nytimes.com/2009/03/26/nyregion/26rockefeller.html.

Peters, Roger, and Harry Wexler, eds. 2005. *Substance Abuse Treatment for Adults in the Criminal Justice System: A Treatment Improvement Protocol (TIP 44)*. Substance Abuse and Mental Health Services Administration (SAMHSA). Rockville: U.S. Department of Health and Human Services.

Petersilia, Joan, ed. 1998. "A Crime Control Rationale for Reinvesting in Community Corrections." In *Community Corrections: Probation, Parole, and Intermediate Sanctions*, 20–28. New York: Oxford University Press.

——. 2003. *When Prisoners Come Home: Parole and Prisoner Reentry*. New York: Oxford University Press.

Peterson, Alan, and Deborah Lupton. 1996. *The New Public Health: Health and Self in the Age of Risk*. London: Sage Publications.

Pew Center on the States. 2009. *One in 31: The Long Reach of American Corrections*. Washington, D.C.: Pew Charitable Trusts. www.pewtrusts.org/~/media/assets/2009/03/02/pspp_1in31_report_final_web_32609.pdf.

Peyton, Elizabeth, and Robert Gossweiler. 2001. "Treatment Services in Adult Drug Courts." In *Drug Courts Resource Series*. Washington, D.C.: Substance Abuse and Mental Health Services Administration, National Treatment Accountability for Safer Communities (National TASC). NCJ 188086.

Phelps, Michelle. 2011. "Rehabilitation in the Punitive Era: The Gap between Rhetoric and Reality in U.S. Prison Programs." *Law & Society Review* 45 (1): 33–68.

. 2012. "The Place of Punishment: Variation in the Provision of Inmate Services Staff Across the Punitive Turn." *Journal of Criminal Justice* 40 (5): 348–57.

Piven, Frances Fox, and Richard Cloward. 1998. *The Breaking of the American Social Compact*. New York: The New Press.

Pollack, Shoshana. 2007. " 'I'm Just Not Good in Relationships': Victimization Discourses and the Gendered Regulation of Criminalized Women." *Feminist Criminology* 2: 158–74.

Pollock-Byrne, Joycelyn. 2002 [1990]. *Women, Prison & Crime*. Belmont, CA: Wadsworth Cengage Learning.

Porter, Rachel. 2000. *Implementing a Drug Court in Queens County: A Process Evaluation*. New York: Vera Institute of Justice.

——. 2001. *Treatment Alternatives in the Criminal Court: A Process Evaluation of the Bronx County Drug Court*. New York: Vera Institute of Justice.

Price, David. 2016. *Cold War Anthropology: The CIA, the Pentagon, and the Growth of Dual Use Anthropology*. Durham, NC: Duke University Press.

Puar, Jasbir. 2007. *Terrorist Assemblages: Homonationalism in Queer Times*. Durham, NC: Duke University Press.

Pugh, Tracy, Julie Netherland, Ruth Finkelstein, Kassandra Frederique, Simone-Marie Meeks, and Gabriel Sayegh. 2013. *Blueprint for a Public Health and Safety Approach to Drug Policy*. New York: New York Academy of Medicine and Drug Policy Alliance, March. www.drugpolicy.org/sites/default/files/3371_DPA_NYAM_Report_FINAL_for_WEB%20April%2019%202013.pdf.

Quest Diagnostics. 2016. *Quest Diagnostics Drug Testing Index*, Full Year 2016 Tables. www.questdiagnostics.com/dms/Documents/Employer-Solutions/Brochures/drug-testing-index-2017-report--tables/drug-testing-index-2017-report-tables.pdf.

Rafaeli, Anat, and Robert Sutton. 1991. "Emotional Contrast Strategies as Means of Social Influence: Lessons from Criminal Interrogators and Bill Collectors." *Academy of Management Journal* 34 (4): 749–75.

Rawlings, Barbara, and Rowdy Yates, eds. 2001. *Therapeutic Communities for the Treatment of Drug Users*. London: Jessica Kingsley Publishers.

Ray, Carina. 2012. "A Troubled Experiment's Forgotten Lesson in Racial Integration." *Huffington Post*, April 1. www.huffpost.com/entry/racial-integration_b_1384979.

Reeser, Todd. 2011. *Masculinities in Theory: An Introduction*. West Sussex, UK: Wiley-Blackwell.

Rempel, Michael, Dana Fox-Kralstein, Amanda Cissner, Robyn Cohen, Melissa Labriola, Donald Farole, Ann Bader, and Michael Magnani. 2003. *The New York State Adult Drug Court Evaluation: Policies, Participants and Impacts*. New York: Center for Court Innovation.

Rhine, Edward. 1997. "Probation and Parole Supervision: In Need of a New Narrative." *Corrections Management Quarterly* 1 (2): 71–75.

Rhodes, Lorna. 2002. "Psychopathy and the Face of Control in Supermax." *Ethnography* 3 (4): 442–66.

——. 2004. *Total Confinement: Madness and Reason in the Maximum Security Prison*. Berkeley: University of California Press.

Richman, Josh. 2011. "Money Is Gone, but Proposition 36's Drug-Treatment Mandate Remains." *East Bay Times*, February 20. www.eastbaytimes.com/2011/02/20/money-is-gone-but-proposition-36s-drug-treatment-mandate-remains.

Riddle, Jennifer, Sena Loyd, Stacy Branham, and Curt Thomas. 2012. *Images of America: Nevada State Prison*. Charleston, SC: Arcadia Publishing.

Rinella, Vincent. 1976. "Rehabilitation or Bust: The Impact of Criminal Justice System Referrals on the Treatment of Drug Addicts and Alcoholics in a Therapeutic Community (Eagleville's Experience)." *American Journal of Drug and Alcohol Abuse* 3 (1): 53–58.

Roberts, Dorothy. 1993–1994. "The Value of Black Mothers' Work." *Connecticut Law Review* 26 (3): 871–78.

Roberts, Neil. 2015. *Freedom as Marronage*. Chicago: University of Chicago Press.

Roberts, Samuel. 2012. "'Rehabilitation' as Boundary Object: Medicalization, Local Activism, and Narcotic Addiction Policy in New York City, 1951–62." *Social History of Alcohol and Drugs* 26 (2): 147–69.

Robinson, Cedric. 1983. *Black Marxism: The Making of the Black Radical Tradition*. Chapel Hill: University of North Carolina Press.

Robinson, Gwen. 1999. "Risk Management and Rehabilitation in the Probation Service: Collision and Collusion." *Howard Journal of Crime and Justice* 38 (4): 421–33.

Roediger, David. 2017. *Class, Race, and Marxism*. New York: Verso Press.

Rogoff, Irit, and David Van Leer. 1993. "Afterthoughts . . . A Dossier on Masculinities." *Theory and Society* 22 (5): 739–62.

Rose, Nikolas. 1999a. *Powers of Freedom: Reframing Political Thought*. Cambridge: Cambridge University Press.

——. 1999b. *Governing the Soul: the Shaping of the Private Self*. London: Free Association Books.

Rosenthal, Mitchell. 1974. "The Phoenix House Therapeutic Community: An Overview." In *Phoenix House: Studies in a Therapeutic Community (1968–1973)*, ed. George De Leon, 12–24. New York: MSS Information Corporation.

Rossman, Shelli, Jeffrey Butts, John Roman, Christine DeStafano, and Ruth White. 2004. "What Juvenile Drug Courts Do and How They Do It." In *Juvenile Drug Courts and Teen Substance Abuse*, ed. Jeffrey Butts and John Roman, 55–106. Washington, D.C.: Urban Institute Press.

Rossman, Shelli, John Roman, Janine Zweig, Christine Lindquist, Michael Rempel, Janeen Buck Willison, P. Mitchell Downey, and Kristine Fahrney. 2011. *The Multi-Site Adult Drug Court Evaluation: Study Overview and Design*. Washington, D.C.: Urban Institute, Justice Policy Center. https://www.ncjrs.gov/pdffiles1/nij/grants/237109.pdf (see also www.nij.gov/topics/courts/drug-courts/pages/madce.aspx).

Rotskoff, Lori. 2002. *Love on the Rocks: Men, Women, and Alcohol in Post-World War II America*. Chapel Hill: University of North Carolina Press.

Rousseau, Jean-Jacques. 1992 [1762]. *The Social Contract*. Trans. George Cole. New York: Knopf.

Rowan, Noell, David Jenkins, and Cheryl Parks. 2013. "What Is Valued in Gay and Lesbian Specific Alcohol and Other Drug Treatment?" *Journal of Gay & Lesbian Social Services* 25 (1): 56–76.

Rubio, Dawn, Fred Cheesman, and William Federspiel. 2008. *Performance Measurement of Drug Courts: The State of the Art*. Statewide Technical Assistance Bulletin, v.6. Williamsburg: National Center for State Courts, July.

SAMHSA (Substance Abuse and Mental Health Services Administration), Center for Behavioral Health Statistics and Quality. 2015. *Treatment Episode Data Set (TEDS): 2003–2013. National Admissions to Substance Abuse Treatment Services*. BHSIS Series S-75, HHS Publication No. (SMA) 15–4934. Rockville, MD: Substance Abuse and Mental Health Services Administration.

——. 2016. *National Survey of Substance Abuse Treatment Services (N-SSATS): 2016. Data on Substance Abuse Treatment Facilities*. BHSIS Series S-39, HHS Publication No. (SMA) 17–5039. Rockville, MD: Department of Health and Human Services.

——. 2017. *Treatment Episode Data Set (TEDS): 2005–2015, National Admissions to Substance Abuse Treatment Services*. BHSIS Series S-91, HHS Publication No. (SMA) 17–5037. Rockville, MD: Department of Health And Human Services.

Sanders, Eli. 2011. "The War on Drug Courts: King County's Drug Courts are Successful, So Why Are DC Progressives Against Them?" *The Stranger*, August 11. www.thestranger.com/seattle/the-war-on-drug-courts/Content?oid=9540197

Sanjurjo, Libni. 2014. "No todo es como lo pintan." *Primera Hora*, January 20. www.primerahora.com/noticias/puerto-rico/nota/notodoescomolopintan-983978.

Satel, Sally, and Frederick Goodwin. 1998. *Is Drug Addiction a Brain Disease?* Washington, D.C.: Ethics and Public Policy Center's Program on Medical Science and Society.

Schecter, Arnold, Harold Alksne, and Edward Kaufman, eds. 1978. *Drug Abuse: Modern Trends, Issues, and Perspectives*. New York: Marcel Dekker.

Schein, Edgar. 1961. *Coercive Persuasion*. New York: Norton.

—. 1962a. "New Horizons for Correctional Therapy." *Corrective Psychiatry and Journal of Social Therapy* 8 (2): 57–59.

—. 1962b. "Man Against Man: Brainwashing." *Corrective Psychiatry and Journal of Social Therapy* 8 (2): 90–97.

—. 1973. "The Torture Cure." *Harper's Magazine* (Letters section), November: 128.

—. 1999. "Kurt Lewin's Change Theory in the Field and in the Classroom: Notes Toward a Model of Managed Learning." *Reflections: The SoL Journal* 1 (1): 59–74.

Schein, Edgar, and J. Steven Ott. 1962. "The Legitimacy of Organizational Influence." *American Journal of Sociology* 67 (6): 682–89.

Schept, Judah. 2015. *Progressive Punishment: Job Loss, Jail Growth and the Neoliberal Logic of Carceral Expansion*. New York: New York University Press.

Schrage, Michael. 2000. *Serious Play: How the World's Best Companies Simulate to Innovate*. Boston: Harvard Business School Press.

Schram, Pamela, and Merry Morash. 2002. "Evaluation of a Life Skills Program for Women Inmates in Michigan." *Journal of Offender Rehabilitation* 34 (4): 47–70.

Schram, Sanford. 2000. "In the Clinic: The Medicalization of Welfare." *Social Text* 18 (1): 81–107.

—. 2015. *The Return of Ordinary Capitalism: Neoliberalism, Precarity, Occupy*. Oxford: Oxford University Press.

Seddon, Toby. 2010. *A History of Drugs: Drugs and Freedom in the Liberal Age*. New York: Routledge.

Sedgwick, Eve. 1993. *Tendencies*. Durham, NC: Duke University Press.

Senechal, Marjorie. 2003. "Narco Brat." In *Of Human Bondage: Historical Perspectives on Addiction*, vol. 52 of *Smith College Studies in History*, ed. Douglas Patey, 173–200. Northampton, MA: Smith College.

Senreich, Evan. 2009. "A Comparison of Perceptions, Reported Abstinence, and Completion Rates of Gay, Lesbian, Bisexual, and Heterosexual Clients in Substance Abuse Treatment." *Journal of Gay & Lesbian Mental Health* 13 (3): 145–69.

—. 2015. "Self-Identified Heterosexual Clients in Substance Abuse Treatment with a History of Same-Gender Sexual Contact." *Journal of Homosexuality* 62 (4): 433–62.

Shane, Scott. 2008. "China Inspired Interrogations at Guantanamo." *New York Times*, July 2.

Shaw, Randy. 2010. *Beyond the Fields: Cesar Chavez, the UFW, and the Struggle for Justice in the 21st Century*. Berkeley: University of California Press.

Sheehy, Peter. 2002. "The Triumph of Group Therapeutics: Therapy, the Social Self, and Liberalism in America, 1910–1960." PhD Diss., University of Virginia.

Sheen, Martin. 2000. "Prop. 36 Would Devastate the Drug Court System." *Los Angeles Times*, August 7.

Shelly, Joseph, and Alexander Bassin. 1965. "Daytop Lodge—A New Treatment Approach for Drug Addicts." *Corrective Psychiatry and Journal of Social Therapy* 11: 186–95.

Shuker, Richard, and Elizabeth Sullivan. 2010. *Grendon and the Emergence of Forensic Therapeutic Communities*. West Sussex, UK: John Wiley & Sons.

Simmons, J. Q., and B. J. Reed. 1969. "Therapeutic Punishment in Severely Disturbed Children." *Current Psychiatric Therapies* 9: 11.

Simon, Jonathan. 1993. *Poor Discipline: Parole and the Social Control of the Underclass, 1890–1990*. Chicago: University of Chicago.

——. 2007. *Governing Through Crime: How the War on Crime Transformed American Democracy and Created a Culture of Fear*. New York: Oxford University Press.

Simpson, D. Dwayne, George Joe, Kirk Broome, Matthew Hiller, Kevin Knight, and Grace Rowan-Szal. 1997. "Program Diversity and Treatment Retention Rates in the Drug Abuse Treatment Outcome Study (DATOS)." *Psychology of Addictive Behaviors* 11 (4): 279–93.

Singh, Nikhil. 2017. *Race and America's Long War*. Oakland: University of California Press.

Skinner, B. F. 1953. *Science and Human Behavior*. New York: The Free Press.

——. 1971. *Beyond Freedom and Dignity*. New York: Knopf.

Smith, Aminda. 2012. "Remoulding Minds in Postsocialist China: Maoist Reeducation and Twenty-First-Century Subjects." *Postcolonial Studies* 15 (4): 453–66.

Smith, David. 1976. "The Free Clinic Movement in the United States: A Ten Year Perspective (1966–1976)." *Journal of Drug Issues* 6 (4): 343–55.

Smith, David, Lauren Kabat Linda, and Stuart Loomis. 1974. "Experiences of the Haight-Ashbury Free Clinic's Community Based Drug Rehabilitation Program." *Journal of Psychedelic Drugs* 6 (2): 243–51.

Smith, Roger. 1977. *Drug Programs in Correctional Institutions*. Washington D.C.: National Institute of Law Enforcement and Criminal Justice.

Sommer, Robert. 1976. *The End of Imprisonment*. New York: Oxford University Press.

Sommers, Ira, and Deborah Baskin. 1990. "The Prescription of Psychiatric Medications in Prison: Psychiatric Versus Labeling Perspectives." *Justice Quarterly* 7 (4): 739–55.

Soss, Joe, Richard Fording, and Sanford Schram. 2011. *Disciplining the Poor: Neoliberal Paternalism and the Persistent Power of Race*. Chicago: University of Chicago Press.

Spade, Dean. 2011. *Normal Life: Administrative Violence, Critical Trans Politics, and the Limits of Law*. Durham, NC: Duke University Press.

Spillers, Hortense. 1987. "Mama's Baby, Papa's Maybe: An American Grammar Book." *Diacritics* 17 (2): 64–81.

Stack, Carol. 1974. *All Our Kin: Strategies for Survival in a Black Community*. New York: Harper & Row Publishing.

Starks, Michael. 1982. *Cocaine Fiends and Reefer Madness: An Illustrated History of Drugs in the Movies*. New York: Cornwall Books.

Steinert, Heinz. 1985. "The Amazing New Left Law & Order Campaign: Some Thoughts on Anti-Utopianism and Possible Futures a propos Alan Hunt's 'The Future of Rights and Justice.' " *Contemporary Crises* 9 (4): 327–33.

Stephens, Richard. 1985. "The Sociocultural View of Heroin Use: Toward a Role-Theoretic Model." *Journal of Drug Issues* 15 (4): 433–46.

Stevens, Alisa. 2013. *Offender Rehabilitation and Therapeutic Communities: Enabling Change the TC Way*. New York: Routledge.

Stevens, Sally. 2012. "Meeting the Substance Abuse Treatment Needs of Lesbian, Bisexual and Transgender Women: Implications from Research to Practice." *Substance Abuse and Rehabilitation* 3 (1): 27–36.

Steyee, Jimmy. 2013. *Program Performance Report: Implementation Grantees of the Adult Drug Court Discretionary Grant Program.* Rockville, MD: Bureau of Justice Assistance.

Stine, Linda, Sherman Patrick, and Josephine Molina. 1982. "What is the Role of Violence in the Therapeutic Community?" *International Journal of the Addictions* 17 (2): 377–92.

Strawson, Galen. 2011. *Locke on Personal Identity.* Princeton, NJ : Princeton University Press.

Sufrin, Carolyn. 2017. *Jailcare: Finding the Safety Net for Women Behind Bars.* Oakland: University of California Press.

Sugarman, Barry. 1970. "The Therapeutic Community and the School." *Interchange* 1 (2): 77–96.

—. 1974. *Daytop Village: A Therapeutic Community.* New York: Holt.

Sullum, Jacob. 2016. "In Opinion: Attorney General Pick Sessions Is a Drug War Dinosaur." *Newsweek*, December 4. www.newsweek.com/attorney-general-pick-sessions-drug-war-dinosaur-527215.

Sung, Hung-en, and Steven Belenko. 2006. "From Diversion Experiment to Policy Movement: A Case Study of Prosecutorial Innovation." *Journal of Contemporary Criminal Justice* 22: 220–40.

Sykes, Gresham. 1956. "Men, Merchants, and Toughs: A Study of Reactions to Imprisonment." *Social Problems* 4 (2): 130–38.

Szalavitz, Maia. 2006. *Help at Any Cost: How the Troubled-Teen Industry Cons Parents and Hurts Kids.* New York: Riverhead Books.

—. 2007. "The Cult that Spawned the Tough-Love Teen Industry." *Mother Jones*, September/October. www.motherjones.com/politics/2007/08/cult-spawned-tough-love-teen-industry.

—. 2015. "How America Overdosed on Drug Courts." In *Pacific Standard*, May 18. https://psmag.com/news/how-america-overdosed-on-drug-courts.

Talbot, David. 2015. *The Devil's Chessboard: Allen Dulles, the CIA, and the Rise of America's Secret Government.* New York: Harper Collins.

Tan Chen, Victor. 2015. *Cut Loose: Jobless and Hopeless in an Unfair Economy.* Berkeley: University of California Press, 2015.

Tauber, Jeffrey. 1994. "Drug Courts: A Judicial Manual." *CJER Journal*, Special Issue (Summer). San Francisco: California Center for Judicial Education and Research. www.reentrycourtsolutions.com/wp-content/uploads/2010/11/TAUBER-Drug-Courts-a-Judicial-Manual.pdf.

—. 2000. "The Critical Need for Jail as a Sanction in the Drug Court Model." *National Drug Court Institute Drug Court Practitioner Fact Sheet* II (3). Alexandria, VA: National Drug Court Institute.

Taxman, Faye, Matthew Perdoni, and Lana Harrison. 2007. "Drug Treatment Services for Adult Offenders: the State of the State." *Journal of Substance Abuse Treatment* 32: 239–54.

Taxman, Faye, David Soule, and Adam Gelb. 1999. "Graduated Sanctions: Stepping into Accountable Systems and Offenders." *Prison Journal*, 79 (2): 182–204.

Thompson, Anthony. 2002. "Courting Disorder: Some Thoughts on Community Courts." *Washington University Journal of Law and Policy* 10: 63–99.

——. 2008. *Releasing Prisoners, Redeeming Communities: Reentry, Race, and Politics*. New York: New York University Press.

Thompson, Edward Palmer. 1967. "Time, Work-Discipline, and Industrial Capitalism." *Past & Present* 38: 56–97.

Thompson, Mark. 2006. "Hug-a-Thug Pays Off: Drug Courts Aren't a Panacea for Drug Addiction, but They Have Won Hearts and Opened Pocketbooks in State Legislatures." *State Legislatures* 32: 2–3.

Tiebout, Harry. 1944. "Therapeutic Mechanisms of Alcoholics Anonymous." *American Journal of Psychiatry* 100: 468–73.

——. 1953. "The 12 Steps as Ego Deflating Devices." *Recovery Daily* (website). http://recoverydaily.com/tiebout/tibout_ego.html.

——. 1958. "Direct Treatment of a Symptom." In *Problems of Addiction and Habituation*, ed. Paul Hoch and Joseph Zubin. New York: Grune & Stratton.

Tiger, Rebecca. 2008. "Drug Court and Coerced Treatment: The Social Construction of 'Enlightened Coercion.'" PhD diss., City University of New York.

——. 2013. *Judging Addicts: Drug Courts and Coercion in the Justice System*. New York: New York University Press.

——. 2017. "Race, Class, and the Framing of Drug Epidemics." *Contexts* 16 (4): 46–51

Time. 1977. "Nation: Life at Synanon Is Swinging." December 26. http://content.time.com/time/subscriber/article/0,33009,919202-1,00.html.

Tonry, Michael. 1998. "Evaluating Intermediate Sanction Programs." In *Community Corrections: Probation, Parole, and Intermediate Sanctions*, ed. Joan Petersilia, 79–96. Oxford: Oxford University Press.

Torruella, Rafael. 2010. "¿Allá en Nueva York Todo es Mejor? A Qualitative Study on the Relocation of Drug Users from Puerto Rico to the United States." PhD diss., City University of New York.

Tourish, Dennis, and Tim Wohlforth. 2000. *On the Edge: Political Cults Right and Left*. Armonk, NY: M.E. Sharpe.

Trebach, Arnold. 2005. "Moral Integrity and Presidential Appointees: The Straight Skinny." *The Trebach Report*. http://survivingstraightinc.com/StraightArticlesandInformation/The-Trebach-Report-Straight-Skinny-2000-page1_Combine.pdf.

Trotter, Sharland, and Jim Warren. 1974. "The Carrot, the Stick and the Prisoner." *Science News* 105 (11): 180–81.

Tsemberis, S., L. Gulcur, and M. Nakae. 2004. "Housing First, Consumer Choice, and Harm Reduction for Homeless Individuals with a Dual Diagnosis." *American Journal of Public Health* 94: 651–56.

TSS&HA (Toronto Shelter Support & Housing Administration). 2007. *What Housing First Means for People: Results of Streets to Homes 2007 Post-Occupancy Research*. Toronto: Toronto Shelter, Support & Housing Administration.

Turnbull, Sarah, and Kelly Hannah-Moffat. 2009. "Under These Conditions: Gender, Parole, and the Governance of Reintegration." *British Journal of Criminology* 49: 532–51.

Turner, Susan, Suzanne Wenzel, Peter Greenwood, Adele Harrell, Faye Taxman, and Judith Greene. 2002. "A Decade of Drug Court Research." *Substance Use and Misuse* 37 (12–13): 1489–527.

Upegui-Hernandez, Debora, and Rafael Torruella. 2015. *Humiliation and Abuses in Drug "Treatment" Centers in Puerto Rico.* Fajardo: Intercambios Puerto Rico. http://intercambiospr.org/wp-content/uploads/2015/11/Humiliation-Abuse-in-Drug-Treatment-in-Puerto-Rico-Intercambios-PR-2015.pdf.

Urbanoski, Karen. 2010. "Coerced Addiction Treatment: Client Perspectives and the Implications of Their Neglect." *Harm Reduction Journal* 7: 13–22.

USA Today. 2008. "Our View on Crime and Punishment: 'Therapy with Teeth.' " Editorial. October 21. http://drugcourtsurvival.blogspot.com/2010/01/our-view-on-crime-and-punishment.html.

U.S. Congress. 1974a. *Congressional Hearings on Behavioral Modification Programs in the Bureau of Prisons Before the Subcommittee on Courts, Civil Liberties, and the Administration of Justice of the House Commission on the Judiciary*, serial 26, 2nd Session (66) 93rd Congress. Washington, D.C.: U.S. Government Printing Office.

——. 1974b. *Individual Rights and the Federal Role in Behavior Modification*. Committee on the Judiciary, U.S. Senate Subcommittee on Constitutional Rights. 2nd Session (66), 93rd Congress. Washington, D.C.: U.S. Government Printing Office.

——. 2001. *Oversight of the Office of Justice Programs: Program Performance—Drug Courts.* U.S. House of Representatives, Committee on the Judiciary. Washington D.C.: U.S. Government Printing Office.

——. 2017. *Examining Concerns of Patient Brokering and Addiction Treatment Fraud.* House of Representatives, Energy and Commerce Subcommittees, December 12, 2017. https://energycommerce.house.gov/hearings/examining-concerns-patient-brokering-addiction-treatment-fraud.

USDoJ (U.S. Department of Justice). 1975. *Behavior Modification Programs: The Bureau of Prisons' Alternative to Long Term Segregation*. Report by the Comptroller General of the U.S. (Elmer Staats). GGD-75-73. www.gao.gov/assets/120/114301.pdf.

——. 2007. "Adult Drug Court Discretionary Grant Program, FY 2008 Competitive Grant Application." Office of Justice Program, Bureau of Justice Assistance. November 13. www.bja.gov/Funding/08DrugCourtsSol.pdf.

——. 2017. "Department of Justice Awards Nearly $59 Million to Combat Opioid Epidemic, Fund Drug Courts." September 22. www.justice.gov/opa/pr/department-justice-awards-nearly-59-million-combat-opioid-epidemic-fund-drug-courts.

USGAO (U.S. General Accounting Office). 1995. *Drug Courts: Information on a New Approach to Address Drug-Related Crime.* Briefing Report to the Committee on the Judiciary. www.gao.gov/products/GGD-95-159BR.

——. 1997. *Drug Courts: Overview of Growth, Characteristics, and Results.* Briefing Report to the Committee on the Judiciary. www.gao.gov/products/GAO/GGD-97-106.

——. 2002. *Drug Courts: Better DOJ Data Collection and Evaluation Efforts Needed to Measure Impact of Drug Court Programs.* Briefing Report to the Committee on the Judiciary. www.gao.gov/products/GAO-02-434.

——. 2005. *Adult Drug Courts: Evidence Indicates Recidivism Reductions and Mixed Results for Other Outcomes.* Briefing Report to the Committee on the Judiciary. www.gao.gov/products/GAO-05-219.

——. 2007. *Residential Treatment Programs: Concerns Regarding Abuse and Death in Certain Programs for Troubled Youth.* Briefing Report to the Committee on the Judiciary. www.gao.gov/products/GAO-08-146T.

——. 2011. *Adult Drug Courts: Studies Show Courts Reduce Recidivism, But DOJ Could Enhance Future Performance Measure Revision Efforts.* Briefing Report to the Committee on the Judiciary. www.gao.gov/products/GAO-12-53.

U.S. Government. 2014. *Essential Guide to Interrogation and Torture: CIA KUBARK Counterintelligence Interrogation Manual, Human Resource Exploitation Training Manual, Art and Science of Interrogation.* Washington, D.C.: Progressive Management Publications.

Valverde, Mariana. 1996. " 'Despotism' and the Ethical Liberal Subject." *Economy and Society* 25 (3): 357–72.

——. 1998. *Diseases of the Will: Alcohol and the Dilemmas of Freedom.* New York: Cambridge University Press.

van der Meer, Chris. 1997. "Inpatient Treatment, and Update." In *Proceedings From the Third European Conference on Rehabilitation and Drug Policy*, ed. S. Sollhakken. Oslo: Norwegian Directorate for the Prevention of Alcohol and Drug Problems.

Vandevelde, Stijn, Eric Broekaert, Rowdy Yates, and Martien Kooyman. 2004. "The Development of the Therapeutic Community in Correctional Establishments: A Comparative Retrospective Account of the 'Democratic' Maxwell Jones TC and the Hierarchical Concept-Based TC in Prison." *International Journal of Social Psychiatry* 50 (1): 66–79.

van Gelder, Lawrence. 1997. "Charles Dederich, 83, Synanon Founder, Dies." *New York Times*, March 4. www.nytimes.com/1997/03/04/us/charles-dederich-83-synanon-founder-dies.html.

Varney, Steven. 2015. "Practicing Medicine Without a License: Medication-Assisted Treatment in the Courts." *The Fix*, October 28. www.thefix.com/practicing-medicine-without-license-medication-assisted-treatment-courts.

Vrecko, Scott. 2010. " 'Civilizing Technologies' and the Control of Deviance." *BioSocieties* 5 (1): 36–51.

Wacquant, Loic. 1997. "Elias in the Dark Ghetto." *Amsterdam Sociologisch Tijdschrift* 24 (3–4): 340–48.

——. 1998. "Inside the Zone: The Social Art of the Hustler in the Black American Ghetto." *Theory, Culture and Society* 15 (2): 1–36.

——. 2001. "Deadly Symbiosis: When Ghetto and Prison Meet and Mesh." In *Mass Imprisonment: Social Causes and Consequences*, ed. David Garland, 82–120. Thousand Oaks, CA: Sage Publications.

—. 2008. "Ordering Insecurity: Social Polarization and the Punitive Upsurge." *Radical Philosophy Review* 11 (1): 9–27.

—. 2009a. *Punishing the Poor: The Neoliberal Government of Social Insecurity*. Durham, NC: Duke University Press.

—. 2009b. *Prisons of Poverty*. Minneapolis: University of Minnesota Press.

Wagner, Chris, and Wayne Conners. 2003. "The Philosophy Behind Motivational Interviewing." www.motivationalinterview.org/clinical/philosophy.html.

Waldorf, Dan. 1971. "Social Control in Therapeutic Communities for the Treatment of Drug Addicts." *International Journal of the Addictions* 6 (1): 29–43.

Wallace, Susan, Bernadette Pelissier, Daniel McCarthy, and Donald Murray. 1990. "Beyond 'Nothing Works': History and Current Initiatives in BOP Drug Treatment." *Federal Prisons Journal* 1 (4): 23–26.

Walsh, Nastassia. 2011. *Addicted to Courts: How a Growing Dependence on Drug Courts Impacts People and Communities*. Washington, D.C.: Justice Policy Institute. www.justicepolicy.org/uploads/justicepolicy/documents/addicted_to_courts_final.pdf.

Walters, Glenn. 1995. "Predictive Validity of the Drug Lifestyle Screening Interview: A Two-Year Follow-Up." *American Journal of Drug and Alcohol Abuse* 21 (2): 187–94.

Walther, Michael. 2012. "Insanity: Four Decades of U.S. Counterdrug Strategy." Washington, D.C.: United States Department of Justice.

Ward, Robert. 2000. "From Courtroom Advocacy to Systems Advocacy: Lessons Learned by a Drug Court Public Defender." *Indigent Defense*, March/April. https://jpo.wrlc.org/handle/11204/4311.

Warner, Michael. 2000. *The Trouble with Normal: Sex, Politics, and the Ethics of Queer Life*. Cambridge: Harvard University Press.

Warren-Holland, David. 2006. "Some Reflections of a Decade of Experiences in British and American Concept House Therapeutic Communities, 1967 to 1977: A Personal Experience." *Therapeutic Communities* 27 (1): 13–29.

Weheliye, Alexander. 2014. *Habeas Viscus: Racializing Assemblages, Biopolitics, and Black Feminist Theories of the Human*. Durham, NC: Duke University Press.

Weinberg, Darin. 1996. "The Enactment and Appraisal of Authenticity in a Skid Row Therapeutic Community." *Symbolic Interaction* 19 (2): 137–62.

—. 2000. "Out There: The Ecology of Addiction in Drug Abuse Treatment Discourse." *Social Problems* 47 (4): 606–21.

—. 2005. *Of Others Inside: Insanity, Addiction, and Belonging in America*. Philadelphia: Temple University Press.

Weitzman, Jamey. 1995. "Drug Courts: A Manual for Planning and Implementation." Washington, D.C.: American Bar Association.

Weppner, Robert. 1983. *The Untherapeutic Community: Organizational Behavior in a Failed Addiction Treatment Program*. Lincoln: University of Nebraska Press.

Werb, Dan, Adeeba Kamarulzaman, Meredith Meacham, Claudio Rafful, Benedikt Fischer, Steffanie Strathdee, and Evan Wood. 2016. "The Effectiveness of Compulsory Drug Treatment: A Systematic Review." *International Journal of Drug Policy* 28: 1–9.

Wexler, David. 1972. "Therapeutic Justice." *Minnesota Law Review* 57: 289–338.

——. 1990. *Therapeutic Jurisprudence: The Law as a Therapeutic Agent*. Durham, NC: Carolina Academic Press.

——. 2000. "Therapeutic Jurisprudence: An Overview." *Thomas M. Cooley Law Review* 17: 125–34.

Wexler, David, Michael Perlin, Michael Vols, Pauline Spencer, and Nigel Stobbs. 2016. "Guest Editorial: Current Issues in Therapeutic Jurisprudence." *QUT Law Review* 16 (3): 1–3.

Wexler, David, and Bruce Winick. 1991. *Essays in Therapeutic Jurisprudence*. Durham, NC: Carolina Academic Press.

Wexler, Harry. 1995. "The Success of Therapeutic Communities for Substance Abusers in American Prisons." *Journal of Psychoactive Drugs* 27 (1): 57–66.

Wexler, Harry, John Blackmore, and Douglas Lipton. 1991. "Project Reform: Developing a Drug Abuse Treatment Strategy for Corrections." *Journal of Drug Issues* 21 (2): 469–90.

Wexler, Harry, and Douglas Lipton. 1993. "From REFORM to RECOVERY: Advances in Prison Drug Treatment." In *Drug Treatment and Criminal Justice*, ed. James Inciardi, 209–27. Newbury Park, CA: Sage Publications.

Whetstone, Sarah, and Teresa Gowan. 2011. "Diagnosing the Criminal Addict: Biochemistry in the Service of the State." In *Sociology of Diagnosis*, vol. 12 of *Advances in Medical Sociology*, ed. PJ McGann and David Huston, 309–30. Howard House, UK: Emerald Group Publishing.

——. 2017. "Carceral Rehab as Fuzzy Penality: Hybrid Technologies of Control in the New Temperance Crusade." *Social Justice* 44 (2–3): 83–112.

White House. 2016. *FY 2017 Budget and Performance Summary: Companion to the National Drug Control Strategy*. Washington, D.C.: Executive Office of the President of the United States. https://obamawhitehouse.archives.gov/sites/default/files/ondcp/policy-and-research/fy2017_budget_summary-final.pdf.

——. 2017a. "America First: A Budget Blueprint to Make America Great Again, Budget of the United States Government, Fiscal Year 2018." www.govinfo.gov/app/details/BUDGET-2018-BLUEPRINT.

——. 2017b. *The President's Commission on Combating Drug Addiction and the Opioid Crisis*. Washington, D.C.: Commission on Combating Drug Addiction and the Opioid Crisis. www.whitehouse.gov/sites/whitehouse.gov/files/images/Final_Report_Draft_11-1-2017.pdf.

White, William. 1998. *Slaying the Dragon: The History of Addiction Treatment and Recovery in America*. Bloomington, IL: Chestnut Health Systems.

White, William, and William Miller. 2007. "Confrontation in Addiction Treatment: History, Science and Time for Change." *Counselor: The Magazine for Addiction Professionals* 8 (4): 12–30.

Whitehead, Tony. 1985. "Use of Psychiatric Drugs in Prison." In *Prison Medicine: Ideas on Health Care in Penal Establishments*, ed. Sarah Cawthra and Catherine Ginity, 71–82. London: Prison Reform Trust.

Willhelm, Sidney, and Edwin Powell. 1964. "Who Needs the Negro?" *Trans-action* 1 (6): 3.

Williams, Andrew. 2016. "Spiritual Landscapes of Pentecostal Worship, Belief, and Embodiment in a Therapeutic Community: New Critical Perspectives." *Emotion, Space and Society* 19: 45–55.

Williams, Vergil. 1996. *Dictionary of American Penology*. Westport, CT: Greenwood.

Willoughby-Herard, Tiffany. 2015. *Waste of a White Skin: the Carnegie Corporation and the Racial Logic of White Vulnerability*. Berkeley: University of California Press.

Willse, Craig. 2015. *The Value of Homelessness: Managing Surplus Life in the United States*. Minneapolis: University of Minnesota Press.

Wilper, Andrew, Steffie Woolhandler, J. Wesley Boyd, Karen Lasser, Danny McCormick, David Bor, and David Jimmelstein. 2009. "The Health and Health Care of US Prisoners: Results of a Nationwide Survey." *American Journal of Public Health* 99 (4): 666–72.

Wilson, John, and Jon Snodgrass. 1969. "The Prison Code in a Therapeutic Community." *Journal of Criminal Law, Criminology, and Police Science* 60 (4): 472–78.

Wilson, William Julius. 1996. *When Work Disappears: The World of the New Urban Poor*. New York: Vintage.

Wilton, Robert, Geoffrey DeVerteuil, and Joshua Evans. 2013. " 'No More of This Macho Bullshit': Drug Treatment, Place and the Reworking of Masculinity." *Transactions of the Institute of British Geographers* 39 (2): 291–303.

Winick, Bruce. 2003. "Therapeutic Jurisprudence and Problem Solving Courts." *Fordham Urban Law Journal* 30 (3): 1055–103.

Winick, Bruce, and David Wexler, eds. 2003. *Judging in a Therapeutic Key: Therapeutic Jurisprudence and the Courts*. Durham, NC: Carolina Academic Press.

Winnubst, Shannon. 2006. *Queering Freedom*. Bloomington: Indiana University Press.

Winslow, Walker. 1960. "Frontiers: Ex-Addicts, Incorporated." *MANAS* 13 (37): 11–14.

—. 1961. "Synanon Revisited." *MANAS* 14 (6): 1–6.

Wolch, Jennifer. 1990. *The Shadow State: Government and Voluntary Sector in Transition*. New York: The Foundation Center.

Woodcock, Thomas. 2003. *Legal Habits: A Brief Sartorial History of Wig, Robe and Gown*. London: Good Books Publications.

Woods, Christian. 2016. "Proposition 47: The Unintended Consequence." *University of La Verne Law Review* 38: 83–98.

Wynter, Sylvia. 1996. "Is Development a Purely Empirical Concept or Also Teleological? A Perspective from We the Underdeveloped." In *Prospects for Recovery and Sustainable Development in Africa*, ed. Aguibou Yansane, 299–316. Westport, CT: Greenwood Press.

—. 2003. "Unsettling the Coloniality of Being/Power/Truth/Freedom Towards the Human, After Man, Its Overrepresentation-An Argument." *New Centennial Review* 3 (3): 257–337.

—. 2015. "The Ceremony Found: Towards the Autopoetic Turn/Overturn, its Autonomy of Human Agency and Extraterritoriality of (Self-)Cognition." In *Black Knowledges / Black Struggles: Essays in Critical Epistemology*, ed. Jason Ambrose and Sabine Broeck, 184–252. Liverpool, UK: Liverpool University Press.

Yablonsky, Lewis. 1962. *The Violent Gang*. Baltimore, MD: Penguin Books.

——. 1965. *The Tunnel Back: Synanon.* New York: MacMillan Company.

——. 1989. *The Therapeutic Community: A Successful Approach for Treating Substance Abusers.* New York: Gardner Press.

——. 2002. "Whatever Happened to Synanon? The Birth of the Anticriminal Therapeutic Community Methodology." *Criminal Justice Policy Review* 13 (4): 329–36.

Young, Douglas. 2002. "Impacts of Perceived Legal Pressure on Retention in Drug Treatment." *Criminal Justice and Behavior* 29 (1): 27–55.

Young, Douglas, Reginald Fluellen, and Steven Belenko. 2004. "Criminal Recidivism in Three Models of Mandatory Drug Treatment." *Journal of Substance Abuse Treatment* 27: 313–23.

Young, Jock. 1986. "The Failure of Criminology: The Need for a Radical Realism." In *Confronting Crime*, ed. Roger Matthews and Jock Young. London: Sage Publications.

——. 1992. "Realist Research as a Basis for Local Criminal Justice Policy." In *Realist Criminology: Crime Control and Policing in the 1990s*, ed. John Lowman and Brian MacLean. Toronto: University of Toronto Press.

——. 2002. "Ten Points of Realism." In *Criminology: A Reader*, ed. Yvonne Jewkes and Gayle Letherby. London: Sage Publications.

——. 2011. *The Criminological Imagination.* Cambridge: Polity Press.

Zelvin, Elizabeth, and Alissa Mallow. 2005. "Through the Looking Glass: How a TC Graduate Brings a Social Work Perspective to the Therapeutic Community: An Interview with Jeffrey Savoy." *Journal of Social Work Practice in the Addictions* 5 (3): 91–98.

Index